Organizational Network Analysis

The integrated meta-model for organizational resource audit is a consistent and comprehensive instrument for auditing intangible resources and their relations and connections from the network perspective. This book undertakes a critically important problem of management sciences, poorly recognized in literature although determining the current and future competitiveness of organizations, sectors, and economies. The author notes the need to introduce a theoretical input, which is manifested by the meta-model. An expression of this treatment is the inclusion of the network as a structure of activities, further knowledge as an activity, and intangible assets as intellectual capital characterized by a structure of connections. The case study presented is an illustration of the use of network analysis tools and other instruments to identify not only the most important resources, tasks, or actors, as well as their effectiveness, but also to connect the identified networks with each other. The author opens the field for applying her methodology, revealing the structural and dynamic features of the intangible resources of the organization. The novelty of the proposed meta-model shows the way to in-depth applications of network analysis techniques in an intra-organizational environment.

Organizational Network Analysis makes a significant contribution to the development of management sciences, in terms of strategic management and more strictly a resource approach to the company through a structural definition of knowledge; application of the concept of improvement-oriented audit, abandoning a narrow understanding of this technique in terms of compliance; reliable presentation of audits available in the literature; rigorous reasoning leading to the development of a meta-model; close linking of knowledge and resources with the strategy at the design stage of the developed audit model, including the analysis of link dynamics and networks together with an extensive metrics proposal; and an interesting illustration of the application with the use of metrics, tables, and figures. It will be of value to researchers, academics, managers, and students in the fields of strategic management, organizational studies, social network analysis in management, knowledge management, and auditing knowledge resources in organizations.

Anna Ujwary-Gil is a professor at the Institute of Economics, Polish Academy of Sciences, in Warsaw, Poland, where she is also a director of two MBA studies. She received her PhD in economics and management from the Warsaw School of Economics, Poland. She is a founder and editor-in-chief of *Journal of Entrepreneurship, Management and Innovation*. In 2010, her book *Kapitał intelektualny a wartość rynkowa przedsiębiorstwa* [*Intellectual Capital and the Market Value of a Company*] (CH.Beck) won the Polish Academy of Sciences monographs award. Among numerous projects, she was a project supervisor in the Sonata competition of the National Science Center, and an experienced researcher in the EU Marie Curie Industry-Academia Partnerships and Pathways program. For more than 18 years, she has been the conference director and academic supervisor of annual academics' and business professionals' conferences held every June and is founder and president of the Cognitione Foundation for the Dissemination of Knowledge and Science. Her research interests include organizational network analysis, knowledge management, intellectual capital, resource-based views, and dynamic approaches to organization and management.

Routledge Studies in Business Organizations and Networks

Location Behaviour and Relationship Stability in International Business Networks
Evidence from the automotive industry
Bart Kamp

Privatization and Financial Collapse in the Nuclear Industry
The Origins and Causes of the British Energy Crisis of 2002
Simon Taylor

Decisions: Risk and Reward
Edited by Johnnie Johnson and Alistair Bruce

Deregulation, Innovation and Market Liberalization
Electricity Regulation in a Continually Evolving Environment
L. Lynne Kiesling

Procuring Complex Performance
Studies of Innovation in Product-Service Management
Edited by Mickey Howard and Nigel Caldwell

Uniting Diverse Organizations
Managing Goal-Oriented Advocacy Networks
Angel Saz-Carranza

Customer Loyalty and Supply Chain Management
Business-to-Business Customer Loyalty Analysis
Ivan Russo and Ilenia Confente

Organizational Network Analysis
Auditing Intangible Resources
Anna Ujwary-Gil

For a full list of titles, please visit: www.routledge.com/Routledge-Research-in-Architecture/book-series/RRARCH

Organizational Network Analysis

Auditing Intangible Resources

Anna Ujwary-Gil

Routledge
Taylor & Francis Group
NEW YORK AND LONDON

First published 2020
by Routledge
52 Vanderbilt Avenue, New York, NY 10017

and by Routledge
2 Park Square, Milton Park, Abingdon, Oxon, OX14 4RN

Routledge is an imprint of the Taylor & Francis Group, an informa business

Library of Congress Cataloging-in-Publication Data
A catalog record for this book has been requested

ISBN: 978-0-367-37007-7 (hbk)
ISBN: 978-0-367-40894-7 (ebk)

Typeset in Sabon
by Apex CoVantage, LLC

To Maria

Contents

Figures

Tables

Acknowledgments

Thank you to Professor Kathleen M. Carley for her inspiration to write this book. I particularly appreciated the opportunity to take part in the Summer Institute she held at the Carnegie Mellon University, School of Computer Science Institute for Software Research—CASOS, USA, where Geoffrey Morgan and his workshop were especially memorable. For their assistance with technical aspects of using the ORA software for data analysis, I would like to thank Professor Rick Carley, Jeff Reminga, and Jon Storrick.

Also, I would like to thank Professor Wojciech Czakon for his review and valuable comments. I am especially grateful to Piotr Wąs, Connecto Ltd. Board Member and Head of Implementation Department, for allowing me to perform the research in his company, for his welcoming and open attitude, and for his support at all times.

The book was supported by the Cognitione Foundation for the Dissemination of Knowledge and Science (KRS 0000587704) and the National Science Centre project allocated on the basis of the decision number DEC-2012/05/D/HS4/01338.

Preview

The saying it is not who you know, but what who you know speaks to the power of intangible resources. This work goes a step further by also showing the power of what who you know does and what resources they have at their disposal. I have long espoused the value of these high-dimensional or meta-networks and their dynamics for understanding real-world issues. These ideas are operationalized in a sophisticated toolkit for high-dimension network analysis, visualization, and what-if analysis referred to as ORA. I teach ORA and this approach at Carnegie Mellon University during the CASOS Summer Institute (SI). This is how I met Anna. She was a participant in 2015. She instantly grasped the power of this approach and its value for understanding organizations. This book came out of that beginning.

In this book, *Organizational Network Analysis: Auditing Intangible Resources*, Anna goes far beyond the basic methodologies. She situates this approach by building on the theories that underlie team science and resource management. She empirically grounds this approach and builds relevance through numerous real-world examples. In these examples, she shows in detail how to apply dynamic meta-networks to real-world organizations and describes what new insights this application brings to our understanding of the organization at work. She helps the reader understand how network forces impact performance at all levels and across humans and intangible resources. It has long been recognized that informal networks of who talks to whom are key to promotion, to how things get done, and to organizational gaps. This book is unique in that it goes several steps further and builds on the networks connecting people, resources, knowledge, and tasks to each other. This broader perspective is critical for understanding the organization at work. Using this perspective one can measure and reason about policies for effecting organizational needs such as workload distribution, congruence, team stability, and just-in-time teaming. Illustrative examples show how this meta-network approach enables corporate leaders to manage intangible resources as they hire new personnel, reorganize, and build connections among groups. Going still another step the author shows how the application of dynamic network analysis provides the manager or researcher with a merged picture of the flow of information and knowledge through the organization. Anna has moved organizational network analysis beyond simple assessment of informal networks into the realm of high-dimensional (meta-network) and dynamic network analytics. As such she is able to provide a sophisticated, usable, and practical approach to auditing intangible resources. The universality of the approach means that the metrics and processes are relevant to any organization or group, even one composed of humans and robots.

Scientists and practitioners will find this book of value – as it contains both methodological contributions and detailed practical applications. It provides a promising and systematic data-driven approach for addressing the challenges of identification, measurement, and evaluation of organizational resources. The methods used are sophisticated, but easily understood and employed by doctoral students and MBAs. The approach is scalable and can be used both at the small team level such as a group of five to coordination across the entire space of GitHub. All in all, this is a key contribution to team science.

Earl Nightingale once said, "All you need is the plan, the roadmap, and the courage to press on to your destination." In this book, Anna has given organizational scholars and practitioners the roadmap. Enjoy.

Dr. Kathleen M. Carley

Prof. of Societal Computing
Director of the Center for Computational Analysis of Social and Organizational Systems (CASOS) at Carnegie Mellon University, Pittsburgh.
August, 2019

Introduction

Value creation in an organization is largely dependent on intangible resources, as shown by research on the modern economy, which is transforming into a knowledge- and innovation-based economy, and increasingly—a network economy. The combination of the entirety of employees' skills, knowledge, and experiences improves the way the organization uses its intangible resources for value creation (Bukowitz & Petrash, 1997). The evolution of a knowledge-based economy toward a network-based economy demonstrates its gradual passage into the next stage of development, dominated by knowledge—seen as a strategic intangible resource of an organization (Zack, 1999)—and intra- and inter-organizational relations based on the exchange and flow of resources (including knowledge and information). Due to the complexity of interrelations between the intangible resources of an organization, and particularly their indeterminacy and elusiveness, the issue of their assessment and control in the management process remains open. In the 21st century, the success of an organization, especially one operating in a competitive market, depends on investments in the development of intangible resources: information, knowledge, and intellectual capital. In order to understand the complexity of an organization's functioning, it is worthwhile to investigate the dynamics and relations of these resources by formulating and verifying new hypotheses.

Besides network theory, actor–network theory, and activity theory, the primary theoretical approaches of this book are resource-based approaches, including knowledge- and intellectual capital–based views and resource dynamics. Within these approaches, researchers analyze internal differences in economic outcomes, aiming to explain why some companies perform better than others by identifying resources specific to an organization or the effectiveness of resource use. The dynamics and connections of intangible resources are analyzed less frequently. The resource-based view includes both tangible and intangible resources. However, the fact that these resources are equifinal and may be used interchangeably is not considered here. In this approach, the issue of direct causal relationships between physical resources and their use remains open.

The present research led to the development of a methodology for organizational intangible resource audit,[1] including in particular an assessment of these resources' relationships, flows, and intensity (prominence) in the organization. The methodology should allow for developing and interpreting findings, planning the course of action, and identifying all aspects of the defined issues. This methodology has been used to diagnose the organizational requirements for the effective performance of an intangible resource audit. No similar research had been performed, and literature on the subject is scarce to the point of being non-existent. There are noteworthy concepts of information, knowledge, and intellectual capital audit developed by authors, and these concepts have been used by the author as the basis for a *meta-model* of organizational intangible resource audit. Notably, most of these methodologies are static, and thus do not sufficiently include the dynamic nature of intangible resources in relation to organizational tasks. These include the *InfoMap* concept by Burk and Horton (1988) and *Information Audit* by Henczel (2000) and Buchanan and Gibb (1998). In other methodologies, authors only highlight the flow of information, for example, in Orna (1999) or the more recent Buchanan and Gibb approach (2007; 2008). However, all of these lack an approach to information process modeling.

The concepts of organizational knowledge audit are interesting. However, many authors do not differentiate between the relevant definitions, treating information audit as knowledge audit and *vice versa* (see Wang & Xiao, 2009). This is directly related to viewing information and knowledge as organizational resources. In many cases, hypotheses and assumptions lack precision. Particularly noteworthy are knowledge audit methodologies by Debenham and Clark (1994); Helms, Bosua, and Ignatio (2009); Choy, Lee, and Cheung (2004); Gourova, Antonova, and Todorova (2009); Liebowitz et al. (2000); and Reinhardt (2003). Here, knowledge audit is mainly approached from the process perspective, with authors attempting to identify the major audit stages and map knowledge processes and flows, without key audit components, that is, assessment and control of organizational knowledge resources or dynamics of changes and connections of these resources in the analysis period.

As to intellectual capital audit concepts, they are not common, contrary to the widely known and accepted classification of organization intellectual capital measurement and assessment methods (see: Sveiby classifications at www.sveiby.com). Out of the numerous qualitative and quantitative methods for intellectual capital assessment and valuation, two can be classified as intellectual capital audit methods.[2] These are the *Technology Broker* by Brooking (1996) and the *Intellectual Capital Statement* (Mertins, Wang, & Will, 2007). The Technology Broker defines the intellectual capital audit cycle but lacks a precise indication of the stage where the author suggests valuating each resource (human, market, infrastructure, and intellectual property). The Intellectual Capital Statement comprises two models, a structural and a procedural one, providing a theoretical framework for defining and performing an intellectual capital audit in an organization.

The objective of this book is to develop a methodology for organizational intangible resource audit using organizational network analysis. The audit is seen here as a procedure oriented toward documented systems and processes, which is advisory in nature and used for organizational improvement. A preliminary review of literature on the subject shows that this is a new area of research that has yet to be explored, especially in terms of theoretical precepts regarding intangible resources and their definition, auditing, and analysis of the dynamics of their interrelations in an organization. The downside of inadequate intangible resource management is that efforts are duplicated, resulting in the acquisition and reproduction of the same information, that is, the creation of already existing knowledge due to unawareness of its existence. One issue that had not been investigated before, and is at the core of the present discussion, is the identification of the dynamic interrelations between resources, and their inclusion in the intangible resource audit methodology. An analysis of existing audit models, specifically including organizational information, knowledge, and intellectual capital audits, resulting in the creation of a *meta-model*, is an important part of this research. The *meta-model* is formed by way of comparisons and creative integration of the non-conflicting assumptions of the existing models. Abductive reasoning has been used in order to explain events and systems that already exist and are known. This explanation is based on experiment results and theoretical principles. Abduction has been used in order to name the model components and to include specific audit elements (stages) in the *meta-model*. This approach aims at producing a *meta-model* created out of the least common denominators of all the activities described in the audit processes (stages and steps). The integrated audit model will comprise those steps that best reflect the overall process of intangible resource audit. Thus, also central to the present discussion is the very concept of intangible resource audit, understood as a control, management, and advisory instrument for the ongoing diagnosis of intangible resources from the perspective of the network of interrelations between an organization's resources and their dynamics.

The interpretation of static and dynamic concepts of intangible resources and their audit is equally important. The static approach is dominant in the literature on the subject and involves the characterization of the *status quo* of organizational intangible resources (information, knowledge, and intellectual capital). Notably, resources such as information, knowledge, and skills are integral to the tasks performed by an organization's employees. The use of these resources in action makes them dynamic, which entails the identification of a network of relations. There is likely no methodology combining the static and dynamic approaches to audit. A standardized methodology for organizational intangible resource audit is also lacking, which means that audits are performed in a variety of ways in various environments.

Moreover, no audit methodology provides a comprehensive, holistic view of intangible resources rather than a fragmented one. Such a holistic approach would enable intangible resources to be analyzed in a complementary manner, together with their interrelations, flows, and contribution to organizational value creation. Audits described in the literature are mainly performed for a specific purpose, such as a merger or acquisition process, or the implementation of new technology. This is true, for example, in the case of internal audit concepts, which, however, are not the focus of this book.

In many cases, the strictly defined scope and purpose of audit do not allow for universal adaptation in the organization, and thus do not provide comprehensive analyses or indicate the proper tools required for their performance. The development and implementation of instruments for intangible resource auditing are integral to the study procedure. From the process perspective, intangible resource audit is a complex, multitiered fact-finding process, involving an analysis of both quantitative and qualitative data. The purpose of such an audit is to: identify intangible resources, assess their value for the organization, identify individuals that are obstacles to information and knowledge proliferation or intermediaries (brokers) in the process, identify knowledge and information overload in the organization, and diagnose the dynamics of intangible resource flow.

Developing a methodology for organizational intangible resource audit requires a detailed analysis of terminology related to such an audit, the relevant theoretical framework, and the conditions created in the organization in order to understand the dynamics, relations, and flows of intangible resources that are the focus of the investigation. The research should be structured so as to comprise three stages:

1. Concept (defining the precepts, restrictions, and conditions of the research process).
2. Creation (developing research instruments).
3. Verification (testing the instruments).[3]

The primary research problem can be formulated as a question: How can one identify an organization's intangible resources and their relations in the information network, knowledge network, task network, and resource network? This gives rise to the following specific research questions:

1. How, in the light of network and management theories, should one develop a methodology for organizational intangible resource audit,

bearing in mind the uniqueness both of the intangible resources and their relations, and of the organization itself?
2. What prerequisites should be met by an organization for intangible resource audit to be feasible and effective?
3. Can organizational intangible resource audit be considered a valuable management technique in the modern knowledge-based economy?
4. How can intangible resources be measured, evaluated, and included in audit planning and performance using the network-based view?

The general objective is to develop a methodology for organizational intangible resource audit using the network-based view and organizational network analysis methods. The specific objectives include:

1. Developing a concept for organizational intangible resource audit, based on an exploration of theoretical precepts, where the author shall creatively combine his or her own and other researchers' concepts.
2. Creating a methodology for organizational intangible resource audit based on approaches developed by Hong, Van den Goor, and Brinkkemper (1993), and Brinkkemper (1996).
3. Identifying and analyzing the dynamics of connections and relations between intangible resources, on the basis of network and resource theories.
4. Providing an empirical basis for intangible resource audit, and in particular for its key stage, that is, performance, using organizational network analysis techniques.
5. Testing selected instruments indispensable for the diagnosis and operationalization of the relations and connections of intangible resources in an organization.
6. Formulating the findings from the organizational intangible resource audit, highlighting study limitations and areas for further investigation.
7. The developed intangible resource audit may become another important component of the *meta-model* and *meta-process* approach to audit for other authors' future research.

Based on a literature review and an innovative combination of the intangible resource audit *meta-model* with the network-based view, the author has formulated the following assumptions:

- Organizational network analysis is an instrument in intangible resource auditing, allowing one to view the resources from the perspective of a network of relations and connections.
- Understanding of information, knowledge, and intellectual capital audit concepts, and of organizational network analysis techniques, is a prerequisite for designing an integrated intangible resource audit model.

- The network-based view, in the form of organizational network analysis, is a comprehensive instrument for intangible resource audit, enabling the auditing of relations and dynamics of the resources, and thus going beyond the standard methodology of simply measuring the resources themselves.
- Developing and implementing a measurement system comprising metrics of intangible resource relations and dynamics assists in organizational intangible resource auditing in the aspect of interrelatedness of the resources.
- Simulating changes of each resource in the relationship network allows for shaping conditions optimal for an organization's performance.

The present study is qualitative in nature due to the complexity of problems associated with the analysis, assessment, and investigation of relations between organizational intangible resources. It is primarily oriented toward a nomothetic explanation based on case study analysis, useful in the development and verification of economic theories. The choice of this research method is motivated by the complexity of the issue and the scarcity of research on the subject. It allows for the explanation of causal relationships that are too complex for survey-based research, and impossible to analyze in experiments, with a detailed description of the context of the focus of research (intangible resources). Selection of cases for the analysis was based primarily on the prominence (intensity) of intangible resources in the functioning of each organization. The pilot study included a higher education organization and a joint-stock company operating in the medical sector. The main study was performed in an IT company. Research instruments were tested during the pilot study in one of the largest Polish university libraries and a medical company. Case study guidelines indicate that a minimum of two to four cases should be included, up to a maximum of 15 (Perry, 1998). As the analyses performed are highly complex and time-consuming, the number has been reduced to a single case, which is the dominant approach in network analyses (see, e.g., de Oliveira Maciel & Chaves, 2016; Tsai & Ghoshal, 1998). Two other cases were additionally selected for pilot study purposes. The current state of knowledge was confronted with the specifically selected case in order to enable the formulation of empirically founded propositions. The credibility of findings from the case study was enhanced using triangulation (Stake, 1995), including secondary data analysis, surveying (which is a part of the organizational intangible resource audit methodology, and must be adjusted to the characteristics and environment of a given organization), interviews, and study result processing. Statistical analyses (survey result analysis, means, standard deviations, and other measures) and qualitative analyses were also used. For network data analysis, the *Organizational Risk Analyzer* (ORA-NetScenes) software was used. Statistical analyses were performed using the SPSS and UCI-NET packages, and in particular the QAP and MRQAP tools. Bibliographic databases were also used, including Web of Science and Scopus.

The research plan is illustrated below (Figure 0.1):

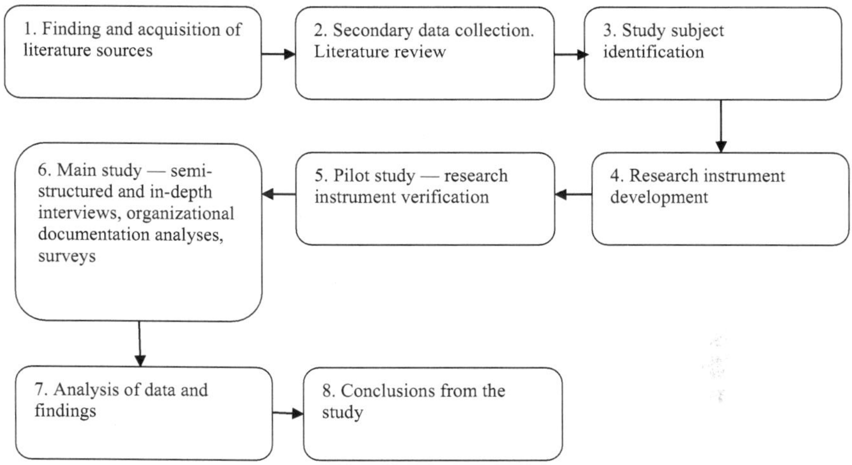

Figure 0.1 Research plan

This book has five chapters. Contents have been organized around network approaches, intangible resources, and the concept of organizational intangible resource audit. The first two chapters have a theoretical focus. Chapter 1 discusses theoretical approaches to networks in the organizational context, including network theory, actor–network theory, and activity theory, selected for their relevance to the study focus, that is, the intangible resources of an organization and the audit process for these resources. Hence the inclusion of resource-based theoretical approaches. In the book, intangible resources are subjected to organizational network analysis, which is therefore particularly emphasized. Social network analysis and dynamic network analysis are also discussed. Chapter 2 is a conceptual one. The author undertakes to develop a *meta-model* for organizational intangible resource audit on the basis of existing concepts for information, knowledge, and intellectual capital audit. Importantly, the *meta-model* includes network-based metrics for intangible resource audit.

The methodology section discusses the research focus, questions, and objectives. The study methodology is comprehensively presented, including in particular the need for further investigations and a larger number of cases that would allow for the empirical verification of the proposed intangible resource audit methodology. Within the present case study, it has only been possible to exemplify the hypotheses based on abductive reasoning, to showcase the primary network research instruments in the context of the scope and purpose of intangible resource audit in a specific organization. The hypotheses do not concern a verification of intangible resource audit methodology, but only the social-based research process focusing on intangible resources and their use. Qualitative, quantitative, and network-based research methods are discussed separately, as each category requires a slightly different approach.

In the empirical section, the findings and conclusions from the organizational intangible resource audit are presented, categorized by network level (entire network, dyads, nodes). Changes in positions of actors in the information and knowledge networks are also discussed, as an example of network simulation and the dynamic approach. Another aspect of the analysis concerns changes in selected metrics following the removal of prominent nodes (knowledge, tasks, and resources). Finally, conclusions regarding the developed concept for intangible resource audit methodology and its exemplification in the selected case study are presented.

The author hopes that the development of a new organizational intangible resource audit methodology, as well as the systematization of theoretical aspects of each audit type and their definitions, differences, and approaches to identifying and analyzing intangible resources will offer a valuable contribution to the literature on the subject.

Notes

1. In this book, the terms "intangible resource audit," "organizational intangible resource audit," "integrated intangible resource audit," and "*meta-model*" are used interchangeably.
2. Others include, for example, the RICARDIS project (Reporting Intellectual Capital to Augment Research, Development and Innovation in SMEs), MERITUM (MEasuRing Intangibles To Understand and improve innovation Management), DMSTI (Danish Ministry of Science Technology and Innovation), PRISM (Policy-Making Reporting and Measurement Intangibles Skills Development Management), DATI (Danish Agency for Trade and Industry), and Scandia Navigator.
3. Empirical verification of the intangible resource audit methodology is not possible, as a considerably larger number of cases would be required for any generalizations.

References

Brinkkemper, S. (1996). Method engineering: Engineering of information systems development methods and tools. *Information and Software Technology*, *38*(4), 275–280.

Brooking, A. (1996). *Intellectual capital: Core asset for the third millennium* (1st ed.). London: International Thomas Business Press.

Buchanan, S., & Gibb, F. (1998). The information audit: An integrated strategic approach. *International Journal of Information Management*, *18*(1), 29–47. https://doi.org/10.1016/S0268-4012(97)00038-8

Buchanan, S., & Gibb, F. (2007). The information audit: Role and scope. *International Journal of Information Management*, *27*(3), 159–172. https://doi.org/10.1016/j.ijinfomgt.2007.01.002

Buchanan, S., & Gibb, F. (2008). The information audit: Methodology selection. *International Journal of Information Management*, *28*(1), 3–11. https://doi.org/10.1016/j.ijinfomgt.2007.10.002

Bukowitz, W. R., & Petrash, G. P. (1997). Visualizing, measuring and managing knowledge. *Research Technology Management*, *40*(4), 24.

Burk, C. F., & Horton, F. W. (1988). *Infomap: A complete guide to discovering corporate information resources*. Englewood, NJ: Prentice Hall.

Choy, S. Y., Lee, W. B., & Cheung, C. F. (2004). A systematic approach for knowledge audit analysis: Integration of knowledge inventory, mapping and knowledge flow analysis. *Journal of Universal Computer Science*, *10*(6), 674–682.

Debenham, J., & Clark, J. (1994). The knowledge audit. *Robotics and Computer-Integrated Manufacturing*, *11*(3), 201–211.

Gourova, E., Antonova, A., & Todorova, Y. (2009). Knowledge audit concepts, processes and practice. *WSEAS Transactions on Business and Economics*, *12*(6), 605–619.

Helms, R., Bosua, R., & Ignatio, R. (2009). Impact assessment of knowledge sharing bottlenecks: The Knowledge Sharing Environment Model (KSEM). *20th Australasian Conference on Information Systems, Melbourne, Australia*. Retrieved from http://aisel.aisnet.org/cgi/viewcontent.cgi?article=1013&context=acis2009

Henczel, S. (2000). The information audit as a first step towards effective knowledge management: An opportunity for the special librarian. *Inspel*, *34*(3/4), 210–226.

Hong, S., Van den Goor, G., & Brinkkemper, S. (1993). A formal approach to the comparison of object-oriented analysis and design methodologies. *Proceeding of the Twenty-Sixth Hawaii International Conference on Systems Sciences*, *4*, 689–698. Retrieved from http://ieeexplore.ieee.org/xpls/abs_all.jsp?arnumber=284253

Liebowitz, J., Rubenstein-Montano, B., McCaw, D., Buchwalter, J., Browning, C., Newman, B., & Rebeck, K. (2000). The knowledge audit. *Knowledge and Process Management*, *7*(1), 3–10.

Maciel, Cristiano de O., & Chaves, C. E. L. (2017). Informational status in intra-organizational networks: The role of knowledge sharing and structural holes. *Revista de Administração*, *52*(2), 189–198. https://doi.org/10.1016/j.rausp.2016.12.008

Mertins, K., Wang, W-H., & Will, M. (2007). How to ensure the quality and reliability of intellectual capital statements? *Electronic Journal of Knowledge Management*, *5*(4), 437–447.

Orna, E. (1999). *Practical information policies* (2 Sub ed.). Aldershot, UK; Brookfield, VT: Gower Pub Co.

Perry, C. (1998). Processes of a case study methodology for postgraduate research in marketing. *European Journal of Marketing*, *32*(9/10), 785–802.

Reinhardt, R. (2003). Theoretical basis of a knowledge audit: An integrative measurement approach. *Proceedings of I-KNOW '03–3rd International Conference on Knowledge Management* (pp. 389–397). Graz, Austria: Graz University of Technology.

Stake, R. E. (1995). *The art of case study research*. London: Sage Publications.
Tsai, W., & Ghoshal, S. (1998). Social capital and value creation: The role of intrafirm networks. *Academy of Management Journal*, *41*(4), 464–476.
Wang, J., & Xiao, J. (2009). Knowledge management audit framework and methodology based on processes. *Journal of Technology Management in China*, *4*(3), 239–249. https://doi.org/10.1108/17468770911013546
Zack, M. H. (1999). Developing a knowledge strategy. *California Management Review*, *41*(3), 125–134.

1 Theoretical Foundations of Networks and Resource-Based Approaches in Organization Management

At present, looking at organizations from the point of view of a network of relations and connections has become an attractive, yet still poorly examined field of management research, in particular in terms of identifying and analyzing intangible resources and the dynamics of their connections. Until now, the system approach to organizations dominated, emphasizing the human factor. It concentrates on the inside of the organization as a socio-technical system and strongly emphasizes the relations between its components (sociogram and technogram). Chapter 1 focuses on the theoretical framework for the intangible resource audit model discussed here, which uses the network-based view for identifying and analyzing those resources. It is crucial to present theoretical approaches to networks in the organizational context, including the emerging network theory as one of the disciplines in network science. In network science, network theory, including social network theory, intertwines with social network analysis techniques, algebra, and statistics, which become the basic tools for formulating and testing network theories.

Defining basic terms related to networks and organizations is of prime importance in the debate. Since network theory (including social network theory) concerns mainly human actors, the reader must be familiar with the concepts of social capital and social network. However, the concept of intangible resource audit goes beyond the dominant aspect of social network actors. Therefore it is important to look more broadly at networks and to include both nonhuman actors (actor–network theory) and human actors' activities (activity theory), which interact with one another to create an organization, as an organization does not solely include social actors. It is in an ongoing process of creating various relations between people, resources, and activities performed by individuals in the workplace, depending on their knowledge and skills. Actor–network theory and activity theory seem to be among the most interesting approaches to organizations from the network perspective, which "animates" the system we know so well through various translations, flows, relations, connections, or ties.

The basic research tools of the network-based view of intangible resources are social, organizational, and dynamic network analysis (SNA, ONA, DNA) techniques. In organizational network analysis, the multimode view of the network was highlighted, where the network comprises both human (animate) and nonhuman (inanimate) actors, creating a network of information, knowledge, tasks, and resources. Through a comprehensive approach to these three techniques, the SODNA model (a combination of SNA, ONA, and DNA) was presented, as a tool for managing intangible resources in the organization.

In order to include the concept of intangible resources and their audit using the aforementioned techniques, the well-known resource-based, knowledge-based, and intellectual capital–based views were used. Therefore, this chapter looks at the organization and intangible resources from the point of view of selected theoretical approaches and social, organizational, and dynamic networks.

1.1 Theoretical Approaches to Networks in the Organizational Context

1.1.1 Network Theory

Network theory[1] is one of the disciplines of network science that developed significantly in the 21st century and has become one of the most prolific fields of interdisciplinary research promoting the idea that "networks are everywhere" (Barabási, 2016; Christakis & Fowler, 2011; Newman, 2010). Network science, network theory, social network theory, and social network analysis stem from social psychology, sociology, and anthropology (Brandes, Robins, McCranie, & Wasserman, 2013), where the network perspective allows one to pose research questions concerning human, biological, and economic systems. Network research is also deeply rooted in graph theory, as well as matrix algebra (Luce & Perry, 1949; Shimbel, 1951) and network statistics. Both matrix algebra and network statistics are important tools used in social network analysis (Figure 1.1).

It is believed that network science was born in 1736 when the physicist Leonhard Euler used a graph to formulate the "Seven Bridges of Königsberg" problem—how to plan a walk through the city that would cross each of those bridges once and only once (Wilson, 2012). According to Lewis (2009), the history of network science can be divided into three periods: the years 1736–1966, strongly related to the mathematical graph theory; the years 1967–1997, when it focused on applying network concepts derived from literature research; and the years from 1998 onward, when the significance of networks in the real world and their universal character have been observed.

A common concept in network science is identifying and studying complex structures and behaviors occurring between individuals (entities)

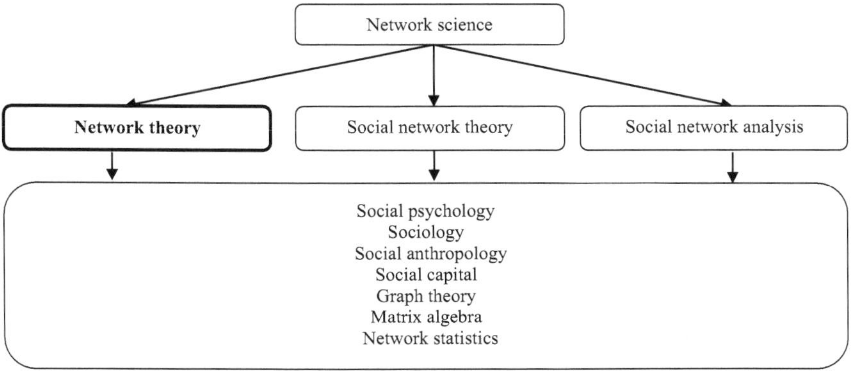

Figure 1.1 The roots of network theory and its position within network science

who are the subjects of network research. Usually, these are people or other entities (e.g., organizations) called "social networks." What makes them different from other networks is the fact that their actors' actions are intentional. Complex structures of relationships between the examined objects (broadly understood *actors*[2]) and the achieved results based on the structures of *relations* are what distinguishes network science from other approaches (Robins, 2015). For example, reductionism divided complex systems in a way that enabled studying separated, individual nodes and their connections. Network theory, one of the disciplines in network science, returns to the study of the entirety and the consequences of mutual relationships. Wellman (1997) and Parkhe, Wasserman, and Ralston (2006) observe that network theory shifts the balance from an atomistic explanation of phenomena and independent cases to relations between the interdependent components of the system. This is a different approach than the search for the smallest, most fundamental component of society, that is, according to Weber (1978), the social actor (acting individual) and its actions.

Two important terms recur throughout the book, "structure" and "network." The *Oxford Dictionary* defines *structure* (http://oxforddictionaries.com/definition/english/structure) as "the arrangement of and relations between the parts or elements of something complex." *Network* (http://oxforddictionaries.com/definition/english/network) is defined as "a group or system of interconnected people or things based on specific types of relations between them."

Networks are omnipresent in science, technology, and business. In order to understand the complexity of a *system*, understood as a complex whole composed of things (elements) working together as parts of a mechanism or an interconnecting network, one must deeply penetrate the network of relations and connections comprising a given system (Barabási, 2016). The complexity of the system itself (for example, a *socio-technical* system) depends on the diversity of its components, their dynamics (inclusion and exclusion), and evolution. Intangible resource management is embedded in a dynamic and complex socio-technical system. At the macro level, the system includes social and technical elements. At the micro level, numerous factors are involved in every part. Technical elements include, for example, the processes, tasks, techniques, knowledge, and resources used for value creation and proposition. Social elements include people, their behaviors, attitudes, organizational norms, principles, and culture.

Network science can be attributed significance as a new emerging paradigm, understood as per Kuhn (1962), namely as a set of terms and theories creating the foundation of science. According to the author, science undergoes periodical paradigm shifts. Today we witness such a shift—the emergence of network science as an academic discipline (Lewis, 2009) and the network paradigm, inspired mainly by empirical studies on networks in the real world. These include: technological networks (e.g., Balthrop, Forrest, Newman, & Williamson, 2004; Gemünden & Heydebreck, 1995), biological networks (e.g., Li, Liakata & Rebholz-Schuhmann, 2014), information networks (e.g., Wellman, 2001), and social networks (e.g., Scott, 2012; Wasserman & Faust, 1994), as well as the discovery of common rules that govern them. Thus, network science examines complex networks related to various fields of research. An engineer, a sociologist, an entrepreneur—each of them will be interested in different kinds of networks, from communications networks, to networks of influence in social organizations, to informal networks that enable organizations to function.

A network is described through its structure (nodes and relations), dynamics, and behaviors. The study of structural and dynamic properties of the above-mentioned network representations is called network science (Watts, 2004). Furthermore, it is also a science of network (relationship) data collection, management, analysis, interpretation, and presentation, as well as an examination of network models (Brandes et al., 2013). Network models constitute representations of a given phenomenon within the network concept, with the help of network data and observations, which are mutually dependent.

It should be assumed that a network is a representation or a model of the observed reality and not the reality itself. The abstraction of a network into a model and its representation requires a set of basic elements: nodes, which can be any animate or inanimate thing (see: actor–network theory), a relationship between at least one pair of nodes (dyad), and an identified network structure. Conceptualizing the *organization* as a network, in which various social and technical elements are combined to create a system, is the fundamental premise of organizational network theory. Organizational management can be described as a science of managing relations in networks in a way ensuring the achievement of organizational goals, such as high efficiency and value creation. In management, social networks are used to understand various research problems related to forming dependency networks (coalitions) in project management (Pryke, 2012), professional achievements (Burt, 2009), the functioning of organizational research and development teams (Allen, James, & Gamlen, 2007; Reagans & Zuckerman, 2001), innovation and creativity (Burt, 2004; Obstfeld, 2005), new product development (Leenders & Dolfsma, 2016), and many others.

In strategic management and organization theory, the new network model for examining competition and value creation provided an impulse for starting a debate on the network paradigm (e.g., Borgatti & Foster, 2003). According to Czakon (2011), the paradigm includes three reference theories: the sociological theory of social networks; resource theory, where the network is understood as a strategic resource; and transaction costs theory, as a method of coordinating cooperation. As the author emphasizes (Czakon, 2011), the "structural order" measured by social network analysis (discussed in more detail in Section 1.2.1) is crucial for the network paradigm. Many authors (e.g., Everton, 2012; Hennig, Brandes, Borgatti, Pfeffer, & Mergel, 2012; Leinhardt, 2013; Prell, 2012; Valente, 2010) perceive the network paradigm from the point of view of network analysis, which includes the techniques, models, and methods useful in solving many social and behavioral problems. The concept of social structure is not purely symbolic, and has been described and analyzed. Emirbayer and Goodwin (1994) identified three social network paradigms that researchers refer to: structural determinism, structural instrumentalism, and structural constructionism. In structural determinism, there is no room for human agency, free will, culture, actors' beliefs, or values that could play a role in social processes and historical change. People are seen as biological organisms, and the social phenomenon is a property of the social network (organization). Structural instrumentalism, on the other hand, accepts human agency understood as a rational choice—a pragmatic action motivated by financial gain and maximization of benefits. Similarly, in structural constructionism, human agency is present in social transformations, and actors are motivated by intangible factors (values, norms, responsibilities resulting from the culture of a given society in which the individual is embedded). These three paradigms define relations among culture, agency, and social structure.

Borgatti and Foster (2003) characterized four dimensions of network research: the direction of causality (network structure as a cause or consequence), the level of analysis (actor, dyad, entire network), explanatory objectives, and mechanisms. In the dimension of network-as-a-consequence, the authors analyze objectives and mechanisms explaining the functioning of the network. The objectives concern the results and the homogeneity of social capital. Mechanisms are used to discuss the structural and connectionist dimension of networks. Both elements address issues related to topology, the equivalence of network (structural dimension) and flows, and the cohesion and relations of network actors (connectionist dimension). This general classification served to create a typology for research on the consequences of network factors comprising the following subjects: structural capital in the social network, access to resources, convergence (structural equivalence), and contagion (sharing attitudes, culture, practices, ideas, or tangible objects as a result of an interaction and interpersonal transmission). As the authors point out, the presented dimensions and typology of network research form a network paradigm in organizational research.

Barabasi and Frangos (2002) claim that network science is an attempt to understand networks existing in nature, technology, and society using uniform sets of tools and principles. Those tools (more broadly discussed in Section 2.3.2) allow for studying the topography and structure of networks, as well as their behaviors and evolution.

The development of network science is based on three approaches: mathematical analysis of social networks, qualitative methodology used in social sciences, and complex networks studied in statistical physics and complexity theory. The present work is based on the first two, where quantitative and qualitative approaches to network analysis have actually become increasingly common tools used in research on organizations and management (Fombrun, 1982; Hollenbeck & Jamieson, 2015; Hoppe & Reinelt, 2010; Tichy & Fombrun, 1979; Tichy, Tushman & Fombrun, 1979).

At present, network science poses several challenges (Kocarev & In, 2010) related to the methods for drawing conclusions from actual network data; describing a network, its structure, and its properties; and the nature of processes that occur in a network. These challenges are related to a number of problems, for example, the problem of missing links in a network or understanding the dynamics of the processes occurring in networks. There are almost as many dynamic phenomena as networks. Still, we are far from understanding the mechanisms of network flows, the long-term dynamics, or the interdependencies existing in networks.

The development of this scientific discipline is accompanied by the emergence of new academic journals and countless events (conferences, symposiums, seminars, etc.). In 2016, the number of journals featuring the word *network* or *networks* in the title stood at 113 (data from the SCImago Journal & Country Rank), mostly in the fields of IT, medicine, or physics. In social sciences, the *Social Networks* journal has a high impact factor. In 2013, a new journal appeared, strictly related to this discipline, namely *Network Science* published by the Cambridge University Press. After merely three years of presence in the market, the journal had 79 citations, according to the *Web of Science* database. In 2009,

Science issued a special edition entirely devoted to networks (*Complex Systems and Networks*), and one of the first chapters of the monograph devoted to network science was written by Börner, Sanyal, and Vespignani (2007).

Considering the above, it seems that network theory is one of the disciplines in network science. The main objective of network theory is to understand the roots and features of networks that consolidate the network elements into various complex systems. Key aspects include structure and position in the network, its function (e.g., distribution or flow), and examining the way in which the network structure supports a given process (e.g., resource distribution or information flow). Social network analysis (SNA), which is further discussed in Section 1.2.1, is a methodical procedure used in network theory development. It is a popular tool in human resources development (Brass, 2003; Hatala, 2006; Parise, 2007), useful for examining dynamics between individuals and their impact, with a focus on interaction. The general thesis in network theory is that the position of an actor in the network determines its limitations and opportunities in terms of its achievements, behaviors, and beliefs. On the group level, what happens in a group of actors is a function of the structure of connections between them.

According to Borgatti and Halgin (2011), depending on whether the network is an independent (preceding) or dependent (resulting) variable, a distinction must be made between "network theory" and "the theory of network." The theory of network refers to the mechanisms and processes that act together with network structures in order to achieve specific results for individuals and groups (e.g., having many relations, achieving a prominent position). Network theory, in turn, deals with processes that determine why networks have a specific structure (for example, centralization, small worlds—Buchanan, 2003).

Very often, two popular concepts are mentioned in the context of the emerging network theory: the strength of weak ties (Granovetter, 1973, 1983), and structural holes (Burt, 2009), in which the key role is played by structure and position in the network and by the explanation of the relationship between the structure and outcomes of a network. According to Granovetter, the stronger the ties between a pair of people or actors (e.g., A01[3] and A02; A02 and A03) in a given society (e.g., organization), the higher the likelihood of weaker ties with the relevant third parties (A01 and A03). Strong ties in the same social group do not, however, foster the exchange of new knowledge or access to new information and the latest innovative trends. There is a risk that redundant (excessive) ties will emerge, activities will be duplicated, and the same information and knowledge will be exchanged—all of which does not promote value creation. Therefore the author points to the bridging connections (usually weak ties), which are the potential source of new information and knowledge.

The other is Burt's concept of structural holes (2009), which mainly refers to the shape of the ego network of a given actor and the pattern of relations in at least two unrelated social networks. Therefore, relations with many other networks, in which actors do not have relations with the given networks, are beneficial for the ego. This leads to a larger number of so-called structural holes. In the context of the aforementioned redundancy, the ego network with many structural holes has a chance to receive more nonredundant (new) information. Based on these two concepts, Borgatti and Halgin (2011) suggest two network models: the flow model (e.g., information flow) and the coordination model.

The variant of network theory in which social networks (of individuals or groups of individuals) play a dominant role is called social network theory (Kilduff & Tsai, 2003). It explains the interpersonal mechanisms and social structures that exist among cooperating individuals: small and large groups, an organization's departments, and entire organizations (Wasserman & Faust, 1994), making it possible to determine how the relationships of a given individual, group, or organization influence beliefs or behaviors. Scientists measure the interactivity of people by mapping relations, and thus discover the group dynamics and the way people use their connections in order to achieve the desired results (Coleman, 1988). Social network theories were tested by applying the empirical rigor of social network analysis. Kilduff and Tsai (2003) identified three fields that inspired social network theory:

- imported theories and concepts (mathematics, in particular, graph theory; social psychology: balance theory and social comparison theory);
- original concepts (heterophily: weak ties theory, structural holes; structural roles: structural equivalence, structural cohesion, role equivalence);
- organization theories[4] (resource dependency theory, situational determinant theory, organizational ecology theory, transactional costs theory, knowledge-based view).

In the context of social networks, graph theory provides means for assessing the cohesion of a given social system, its hierarchy, and organizational efficiency. A cohesive (connected) social system in an organization promotes cooperation and resource-sharing, while a lack of connections in the network leads to divisions and communication breakdown (Powell, Koput, & Smith-Doerr, 1996). A high level of organizational hierarchy (a mechanistic organization) involves top-down dependency. Networks make it possible to picture informal relations and look at a given network from many levels (Moliterno & Mahony, 2011), including a bottom-up perspective. Network efficiency is evaluated in terms of its fragmentation (division of the network into smaller parts) and redundancy of nodes or connections.

Kilduff and Tsai (2003) borrowed the term "supremum" from graph theory to describe a pair of actors who have access to a third party in the organization. In the group of imported concepts and theories, social psychology plays an important role, including in particular Heider's balance theory (Cartwright & Harary, 1956; Heider, 1958) and the theory of social comparisons (Festinger, 1954; Goethals & Darley, 1987).

According to balance theory, if two people (A01 and A02) cooperate, and A01 provides information to A03 within one department, then A01 assumes that A02 will also provide information to A03. In the case of a two-mode network, the cooperation between A01 and A02 might lead to the same resources (R) being used in the organization. Therefore, Heider uses various combinations of dyads and triads in which networks can be created by animate (e.g., A01 and A02) and inanimate (e.g., R) entities. Relations can be either positive or negative. Imbalance occurs when relations of conflicting nature exist (in a given constellation: triad—both negative and positive). Social comparison theory (Festinger, 1954) emerged in connection with balance theory, and assumes that people learn from one another by comparing themselves to others, that they choose people similar to themselves with whom they can compete, and that social comparison strongly affects attitudes and opinions. Festinger refers to the notion of cognitive dissonance, experienced when one's environment is in a state of imbalance. Elimination of intransitivity restores balance to the triad. Homophily (McPherson, Smith-Lovin, & Cook, 2001) also plays an important role in this theory. It is a tendency to cooperate and form relations with people having the same network attributes (e.g., gender, age, culture, beliefs, experiences, location, views, social status, etc.). For instance, in the organizational context, dividing managers into two ideologically conflicting groups with different views regarding the development of an organization jeopardized its future research and development activities (White, 1961).

The next category, called "original network concepts," includes the strength of weak ties and structural holes concepts, already introduced above. Other notable notions include structural equivalence, role equivalence, and structural cohesion theories. Equivalence means that actors play similar roles, control information, and have access to resources in the same or different networks. Structural equivalence is observed when an actor has the same relationships within the same network as another actor (comparisons within the same network). However, if the actor has a similar position in a different network, then the equivalence of role is observed (comparisons between networks). Network cohesion is observed in the behavior of the so-called cliques, or subgroups, and their impact on actors' behaviors, which become limited by the structure of the group to which they belong (they may experience pressure from other actors and behave similarly).

As shown in Figure 1.1, network theory, social network theory, and social network analysis are deeply rooted in social capital and sociology. A vast majority of researchers use social networks and social network analysis to study selected fragments of organizational reality and the organization as a group, in which things are perceived from the perspective of the network (relationships). Organizations are established through expansion of interpersonal relations and their networks. Within an organization understood in this way, social capital is created, which requires the existence of more or less institutionalized relations (Bourdieu, 1980, as cited in Lin, 1999). As opposed to Bourdieu, Coleman (1988) highlights the benefits of the community network, leading to higher effectiveness, rather than benefits that an individual can gain in the network of relationships.

According to Simmel (Simmel & Wolff, 1950), sociology can disregard an individual and a community, taking into account the forms of interpersonal relations and emphasizing relations between the elements rather than the entirety or particular individuals. Simmel uses a geometrical metaphor to define shapes and social forms, understood as various configurations of social relations that result in the formation of organizations. Now, these relationship forms would be called knowledge networks, information networks, task networks, or resource networks, expressing mutual relations between individuals in an organizational setting. The importance of human actions and communications is the central aspect of social reality for Mead (1934) and Blumer (1986), for whom the interaction between individuals is the most important element of society, as well as of organization and labor division. However, Mead, similarly to Simmel, rejects the existence of objectified nonhuman objects, which is the case in actor–network theory, where it is taken for granted. Nonhuman objects (which include intangible resources) are essential to organizational network analysis, as without them, a complete network analysis of intra-organizational relations would be impossible.

Social capital is strongly related to the network-based view (Diez-Vial & Montoro-Sanchez, 2014), in which access to new sources of knowledge is one of the main benefits of social capital. It refers to embedded knowledge, available as a result of interactions between people and their network of connections. It is a commonly used concept, which allows for observing the consequences of the social network for its members (Adler & Kwon, 2002). The term "social capital," also in the organizational context, was first used in 1916 by Lyda J. Hanifan (1916), one of the first scholars to make comparisons between an informal community and a company or corporation. He was an activist working to engage the local school community in efforts to improve the quality of teaching and create a parent community. Nahapiet and Ghoshal (1998) defined social capital as the sum of real and potential resources, embedded in the network and available through it, derived from the network, or possessed by an individual or a social group. Therefore, social capital includes both the network and the assets that can be used through the network of relations in the organization. Another angle is provided by Bourdieu (as cited in Richardson, 1986), for whom social capital is a collection of real and potential resources associated with the existence of a permanent network of institutionalized relations based on personal contacts or on entering into personal relationships for personal gain. In Coleman (1988), social capital is viewed in the light of its functions. It is positioned in the structure of relations between actors and actions. The author refers to the agency of social capital, which enables the achievement of objectives which would be unattainable without it. As opposed to Bourdieu, Coleman emphasizes the benefits of the network for a group—it is a property of the group, which makes their actions more successful. Similarly, in Putnam (1995), social capital refers to the features of social organizations such as networks, norms, and social trust, which improve coordination and cooperation for mutual benefit. Here, social capital has both an individual and a group aspect; it shapes social networks and norms of reciprocity, as well as the trust built on them.

This notion points to the network of individual and collective relations understood as a resource that can be exchanged for other goods or services. The influence of social ties and networks on the actions of members, which results from the context, is the central mechanism making it possible for networks to provide participants with resources and structural benefits that form social capital (Granovetter, 1985; Moran, 2005). This mechanism is referred to as embeddedness. Since individuals in organizational settings are deeply rooted in the network of interpersonal relations, their actions are inevitably affected by the consequences of network embeddedness. This embeddedness represents the history of interactions between the members of the network, which leads to the emergence of routines and stabilizes network relations. Embeddedness results from personal relations and is a function of the configuration of the whole network. It takes two forms (Moran, 2005): relational and structural embeddedness (Table 1.1).

Relational embeddedness focuses on the results of network confinement resulting from strong ties and cohesion in the network, which may promote trust, cooperation, and support among actors. On the other hand, it may also limit their freedom due to strong norms and common expectations (Coleman, 1988; Granovetter, 1973). Structural embeddedness emphasizes the implications of structural features of the network, such as structural equivalence and structural holes, which generate costs and benefits for the network members (Burt, 2009). Embeddedness reflects mechanisms through which users experience the consequences of social capital (e.g., access to diverse information and knowledge).

Table 1.1 Forms of embeddedness and its elements

Relational embeddedness	*Structural embeddedness*
Strong ties	Weak ties
Dense network	Loose network
Trust, cooperation, reciprocity	Structural equivalence
Limited freedom	Structural holes
Strong norms and expectations	Access to more diverse information and knowledge
Interpersonal trust and credibility	
Overlapping identities and a sense of intimacy	
Interpersonal solidarity	

Source: Based on Granovetter (1985) and Moran (2005).

The above theoretical deliberations introduce us to subsequent approaches, actor-network theory and activity theory, that highlight the nonhuman elements of networks. Recognition of both nonhuman and human elements of a network and identification of their interrelationships within an adopted socio-technical system (organization) is an important element of organizational network analysis.

1.1.2 Actor–Network Theory

Actor–network theory (ANT) is strongly associated with science and technology studies, a field of research concerned with the history of science, technology, and innovation. This discipline emerged in the 1970s in the Sociology of Scientific Knowledge program (the Edinburgh School), which in ANT is the ontology of community transformations (Latour, 1999). Here, the community includes both human and nonhuman factors. The most notable representatives of ANT are Bruno Latour, Michael Callon, and John Law (Law & Hassard, 1999). ANT rejects the category of knowledge as something static and inhabiting the mind, in favor of building the network and seeing the knowledge-generating processes in the context of connections between heterogeneous actors, including dynamic relations between people and nonhuman factors. Rather than describing the network as an object, ANT concentrates on the practice of network formation and stabilization, as well as on the emergence of new actors (Latour, 1988; Law & Hassard, 1999). In the organizational reality (in which the organization can be an actor or an actor-network), ANT sees issues as complex, cohesive, and mutually dependent. Similarly to social network analysis, organizational network analysis (ONA), or dynamic network analysis (DNA), transformations related to an individual actor (both positive and negative) often affect the whole network (its development, impairment, or in extreme cases—destruction).

The literature on networks, mainly inter-organizational, social, or strategic, is increasingly available and interdisciplinary, making references to many fields—not only organization theory and strategic management, but also IT, epidemiology, public administration, sociology, communication, and psychology. In this context, ANT can be seen as an instrument that explains the dynamics of the organizational network at both the micro and macro level. Actor-network, translation, and actor (actant) are the basic elements in ANT, as shown in Figure 1.2.

What distinguishes ANT (also known as the sociology of translation) among other network theories is the agency of nonhuman actors. Any animate (person) or inanimate (e.g., item, idea) object alike can be an actor or actant (Latour, 1987). This means that all socio-technical elements of an organization have the same impact on the organizational reality. In ANT, this phenomenon is called "generalized symmetry" (Callon, 1984), and its elements can be described with the same terms.

The term *network* is defined as a group of unspecified relationships between entities of which nature itself is undetermined (Callon, 1993). The actor-network is not limited to social entities and includes two notions: the sociogram (people) and the technogram (objects). In the case of the sociogram, sociological analysis, for example, social network analysis, focuses on a collection of alliances (Wasserman & Faust, 1994). The technogram, on the other hand, comprises all locally specific technical elements that connect people. Therefore, it seems incorrect to study these systems separately, as they are linked. Any change in the technogram usually entails a reduction of limitations in the sociogram, and vice versa (Latour, 1987). Correlations between the sociogram and the technogram become apparent, for example, when a resource is not used by its specified user. One way of reacting to this mismatch is changing the resource, which may be accepted by the users (sociogram change) or changing the user. In order to understand the dynamics on one level of the network, it is necessary to study the dynamics of the other. The actor and the network are mutually constitutive. The actor cannot operate without the network, and the network is composed of actors. This dependency is

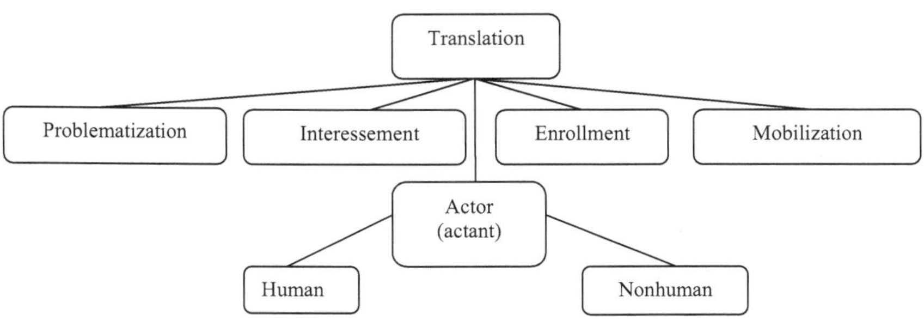

Figure 1.2 Elements of actor–network theory

Source: Based on Callon (1984).

highlighted in one more definition of an actor, as any element that bends space around itself, makes other elements dependent upon itself, and translates their will into the language of its own (Callon & Latour, 1981).

One of the main elements of ANT is the notion of translation (Callon, 1984), which refers to the process of creating an actor-network. Actors can be simultaneously engaged in many different translation processes, each of them having a different character and sequence of actions. The number of actors seems indefinite, which means that the analysis of translation usually occurs from the point of view of a chosen (main) actor and is iterative in nature (the actor-network can be the next defined actor, which thus becomes the main actor). The basic stages of the translation process, or creation of the actor-network, are: problematization, interessement, enrollment, and mobilization. In problematization, the identified main actor formulates interests of other actors (allies) according to its own interests, thus becoming the so-called obligatory passage point (OPP). Interessement consists of convincing other actors to follow the formulated interests of the main actor (for example, by adopting a given role or function) and to become engaged. Enrollment involves the adoption of interests (roles, functions) by other actors. The last element of the translation process is mobilization of the allies, which allows for determining representation (who represents whom). In ANT, there are no elements existing outside of the network. Inclusion in the network of relationships is inevitable, which makes all the elements of the actor-network connected (by interests, roles, functions, etc.). These relations make the system (the actor or actant that behaves in a certain way) dynamic, and the dynamics are present in constantly developing and evolving relations. These four forms of translation intermingle and create a network of relations.

The analysis of network heterogeneity can be a path to mapping the complexity and diversity of resources in organizations. Such socio-technical networks can become the foundation for future technological development. If resources are sustainable, the stabilization of translations resulting from these resources must be explained. ANT also explains why and how networks function by analyzing the network of influences that shape social behaviors. ANT assumes that each actor is equally important for the social network, while social order results from efficient functioning of the actor-network. This order may be disrupted if one or more actors are removed. This approach entails an increased level of specificity and accuracy in network studies. Since social and technical elements must be combined, one is encouraged to describe the particular mechanisms linking the networks in more detail, including their context-specific nature and location within social relations and power dynamics (Steen, 2010).

One interesting aspect of ANT is its dynamic view of the network, which is not emphasized in network theory or SNA. At present, it is not enough to look at the organization only in terms of possession and evaluation of resources. This perspective is certainly static. It must be complemented with the notion of "organizing," or constructing a network of activities (Czarniawska, 2017). Resource dynamics in the process of value creation, activities, and skill transformation are crucial (Kianto, 2007). This is the perspective from which intangible resources are discussed in Chapter 2.

1.1.3 Activity Theory

Activity theory (AT) is mainly associated with authors such as Vygotsky (1978) and (Leont'ev, 2000). It is also called "cultural and historical activity theory," as it considers the environment, history, culture, and the role of artifacts, motivation, and complexity in actual human activity. Though rooted in psychology, it is an interdisciplinary approach, oriented, for example, toward researching labor and technology (Engeström, 2000; Nardi, 1996). Its main premise is the understanding of complex dynamics of collective effort. AT emphasizes the importance of systemic analysis of the organizational environment, considering it a network of interrelated activities. It offers an analysis of direct and indirect relations linking individuals and the community. In order to achieve the desired result, it is necessary to identify objects, which can be tangible or intangible, and may include, besides many others, knowledge, products, or processes. Human activity is mediated by tools and artifacts, depending on the specific actions. Activities are also mediated by communities, which might support the activity or not (e.g., facilitate or obstruct access to resources); and impose rules regarding types of products, knowledge, experiences, which might be enforced by some form of labor division (Figure 1.3). Activity patterns within an activity system, including interactions, conflicts, transformations, and past, present, and future activities, are examined and explained.

The activity-based view assumes that value is increasingly dependent on the micro activities of managers and other people in the organization (Johnson, Melin, & Whittington, 2003; Morgan & Carley, 2019). It penetrates the organization and its strategies and processes in order to determine what is done and by whom. Many resource-based studies disregard the activity that takes place in the organization. However, the value of resources depends not on their existence, but on their utilization. At the micro scale, the analysis begins not with the organization as an entirety, or its business units, but with the actions of individuals, groups, or networks of people involved in core processes and practices.

In an organization, many unique activities are observed, together with their influence on the organization's members and development potential, forming more or less sustainable systems of collective human activity. In Poland, the most reputable authors in the field of praxeology (the study of

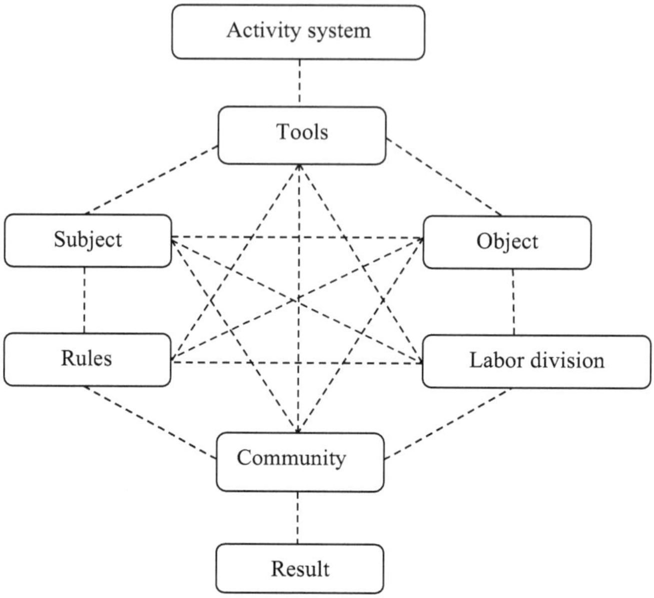

Figure 1.3 The structure of the activity system
Source: Based on Engeström (2014).

human action) include Gasparski (1999), Kotarbiński (1982), and Zieleniewski (1981). These systems are socio-technical in nature and include between three and six components[5] of collective activity (Engeström, 2014; Kuutti, 1996), as shown in Figure 1.3. These are object, subject, tools (resources, signs), rules, community, and labor division. All these components constitute a specific infrastructure, which enables employees to gain knowledge, perform tasks, use resources (Blackler, 1995), and be a part of a complex network of interactions. By adopting the activity system as an analysis unit, AT avoids simple causal explanations and describes the organization as a set of multiple systematically interacting elements, some of which (tools, social rules, labor division) play an intermediary role. The studied activity system can be, for example, a sector, an industry, an organization, a business unit, a society (group), a business model, or even a business process. An organization as an activity system is useful for discovering the character of work (performing tasks, using resources), knowledge, and organizational skills. In this approach, knowledge depends on actors and activities, and is produced by discourse and interpersonal communication (Blackler, 1993). From the organizational point of view, the main reason for sharing knowledge is to enable transforming an object of activity into a desired result.

Activity is the key term in AT, and is understood as purposeful, evolving, and transforming interactions between subjects (participants) and objects. The essence of activity is work and the so-called transformation of elements into a complex result, which is social in character. This points to the social roots of motivations and helps explain the cohesion of various activities (Blackler, 1993). Activity is also a dynamic phenomenon, in which a key role is played not only by stability and consensus, but also by conflicts, disruptions, and divisions. They result from relationships among tangible and intangible activities, the actor (intentions, behaviors), and the community (collective practices) (Blackler, 1993). Engeström (2014) emphasizes that the analysis of human activity is moving from researching tangible activities and communication processes to the analysis of the context of activities in which people, objectives, tools, and language are located in a broader social and structural setting.

In an organization, the elements of the activity system interact. The notion of intermediation is also important (Blackler & Regan, 2009; Engeström, 2014; Vygotsky, 1978). Tools are intermediaries between the subject and the object, rules—between the community and the subject, division of labor—between the community and the object. They are presented as the transformations of the nature of context in which people operate. Engeström emphasizes that people do not only think—they also operate in practice, modeling (shaping) their intangible environment in cooperation with others. Intermediations are perceived as constitutive features of human activity. They combine the thoughts and actions of an individual with cultural, social, and technological tools (Blackler & Regan, 2009).

Regarding the subject (the actor, group of actors, or community), the relationship between artifacts (tools) boils down to their availability and utility to the subject (e.g., whether an actor can work with specific software). On the other hand, the object is related to the possibility of being transformed into the desired effect (result), for example, through effective methods of object transformation. The object of activity should not be confused with its objectives. In AT, the object can be a product, project, or even a business process, whereas objectives are the intended result of project or process implementation (Blackler & Regan, 2009). The intermediary role of labor division in relation to the object concerns the mode of work and task division or integration with a view to achieving the desired result (transformation of the object). By applying this relation to the subject (labor division–subject), one can examine the role that the subject plays in the overall activity, or the restrictions on the subject's behavior resulting from labor division. At the group level, this relation is similar in character, enabling an examination of the number and complexity of tasks performed by a given group of actors (community). In a different relation: rules–subject (community), the interaction concerns the scope and internalization of the rules by the subject (community), taking into account personal interest of the subject (community). At the same time, the subject (community) can contribute to the development of social rules (principles), and the social rules (principles) can restrict the behavior of the subject (community).

These are only some relations and interpretations of intermediations (by tools, rules, labor division) to be found in the activity system (e.g., at the organization or business process level). The so-called socio-spatial expansion (Engeström, 2000, 2001) allows for the expansion of the activity area from individual relations to complex networks of relations (connections) engaged in the activity. Collective action is capable of solving conflicts and expanding the activity from a single interaction to the whole network of relations, and from single occurrences to long-term transformations of the objective. Individuals are capable of moving from one activity to another, resolving conflicts between them.

In addition to analyzing relations between elements, the activity system structure also enables identification of conflicts between the elements of this structure. These are defined as historically conditioned properties of the structures, suggesting disruptions and tensions in activity systems (Blackler & Kennedy, 2004). In AT, each activity in the system is affected by the primary conflict resulting from the capitalist order of production, that is, that between the use value and the exchange value of goods. Engeström (1993) uses the example of fundamental conflicts experienced by physicians in their work, where they play the role of gatekeepers and cost-efficient producers on the one hand, and of healers and consultants on the other. Furthermore, activity systems are prone to secondary conflicts, because they are open systems, and every novelty introduced in an element of the activity system can change the quality of the system and, as a consequence, produce conflicting relations between the transformed element and the other elements of the system. Conflicts associated with disruptions and tensions are seen as sources of learning, development, and innovation. They can lead to the emergence of new work and new methods of organization.

Zott and Amit (2010) present an interesting concept of applying AT in business model analysis. The authors define a business model as an activity system comprising two complex parameters: the architecture and the sources of value creation. The architecture includes content, structure, and the activity management system. The content of the activity system includes the selection of activities, and the structure defines how activities are related to one another, while management defines who will perform the activity. In practice, these elements demonstrate how organizations do what they do through a specific business model (Balboni & Bortoluzzi, 2015; Freiling, 2015; Günzel-Jensen & Holm, 2015; Jokela & Elo, 2015; Straker & Wrigley, 2015). The second parameter describes sources of value creation, which comprise novelty, lock-in (difficulty of change resulting from high costs of switching and engagement), complementarities, and efficiency.

Both ANT and AT assume that value creation is always relational, and emphasize the importance of human and nonhuman actors in forming and maintaining knowledge-based relations (Frith, 2014). The next section discusses social network analysis, organizational network analysis, and dynamic network analysis. It seems that ANT and AT, as opposed to SNA, are much better suited to analyzing the heterogeneous nature of the network. These shortcomings are compensated for in ONA and DNA, further discussed in subsequent sections (1.2.2 and 1.2.3, respectively).

1.2 Social Network Analysis vs. Organizational Network Analysis—Toward the Dynamic Approach

1.2.1 Social Network Analysis

The first publications using the phrase "social network analysis" appeared in the 1970s, written by authors including Breiger, Boorman, and Arabi (1975). Nonetheless, most articles and books including the phrase in their title, abstract, or keywords were published in the last five years. This rapid growth demonstrates that SNA has been accepted by scientific and academic circles, and even by practitioners and consultants, as a justified and useful way of understanding networks, organizations, and phenomena. This occurred partially because it became easier to obtain and analyze large amounts of relational data (Burt, Kilduff, & Tasselli, 2013). Due to the growing popularity of the social network approach, scientists found ways to include it in their research. Wasserman and Faust (1994) claim that the rapid development of quantitative analytical, mathematical, and statistical techniques for representing network data, and the possibility of visualizing network relations, are the two pillars of SNA.

In the broadest sense, SNA has been defined as a study of actors and the relations that connect or divide them (Freeman, 2004). It stems from the work of Moreno (1934 and the measurement of interpersonal relations in small groups (Wasserman & Faust, 1994). Moreno (1934) introduced the notion of sociometry—a mathematical analysis of psychological properties of the population, also defined as a method of measuring the kinship between people. Moreno tried to explain an outbreak of runaways from the New York Training School for Girls in Hudson. His analysis showed that the ability to predict which girls run away had very little to do with their individual features and attributes, but was strongly determined by relational connections and cliques existing among the girls (Borgatti, Mehra, Brass, & Labianca, 2009). Finding a method for modeling the observed social phenomena remained a challenge for Moreno in the early years. Hence the emergence of the sociogram—a picture in which all social individuals are represented as points in a two-dimensional space, and relations between pairs of people are represented by lines joining the respective points (Wasserman & Faust, 1994). By mapping the social network of the school, Moreno was capable of understanding the course of social influence and the flows of ideas between the girls, as well as the social factors that caused some of the girls to run away. From that moment on, many scientists and scholars (e.g., Hollenbeck & Jamieson, 2015; Kim, Howard, Pahnke, & Boeker, 2016) have used the methods and terminology required for more advanced quantitative analyses, which evolved into what we now know as social network analysis.

The importance of SNA is based on three basic assumptions concerning patterns of relations and their consequences. First of all, structural relations are more important in understanding observed behaviors than the features (attributes) of the individual. Standard research, social, and behavioral methods focus on the attributes of individual actors, while modern social research focuses mainly on the structure of relations existing between the subjects (Scott, 2012). Many attributes remain unchanged in various social contexts in which the subjects participate, while the structural relations only exist in a specific place and time and are dependent on the participants. The transition to attributes in relations involves changes in theoretical frameworks, from monadic to dyadic variables, mainly comprising social relations and repetitive interactions. In a dyad, ties are formed through shared nodes, creating a field or a system of interrelations called a network (Borgatti, Brass, & Halgin, 2014). Second of all, social networks affect perceptions, beliefs, and activities through various structural mechanisms, that is, socially constructed relations between individuals. Direct contact and more intense interactions mean that individuals have better information, higher awareness and sensitivity, and are more influential or influenced. Third of all, structural relations should be perceived as dynamic processes (see Section 1.2.3 on dynamic network analysis below). This rule indicates that networks are not static; they constantly change at the individual, group, or organizational level. Since network analysis comprises both structures and subjects, it should provide concepts and tools for combining changes occurring at the individual (micro) level and the structural (macro) level.

Network research adopts a characteristic perspective, which focuses on relations between subjects. In SNA, these are usually individuals, administrative units (departments, branches), or organizations. In this perspective, actors are embedded in a network of connected relations, which affect social behaviors of those involved. It differs from the traditional perspectives of organizational research where particular subjects are studied in isolation. What dominates in the network approach is focus on relations rather than attributes, and on organized patterns of interaction rather than singular features of specific actors (Brass, Galaskiewicz, Greve, & Tsai, 2004).

SNA aims at understanding formal and informal interactions and interrelations in the work environment. These relations between employees are fundamental for understanding the way in which information, data, work instructions, skills, and advice are shared and distributed among colleagues at various levels of management (see research on communication networks, information sharing, advice networks in public health organizations: Benham-Hutchins, Carley, Brewer, Effken, & Reminga, 2018; Brewer, Carley, Benham-Hutchins, Effken, & Reminga, 2018; Brewer, Carley, Benham-Hutchins, Effken, Reminga, et al., 2018). SNA includes a unique set of tools that allows for revealing patterns of human interaction. It is both an approach and a set of techniques used for investigating resource exchanges between subjects (Scott, 2012). For example, according to Müller-Prothmann (2007), SNA can be useful in knowledge management, including:

- assessment of knowledge availability and distribution;
- development of strategic organizational knowledge;
- identifying personal knowledge and experience;
- transferring and securing tacit knowledge;
- development of key capabilities;
- identifying the community of practice;
- creating and discovering opportunities for improving communication and efficiency.

Networks and the relational view can explain the organizational effects, which could not be fully understood with the use of traditional research methods or conceptual frameworks involving individual attributes. The book by Wasserman and Faust (1994) is a comprehensive source of information, definitions, and terminology used in SNA. It is also the most cited one—with 25,456 citations according to Google Scholar as of September 2016. As such, it is a good starting point for introducing some key principles and foundations of SNA. Thus, there is no need to discuss all the textbook elements of SNA, such as network data, network characteristics of actors, global network properties, or groups within networks in detail. Some of these are discussed in sections devoted to network metrics for intangible resource audit (Section 2.3.2) and the study design and identification of basic nodes (Chapter 3).

The social network perspective includes theories, models, and applications that are expressed in relational categories of notions and processes. Organizational environment, from the perspective of social networks, is represented as a pattern of relations between the participants of interactions. The social network perspective assumes that subjects exist in a network of relations with other subjects (Brass, 2003). The expression *social network* refers to a set of actors and the presence or absence of social ties between them (Wasserman & Faust, 1994). A social network can also be seen as a specific set of ties between the subjects and their properties, which, as a whole, can be used for interpreting social behaviors of the involved subjects (Tichy, Tushman, & Fombrun, 1979).

SNA allows for modeling the structure of relations between people in order to understand the social environment of a given group. It is possible, then, to study the influence of this structure on the functioning of the group and its influence on its members. Apart from the fact that they use relational terms, Wasserman and Faust (1994) define the following principles important for the social perspective of the network:

- actors and their activities are seen as interrelated, not as independent, autonomous units; ties between subjects are channels for transfer or flow of tangible and intangible resources;
- network models concentrating on the individual capture its structural network environment, which provides opportunities for individual actions or restricts them;
- network models conceptualizing social, economic, and political structures are permanent patterns of relations between subjects.

A combination of SNA and social capital theory, discussed in the previous section (1.1.1), reveals relations between individuals and the development of social network structure (Adler & Kwon, 2002). The network structure reflects an analysis of structural attributes in the network on three levels: node, dyad, and entire network. The network structure includes two main concepts: cohesion and location (Burt, 2001). The research aims at developing a permanent pattern of connections and disconnections between subjects (Kilduff & Brass, 2010), developing theoretical frameworks capturing the structural features of the network, and studying their influence on network members, patterns of creation, and transformations. Cohesion stands for the level of mutual socialization between two subjects, and is rooted in their interaction, shared experiences, and emotional intimacy. Location refers to the positions of the main actors in the whole network, and defines a general pattern of their connections with other subjects. Cohesion defines the content of resource flow. Highly cohesive connections facilitate the exchange of resources between partners, who act in accordance with mutual expectations. In turn, social ties with low cohesion enable participants to reach partners with unique resources and to access diverse resources (Burt, 1987; Coleman, 1990). On the other hand, actors' locations and positions in the whole network demonstrate the overall situation of actors, available resources and their roles, and actions and interactions in the network (Borgatti & Foster, 2003).

The social network as a social structure is composed of nodes connected by a set of specific ties. In social network research, ties can be strong or weak, direct or indirect. Relationships can take the form of clusters or small worlds. Positions in the network are described by centrality, betweenness, and closeness. At the node level, the network structure constructs demonstrate the actor's position in the network. One essential example of an actor's position in the network is *centrality*, which refers to the degree to which the actor is central, or important, to the network (Brass et al., 2004). The *strength of ties* can represent the frequency and intensity of interactions, the duration of a relationship, or the closeness between two actors (Granovetter, 1973). At the network level, structural features include network density and network cohesion (Scott, 2012).

An increasing number of publications discuss the use of network techniques in organizations and management. Among the top 30[6] journals in the fields of business, management, and accounting, and in the "Management and strategy" category, according to the Scimago Journal Ranking (2015), were journals listed in Table 1.2, which published articles featuring the phrase "social network analysis" in their title or abstract. The Web of Science database was used to select the articles, 48 in total.

Most articles published in prestigious management journals concerned inter-organizational networks of relations, which are not the subject of this book. The remaining 15 articles concerned intra-organizational relations. However, the subject matter was varied, even if we only consider networks in an organizational setting. One topic concerns formal (resulting from hierarchy and centralization) and informal coordination mechanisms affecting ways knowledge is shared in a large organization

Table 1.2 Ranking of journals in the "management and strategy" category

Rank	*Title*	*No. of papers*	*Hirsch index*
2	*Academy of Management Review*	2	193
3	*Organization Science*	7	167
4	*Journal of Management*	2	145
5	*Strategic Management Journal*	3	199
7	*Journal of Operations Management*	4	134
11	*Academy of Management Perspectives*	2	88
13	*Organization Studies*	2	102
14	*Omega*	2	90
15	*Research Policy*	14	160
22	*Tourism Management*	1	110
24	*Journal of Product Innovation Management*	3	101
25	*International Journal of Operations and Production Management*	2	94
26	*Human Relations*	2	90
28	*Long Range Planning*	2	69
	Total	48	

(Tsai, 2002) that has many cooperating and/or competing parts. Knowledge sharing between individuals and organizational units can enhance general organizational capabilities through collective learning and synergistic benefits resulting from the exchanges of information, know-how, and local knowledge. Knowledge is asymmetrically distributed in various units inside an organization. Without efficient coordination, knowledge is unequally distributed in the organization, and thus the reduction of limitations resulting from hierarchy and centralization can increase social relations between units, leading to internal flow of knowledge.

In Currie and White (2012), brokering (intermediary transfer) of knowledge in an organization is characterized by the professional hierarchy. Professional affiliation and authority differentiate the influence resulting from knowledge brokering on individual and group levels in the organization. Social structures can be studied at any level of the organizational hierarchy. Knowledge development is reflected in both formal and informal organizational procedures, which create social relations extending beyond professional hierarchy. This promotes knowledge brokering (transfer). One of the fields where SNA is commonly applied is human resource management (Hollenbeck & Jamieson, 2015), as it can be useful for identifying and selecting the most efficient employees, improving training and development programs, and implementing knowledge management programs. The topic of knowledge and methods of measuring it still fires up the imagination of researchers. One example is measuring individual organizational knowledge using an extensive and complex method called a "knowledge account" (Massingham, 2016), which uses network metrics.

In another study, Brass, Butterfield, and Skaggs (1998) analyze how the type of relation (strength of ties, status, diversity of relations, and the asymmetry of relations), organizational factors (climate, reward system, norms, and code of conduct), individual factors (level of control, morale, level of Machiavellianism), behavioral factors (gravity of consequences, social consequences, likelihood of effect occurrence, intimacy), and the structure of relations (density, cliques, structural holes, centrality) affect unethical conduct in the organization. Aven (2015) conducted a study concerning corruptive behaviors, using SNA to analyze the impact of corruption on communication (the role of information) among members of a project group. The study of negative relations also includes topics related to the analysis of aggressive behaviors in a governmental organization. The authors (Lamertz & Aquino, 2004) study the impact of the social structure model—power and status—on victimization in the workplace.

In their paper, Morel and Ramanujam (1999) focus on applying complex systems theory to organization theory. In complex systems theory, the authors include the concept of the evolution of an organization as a biological entity and SNA, specifically the combination of graph theory with the study of self-organization in a network. In a different study, Moliterno and Mahony (2011) point out that organizations are multitiered systems, and thus the theory of organizational network should also be multitiered and include networks at the individual, group (team), departmental, organizational, national, and international levels.

SNA and structural models are used to identify alternative mechanisms of interaction (Meyer, 1994), such as contact, norms defining group cohesion, or structurally equivalent positions or roles. The relative efficiency of various structural configurations in predicting similarities of perceptions and attitudes concerning the organization is assessed, and the mechanisms are analyzed from the perspective of social information processing in an organization.

SNA was also used in the methodology of new product development, based on an approach that can be planned, optimized, and verified (Leenders, Van Engelen, & Kratzer 2007; Leenders & Dolfsma, 2016). This approach is called a "systematic design method," and is associated with team creativity, mediated by patterns of social communication in the team. Features of communication, such as hierarchical decomposition, systematic change, satisfaction, and discursiveness, affect communication through subgroup creation, frequency of communication, level of compatibility and incompatibility in a team, or level of communication centralization. The study by Björk and Magnusson (2009) on the innovativeness of an idea (product or service) uses SNA to analyze interrelations between the quality of innovative ideas and the connectivity of the network of the idea provider. The analysis points to a clear relationship between connectivity in a network and the quality of ideas generated, measured by the level of novelty and utility for the organization. Ideas delivered by individuals with more numerous and varied relations inside and outside of the network are more innovative and of higher quality, as opposed to a dense network of relations in a single group, which results in less innovative and useful ideas.

One original study concerned the so-called "affective primacy" (Casciaro & Lobo, 2014) in task division and performance in the organization. The affect identifies cognitive and motivational mechanisms through which the affective value of social interactions (positive influence of interaction with a colleague) gives rise to instrumental value (subjective assessment of interaction when performing the assigned tasks). The study concerned the influence of positive emotions—excitement (a subjective state of feeling energized) and pleasantness (a subjective state of feeling gratified)—on performing tasks in a network. In a different study (DeRue, Nahrgang, & Ashford, 2015), patterns of interpersonal perception are used to explain the emergence of informal management structures. The origins of a group leader's experience from a social system (working with different people) and a technical system (the experience of a group leader involving managing projects from the same field), and its influence on team improvement, are presented in a study by Easton and Rosenzweig (2015).

The above overview of research interests demonstrates that SNA can be applied in diverse organizational studies. Some publications are empirical, while others are theoretical. In empirical studies, the authors most often use centrality indicators (degree, closeness, betweenness), and for the level of the whole network—density and centralization. They also use structural holes and subgroup (clique) analysis as the elements of the network structure. The diversity of topics also suggests that SNA can be used in all areas of organizational functioning and management where relations and ties exist.

The next section covers organizational network analysis, which is an extension of social network analysis, where network nodes (elements) can include people and network actors (including organizations or countries), and nonhuman elements (resources, tasks). SNA and ONA have become important parts of management science and its set of quantitative, qualitative, and graphic instruments, which allow for depicting and examining any fragment of the organizational reality from the point of view of relations and dependencies. In research, ONA takes the form of a meta-network, which means that it comprises not only human actors, but also (among many others) resources, tasks, and knowledge as network nodes (vertices). ONA is strongly associated with authors such as Cross and Parker (2004), mainly due to the embedding of SNA in the organizational context, though the authors mainly refer to the (human) actors of the network and do not mention the meta-network in their book.

1.2.2 Organizational Network Analysis

The previous section introduced the concept of SNA, and in this one, organizational network analysis will be discussed in more detail. There is no need to repeat the substantial and methodological foundations of the SNA that are also applied in ONA. (Intra)organizational networks are a way of thinking about the socio-technical system focused on connections between broadly understood actors (animate and inanimate). Every actor in the network has a feature that distinguishes it from other actors, referred to as an "attribute." The attributes of animate actors (people, teams, organizations) can include gender, age, experience, education, location, nationality, wealth, and many others, depending on the level of analysis (micro, meso, and macro). The macro level mainly concerns relations between organizations, which are not the subject of this book. Examples of inanimate objects' attributes include field of knowledge, level of innovation, heterogeneity, applicability to problem-solving (for knowledge), tangibility, intangibility (for resources), and associated business process (for tasks).

Similarly to SNA, ONA includes three areas of study: actor, dyad, and the whole network. At the level of an individual actor, we study, for instance, whether an actor with a larger number of international contacts achieves better results in sales. The dyadic level involves the analysis of a pair of actors who interact and create a relation (network). Then, we can study two matrices representing two different relations (e.g., professional and personal) and their influence on negotiating contracts. The network level is an aggregation of dyadic relations and their measurement. Here, areas of interest can include network density (the number of relations) and its influence on an organization's innovativeness. In dense networks, it is likely that actors will be assigned to similar tasks, and use of knowledge will occur much more frequently than development of (new) knowledge.

As has already been emphasized on numerous occasions, the notion of a network is derived from interpersonal relations within which social connections exist. Therefore, the *organizational network* is understood as a system of connections between people or organizational units (e.g., departments), created in order to exchange information, knowledge, ideas, and resources. Significant aspects of this network are internal relations, creation, flow, and use of information and knowledge. Utilization of information and knowledge in an organization is seen more broadly, as it is related to the performance of tasks that determine value creation or proposition. An organizational network is a form of informal cooperation among many independent actors, based on labor division among people and value creation through synergy. Social forms are, in other words, various configurations of interpersonal relations, which include variants of relations between people and information, knowledge, tasks, and resources. Organizational functioning is primarily based on interactions, that is, an ongoing exchange of knowledge and information occurring between people undertaking joint actions. By interacting, people create relations. The form and intensity of relations create the *network structure* (Alba, 1982).

In the organizational context, the inside of the organization (what is happening within its borders) determines the network structure of relations between the elements of this organization. Mead (1934) emphasizes the importance of human actions and information exchanges, rather than the social forms, because people bond with others through actions. These mutual ties of ongoing activities are what creates an organization (Blumer, 1986; Weber, 2015). Organizations referred to by Granovetter (1973) as larger social entireties are created by extending interpersonal relations and their networks at the micro and macro level.

In the intra- and inter-organizational context, many types of organizational networks exist, which can be classified as social or nonsocial, and one- or two-mode (Figure 1.4). One-mode social networks (AA, OO) include those networks whose members are actors (people or groups of people—A) and organizations (O), creating networks of information flows or inter-organizational business relationships. Two-mode social networks are created, for example, by assigning a location (L) to an

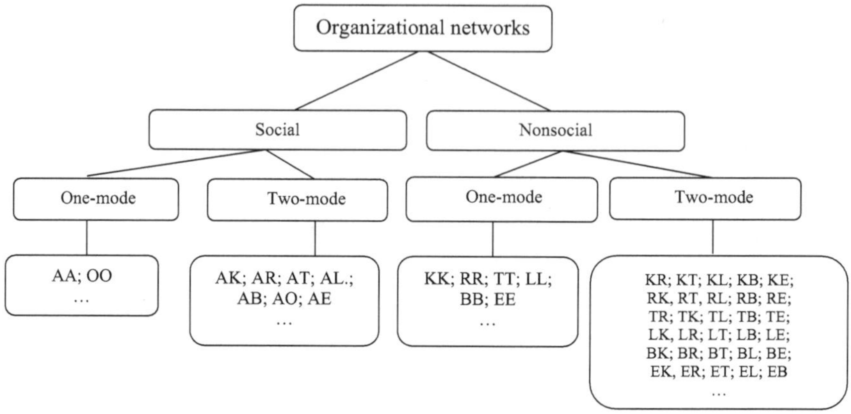

Figure 1.4 Types of organizational networks

Key: A—actor; O—organization; K—knowledge; R—resource; T—task; L—location; B—beliefs; E—event.

organization (O), or by beliefs (B) determining the organizational culture. In the case of nonsocial one- and two-mode networks, inanimate nodes, as understood in actor–network theory, can include knowledge (K), resources (R), tasks (T), or events (E), knowledge networks (AK), resource networks (AR), task networks (AT), and many others. The more nodes there are, the more combinations are possible.

The above-mentioned types of organizational networks create ontological classes, providing methods for classifying and segmenting nodes. Taking into consideration two ontological classes, one or more networks exist that are created by a given type of relation between two nodes. Some of these networks are one-mode, for example, social networks. Two-mode networks, on the other hand, combine node networks in one ontological class with another (e.g., employment location). As Carley (1999) points out, networks can be interpreted in the context of their ecology, which means that many networks exist (e.g., of information, knowledge, tasks) that mutually affect one another. In an organization, the social network (who contacts whom) is related to many other networks, including the task structure (to which task an employee is assigned) or knowledge structure (what knowledge the employee has and uses). Changes in any part of this network ecology affect all other parts, and maintenance of the whole system depends on the identification of how these networks are connected. An organization, or even a group or society, is in a constant state of flow. This flow often takes the form of transformations in the fundamental social and organizational networks; a phenomenon referred to as "network evolution." These networks influence the speed of information diffusion among people and in organizations, as well as the capability of individuals to acquire and use information, and the speed, quality, and accuracy of organizational decision-making. Therefore, transformations of these networks and their development can have far-reaching social and organizational consequences.

An *organization* is thus composed of interrelated actions (activities, tasks) implemented by people who are connected and use their knowledge and resources in these actions. It is a network of people who exchange and process information and knowledge in order to design the relational and process architecture of the organization. In this definition, the organization is seen from the point of view of dynamic interrelations between network actors, knowledge, resources, and tasks, which are crucial for its existence and development. The scope of actions here is very broad, covering all essential organizational activity (determined by business processes) that results (directly or indirectly) in value creation. These actions are humanistic, intentional, and causal in nature, as they concern people. In every action, a person uses the available information, knowledge, and resources to perform the assigned task. The organization is seen from the point of view of internal networking of actors (Agbim, 2019), including knowledge, resources, and tasks, in which an important role is played by the modeling of networks, flows, transfers, and exchanges. The flow of information, knowledge, resources, and tasks is inherently dynamic, and provides a valuable insight into the patterns of interactions between people or departments in the organization. When focus is placed on the efficiency of value creation in the whole system, less significance is attributed to whether an entity is technically an employee, a client, a colleague, or a supplier. What is important is whether this relation generates value.

Thus, an *organization* is as a collection of connected actors (animate and inanimate) who collaborate or interact in various, unlimited constellations (combinations of connections), thus creating a socio-technical system. Figure 1.4 by no means exhausts the types of networks and relations, which can also be discussed in association with the multitiered nature of networks (Brass, Galaskiewicz, Greve, & Tsai, 2004; Lomi, Robins, & Tranmer, 2016; Moliterno & Mahony, 2011).

In social research, social networks are very well identified. One-mode social networks (AA; OO) include relations distinguished by Borgatti, Everett, & Johnson (2018):

- similarity—including the similarity of location, participation, attributes (gender, age, attitudes);
- social roles—kinship, professional subordination;
- cognition—affect (to like, to hate);
- perception (to know);
- events—interactions (to sell, to talk, to help), flows (of information, money).

In two-mode social networks (Table 1.3), each actor (A) is assigned another type of node, which can be nonhuman, such as knowledge (K) or a resource (R) the person has or uses (network AK or AR), or a task (T) that the person can or does perform (network AT). Nonsocial networks, one- or two-mode, are not a popular topic in literature on management, and are usually associated with social networks. This is a field that requires further and more detailed examination by researchers, especially since, in the organizational context, nodes can take any form. The first attempts to identify and analyze nonsocial networks were undertaken by Krackhardt and Carley (1998). Networks and their various configurations shown in Figure 1.4 and Table 1.3 are called a *meta-network*, and enable one to simultaneously analyze many connected elements in the organizational (socio-technical) system. In the present book (see Chapter 3), an attempt is made to analyze, among many others, nonsocial two-mode networks KT (knowledge assigned to tasks) and RT (resources assigned to tasks).

The meta-network (multimodal) approach to organizations is a promising one, as it may help clarify complex relations and interactions in the organizational network. Meta-networks include additional modules, which go beyond interactions between actors (here: people), and are therefore multimodal (Carley, 1999). Using the multimodal perspective and the modeling opportunities available, one can accurately measure and diagnose how tasks are carried out and how knowledge and information are shared and resources used, contributing to the optimization of the planned and assigned activities. Usually, the meta-network is represented by several graphs for one organization or group. Each network is a reflection of its matrix, and therefore, by analogy, matrices and meta-matrices can be one-mode or two-mode, which means they can comprise a single type of elements or two different types (Tsvetovat & Carley, 2004). This flexibility allows for advanced and comprehensive analysis of socio-technical networks, which exceeds the standard analyses of individual nodes (social actors). With four groups of nodes (e.g., A, K, R, T), certainly, more than six different types of networks can be identified. In this book, only six combinations are discussed (AA, AK, AR, AT, KT, RT), as shown in Table 1.3. Based on these combinations, more complex network metrics have been developed, discussed in Section 2.3.2.

Table 1.3 Types of organizational networks forming a meta-network

Node	*Network*
Actor—A	Information network—actor to actor—AA
Knowledge and skills—K	Knowledge network—actor to knowledge—AK
Resource—R	Resource network—actor to resource—AR
Task—T	Task network—actor to task—AT
	Knowledge to task network—KT
	Resource to task network—RT

Source: Based on Krackhardt and Carley (1998)

Analysis of each network structure can provide a different insight into the organization. The information network (AA) serves to analyze, for example, the connections between employees in an organization. The knowledge, task, and resource networks (AK, AT, AR) enhance organizational perception in terms of what knowledge and resources employees have and use, and how they perform tasks. This is consistent with the concept of multiplexity of network relations, which, in the social relations only, can refer to various types of connections, not necessarily related to professional activity (Beckman & Haunschild, 2002). Attributes assigned to specific nodes in the network play an important role. For example, in the information network, they allow for identifying information silos associated with the position in organizational hierarchy, location, professional experience, and even gender or age.

As pointed out in Section 1.1, graph theory was one of the first attempts at interpreting and analyzing networks. The most frequently used mathematical conceptualization of a network is graph G (V, E), which is an object composed of a set of vertices (nodes) V and a set of edges (links) E. Each graph represents a different type of relations, which usually has a different structure. Graph H (V, A) represents a different relation in the same group of nodes. If two nodes (u, v) are linked by an edge, then (u, v)$\in$E(G). Graphs can be directed (if edges have a direction) or undirected (if edges or connections do not have a direction). Directed graphs can include reciprocated or unidirectional (unreciprocated) relations (Wilson, 2012). In order to understand the direction of a relation, let us assume that actor A01 provides information to actors A02, A06, and A09 (Figure 1.5). This relation is not reciprocated. Actors A02 and A09 do not provide information to A01. A mutual relation (e.g., providing and receiving information) occurs only between actors A01 and A02. For

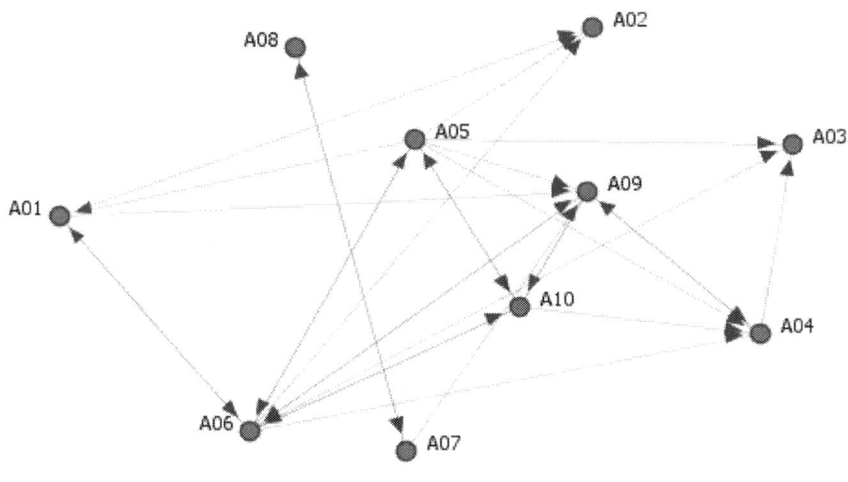

Figure 1.5 Example of a directed one-mode graph

a relation that involves providing and receiving information, two distinct matrices can be created. An example of a directed graph (one-mode AA, e.g., providing information) is shown in Figure 1.5.

In an organization, the vast majority of networks are represented by directed graphs, in which the direction of relation is significant. Many types of relations exist in an organization: interactions, actions, and flows, for which the centrality degree indicates the number of incoming and outgoing connections. These relations, even if they are undirected (reciprocated), cannot simply be assumed. They result from complex and diverse organizational interactions, as well as from formal and informal ties in the organization.

An adjacency matrix is a common form of presenting network data. In this case, rows and columns refer to nodes. A connection between row *i* and column *j* denotes the existence (a*ij* = 1) or lack of relation (a*ij* = 0) in the binary matrix. Figure 1.5 shows such a matrix (Table 1.4).

In each cell, the numbers in the matrix represent the existence or lack of a direct connection between the nodes. A value of 2 or greater indicates the frequency or strength of the relationship (Scott, 2012). Strong relationships can lead to more efficient communication, owing to the development of specific relations (Uzzi, 1997) or of inalienable, shared knowledge between the parties (Grant, 1996).

An *information network*[7] (AA) is based on a one-mode network whose nodes are actors (A) understood as employees (staff) of the organization, who are capable of working, and contribute to the exchange of information, social contacts, task division, and/or control over the resources. In organizational network AA, actor *i* is associated with actor *j* (AA*ij*) if actor *i* provides and/or receives information related to the work of actor *j*. In this case, the cell of the matrix for elements *ij* = 1.

Information is seen as omnipresent and widely distributed among employees in an organization. Uncertainty, understood as the difference between the amount of information needed to perform the tasks and the

Table 1.4 Example of an adjacency matrix (one-mode)

	A01	*A02*	*A03*	*A04*	*A05*	*A06*	*A07*	*A08*	*A09*	*A10*
A01	0	1	0	0	0	1	0	0	1	0
A02	0	0	0	0	0	0	0	0	0	0
A03	0	0	0	0	0	0	0	0	0	0
A04	0	0	1	0	0	0	0	0	1	0
A05	1	1	1	1	0	1	0	0	1	1
A06	1	1	1	1	1	0	0	0	1	1
A07	0	0	0	0	0	0	0	1	1	0
A08	0	0	0	0	0	0	1	0	0	0
A09	0	0	0	1	0	1	0	0	0	1
A10	0	0	0	1	1	1	0	0	1	0

amount of information already in possession of the organization, forces organizations to process information efficiently and effectively (Galbraith, 1974). ONA stems from the belief that traditional organizational patterns and process maps are not enough to grasp the complex network of informational interactions. The exchange of information is not clear cut, which is why it seems to be an uncontrollable process in most organizations. Therefore, ONA provides both graphic and qualitative analysis of complex socio-technical systems, including the flow of information in organizations, with results interpreted with reference to the formal organizational hierarchy, providing an opportunity to discover areas for improvement. By mapping these relations, information networks help reveal informal patterns of communication and compare them with the existing formal structures in order to explain the processes occurring in the organization. The position of an individual in the social structure of the organization helps explain its situation and control over information, based on the observed relations (Burt, 1987). Such a relational approach to understanding organizations includes a range of relations and interactions between individuals in a way that decreases uncertainty in the environment, which results from information shortage or overload. In the context of relationship network coordination, organizational integration based on informal social mechanisms contributes to collective problem-solving. According to the theory of information processing, members of the organization reach out for guidelines from both official and unofficial sources in order to give them a true sense, because behaviors are to a large extent driven by shared interpretations of events and actions (Soda & Zaheer, 2012). Therefore, informal networks are fundamental for the understanding of organizational learning, because they include a wide range of resources that can improve efficiency and potentially help coordinate actors in the organization (Hortoványi, Szabó, & Szabó, 2006).

The flow of information defines how information moves around in the organization. It is the key component of organizational learning and adaptation because how information is distributed in the organization defines the speed at which people can work and plan their future actions (Cricelli & Grimaldi, 2008; Wu, Huberman, Adamic, & Tyler, 2004). ONA serves as a useful technique for determining whether an employee in a given network position provides information to the remainder of the network. Employee positions defined as information suppliers are associated with a high level of information exchange. Early research into organizational networks demonstrated (Leavitt, 1951) how network structure affects the speed of information diffusion and the capabilities of a person to acquire and use information, which in turn affects the speed, quality, and accuracy of decision-making. Any changes in the information network correspond to changes in other networks, such as knowledge, task, and resource networks, affecting general organizational efficiency. Understanding the flow of information is an important factor in transforming information into knowledge. When we describe patterns of interactions between people and information in the organization, we gain an opportunity to analyze the flow of knowledge (created based on collective problem-solving and information exchange) beyond the functional and organizational boundaries, and to find areas where increased flow of knowledge will have the largest impact on overall performance and value creation.

Relational variables in the information network are understood here (per Cross & Parker, 2004) in a number of ways. They can take the form of communication (information flow), in which actor A01 provides information to actor A02, or actor A01 receives information from actor A05 (see Table 1.4). ONA also uses various indices of similarity between employees (homophily, similarity of relation due to experience, department, professional qualifications, etc.) concerning the representation of social structures and social positions in the organization. These representations are important for describing the work environment and its influence on the efficiency of information flow and the capability of an individual to acquire new knowledge.

ONA, within which *knowledge networks* are analyzed (one-mode—AA, and two-mode—AK), is a technique that allows one to define flows and bottlenecks related to knowledge inside the organization from the network perspective. This technique uses network knowledge graphs to visualize flows of specific knowledge between actors (AlDahdouh, Osório, & Caires, 2015), instrumental relations (with whom I discuss or solve complex problems at work), and the "knowing who" has what knowledge and skills. Network predictions of information diffusion, especially in the case of information concerning the knowledge and actions of other actors, are good indicators of the performance of the group (Carley, 2005). Knowledge lives in the minds of different people, and in order to use it effectively, one has to know who knows what. Both the creation and the utilization of knowledge is undoubtedly a social process, just like information is an element of the social network (Brown & Duguid, 2000). In reality, the network knowledge graph replaced the notion of a knowledge map in the knowledge audit. Actors of the knowledge network meet around a common goal. They are connected with one another by interdependent relations of exchange (informal networks) or formalized rules and procedures (Pugh & Prusak, 2013). The knowledge network, similarly to the network according to Wasserman and Faust (1994), is defined as a collection of individuals and teams who meet in various organizations in order to create and share knowledge, coordinate, learn, create innovation, and support individual members both inside and outside of the organization (Bourouni, Noori, & Jafari, 2015). In this network, nodes simultaneously provide and receive information and knowledge. Employees are not isolated from others in the organization, or are isolated only in singular cases. Through the network, an individual can gain access to valuable information and knowledge. Networking promotes knowledge sharing and transfer among actors, and provides employees with opportunities to learn and cooperate. The knowledge-sharing network is a process of social interaction which, by socialization and interaction, causes members to share information, ideas, and professional knowledge with others. In the knowledge network, every employee is a part of the network and occupies a different position in the network, which provides various opportunities of accessing new knowledge required to perform tasks (Wu, Yeh, & Hung, 2012).

A two-mode *knowledge network* (AK) is composed of two types of nodes: actor nodes (A) and knowledge nodes (K). Knowledge is perceived here as a set of coherent elements of procedural or declarative information, usually concerning the correct performance of organizational tasks. It allows for defining "who knows what" in an organization, but also how interpersonal network structures affect the level of knowledge utilization. The knowledge network comprises actors, knowledge, resources, and their relations established in the process of knowledge utilization. Since the knowledge network is constantly expanded with the knowledge gained in the learning process, it should be treated as a dynamic structure that combines various levels and areas of knowledge. It is important to foster the creation of networks between various types of knowledge, levels (individual, group, organizational), and areas of knowledge (such as knowledge about the market, a client, or a product). To demonstrate one example out of the many two-mode networks discussed in this book, a two-mode matrix (actors A and knowledge K) and the network that reflects it (AK) are shown in Figure 1.6 and Table 1.5. Rows include actors (A), while columns include areas of knowledge and skills (K). The connection AK*ij* in network AK demonstrates that actor *i* is connected to knowledge *j* if actor *i* has or uses knowledge *j* in his or her work.

The interpretation of each matrix starts with rows, for example, actor A01 has or uses knowledge and skills K04, K05, K08, and K12. Similarly, it is possible to show the *resource network*[8] (AR) by inserting tangible and intangible resources in columns. Resources in the network are passive organizational elements—they are tools for performing tasks and can be controlled by actors. The resource network (AR) defines access to resources (R) and their use by particular actors (A). The connection AR*ij* in network AR demonstrates that actor *i* is connected to resource *j* if actor *i* has or uses the resource in their work.

Coordinating the balance between information transfer, use of knowledge and resources, and performance of tasks is important for the organization. In the knowledge network, each actor is assigned a knowledge domain, and the ultimate relation, that is, connection of knowledge with the actor, depends on whether the actor uses the given knowledge when performing a task. The ability of actors to use their knowledge in association with

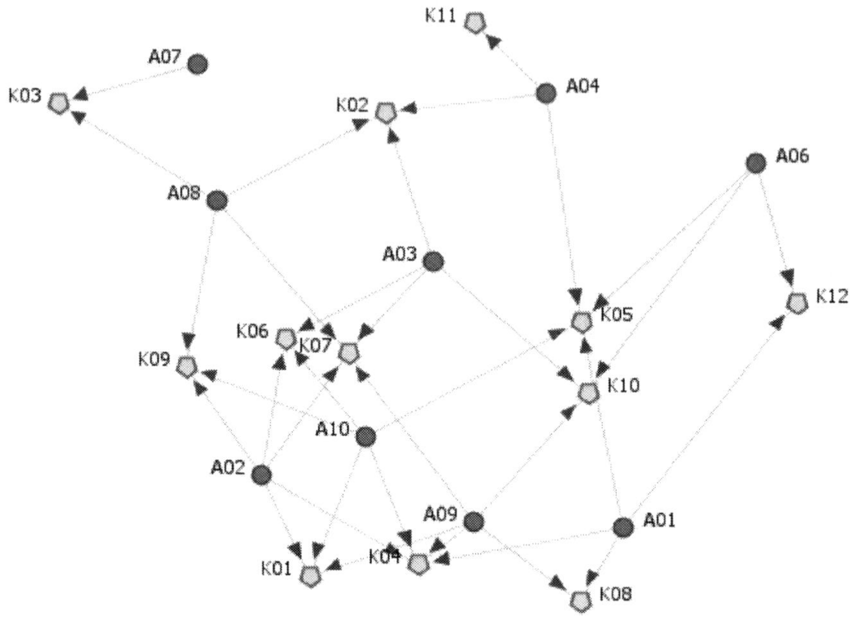

Figure 1.6 Example of a directed two-mode graph

Table 1.5 Example of an adjacency matrix (two-mode)

	K01	*K02*	*K03*	*K04*	*K05*	*K06*	*K07*	*K08*	*K09*	*K10*	*K11*	*K12*
A01	0	0	0	1	1	0	0	1	0	0	0	1
A02	1	0	0	1	0	1	1	0	1	0	0	0
A03	0	1	0	0	0	1	1	0	0	1	0	0
A04	0	1	0	0	1	0	0	0	0	0	1	0
A05	0	0	0	0	0	0	0	0	0	0	0	0
A06	0	0	0	0	1	0	0	0	0	1	0	1
A07	0	0	1	0	0	0	0	0	0	0	0	0
A08	0	1	1	0	0	0	1	0	1	0	0	0
A09	1	0	0	1	0	0	1	1	0	1	0	0
A10	1	0	0	1	1	1	0	0	1	0	0	0

tasks depends on how this knowledge is distributed among the members of the organization. Isolation of knowledge and actors makes it more difficult for the team to coordinate their tasks. When some actors have knowledge that is inaccessible to others, it is difficult to engage all people required to perform the task. Shared knowledge helps teams because it makes it possible to understand expectations, explain the task, and plan the actions in agreement with the whole team (Espinosa & Clark, 2014).

Knowledge utilization is seen as a process related to a specific task (the *knowledge–task network*, KT) to which knowledge is applied. The connection KT*ij* between knowledge and a task in network KT occurs when knowledge *i* is required to perform task *j*. Knowledge use can be measured in these relations. Task assignments (relations between actors and tasks—the *task network*, AT) play a particularly important role in measuring knowledge use. Tasks are the key element of business processes that must be performed by specific actions of the actor, usually with the participation of resources and knowledge. Using simulation focusing on nodes, that is, actor, knowledge, tasks, one can show how network features affect the level of knowledge utilization in the entire organization, as well as the coordination of the use and acquisition of knowledge. The task elements are the reflection of how resources are organized in order to execute a specific business process. Each of the tasks with the assigned resources becomes a separate class of nodes in the meta-network model, in which relations are modeled in the form of graphs. The connection AT*ij* = *v* between the actor and the task occurs in network AT if actor *i* can or does perform task *j*. Intra-organizational relations (determined by matrices) must be coordinated in order to achieve the required levels of information and knowledge sharing, and knowledge and resource utilization. The level of knowledge utilization depends on whether the acquired knowledge can be (re-)used. For example, the performance of a task requires a person who knows how to perform this task. However, the person assigned this task can only have partial knowledge on how to perform the task or even none at all. In this case, knowledge would not be used, or it would be used only partially. Therefore, the level of knowledge use is a function of task assignment to people with relevant knowledge. By understanding the complexity of information, knowledge, resource, and task flows among the employees in the organization, it is possible to identify ways for improving accessibility, utilization, and sharing of knowledge, to increase efficiency and value creation.

Penrose's groundbreaking work (1995) remains very popular to this day, as it made a massive contribution to the distinction between resources (R) and tasks (T). Resources are the potential for actions. They create the *resource–task network* (RT), which can generate various streams of services or activities. Without assigning specific resources (both tangible and intangible), it is impossible to perform the task (provide the service). When resource and activity nodes are identified, the interrelations created by various types of complementarities can be analyzed to determine the value of a resource (Milgrom & Roberts, 1995). For example, complementary resources may be connected within a given task. Activities can depend on one another when they use resources from the same pool.

The connection (RT*ij*) = *v* between resources and tasks in network RT occurs when resource(s) *i* is or are required to perform task *j*.

The organizational network was presented here are as a meta-network, comprising several connected social and nonsocial networks that form a complex and dynamic socio-technical system. It is impossible to provide an exhaustive analysis of organizational relations based solely on the social elements (employees and stakeholders of the organization), as Cross and Parker suggest (2004). Organizations are multi-agent entities, and nonsocial networks are their inherent part. The analysis of communication, network, and knowledge-sharing networks is not a complete organizational analysis, especially when these networks only include human actors. In this case, it is not known what knowledge and resources the employees share or use, or how they are connected with specific tasks that must be completed. Hence, it is important to analyze organizations from connections existing between the complex elements of the socio-technical system.

The next section details the dynamic approach to organizational networks, called dynamic network analysis, which is to an even larger extent based on the meta-network.

1.2.3 *Dynamic Network Analysis*

The features and regularities of the organization as a whole can be derived from the dynamic configuration of the socio-technical system, which in a way means that the organization is a process—it does not exist, but is constantly in a state of "becoming." Elias (2001) introduced a dynamic dimension into micro-sociological analyses by presenting figurations (dynamics of the network of relations)—the processes of creation and reproduction of interpersonal relations in ongoing interactions between individuals. The dynamic approach to firm growth according to Penrose (1995) is based on identifying key components of the enterprise, which allow one to explain the process of growth by proposing theories on the dynamics existing between the components (Demil & Lecocq, 2010). In this approach, the components are mainly tangible and human resources with incorporated services (tasks) used in value creation. Services provided by resources are a function of their use combined with various types or amounts of other resources. They depend on the managers' capability to extract value from their use and create more or less innovative combinations. The capability to extract services from resources depends on the development of knowledge by the company and can affect its expansion (Demil & Lecocq 2010). Permanent increases in knowledge on the effective use of resources or on new ways of using them can lead to the development of new value offerings. Similarly, the diversity of an actor's contacts in the network increases individual knowledge creation, as such networks provide access to diverse knowledge, which boosts chances of new recombinations (Rodan & Galunic, 2004).

The dynamic aspect of networks (*dynamic networks*) refers to relations and interactions between entities, within which transformations and flows of information, resources, and knowledge occur. Entire networks, in which actors are entangled, also constantly change their shape. These dynamics of the network affect every member of the organization. People change through their relations with other people and through the resources (both tangible and intangible) they create, share, or use in their actions. The dynamic aspect of network analysis in the organizational context was already noticed by Tichy, Tushman, and Fombrun (1979, p. 508). The authors point to the need to study both the static and dynamic aspects of organizations, and connections between the social objects, over time.

Direct references to dynamics in network science are made by Lewis (2009), who sees it as a study of the dynamic behavior of aggregated nodes and connections. In this respect, it tries to respond to a fundamental question: what happens to the network over time, as it develops, and why does that happen? According to Lewis (2009), the dynamic network is defined by a set of "micro-rules," concerning the behavior of nodes and connections, and "macro-rules," which determine the emergence of global properties of networks. A full definition of network G must include both structural and behavioral information, and take into consideration the time factor (Formula 1.1), which determines network evolution and transformation (Lewis, 2009):

$$G\ (t) = \{N\ (t), L(t), f(t): J\ (t)\} \tag{1.1}$$

Where: t—time; N—actor, node; L—links, connections, edges; f: N × N—matrix of connections (one- or two-mode); J—algorithm describing the behavior of nodes and connections at a given time.

As pointed out in the previous section (1.2.2), ONA comprises many types of nodes and unlimited combinations of relations between them, which form a meta-network. Dynamic network analysis is an extension of ONA, just like ONA is an extension of SNA, which is usually static. All of these techniques form a comprehensive *SODNA* model, based on solutions from each of the network models: SNA, ONA, and *DNA*. Table 1.6 presents connections between them based on types and behaviors of networks.

DNA brings together the traditional social network analysis, link analysis, and multi-agent models to simulate the dynamics of socio-technical system components (Carley, 2014; Carley, Martin, & Hirshman, 2009; Galup, Dattero, & Groll, 2011; Louie & Carley, 2008). According to Bonabeau (2002), in multi-agent models:

- each agent has its own individual attributes and behaviors that differ significantly from those of other agents;

Table 1.6 Elements of the SODNA model

Elements	*SNA*	*ONA*	*DNA*
Static approach	x	x	
Dynamic approach	x	x	x
Social networks	x	x	x
Nonsocial networks		x	x
Network combination	x	x	x
Network simulation	x	x	x
Network modeling	x	x	x
Longitudinal study	x	x	x
Cross-sectional study	x	x	

- the modes and topologies of interaction between agents are complex, and agents' behavior can change the behaviors of other agents;
- agent behavior adheres to complex rules, including, in particular, learning and adaptation to the changing environment;
- physical space is significant, and agents move in this space;
- the mapping of the system's process characteristics is a significant aspect.

Characteristics of the model correspond with characteristics of the socio-technical system reflected by the relationship network. Here, the agent is replaced by the actor (similarly to agents, actors can be human or nonhuman, i.e., be persons or resources), also equipped with individual attributes and behaviors (homophily and heterophily studies). The mode and topology of interactions (termed the network structure) are shaped in various ways, affecting and modifying other actors' behaviors. While nodes in the traditional SNA model are static, nodes in the DNA model have learning capabilities. Employees of an organization can acquire new skills or undertake new tasks, thus making the network dynamic. Transformation at the level of one node effects a transformation in another one and so on, leading to the evolution of the whole network. Another common feature of the multi-agent model and the dynamic approach to networks (socio-technical systems) is the physical space that determines the boundaries of the organization in which the actors move. In turn, the process features of the modeled socio-technical system can be reflected based on the identification and analysis of dynamics in the networks, including knowledge networks, resource exchange networks, and task performance networks.

What distinguishes DNA from ONA and SNA is the increased focus on the time factor (longitudinal study), which makes it possible to analyze the dynamics of transformations occurring in the observation period (Wolbers, Groenewegen, Mollee, & Bím, 2013) and to simulate transformations and model the network by adding or eliminating nodes and/

or relations. Certainly, both longitudinal studies and modeling may also be undertaken within SNA and ONA, though this makes them equal with DNA for all intents and purposes. In Table 1.6, only information, knowledge, resource, and task networks are presented, in line with the scope of this book. Network combinations should be understood as any combination of elements (nodes or whole networks) that create an entirety (meta-network), also with the use of matrix algebra operations (e.g., transposing, adding, or multiplying matrices). Network configuration is associated with the arrangement of elements, which can change under the influence of more or less forced circumstances. Within a given configuration, two approaches are examined: simulation and modeling of networks as forms of representation, which allow one to examine how networks evolve and adapt, as well as to study the influence of interventions on the behavior and structure of the network.

Cells of the meta-matrix define the elements that can be used in simulation based on the adopted set of criteria. There are costs and limitations involved in manipulating various aspects of the meta-matrix (Tsvetovat & Carley, 2004). Usually, the cells can be regulated by adding or removing nodes and/or relations or by changing the relations and the strength of ties. The key processes affecting node transformations are fluctuation of people, change in mission (addition or removal of tasks), change in technology (addition or removal of resources and tasks), resource consumption, and purchase or creation of resources. The key processes affecting changes in relations are reassignment of staff, training (knowledge generation), and the evolution of the communication structure. In most organizations, due to shortages of capital and investment funds, it is more difficult to change tasks and resources than personnel and knowledge, at least in the short run. The set of tasks is to a smaller or larger extent defined by the organizational mission and maintained technology, and addition or elimination of tasks or connections can be difficult in the short term. Changes in any (human) node of the network can potentially lead to changes in others. For example, new employees can bring in new knowledge and new connections with knowledge after access to knowledge has decreased due to a previous employee's departure.

Many organizations recognize the value of a person, knowledge, or resources only after they have become unavailable. In order to simulate the loss of nodes within DNA, one can calculate the changes in selected network metrics once a node (person, knowledge, or resource) has been lost. Node removal can be planned or random and can be repeated any number of times, enabling assessment of the eliminated node's impact on the network. DNA allows for simulating of the scenario in which key (central) actors in the network or brokers (intermediaries) between networks are lost. In this situation, the organization should develop a knowledge retention program (Parise, 2007), for instance, to secure the knowledge and experience of key employees that are critical for the organization and to identify their relations.

Network interventions are based on the "diffusion of innovations" theory (Rogers, 2003), which explains how new ideas and practices, distributed in and among communities, emerge. Valente (2012) demonstrates four strategies of using network data to develop programs of planned transformations, including:

- identification of actors (nodes), selected based on their network properties (e.g., centrality degree);
- segmentation, where the intervention is directed toward a group or a team;
- induction, where the network is stimulated to create new interactions between people and activate connections;
- alteration, where interventions change the network.

Depending on the applied centrality metrics, usually the most prominent nodes are selected for simulating network transformations. Specialized software (ORA, UCINET) can be used to help identify the key node. It might be advantageous to selectively add nodes to the network depending on its characteristics, for example, network cohesion. New people, knowledge, or resources should be added to the network, for example, in order to compensate for loosely connected groups or missing knowledge or resources. On the other hand, elimination of a critical network node allows one to examine transformations in the network structure (Valente, 2010). Selection of the right network intervention depends on many factors, including the type and nature of the available network data, type of behavioral change, and environmental or situational context. So far, findings indicate that these efforts produce a substantial amount of scientific knowledge concerning the behavior, development, and flexibility of socio-technical systems. The analysis of critical personal and leadership risks in network organizations, related to intermittent availability of knowledge, skills, and tasks, is a major objective of DNA. These situations might lead to organizational dysfunctions by interfering with the process of learning. Intermittent availability is a risk because insufficient integration of key employees can slow down the process of learning and curb adaptive and flexible responses. This concerns small organizations in particular. Long-term disturbances in information, knowledge, task, or resource networks pose a serious risk for organizations.

A meta-network is a complex socio-technical system, both in terms of its structure and the diversity of connections that reflect organizational dynamics (Schipper, Gerrits, & Koppenjan, 2015). The complexity of this system increases exponentially along with numbers of nodes and connections, which makes the meta-network go way beyond the capabilities of conventional SNA, which is limited to only one class of nodes, usually human actors. The meta-network is a dynamic system capable of adapting to organizational transformations. Nodes of the network (actors, knowledge, resources, and tasks) change correspondingly in order to help achieve the new objectives. Also, the relations between any two nodes can be restructured, transformed, or eliminated (Carley, 2003; Carley, Diesner, Reminga, & Tsvetovat, 2007; Li, Lu, Li, & Ma, 2015). Relationships maintained over time form a relatively stable pattern of network connections. With this network perspective, organizational researchers are capable of explaining the variability of group structure and efficiency or of organizational innovation. DNA can be used to increase organizational efficiency, improve resource utilization, and use new possibilities of modeling network relations. It can identify patterns in those networks and reveal how transformations in networks and relations affect the people and the organization (Valente, 2012).

Both the selected theoretical approaches to networks and the SNA, ONA, and DNA methods have now been placed in the intra-organizational context. This book deals with intangible organizational resources and their audit with the use of ONA; therefore, the next section presents theoretical approaches to intangible resources—information, knowledge, and intellectual capital. Widely known theoretical approaches, such as the resource-based view, knowledge-based view, and intellectual capital-based view, were selected to help understand resources and their role in value creation.

1.3 Resource-Based Theoretical Approaches in the Dynamic Perspective[9]

1.3.1 Resource-Based View

One of the domains of strategic management, besides strategy formulation and implementation, is the creation of value and competitive advantage of the enterprise. The resource-based view (RBV) is a well-recognized approach to strategic management, associated mainly with Amit and Schoemaker (1993), Barney (1991), Peteraf (1993), Rumelt (1984), and Wernerfelt (1984). The knowledge-based view (KBV) and intellectual capital-based view (ICBV) are extensions of the RBV. In these approaches, emphasis is placed on knowledge-based intangible resources and their utilization (Grant, 1996; Kogut & Zander, 1992; Reed, Lubatkin, & Srinivasan, 2006; Spender & Grant, 1996). Since many definitions of knowledge and intellectual capital, which will be further discussed in Section 2.1.3, refer to resources, competitive advantage, and value creation, these approaches provide a natural context for them, especially seeing as any organization needs resources to create value for itself and its customers. Resources are included in business processes, which, by building competitive advantage, create value. They include many approaches to competitive advantage, including those based on dynamic capabilities (Teece, 2009). Resources and their complementarities, configurations, and value creation play a key role here.

Resources are central to the RBV, but their significance is often taken for granted. The weakness of this view results from inclusion of all possible elements in the definition, which makes it difficult to separate resources from skills (Priem & Butler, 2001). Various authors define resources in a variety of ways. For example, for Peppard and Rylander (2001), resources include structures, processes, people, culture, knowledge, and relations. For Barney (1991), they include assets, skills, organizational processes, enterprise attributes, information, knowledge, and so on. Resources also include social and organizational routines, which determine the efficiency with which enterprises transform efforts into results (Collis, 1994; Winter & Szulanski, 2001). Routines understood in this way build skills, which, if systematically repeated, make it possible to benefit from learning and experience. As Kraaijenbrink, Spender, and Groen (2010) suggest, resources should be classified in the context of their contribution to the creation of sustainable competitive advantage. Resources can be classified as tangible and intangible, as well as static and dynamic.

The key question in the RBV is how companies develop strategic resources and what the quality of resources involved in the process of value creation is. However, it does not provide a framework for the involved processes and does not explain how the resulting value is generated. The relationship between resources and enterprise value is assumed but not explained (Peppard & Rylander, 2001; Reed et al., 2006). In the RBV, resources, in particular, intangible resources, contribute to achieving and maintaining efficiency when they are connected or integrated (Barney, 1991). This is similar to the theory of the growth of the firm by Penrose (1995), which is a theory of value creation (Rugman & Verbeke, 2002), where resources and activities of an enterprise are seen as a fundamental part of value creation and do not exist independently of one another. They can be specialized and combined in various configurations. The enterprise, on the other hand, is a creator of added value and core organizational capabilities (Leonard-Barton, 1992; Prahalad, 1993; Prahalad & Hamel, 1990), which are associated with knowledge and technology resources ensuring the success of production and future development of the enterprise. The added value manifests in the price that a customer pays for the benefits obtained from the transaction. In order to achieve added value, the value must be combined with tangible and intangible resources required for its creation, and the resources must be used productively. Within this theory, the enterprise's aims include the interests of its stakeholders, which fits in with the notion of redistribution of the generated added value. It must be noted that the enterprise's rate of growth is determined by the nature and type of its resources, as well as the knowledge and experience of managers. The RBV connects intellectual capital with resources and their allocation. The network of relations between resources can play a significant role in visualizing the configuration capabilities of the company, that is, coherent combinations of resources and skills in the organizational infrastructure, which foster value creation (Nielsen & Montemari, 2012).

A typical example of RBV application is provided by Hedman and Kalling (2003), who analyze an enterprise's business model from the point of view of resources, such as design skills, relations with suppliers, networks of supply, and cultural factors related to leadership and commitment. Similar resources are combined in intellectual capital (discussed further in Section 2.1.3), where design skills are a component of human capital, or, if codified, structural capital (Edvinsson & Malone, 1997). Relations with suppliers and networks of supply are included in social (Nahapiet & Ghoshal, 1998; Reiche, Harzing, & Kraimer, 2009) or relational capital (Bontis, 2001), which goes beyond the internal aspects of the organization that dominate in the RBV (Roos, 1998). Cultural factors are a part of structural capital (Martínez-Torres, 2006). However, the complex and comprehensive nature of intellectual capital cannot be explained solely by the RBV, because resources themselves do not bear any value. Value creation is only possible as a result of resource use or transaction (DaSilva & Trkman, 2014). Therefore, mere possession of resources is considered useless. Far greater significance is associated with improved use of resources by the enterprise (Mahoney & Pandian, 1992; Rubin, 1973) in the dynamic approach to resources, which is not a dominant aspect of the RBV.

1.3.2 Knowledge-Based View

The RBV is enriched by the knowledge-based view, which emphasizes that critical resources and capabilities are those associated with knowledge. According to Amit and Schoemaker (1993), Grant (1996), and Spender and Grant (1996), knowledge processes play a key role in improving an enterprise's performance. The KBV provides significant insight into why enterprises exist and will continue to exist, and why organizational knowledge is an important part of their operation. In order to remain competitive, organizations should efficiently and continuously identify, integrate, and apply knowledge resources, which are distributed among employees and teams (Grant, 1996).

According to the RBV, knowledge resources are strategic organizational resources that distinguish an enterprise from others and provide sustainable competitive advantage. In terms of the KBV, knowledge resources are seen as cognitive artifacts, with resources, which are generated from knowledge or represent knowledge, defining domains of organizational knowledge (Schiuma, 2009). This approach recognizes knowledge as the most important strategic resource and production factor. However, the analysis of knowledge for available assets and resources does not include the transformation factor, their dynamics, and the social processes within which knowledge is created, transferred, and used. Knowledge is more than a resource. Therefore, the key factor is what knowledge-based activities (*knowing*) are undertaken in practice by the company (Orlikowski, 2002). From the point of view of competition, knowledge can be copied and access to it can be gained on comparable conditions. Knowledge in action (*knowing*), which is a feature of the organization included in social relations, is much more difficult to copy. In activity theory, actions generate connectivity between resources and create value through communication activities, in which information and knowledge are in constant movement.

Differences between enterprises result from diversified knowledge resources and skills related to the use and development of this knowledge (Kogut & Zander, 1992; Penrose, 1995). Within this approach, companies are social entities that store internal and external knowledge, which lies at the heart of their survival and success (Martín-de Castro, 2014). Knowledge seen this way comprises both internal and static resources of the enterprise (mainly in a codified form, also known as explicit knowledge). Somewhat contrary to the approach of Yates-Mercer and Bawden (2002), it is assumed that knowledge (especially explicit) is static and formalized in the shape of designs, manuals, documents, and procedures. The dynamic aspect of explicit knowledge only occurs when the collected knowledge stocks are transformed from their passive form into value for the enterprise and customers, as a result of transformations, modifications, and applications. Explicit knowledge can be controlled, used, and traded, as opposed to tacit knowledge (uncodified or codified with difficulty), which can be a source of long-lasting competitive advantage to a far larger extent. This inimitable, intangible, enterprise-specific knowledge is seen as socially complex value protected against imitation (Barney, 1991). The KBV assumes that tacit and contextual knowledge contributes to higher levels of efficiency, as it is not imitable. Subramaniam and Venkatraman (2001) empirically demonstrated how tacit knowledge contributes to marked development of organizational skills that help boost the enterprise's performance. Contextual knowledge, embedded in processes, procedures, and the social context of an enterprise, is particularly difficult to copy and important for building competitive advantage. In this respect, value is created owing to the transfer of knowledge, support for sharing knowledge, and repeated use of knowledge (Kong & Thomson, 2009). Since intellectual capital of enterprises is based on knowledge, the KBV makes a strong case for its role in increasing organizational efficiency (Oliveira, Roth, & Gilland, 2002; Youndt, Subramaniam, & Snell, 2004).

The KBV states that knowledge is crucial for value creation, though it does not fully explain in what way knowledge can contribute to value creation or improvement in the performance of the enterprise. It is necessary to view both tangible and intangible resources from two complementary perspectives, static and dynamic. The static approach is like a snapshot of the status quo. It reflects the state of resources, including knowledge and intellectual capital, in a given moment, and its contribution to value creation. The dynamic approach to knowledge and intellectual capital should be based on the flows and network connections between elements (knowledge and components of intellectual capital), taking into consideration the time factor (change in values of components, as well as in value for the customer and enterprise). Intentional choices associated with the components of intellectual capital are the primary source of their dynamics. Aspects of the dynamic approach to resources and competitive advantage are not prominent in the RBV or the KBV, and can only be found in the ICBV, in particular in Penrose (1995). From the KBV perspective, services rendered with the use of tangible resources depend on how the resources are connected and applied, which in turn depends on organizational *know-how*. Though existing knowledge is important for competitive advantage, new knowledge is even more important. It is created by recombining existing and new knowledge (Hargadon, 2003), and the results of this recombination define the competitive position of the organization, based on dynamic capabilities, creativity, and innovation (Shukla, 2015).

1.3.3 Intellectual Capital–Based View

The KBV is complemented by the intellectual capital-based view (Martín-de-Castro, Delgado-Verde, López-Sáez, & Navas-López, 2010; Reed et al., 2006). Intellectual capital can be divided into the following components: human capital, structural (organizational) capital, and relational (social) capital, which are complementary resources. Both approaches are based on explaining the tacit knowledge-based dynamics, fundamental for the value and competitive advantage of an enterprise. These are also fundamental for the RBV. Youndt et al. (2004) point out that the KBV assesses how effectively management and knowledge-generation tools, such as IT systems and information management systems, are used. As opposed to that, the ICBV concentrates on the stocks and flows of knowledge capital existing in the company, and on its direct relation to financial results. It looks at resource accumulation, allocation, integration, and application to explain value creation by the enterprise (Peppard & Rylander, 2001). Connections between the components of intellectual capital on the one hand, and financial performance, competitive advantage, and innovation on the other, are the main topics of empirical research on the strategic value of this capital (Hsu & Wang, 2012; Subramaniam & Youndt, 2005).

Research by Reed et al. (2006) and their concept of the ICBV is a response to the shortcomings of the RBV, which include:

- impossibility to indicate those resources in which an organization should invest in order to gain advantage;
- lack of clear definition of competitive advantage and the tautology resulting from the fact that resources are defined in relation to results achieved owing to them;
- the vague and overly general nature of the resource-based view;
- equifinality, which means that many potentially beneficial combinations of resources are possible. One must take into account an infinite multitude of permutations of resources and/or combinations, which are at the same time useful and new, as well as knowledge resulting from interactions, which is cumulative and socially determined, and is in itself the context of its creation.

As opposed to the RBV, the ICBV emphasizes external aspects of the enterprise and goes beyond its boundaries by including the social/relational capital and dynamic capabilities in value creation. Knowledge cannot be isolated from tangible resources and the methods of their utilization. Therefore the inclusion of dynamic capabilities in the KBV and ICBV seems warranted. The dynamic capabilities perspective aims at finding the sources of an enterprise's success over time, concentrating on skills that are difficult to replicate and that enable the company to change by configuring and shaping resources, as well as by adapting to the environment (Eisenhardt & Martin, 2000; Teece, Pisano, & Shuen, 1997). The key elements of dynamic capabilities, according to Teece (2007), are the organizational and managerial processes that support the identification and seizing of business, technological, and market opportunities, and the reconfiguration of assets and organizational structures as the enterprise grows and the market changes. It is argued that the application of diverse skills creates value for the customer, and intentional transformations of skills are the essence of dynamic capabilities (Achtenhagen, Melin, & Naldi, 2013). Literature regarding dynamic capabilities (e.g., Mason & Leek, 2008) indicates that the external environment affects enterprise learning, and in a highly uncertain environment, enterprises must expand and configure both existing and new skills.

On the other hand, according to Barreto (2010), a dynamic capability is the firm's potential to systematically solve problems, formed by its propensity to sense opportunities and threats, to make timely and market-oriented decisions, and to change its resource base. Furthermore, dynamic capabilities include the creation of difficult-to-imitate combinations of resources, and the coordination of inter-organizational relations favoring competitive advantage (Griffith & Harvey, 2001). Dynamic capabilities defined this way highlight both the element of learning and the resources and external relations, which are also found in analyses of relational capital, one of the components of intellectual capital. With the above in mind, resources and dynamic capabilities are closely associated with the performance and competitive advantage of the enterprise (Teece, 2007), and are therefore suitable for analysis as part of intellectual capital and the ICBV.

The ICBV is also considered in the context of competitive advantage (Reed et al., 2006; Sydler, Haefliger, & Pruksa, 2014; Zack, 1999). Internal resources of the enterprise are the main source of value creation, and control over critical assets and skills is important for maintaining competitive advantage (Sanchez & Ricart, 2010). Intellectual capital implicitly or explicitly refers to internal capabilities, which are the foundation of competitive advantage. If capabilities lie at the heart of intellectual capital, then advantage can be established around one or more capabilities. This is consistent with the RBV, where the enterprise is seen as a set of resources and capabilities (Barney, 1991). The competitive advantage of an enterprise and its performance rarely result from a single cause, and the cause does not exist in isolation. Therefore, the configuration approach (Fiss, 2007; Meyer, Tsui, & Hinings, 1993) is used to define any multidimensional constellation of various resources, which often occur jointly. Hence the particular suitability of this approach in strategic management studies (Miller, 1996), especially since intellectual capital is a multidimensional construct, which embodies the mechanism of creating competitive advantage resulting from diverse configurations of resources and their use in the enterprise. This approach improves on the causal relationship assumed in the RBV and the ICBV. It allows for equifinality, meaning that some results can be explained by more than one configuration with the same efficiency (Gresov & Drazin, 1997). Competitiveness and value creation can be explained by a set of factors (components of intellectual capital) that do not work separately. Thus, the configuration perspective can help determine in what way a particular pattern of intellectual capital affects the performance of the whole enterprise, taking into consideration the synergistic relations and dependencies.

The three approaches discussed here, the RBV, KBV, and ICBV—regardless of whether they can be justifiably referred to as theories (the debate is still ongoing; see, e.g., Grant, 1996; Kraaijenbrink et al., 2010; Martín-de Castro, 2014))—emphasize, to a lesser or greater extent:

- the internal and external aspects of an enterprise's functioning;
- use of resources (tangible and intangible);
- knowledge (explicit and tacit) and (dynamic) capabilities in the context of value creation for the enterprise and the customer, and of competitive advantage.

Inclusion of the ICBV gives foundations for the analysis of resources going beyond the boundaries of an enterprise and taking into consideration the impact of the environment on the creation, identification, and assessment of value. The RBV takes into consideration the effective organization of processes in the enterprise but does not point to the use of intellectual capital, as is the case in the ICBV. The description of intellectual capital from the point of view of its components justifies the application of the configuration approach, based on identification of configurations or unique arrangements of components providing maximum efficiency.

Full grasp of the complexity of these approaches requires further development toward the accumulation, combination, and heterogeneity of resources, knowledge, and intellectual capital and understanding of their mechanisms. Accumulation of resources by entrepreneurs and employees is not discussed in the RBV, which shows how much the RBV would benefit from an understanding of the process whereby the entrepreneur and employees, operating in a network of relations with actors in the external environment, acquire resources (Eyring, Johnson, & Nair, 2011). Demil and Lecocq (2010) and Nair, Nisar, Palacios, and Ruiz (2012) also discussed the accumulation of resources. Demil and Lecocq see it as a collection of accumulated (acquired) resources and methods of their implementation by organizational management, which can bring about new production opportunities and new products and services in the market. On the other hand, Nair et al. (2012) suggest an interesting concept of knowledge brokering—that is, effective accumulation and transformation of external resources into unique domains, networks, safeguards, capabilities, assets, procedures for learning, skills, actions, processes, and culture—pointing to the acquisition and use of knowledge and ideas from the intersectoral environment of the company.

Accumulation of resources, knowledge, and intellectual capital is the *sine qua non* for their combination. A heuristic approach to creating unique combinations, created on the basis of existing resources, knowledge, and intellectual capital, is important here. Only their combination (configuration) can be new and ground-breaking, resulting in the creation of unique value. Sustained capability for organizational value creation resides not only in the ownership and protection of tangible and intangible resources that guarantee current competitive advantage. It requires the understanding and management of continuous development, distribution, exploitation, and combination of these organizational resources to update, restore, and create organizational skills. Of course, it is not only about collecting resources, but also about how they are transformed into a process, product, reputation, or brand that creates value and subsequently transformed into financial return for stakeholders (Peppard & Rylander, 2001; Schiuma, 2009), in particular since value is incorporated in the products owing to the development of organizational knowledge resources.

An interesting interpretation has been suggested by Morris, Schindehutte, and Allen (2005), for whom the unique combination of resources within the suggested business model, in which every component affects and is affected by other components, offers an opportunity for creating value and increasing return for the enterprise. Value creation is seen similarly by Peppard and Rylander (2001), who state that value can only be generated by combinations and use of resources. Introduction of new components can cause a change in dynamics among the existing components. The importance of resource integration is similar to Teece et al. (1997). It affects the complexity of competitive advantage imitation by competitors, based on combinations of valuable, enterprise-specific resources, because these combinations usually emerge in an organizational process that is causally heterogeneous and socially complex.

These combinations demonstrate how intellectual capital can provide a set of resources as key sources of competitive advantage. They make it possible to examine heterogeneity and help make an input into the RBV by pointing out the way the value of resources depends on how they are connected with other resources, rather than examining them as separate elements (Morris & Snell, 2011). Human capital, even though it is more dynamic, is not the main asset in comparison with structural capital, which can be maintained. The challenge lies in managing the process of intellectual capital development, the collection, recording, and sharing of knowledge, so as to enable creation of value for the enterprise and the customer by identifying, seizing, and using tangible and intangible resources. This concerns both the creation and extraction of value, where the value creation process is conditioned upon new connections, combinations, and social capital (Edvinsson, 1997).

Intangible resources and knowledge support this transformation of goods and services into financial value, enabling innovative combinations of resources and capabilities and the creation of value (Morris et al., 2005). It is, of course, difficult to say how individual resources affect success without considering their connections with other tangible and intangible assets (Beattie & Smith, 2013).

The heterogeneity of resources and the created value depend on how diverse and unique the combination is. Rumelt (1991) writes about company heterogeneity operationalized by variation of profitability resulting from the heterogeneity of resources and their mobility. Here, the emphasis is put rather on the heterogeneity of the value created, which is the result of a unique combination of resources, knowledge, and intellectual capital. Value creation based upon three perspectives, resource-based, financial, and intellectual capital-based (Tseng & Goo, 2005), allows one to understand the dynamics of value creation based on transformation of resources into results. Both intellectual capital and its components make it possible to visualize value creation, mainly driven in the current economy by knowledge and other intangible resources. The way in which this value is created is determined by factors such as key logic of an enterprise's operation, its system of assumptions, the cognitive environment affecting management decisions, and capabilities that support value creation from resources. These factors and their interactions lead to value creation.

The concept of intangible and tangible resources, seen from the network perspective, takes a new meaning: valuable, rare, inimitable, and non-substitutable (VRIN) resources are those resources that are formed in the organizational and inter-organizational network configuration and are not easily duplicated by competitors (Rodan, 2002). Most studies concentrate on inter-organizational networks in the context of the RBV (e.g., Coviello & Cox, 2006; Lavie, 2006). This book emphasizes intra-organizational relations. Regardless of the context (inter- or intra-organizational), resources as such do not create value unless they are appropriately and successfully implemented, transformed, and connected with other tangible and intangible resources in the network of connections and interactions. The network perspective is an attractive approach to studying the behavior of an enterprise based on the RBV (Wills-Johnson, 2008), but also KBV and ICBV, as these frameworks make it possible to analyze interactions between strategic resources and the way these interactions can drive the development of the enterprise.

The next chapter provides definitions of information, knowledge, and intellectual capital. All these approaches have one thing in common: in a way, they are all final products of the information synergy and knowledge transfers between various individuals in an enterprise.

Notes

1. Since network theory is in the phase of development and empirical verification, the term "network theory" is used somewhat tentatively. References are made to Granovetter's labor market theory and Burt's competition theory, most frequently cited in the context of the emerging network theory. The question of how justified associations between these approaches and network theory are, however, merits consideration. This chapter includes attempts at providing a theoretical framework, concepts, techniques, definitions, and research fields, which require further elaboration. An inquisitive reader may find questions that network theory should answer in Salancik (1995).
2. In this book, the words *actor* and *node* are used interchangeably, even though they stem from two different disciplines: sociology and graph theory. However, this is a common way of identifying network elements, regardless of whether the actor is human or nonhuman. The term *relations* between actors (nodes) in the network is used interchangeably with the terms "connections," "links," "ties," or "relationships." A human actor (in particular in the empirical part of the book) is called a "person," "individual," or "employee."
3. "A" denotes a human actor in the network.
4. Out of organization theories, the resource-based view and knowledge-based view are discussed in the following section.

5. In AT, the terms "element," "component," and "category" of the activity system, understood as its constituent part, are used interchangeably.
6. Including a larger number of journals would involve much more extensive analyses, going beyond the scope and aim of this book.
7. Both information and knowledge will be defined and further discussed in Section 2.1, "The Nature of Intangible Resources."
8. Resources in the resource network are understood as the structural capital of the organization. Further explanation is provided in Chapter 2.
9. Reflections in this section can also be found in another publication by the author, but in a slightly different context, involving connections between business models and intellectual capital in organizational value creation (see Ujwary-Gil, 2017).

References

Achtenhagen, L., Melin, L., & Naldi, L. (2013). Dynamics of business models—Strategizing, critical capabilities and activities for sustained value creation. *Long Range Planning*, *46*(6), 427–442. https://doi.org/10.1016/j.lrp.2013.04.002

Adler, P. S., & Kwon, S. W. (2002). Social capital: Prospects for a new concept. *Academy of Management Review*, *27*(1), 17–40.

Agbim, K. C. (2019). Social networking and the family business performance: A conceptual consideration. *Journal of Entrepreneurship, Management and Innovation*, *15*(1), 83–122. https://doi.org/10.7341/20191514

Alba, R. D. (1982). Taking stock of network analysis: A decade's results. *Research in the Sociology of Organizations*, *1*, 39–74.

AlDahdouh, A. A., Osório, A. J., & Caires, S. (2015). Understanding knowledge network, learning and connectivism. *International Journal of Instructional Technology and Distance Learning*, *12*(10), 3–21.

Allen, J., James, A. D., & Gamlen, P. (2007). Formal versus informal knowledge networks in R&D: A case study using social network analysis. *R&D Management*, *37*(3), 179–196. https://doi.org/10.1111/j.1467-9310.2007.00468.x

Amit, R., & Schoemaker, P. J. (1993). Strategic assets and organizational rent. *Strategic Management Journal*, *14*(1), 33–46.

Aven, B. L. (2015). The paradox of corrupt networks: An analysis of organizational crime at ENRON. *Organization Science*, *26*(4), 980–996.

Balboni, B., & Bortoluzzi, G. (2015). Business model adaptation and the success of new ventures. *Journal of Entrepreneurship, Management and Innovation*, *11*(1), 119–140. https://doi.org/10.7341/20151117

Balthrop, J., Forrest, S., Newman, M. E. J., & Williamson, M. M. (2004). Technological networks and the spread of computer viruses. *Science*, *304*(5670), 527–529. https://doi.org/10.1126/science.1095845

Barabási, A. L. (2016). *Network science*. Cambridge, UK: Cambridge University Press.

Barabasi, A. L., & Frangos, J. (2002). *Linked: The new science of networks* (1st ed.). Cambridge, MA: Perseus Books Group.

Barney, J. (1991). Firm resources and sustained competitive advantage. *Journal of Management*, *17*(1), 99–120. https://doi.org/10.1177/014920639101700108

Barreto, I. (2010). Dynamic capabilities: A review of past research and an agenda for the future. *Journal of Management*, *36*(1), 256–280. https://doi.org/10.1177/0149206309350776

Beattie, V., & Smith, S. J. (2013). Value creation and business models: Refocusing the intellectual capital debate. *The British Accounting Review*, *45*(4), 243–254. https://doi.org/10.1016/j.bar.2013.06.001

Beckman, C. M., & Haunschild, P. R. (2002). Network learning: The effects of partners' heterogeneity of experience on corporate acquisitions. *Administrative Science Quarterly*, *47*(1), 92–124.

Benham-Hutchins, M., Carley, K. M., Brewer, B. B., Effken, J. A., & Reminga, J. (2018). Nursing unit communication during a US public health emergency: Natural experiment. *JMIR Nursing*, *1*(1), e11425.

Björk, J., & Magnusson, M. (2009). Where do good innovation ideas come from? Exploring the influence of network connectivity on innovation idea quality. *Journal of Product Innovation Management*, *26*(6), 662–670.

Blackler, F. (1993). Knowledge and the theory of organizations: Organizations as activity systems and the reframing of management. *Journal of Management Studies*, *30*(6), 863–884.

Blackler, F. (1995). Knowledge, knowledge work and organizations: An overview and interpretation. *Organization Studies*, *16*(6), 1021–1046.

Blackler, F., & Kennedy, A. (2004). The design and evaluation of a leadership programme for experienced chief executives from the public sector. *Management Learning*, *35*(2), 181–203.

Blackler, F., & Regan, S. (2009). Intentionality, agency, change: Practice theory and management. *Management Learning*, *40*(2), 161–176.

Blumer, H. (1986). *Symbolic interactionism: Perspective and method*. Berkeley, Los Angeles, London: University of California Press.

Bonabeau, E. (2002). Agent-based modeling: Methods and techniques for simulating human systems. *Proceedings of the National Academy of Sciences*, *99*(S3), 7280–7287.

Bontis, N. (2001). Assessing knowledge assets: A review of the models used to measure intellectual capital. *International Journal of Management Reviews*, *3*(1), 41–60. https://doi.org/10.1111/1468-2370.00053

Borgatti, S. P., Brass, D. J., & Halgin, D. S. (2014). Social network research: Confusions, criticisms, and controversies. *Research in the Sociology of Organizations*, *40*, 1–29.

Borgatti, S. P., Everett, M. G., & Johnson, J. C. (2018). *Analyzing social networks*. London: Sage Publications.

Borgatti, S. P., & Foster, P. C. (2003). The network paradigm in organizational research: A review and typology. *Journal of Management*, *29*(6), 991–1013. https://doi.org/10.1016/S0149-2063_03_00087-4

Borgatti, S. P., & Halgin, D. S. (2011). On network theory. *Organization Science*, *22*(5), 1168–1181. https://doi.org/10.1287/orsc.1100.0641

Borgatti, S. P., Mehra, A., Brass, D. J., & Labianca, G. (2009). Network analysis in the social sciences. *Science*, *323*(5916), 892–895.

Börner, K., Sanyal, S., & Vespignani, A. (2007). Network science. *Annual Review of Information Science and Technology*, *41*(1), 537–607.

Bourouni, A., Noori, S., & Jafari, M. (2015). Knowledge network creation methodology selection in project-based organizations: An empirical framework. *Aslib Journal of Information Management*, *67*(1), 93–74.

Brandes, U., Robins, G., McCranie, A., & Wasserman, S. (2013). What is network science? *Network Science*, *1*(01), 1–15.

Brass, D. J. (2003). A social network perspective on human resources management. In R. Cross, A. Parker, & L. Sasson (Eds.), *Networks in the knowledge economy* (pp. 283–323). New York: Oxford University Press.

Brass, D. J., Butterfield, K. D., & Skaggs, B. C. (1998). Relationships and unethical behavior: A social network perspective. *Academy of Management Review*, *23*(1), 14–31.

Brass, D. J., Galaskiewicz, J., Greve, H. R., & Tsai, W. (2004). Taking stock of networks and organizations: A multilevel perspective. *Academy of Management Journal*, *47*(6), 795–817.

Breiger, R. L., Boorman, S. A., & Arabie, P. (1975). An algorithm for clustering relational data with applications to social network analysis and comparison with multidimensional scaling. *Journal of Mathematical Psychology*, *12*(3), 328–383.

Brewer, B. B., Carley, K. M., Benham-Hutchins, M., Effken, J. A., & Reminga, J. (2018). Nursing unit design, nursing staff communication networks, and patient falls: Are they related? *HERD: Health Environments Research & Design Journal*, *11*(4), 82–94.

Brewer, B. B., Carley, K. M., Benham-Hutchins, M. M., Effken, J. A., Reminga, J., & Kowalchuck, M. (2018). Relationship of staff information sharing and advice networks to patient safety outcomes. *The Journal of Nursing Administration*, *48*(9), 437.

Brown, J. S., & Duguid, P. (2000). *The social life of information*. Boston: Harvard Business School Press.

Buchanan, M. (2003). *Nexus: Small worlds and the groundbreaking science of networks* (Reprint ed.). New York: W. W. Norton & Company.

Burt, R. S. (1987). Social contagion and innovation: Cohesion versus structural equivalence. *American Journal of Sociology*, *92*(6), 1287–1335.

Burt, R. S. (2001). Structural holes versus network closure as social capital. In N. Lin, K. S. Cook, & R. S. Burt (Eds.), *Social capital: Theory and research* (pp. 31–55). New York: Aldine de Gruyter.

Burt, R. S. (2004). Structural holes and good ideas. *American Journal of Sociology*, *110*(2), 349–399.

Burt, R. S. (2009). *Structural holes: The social structure of competition*. Cambridge, MA: Harvard University Press.

Burt, R. S., Kilduff, M., & Tasselli, S. (2013). Social network analysis: Foundations and frontiers on advantage. *Annual Review of Psychology*, *64*, 527–547.

Callon, M. (1984). Some elements of a sociology of translation: Domestication of the scallops and the fishermen of St Brieuc Bay. *The Sociological Review*, *32*(S1), 196–233.

Callon, M. (1993). Variety and irreversibility in networks of technique conception and adoption. In D. Foray & Ch. Freemann (Eds.), *Technology and the wealth of nations: Dynamics of constructed advantage* (pp. 232–268). London, New York: Printer.

Callon, M., & Latour, B. (1981). Unscrewing the big Leviathan: How actors macro-structure reality and how sociologists help them to do so. In K. Knorr-Cetina & A. V. Cocouvel (Eds.), *Advances in social theory and methodology: Toward an integration of micro-and macro-sociologies* (pp. 277–303). Boston; London: Routledge.

Carley, K. M. (2003). Dynamic network analysis. In R. Breiger, K. Carley, & P. Pattison, (Eds.). *Dynamic social network modeling and analysis: Workshop summary and papers* (pp. 133–145). Washington, DC: National Academies Press.

Carley, K. M. (2005). Organizational design and assessment in cyber-space. In W. B. Rouse & K. R. Boff (Eds.), *Organizational simulation* (pp. 389–423). Retrieved from http://onlinelibrary.wiley.com/doi/10.1002/0471739448.ch14/summary

Carley, K. M. (1999). On the evolution of social and organizational networks. *Research in the Sociology of Organizations*, *16*, 3–30.

Carley, K. M. (2014). ORA: A toolkit for dynamic network analysis and visualization. In R. Alhajj & J. Rokne (Eds.), *Encyclopedia of social network analysis and mining* (pp. 1219–1228). Germany: Springer.

Carley, K. M., Diesner, J., Reminga, J., & Tsvetovat, M. (2007). Toward an interoperable dynamic network analysis toolkit. *Decision Support Systems*, *43*(4), 1324–1347. https://doi.org/10.1016/j.dss.2006.04.003

Carley, K. M., Martin, M. K., & Hirshman, B. R. (2009). The etiology of social change. *Topics in Cognitive Science*, *1*(4), 621–650.

Cartwright, D., & Harary, F. (1956). Structural balance: A generalization of Heider's theory. *Psychological Review*, *63*(5), 277.

Casciaro, T., & Lobo, M. S. (2014). Affective primacy in intraorganizational task networks. *Organization Science*, *26*(2), 373–389.

Christakis, N. A., & Fowler, J. H. (2011). *Connected: The surprising power of our social networks and how they shape our lives—How your friends' friends' friends affect everything you feel, think, and do* (Reprint ed.). New York: Back Bay Books.

Coleman, J. S. (1988). Social capital in the creation of human capital. *American Journal of Sociology*, *94*, S95–S120.

Coleman, J. S. (1990). *Foundation of social theory*. Cambridge, MA.: Harvard University Press.

Collis, D. J. (1994). Research note: How valuable are organizational capabilities? *Strategic Management Journal*, *15*(S1), 143–152. https://doi.org/10.1002/smj.4250150910

Coviello, N. E., & Cox, M. P. (2006). The resource dynamics of international new venture networks. *Journal of International Entrepreneurship*, *4*(2–3), 113–132. http://dx.doi.org/10.1007/s10843-007-0004-4

Cricelli, L., & Grimaldi, M. (2008). A dynamic view of knowledge and information: A stock and flow based methodology. *International Journal of Management and Decision Making*, *9*(6), 686. https://doi.org/10.1504/IJMDM.2008.021221

Cross, R. L., & Parker, A. (2004). *The hidden power of social networks: Understanding how work really gets done in organizations*. Boston: Harvard Business Press.

Currie, G., & White, L. (2012). Inter-professional barriers and knowledge brokering in an organizational context: The case of healthcare. *Organization Studies*, *33*(10), 1333–1361.

Czakon, W. (2011). Paradygmat sieciowy w naukach o zarządzaniu. *Przegląd Organizacji*, (11), 3–6.

Czarniawska, B. (2017). Organizing networks: An actor-network theory of organizations. *Organization Studies*, *38*(10), 1483–1484.

DaSilva, C. M., & Trkman, P. (2014). Business model: What it is and what it is not. *Long Range Planning*, *47*(6), 379–389. https://doi.org/10.1016/j.lrp.2013.08.004

Demil, B., & Lecocq, X. (2010). Business model evolution: In search of dynamic consistency. *Long Range Planning*, *43*(2–3), 227–246. https://doi.org/10.1016/j.lrp.2010.02.004

DeRue, D. S., Nahrgang, J. D., & Ashford, S. J. (2015). Interpersonal perceptions and the emergence of leadership structures in groups: A network perspective. *Organization Science*, *26*(4), 1192–1209.

Diez-Vial, I., & Montoro-Sanchez, A. (2014). Social capital as a driver of local knowledge exchange: A social network analysis. *Knowledge Management Research & Practice*, *12*(3), 276–288. https://doi.org/10.1057/kmrp.2014.7

Easton, G. S., & Rosenzweig, E. D. (2015). Team leader experience in improvement teams: A social networks perspective. *Journal of Operations Management*, *37*, 13–30.

Edvinsson, L. (1997). Developing intellectual capital at Skandia. *Long Range Planning*, *30*(3), 366–373. https://doi.org/10.1016/S0024-6301(97)90248-X

Edvinsson, L., & Malone, M. S. (1997). *Intellectual capital: Realizing your company's true value by finding its hidden brainpower* (1st ed.). New York: HarperBusiness.

Eisenhardt, K. M., & Martin, J. A. (2000). Dynamic capabilities: What are they? *Strategic Management Journal*, *21*(10–11), 1105–1121. https://doi.org/10.1002/1097-0266(200010/11)21:10/11 < 1105::AID-SMJ133 > 3.0.CO;2-E

Elias, N. (2001). The *society of individuals*. Oxford, UK: Blackwell.

Emirbayer, M., & Goodwin, J. (1994). Network analysis, culture, and the problem of agency. *American Journal of Sociology*, *99*, 1411–1454.

Engeström, Y. (1993). Developmental studies of work as a testbench of activity theory: The case of primary care medical practice. In S. Chaiklin & J. Lave (Eds.), *Understanding practice: Perspectives on activity and context* (pp. 64–103). Cambridge, UK: Cambridge University Press.

Engeström, Y. (2000). Activity theory as a framework for analyzing and redesigning work. *Ergonomics*, *43*(7), 960–974. https://doi.org/10.1080/001401300409143

Engeström, Y. (2001). Expansive learning at work: Toward an activity theoretical reconceptualization. *Journal of Education and Work*, *14*(1), 133–156.

Engeström, Y. (2014). *Learning by expanding*. Cambridge, UK: Cambridge University Press.

Espinosa, J. A., & Clark, M. A. (2014). Team knowledge representation a network perspective. *Human Factors: The Journal of the Human Factors and Ergonomics Society*, *56*(2), 333–348. https://doi.org/10.1177/0018720813494093

Everton, S. F. (2012). *Disrupting dark networks*. Cambridge, UK: Cambridge University Press.

Eyring, M. J., Johnson, M. W., & Nair, H. (2011). New business models in emerging markets. *Harvard Business Review*, *89*(1–2), 88–95.

Festinger, L. (1954). A theory of social comparison processes. *Human Relations*, *7*(2), 117–140.

Fiss, P. C. (2007). A set-theoretic approach to organizational configurations. *The Academy of Management Review*, *32*(4), 1180–1198. https://doi.org/10.2307/20159362

Fombrun, C. J. (1982). Strategies for network research in organizations. *Academy of Management Review*, *7*(2), 280–291.

Freeman, L. (2004). The development of social network analysis. *A Study in the Sociology of Science*. Retrieved from www.researchgate.net/profile/Linton_Freeman/publication/239228599_The_Development_of_Social_Network_Analysis/links/54415c650cf2e6f0c0f616a8.pdf

Freiling, J. (2015). Business model innovation—A concept between organizational renewal and industry transformation. *Journal of Entrepreneurship, Management and Innovation*, *11*(1), 3–10. https://doi.org/10.7341/20151111

Frith, J. (2014). Social network analysis and professional practice: Exploring new methods for researching technical communication. *Technical Communication Quarterly*, *23*(4), 288–302.

Galbraith, J. R. (1974). Organization design: An information processing view. *Interfaces*, *4*(3), 28–36. https://doi.org/10.1287/inte.4.3.28

Galup, S., Dattero, R., & Groll, J. (2011). DNA model of IT service assets. *International Journal of Service Science, Management, Engineering, and Technology*, 2(2), 16–47.

Gasparski, W. (1999). *Prakseologia*. Warsaw: Oficyna Wydawnicza Warszawskiej Szkoły Zarządzania.

Gemünden, H. G., & Heydebreck, P. (1995). The influence of business strategies on technological network activities. *Research Policy*, *24*(6), 831–849. https://doi.org/10.1016/0048-7333(94)00784-5

Goethals, G. R., & Darley, J. M. (1987). Social comparison theory: Self-evaluation and group life. In B. Mullen & G. R. Goethals (Eds.), *Theories of group behavior* (pp. 21–47). New York: Springer-Verlag.

Granovetter, M. (1983). The strength of weak ties: A network theory revisited. *Sociological Theory*, *1*(1983), 201–233.

Granovetter, M. (1985). Economic action and social structure: The problem of embeddedness. *American Journal of Sociology*, *91*, 481–510.

Granovetter, M. S. (1973). The strength of weak ties. *American Journal of Sociology*, 1360–1380.

Grant, R. M. (1996). Toward a knowledge-based theory of the firm. *Strategic Management Journal*, *17*(S2), 109–122. https://doi.org/10.1002/smj.4250171110

Gresov, C., & Drazin, R. (1997). Equifinality: Functional equivalence in organization design. *The Academy of Management Review*, *22*(2), 403–428. https://doi.org/10.2307/259328

Griffith, D. A., & Harvey, M. G. (2001). A resource perspective of global dynamic capabilities. *Journal of International Business Studies*, *32*(3), 597–606. https://doi.org/10.1057/palgrave.jibs.8490987

Günzel-Jensen, F., & Holm, A. B. (2015). Freemium business models as the foundation for growing an e-business venture: A multiple case study of industry leaders. *Journal of Entrepreneurship, Management and Innovation*, *11*(1), 77–101. https://doi.org/10.7341/20151115

Hanifan, L. J. (1916). The rural school community center. *The Annals of the American Academy of Political and Social Science*, *67*, 130–138.

Hargadon, A. (2003). *How breakthroughs happen: The surprising truth about how companies innovate*. Boston: Harvard Business Press.

Hatala, J. P. (2006). Social network analysis in human resource development: A new methodology. *Human Resource Development Review*, *5*(1), 45–71.

Hedman, J., & Kalling, T. (2003). The business model concept: Theoretical underpinnings and empirical illustrations. *European Journal of Information Systems*, *12*(1), 49–59. https://doi.org/10.1057/palgrave.ejis.3000446

Heider, F. (1958). *The psychology of interpersonal relations*. New York: Wiley.

Hennig, M., Brandes, U., Borgatti, S. P., Pfeffer, J., & Mergel, I. (2012). *Studying social networks: A guide to empirical research*. Frankfurt, New York: Campus Verlag.

Hollenbeck, J. R., & Jamieson, B. B. (2015). Human capital, social capital, and social network analysis: Implications for strategic human resource management. *Academy of Management Perspectives*, *29*(3), 370–385. https://doi.org/10.5465/amp.2014.0140

Hoppe, B., & Reinelt, C. (2010). Social network analysis and the evaluation of leadership networks. *The Leadership Quarterly*, *21*(4), 600–619. https://doi.org/10.1016/j.leaqua.2010.06.004

Hortoványi, L., Szabó, R. Z., & Szabó, R. Z. (2006). Knowledge and organization: A network perspective. *Society and Economy*, *28*(2), 165–179.

Hsu, L. C., & Wang, C. H. (2012). Clarifying the effect of intellectual capital on performance: The mediating role of dynamic capability. *British Journal of Management*, *23*(2), 179–205. https://doi.org/10.1111/j.1467-8551.2010.00718.x

Johnson, G., Melin, L., & Whittington, R. (2003). Micro strategy and strategizing: Towards an activity-based view. *Journal of Management Studies*, *40*(1), 3–22.

Jokela, P., & Elo, M. (2015). Developing innovative business models in social ventures. *Journal of Entrepreneurship, Management and Innovation*, *11*(1), 103–118. https://doi.org/10.7341/20151116

Kianto, A. (2007). What do we really mean by the dynamic dimension of intellectual capital? *International Journal of Learning and Intellectual Capital*, *4*(4), 342–356.

Kilduff, M., & Brass, D. J. (2010). Organizational social network research: Core ideas and key debates. *The Academy of Management Annals*, *4*(1), 317–357.

Kilduff, M., & Tsai, W. (2003). *Social networks and organizations*. London: Sage Publications.

Kim, J. Y., Howard, M., Cox Pahnke, E., & Boeker, W. (2016). Understanding network formation in strategy research: Exponential random graph models. *Strategic Management Journal*, *37*(1), 22–44. https://doi.org/10.1002/smj.2454

Kocarev, L., & In, V. (2010). Network science: A new paradigm shift. *IEEE Network: The Magazine of Global Internetworking*, *24*(6), 6–9.

Kogut, B., & Zander, U. (1992). Knowledge of the firm, combinative capabilities, and the replication of technology. *Organization Science*, *3*(3), 383–397. https://doi.org/10.1287/orsc.3.3.383

Kong, E., & Thomson, S. B. (2009). An intellectual capital perspective of human resource strategies and practices. *Knowledge Management Research & Practice*, *7*(4), 356–364. https://doi.org/10.1057/kmrp.2009.27

Kotarbiński, T. (1982). *Traktat o dobrej robocie*. Wroclaw: Zakład Narodowy im. Ossolińskich.

Kraaijenbrink, J., Spender, J. C., & Groen, A. J. (2010). The resource-based view: A review and assessment of its critiques. *Journal of Management*, *36*(1), 349–372. https://doi.org/10.1177/0149206309350775

Krackhardt, D., & Carley, K. M. (1998). *PCANS model of structure in organizations*. Retrieved from www.ksg.harvard.edu/netgov/files/complexity/Krackhardt-A%20PCANS%20Model%20of%20Structure%20in%20Organization.pdf

Kuhn, T. S. (1962). *The structure of scientific revolutions*. Chicago: University of Chicago Press.

Kuutti, K. (1996). Activity theory as a potential framework for human-computer interaction research. In B. A. Nardi (Ed.), *Context and consciousness: Activity theory and human-computer interaction* (pp. 17–44). Cambridge, MA: MIT Press.

Lamertz, K., & Aquino, K. (2004). Social power, social status and perceptual similarity of workplace victimization: A social network analysis of stratification. *Human Relations*, *57*(7), 795–822.

Latour, B. (1987). *Science in action: How to follow scientists and engineers through society*. Cambridge, MA.: Harvard University Press.

Latour, B. (1988). The politics of explanation: An alternative. *Knowledge and Reflexivity: New Frontiers in the Sociology of Knowledge*, *10*, 155–176.

Latour, B. (1999). For David Bloor . . . and beyond: A reply to David Bloor's "anti-Latour". *Studies in History and Philosophy of Science*, *30*(1), 113–130.

Lavie, D. (2006). The competitive advantage of interconnected firms: An extension of the resource-based view. *Academy of Management Review*, *31*(3), 638–658.

Law, J., & Hassard, J. (1999). *Actor network theory and after*. Oxford, UK: Wiley.

Leavitt, H. J. (1951). Some effects of certain communication patterns on group performance. *Journal of Abnormal Psychology*, *46*(1), 38–50.

Leenders, R. T. A. J., & Dolfsma, W. A. (2016). Social networks for innovation and new product development. *Journal of Product Innovation Management*, *33*(2), 123–131. https://doi.org/10.1111/jpim.12292

Leenders, R. T. A., Van Engelen, J. M., & Kratzer, J. (2007). Systematic design methods and the creative performance of new product teams: Do they contradict or complement each other? *Journal of Product Innovation Management*, *24*(2), 166–179.

Leinhardt, S. (2013). *Social networks: A developing paradigm*. New York: Academic Press.

Leonard-Barton, D. (1992). Core capabilities and core rigidities: A paradox in managing new product development. *Strategic Management Journal*, *13*(S1), 111–125. https://doi.org/10.1002/smj.4250131009

Leont'ev, A. (2000). *Activity, consciousness, and personality*. Englewood Cliffs: Prentice-Hall.

Lewis, T. G. (2009). *Network science: Theory and applications*. Hoboken, NJ: Wiley Publishing.

Li, C., Liakata, M., & Rebholz-Schuhmann, D. (2014). Biological network extraction from scientific literature: State of the art and challenges. *Briefings in Bioinformatics*, *15*(5), 856–877. https://doi.org/10.1093/bib/bbt006

Li, Y., Lu, Y., Li, D., & Ma, L. (2015). Metanetwork analysis for project task assignment. *Journal of Construction Engineering and Management*, *141*(12). https://doi.org/10.1061/(ASCE)CO.1943-7862.0001019
Lin, N. (1999). Building a network theory of social capital. *Connections*, *22*(1), 28–51.
Lomi, A., Robins, G., & Tranmer, M. (2016). Introduction to multilevel social networks. *Social Networks*, *44*, 266–268. https://doi.org/10.1016/j.socnet.2015.10.006
Louie, M. A., & Carley, K. M. (2008). Balancing the criticisms: Validating multi-agent models of social systems. *Simulation Modelling Practice and Theory*, *16*(2), 242–256.
Luce, R. D., & Perry, A. D. (1949). A method of matrix analysis of group structure. *Psychometrika*, *14*(2), 95–116. https://doi.org/10.1007/BF02289146
Mahoney, J. T., & Pandian, J. R. (1992). The resource-based view within the conversation of strategic management. *Strategic Management Journal*, *13*(5), 363–380. https://doi.org/10.1002/smj.4250130505
Martín-de Castro, G. (2014). Intellectual capital and the firm: Some remaining questions and prospects. *Knowledge Management Research & Practice*, *12*(3), 239–245. https://doi.org/10.1057/kmrp.2014.13
Martín-de-Castro, G., Delgado-Verde, M., López-Sáez, P., & Navas-López, J. E. (2010). Towards "an intellectual capital-based view of the firm": Origins and nature. *Journal of Business Ethics*, *98*(4), 649–662. https://doi.org/10.1007/s10551-010-0644-5
Martínez-Torres, M. R. (2006). A procedure to design a structural and measurement model of intellectual capital: An exploratory study. *Information & Management*, *43*(5), 617–626. https://doi.org/10.1016/j.im.2006.03.002
Mason, K. J., & Leek, S. (2008). Learning to build a supply network: An exploration of dynamic business models. *Journal of Management Studies*, *45*(4), 774–799. https://doi.org/10.1111/j.1467-6486.2008.00769.x
Massingham, P. (2016). Knowledge accounts. *Long Range Planning*, *49*(3), 409–425. https://doi.org/10.1016/j.lrp.2015.02.003
McPherson, M., Smith-Lovin, L., & Cook, J. M. (2001). Birds of a feather: Homophily in social networks. *Annual Review of Sociology*, *27*(1), 415–444.
Mead, G. H. (1934). *Mind, self and society*. Chicago: University of Chicago Press.
Meyer, A. D., Tsui, A. S., & Hinings, C. R. (1993). Configurational approaches to organizational analysis. *The Academy of Management Journal*, *36*(6), 1175–1195. https://doi.org/10.2307/256809
Meyer, G. W. (1994). Social information processing and social networks: A test of social influence mechanisms. *Human Relations*, *47*(9), 1013.
Milgrom, P., & Roberts, J. (1995). Complementarities and fit strategy, structure, and organizational change in manufacturing. *Journal of Accounting and Economics*, *19*(2–3), 179–208. https://doi.org/10.1016/0165-4101(94)00382-F
Miller, D. (1996). Configurations revisited. *Strategic Management Journal*, *17*(7), 505–512.
Moliterno, T. P., & Mahony, D. M. (2011). Network theory of organization: A multilevel approach. *Journal of Management*, *37*(2), 443–467.
Moran, P. (2005). Structural vs. relational embeddedness: Social capital and managerial performance. *Strategic Management Journal*, *26*(12), 1129–1151.

Morel, B., & Ramanujam, R. (1999). Through the looking glass of complexity: The dynamics of organizations as adaptive and evolving systems. *Organization Science*, *10*(3), 278–293.

Moreno, J. L. (1934). *Who shall survive* (Vol. 58). Retrieved from www.jstor.org/stable/pdf/2785135.pdf

Morgan, G. P., & Carley, K. M. (2019). Characterizing organizational micro-climates in structural groups. *International Conference on Social Computing, Behavioral-Cultural Modeling and Prediction and Behavior Representation in Modeling and Simulation*, 12–20. Springer.

Morris, M., Schindehutte, M., & Allen, J. (2005). The entrepreneur's business model: Toward a unified perspective. *Journal of Business Research*, *58*(6), 726–735. https://doi.org/10.1016/j.jbusres.2003.11.001

Morris, S. S., & Snell, S. A. (2011). Intellectual capital configurations and organizational capability: An empirical examination of human resource subunits in the multinational enterprise. *Journal of International Business Studies*, *42*(6), 805–827. https://doi.org/10.1057/jibs.2011.14

Müller-Prothmann, T. (2007). Social network analysis: A practical method to improve knowledge sharing. In A. S. Kazi, L. Wohlfart, & P. Wolf (Eds.), *Hands-on knowledge co creation and sharing* (pp. 219–233). Stuttgart: Knowledge Board.

Nahapiet, J., & Ghoshal, S. (1998). Social capital, intellectual capital, and the organizational advantage. *The Academy of Management Review*, *23*(2), 242–266. https://doi.org/10.2307/259373

Nair, S., Nisar, A., Palacios, M., & Ruiz, F. (2012). Impact of knowledge brokering on performance heterogeneity among business models. *Management Decision*, *50*(9), 1649–1660. https://doi.org/10.1108/00251741211266732

Nardi, B. A. (1996). Studying context: A comparison of activity theory, situated action models, and distributed cognition. In B.A. Nardi (Ed.), *Context and consciousness: Activity theory and human-computer interaction* (pp. 69–102). Cambridge, MA: MIT Press.

Newman, M. (2010). *Networks: An introduction*. Oxford, UK: Oxford University Press.

Nielsen, Ch., & Montemari, M. (2012). The role of human resources in business model performance: The case of network-based companies. *Journal of Human Resource Costing & Accounting*, *16*(2), 142–164. https://doi.org/10.1108/14013381211284254

Obstfeld, D. (2005). Social networks, the tertius iungens orientation, and involvement in innovation. *Administrative Science Quarterly*, *50*(1), 100–130. https://doi.org/10.2189/asqu.2005.50.1.100

Oliveira, P., Roth, A. V., & Gilland, W. (2002). Achieving competitive capabilities in e-services. *Technological Forecasting and Social Change*, *69*(7), 721–739. https://doi.org/10.1016/S0040-1625(01)00188-3

Orlikowski, W. J. (2002). Knowing in practice: Enacting a collective capability in distributed organizing. *Organization Science*, *13*(3), 249–273.

Oxford Dictionary. (n.d.). Structure. Retrieved from http://oxforddictionaries.com/definition/english/structure

Oxford Dictionary. (n.d.). Network. Retrieved from http://oxforddictionaries.com/definition/english/network

Parise, S. (2007). Knowledge management and human resource development: An application in social network analysis methods. *Advances in Developing Human Resources*, *9*(3), 359–383. https://doi.org/10.1177/1523422307304106

Parkhe, A., Wasserman, S., & Ralston, D. A. (2006). New frontiers in network theory development. *Academy of Management Review*, *31*(3), 560–568.

Penrose, E. T. (1995). *The theory of the growth of the firm*. Oxford, UK: Oxford University Press.

Peppard, J., & Rylander, A. (2001). Using an intellectual capital perspective to design and implement a growth strategy: The case of APiON. *European Management Journal*, *19*(5), 510–525. https://doi.org/10.1016/S0263-2373(01)00065-2

Peteraf, M. A. (1993). The cornerstones of competitive advantage: A resource-based view. *Strategic Management Journal*, *14*(3), 179–191.

Powell, W. W., Koput, K. W., & Smith-Doerr, L. (1996). Interorganizational collaboration and the locus of innovation: Networks of learning in biotechnology. *Administrative Science Quarterly*, *152*, 116–145.

Prahalad, C. (1993). The role of core competences in the corporation. *Research-Technology Management*, *36*(6), 40–47.

Prahalad, C., & Hamel, G. (1990). The core competence of the corporation. *Harvard Business Review*, *68*(3), 79–91.

Prell, C. (2012). *Social network analysis: History, theory and methodology*. London: Sage Publications.

Priem, R. L., & Butler, J. E. (2001). Is the resource-based "view" a useful perspective for strategic management research? *Academy of Management Review*, *26*(1), 22–40. https://doi.org/10.5465/AMR.2001.4011928

Pryke, S. (2012). *Social network analysis in construction*. Cambridge, UK: John Wiley & Sons.

Pugh, K., & Prusak, L. (2013). Designing effective knowledge networks. *MIT Sloan Management Review*, *55*(1), 79–88.

Putnam, R. D. (1995). Bowling alone: America's declining social capital. *Journal of Democracy*, *6*(1), 65–78.

Reagans, R., & Zuckerman, E. W. (2001). Networks, diversity, and productivity: The social capital of corporate R&D teams. *Organization Science*, *12*(4), 502–517. https://doi.org/10.1287/orsc.12.4.502.10637

Reed, K. K., Lubatkin, M., & Srinivasan, N. (2006). Proposing and testing an intellectual capital-based view of the firm. *Journal of Management Studies*, *43*(4), 867–893. https://doi.org/10.1111/j.1467-6486.2006.00614.x

Reiche, B. S., Harzing, A. W., & Kraimer, M. L. (2009). The role of international assignees' social capital in creating inter-unit intellectual capital: A cross-level model. *Journal of International Business Studies*, *40*(3), 509–526. https://doi.org/10.1057/jibs.2008.86

Richardson, J. (1986). *Handbook of theory and research for the sociology of education*. New York: Greenwood Press.

Robins, G. (2015). *Doing social network research: Network-based research design for social scientists*. London: Sage Publications Limited.

Rodan, S. (2002). Innovation and heterogeneous knowledge in managerial contact networks. *Journal of Knowledge Management*, *6*(2), 152–163.

Rodan, S., & Galunic, C. (2004). More than network structure: How knowledge heterogeneity influences managerial performance and innovativeness. *Strategic Management Journal*, *25*(6), 541–562.

Rogers, E. M. (2003). *Diffusion of innovations* (5th ed.). New York: Simon and Schuster.

Roos, J. (1998). Exploring the concept of intellectual capital (IC). *Long Range Planning*, *31*(1), 150–153. https://doi.org/10.1016/S0024-6301(97)87431-6

Rubin, P. H. (1973). The expansion of firms. *Journal of Political Economy*, *81*(4), 936–949.

Rugman, A. M., & Verbeke, A. (2002). Edith Penrose's contribution to the resource-based view of strategic management. *Strategic Management Journal*, *23*(8), 769–780. https://doi.org/10.1002/smj.240

Rumelt, R. (1991). How much does industry matter. *Strategic Management Journal*, *12*(3), 167–185. https://doi.org/10.1002/smj.4250120302

Rumelt, R. P. (1984). Towards a strategic theory of the firm. *Competitive Strategic Management*, *26*, 556–570.

Salancik, G. R. (1995). Wanted: A good network theory of organization. *Administrative Science Quarterly*, *40*(2), 345–349.

Sanchez, P., & Ricart, J. E. (2010). Business model innovation and sources of value creation in low-income markets. *European Management Review*, *7*(3), 138–154. https://doi.org/10.1057/emr.2010.16

Schipper, D., Gerrits, L., & Koppenjan, J. F. (2015). A dynamic network analysis of the information flows during the management of a railway disruption. *European Journal of Transport and Infrastructure Research*, *15*(4), 442–464.

Schiuma, G. (2009). The managerial foundations of knowledge assets dynamics. *Knowledge Management Research & Practice*, *7*(4), 290 299. https://doi.org/10.1057/kmrp.2009.21

Scott, J. (2012). *Social network analysis*. London: Sage.

Shimbel, A. (1951). Applications of matrix algebra to communication nets. *The Bulletin of Mathematical Biophysics*, *13*(3), 165–178. https://doi.org/10.1007/BF02478225

Shukla, M. (2015). An introduction to knowledge utilization capability and its autopoietic epistemological domain. *Journal of the Knowledge Economy*, *6*(4), 1001–1012. https://doi.org/10.1007/s13132-013-0171-6

Simmel, G., & Wolff, K. H. (1950). *The sociology of Georg Simmel*. New York: The Free Press.

Soda, G., & Zaheer, A. (2012). A network perspective on organizational architecture: Performance effects of the interplay of formal and informal organization. *Strategic Management Journal*, *33*(6), 751–771. https://doi.org/10.1002/smj.1966

Spender, J. C., & Grant, R. M. (1996). Knowledge and the firm: Overview. *Strategic Management Journal*, *17*(S2), 5–9.

Steen, J. (2010). Actor-network theory and the dilemma of the resource concept in strategic management. *Scandinavian Journal of Management*, *26*(3), 324–331.

Straker, K., & Wrigley, C. (2015). The role of emotion in product, service and business model design. *Journal of Entrepreneurship, Management and Innovation*, *11*(1), 11–28. https://doi.org/10.7341/20151112

Subramaniam, M., & Venkatraman, N. (2001). Determinants of transnational new product development capability: Testing the influence of transferring and deploying tacit overseas knowledge. *Strategic Management Journal*, *22*(4), 359–378. https://doi.org/10.1002/smj.163

Subramaniam, M., & Youndt, M. A. (2005). The influence of intellectual capital on the types of innovative capabilities. *The Academy of Management Journal*, *48*(3), 450–463. https://doi.org/10.2307/20159670

Sydler, R., Haefliger, S., & Pruksa, R. (2014). Measuring intellectual capital with financial figures: Can we predict firm profitability? *European Management Journal*, *32*(2), 244–259. https://doi.org/10.1016/j.emj.2013.01.008

Teece, D. J. (2007). Explicating dynamic capabilities: The nature and microfoundations of (sustainable) enterprise performance. *Strategic Management Journal*, *28*(13), 1319–1350. https://doi.org/10.1002/smj.640

Teece, D. J. (2009). *Dynamic capabilities and strategic management: Organizing for innovation and growth*. Oxford, UK: Oxford University Press.

Teece, D. J., Pisano, G., & Shuen, A. (1997). Dynamic capabilities and strategic management. *Strategic Management Journal*, *18*(7), 509–533. https://onlinelibrary.wiley.com/doi/abs/10.1002/%28SICI%291097-0266%28199708%2918%3A7%3C509%3A%3AAID-SMJ882%3E3.0.CO%3B2-Z

Tichy, N., & Fombrun, C. (1979). Network analysis in organizational settings. *Human Relations*, *32*(11), 923–965.

Tichy, N. M., Tushman, M. L., & Fombrun, C. (1979). Social network analysis for organizations. *Academy of Management Review*, *4*(4), 507–519.

Tsai, W. (2002). Social structure of "coopetition" within a multiunit organization: Coordination, competition, and intraorganizational knowledge sharing. *Organization Science*, *13*(2), 179–190.

Tseng, C. Y., & Goo, Y. J. J. (2005). Intellectual capital and corporate value in an emerging economy: Empirical study of Taiwanese manufacturers. *R&D Management*, *35*(2), 187–201. https://doi.org/10.1111/j.1467-9310.2005.00382.x

Tsvetovat, M., & Carley, K. M. (2004). Modeling complex socio-technical systems using multi-agent simulation methods. *Kunstliche Intelligenz*, *18*(2), 23–28.

Ujwary-Gil, A. (2017). The business model and intellectual capital in the value creation of firms: A literature review. *Baltic Journal of Management*, *12*(3), 368–386.

Uzzi, B. (1997). Social structure and competition in interfirm networks: The paradox of embeddedness. *Administrative Science Quarterly*, *42*, 35–67.

Valente, T. W. (2010). *Social networks and health*. Oxford, UK; New York: Oxford University Press.

Valente, T. W. (2012). Network interventions. *Science*, *337*(6090), 49–53.

Vygotsky, L. S. (1978). *Mind in society: The development of higher mental processes*. Cambridge, MA: Harvard University Press. (Original work published 1930, 1933).

Wasserman, S., & Faust, K. (1994). *Social network analysis: Methods and applications*. Cambridge, UK: Cambridge University Press.

Watts, D. J. (2004). The "new" science of networks. *Annual Review of Sociology*, *30*(1), 243–270. https://doi.org/10.1146/annurev.soc.30.020404.104342

Weber, M. (1978). *Economy and society: An outline of interpretive sociology*. Berkeley, CA: University of California Press.

Weber, M. (2015). *On the methodology of the social sciences*. New York: Lulu Press, Inc.

Wellman, B. (1997). Structural analysis: From method and metaphor to theory and substance. *Contemporary Studies in Sociology*, *15*, 19–61.

Wellman, B. (2001). Computer networks as social networks. *Science*, *293*(5537), 2031–2034.

Wernerfelt, B. (1984). A resource-based view of the firm. *Strategic Management Journal*, *5*(2), 171–180. https://doi.org/10.1002/smj.4250050207

White, H. (1961). Management conflict and sociometric structure. *American Journal of Sociology*, *67*, 185–199.

Wills-Johnson, N. (2008). The networked firm: A framework for RBV. *The Journal of Management Development*, *27*(2), 214–224. http://dx.doi.org/10.1108/02621710810849344

Wilson, R. J. (2012). *Introduction to graph theory* (5 ed.). Harlow, UK; New York: Pearson.

Winter, S. G., & Szulanski, G. (2001). Replication as strategy. *Organization Science*, *12*(6), 730–743. https://doi.org/10.1287/orsc.12.6.730.10084

Wolbers, J., Groenewegen, P., Mollee, J., & Bím, J. (2013). Incorporating time dynamics in the analysis of social networks in emergency management. *Journal of Homeland Security and Emergency Management*, *10*(2), 555–585.

Wu, F., Huberman, B. A., Adamic, L. A., & Tyler, J. R. (2004). Information flow in social groups. *Physica A: Statistical Mechanics and Its Applications*, *337*(1–2), 327–335. https://doi.org/10.1016/j.physa.2004.01.030

Wu, W. L., Yeh, R. S., & Hung, H. K. (2012). Knowledge sharing and work performance: A network perspective. *Social Behavior and Personality: An International Journal*, *40*(7), 1113–1120.

Yates-Mercer, P., & Bawden, D. (2002). Managing the paradox: The valuation of knowledge and knowledge management. *Journal of Information Science*, *28*(1), 19–29. https://doi.org/10.1177/016555150224233913

Youndt, M. A., Subramaniam, M., & Snell, S. A. (2004). Intellectual capital profiles: An examination of investments and returns. *Journal of Management Studies*, *41*(2), 335–361. https://doi.org/10.1111/j.1467-6486.2004.00435.x

Zack, M. H. (1999). Developing a knowledge strategy. *California Management Review*, *41*(3), 125–134.

Zieleniewski, J. (1981). *Organizacja i zarządzanie*. Warsaw: Polskie Wydawnictwo Naukowe.

Zott, C., & Amit, R. (2010). Business model design: An activity system perspective. *Long Range Planning*, *43*(2–3), 216–226. https://doi.org/10.1016/j.lrp.2009.07.004

2 Integrated Organizational Intangible Resource Audit as a *Meta-Model* of Information, Knowledge, and Intellectual Capital Audit

The purpose of this chapter is to familiarize the reader with the basic types of intangible resources, that is, information and knowledge, and their combination—intellectual capital. These resources can be presented using three approaches: static, structural, and dynamic. In the static approach, information, knowledge, and intellectual capital are shown from the resource perspective. Notably, a comprehensive view of both information and knowledge is manifested in the notion of intellectual capital, seen as part of strategic management, and not accountancy. Intellectual capital has been extensively covered in literature, so the issue of its measurement will only be discussed in the context of intellectual capital audit. Here, the notion of intellectual capital diverges greatly from its economic and valuation-related connotations. In this book, intellectual capital is viewed as one of the resources upon which strategic decisions are based.

The structural approach lets one view resources from an individual, organizational, and network perspective. The latter is key to the present discussion, as both information and knowledge, and relational capital, are shown in the context of flows and relations, which are the domain of any network. As to the dynamic approach to information, knowledge, and intellectual capital, it is most relevant for the actions that are performed. Therefore, one can view networks and knowledge as actions or structures for actions, where intangible resources constitute intellectual capital with a specific structure of relations. The dynamics are associated with viewing information and knowledge in the light of their relations and their configuration, or transformation into actions (tasks).

This discussion of intangible resources is an introduction to the notions of information, knowledge, and intellectual capital audit. What distinguishes this view of audit from the classical one (e.g., internal audit, quality audit) is the shift of focus from conformity of actions with procedures toward intangible resources viewed from their user's perspective—in other words, compliance has been replaced with improvement. This approach is justified within actor-network theory and activity theory, discussed in Chapter 1. Audit scope concerns the actor (individual, employee), their knowledge and skills, their tasks, and, last but not least, the resources they use. The identification of these components' dynamics is the primary area of improvement in each organization. In order to make improvements, the auditor must first identify the resources.

The key objective of this chapter is to present the notion of intangible resource audit as a *meta-model*, developed on the basis of information audit, knowledge audit, and intellectual capital audit models. Therefore, the present discussion includes a detailed description of a methodology for creating such a *meta-model*. Network metrics selected for use in the intangible resource audit, to measure both information and knowledge flows, and the effectiveness of actions performed using these resources, are particularly relevant. These metrics allow one to view an organization in the light of information and knowledge flows, the prominence of these resources in the network of relationships, resource load, and resource redundancy. As the analyses and network graphs are too extensive to be fully shown here, only the visualizations most relevant to the present discussion are included, with more attention given to results obtained using the selected metrics. This chapter will also contain the essential information on network metrics and on their relevance for intangible resource audit.

2.1 The Nature of Intangible Resources

2.1.1 *The Static Approach to Information, Knowledge, and Intellectual Capital*

Information is in itself intangible and not easily defined. Machlup (1984) recalls that the original meaning of the term *information* is derived from the Latin *informare*, meaning *to give form*. Information, with actual or perceived value in current or future actions or decisions, is composed of data given a form meaningful to its recipient (Bierly III, Kessler, & Christensen, 2000). Information plays a role in forming a context and is the "actor" of influence on the surroundings (Braman, 1989). This is a much broader view of information, including the entire range of processes and phenomena in which information is involved. It can be applied to social structures at all degrees of articulation and complexity, as well as to their flows, and is a significant factor shaping societies and the physical reality. Information is also transmitted by language, which in itself is a social occurrence.

In many studies, data, information, and knowledge are distinguished from one another with specific definitions (Boisot & Canals, 2004; Zins, 2007). Such distinction has been inspired by information theory (Bollinger & Smith, 2001). Data, including numerical data, are the contents of information that can be used as a basis for intentional action. When data are collected, together with their meaning and context, and subsequently processed, they become information. Information is transformed into a component of knowledge when it is analyzed critically, and its fundamental structure is understood in relation to other information components and to a view of the world (Lillrank, 2003).

Within the theory of organizational knowledge creation (Ikujiro Nonaka, Krogh, & Voelpel, 2006), information is generated through systematic processing and refinement (value increase) of data, and, even more importantly, through the application of context and meaning. In daily use, information affects individual and organizational decision-making processes, and its effective management and processing facilitate the creation of intellectual capital, which is the foundation of growth and innovation (Buchanan & Gibb, 2007).

Organizations are aware of the potential information gives them for obtaining competitive advantage and maintaining their success (Porter & Millar, 1985; Prescott, 2016; Vives, 1990). Information is commonly described as a component of assets and resources. Such descriptions appeared particularly frequently in the 1990s (Burk & Horton, 1988; Eaton & Bawden, 1991; Swash, 1997) when the full potential of information in terms of competitive advantage was being explored. In the context of resources, information, its creators, brokers, and users are seen as separate, isolated entities. Therefore, it takes a distributed, fragmented form, not incorporated into the overall flow of information and knowledge (Braman, 1989).

According to Oppenheim, Stenson, and Wilson (2003b), information seen as a resource is characterized by quality and utility (way of use, accessibility, flexibility). The utility attribute is essential for information. Information increases productivity by streamlining the decision-making process and enhancing customer and partner relationships. Notably, information is not synonymous with information assets. It is a component of information assets, as the latter include, according to the cited authors, information on: the market, customers, competitors, management, vendors, specialist knowledge, legal regulations and considerations (e.g., information security), human resource management, organization (organizational learning, change management), or business processes. The above division reflects, in fact, the components of intellectual capital, which are discussed in detail further in the chapter. This demonstrates the difficulty involved in distinguishing clearly between information and knowledge, both elements of intellectual capital (see also Figure 2.1).

The terms "information" and "knowledge" are often used interchangeably, though a clear distinction exists. As emphasized by Nonaka (1994), information is primarily in the relationship (though the relationship itself is bidirectional), while knowledge is created and organized by information flow and focused on the engagement and beliefs of its holder. Seen as a component in a process, information is fragmented and distributed; it is usually timely, but transient. In turn, knowledge as a state (scope,

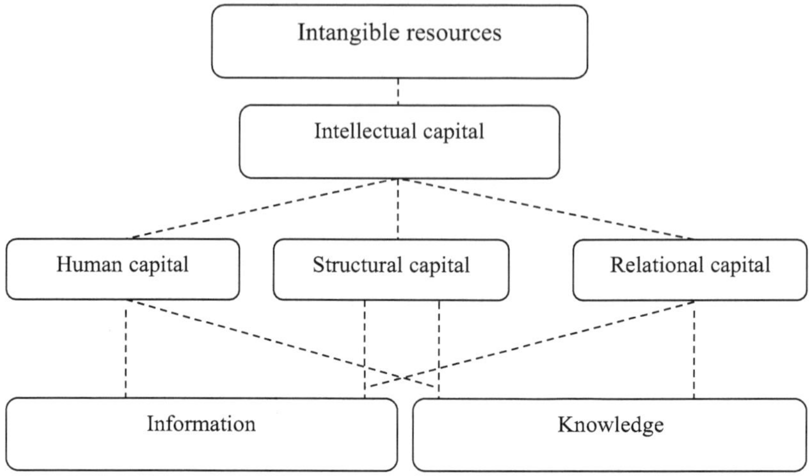

Figure 2.1 Classification of intangible resource components

domain) is, at a given time, organized, coherent, and universal, persistent in time and expansive in space (Machlup, 1984). This does not, however, preclude the active and subjective nature of knowledge, represented by terms such as *beliefs* and *engagement*, deep-rooted in individual value systems.

Two views of knowledge exist (Carlsson, 2003). One is knowledge as a resource, which can be transferred, recombined, licensed, stored in databases, recorded, and used for enterprise value creation. The other is knowledge as a process—the flow of knowledge, "knowing"—which puts the focus on the context within which knowledge is created, exchanged, integrated, and used. These processes become key tasks in network management (Knight & Harland, 2005). Therefore, knowledge processes are designed and structured so as to produce competitive advantage. Importance is assigned to creating new knowledge, sharing knowledge, and applying existing knowledge to problem-solving and task performance thanks to a network of knowledge and resource flows. An organization's capacity for knowledge sharing among its members is the key to competitive advantage (Bock, Zmud, Kim, & Lee, 2005).

Intellectual capital is a widely understood concept in the literature on strategic management and in business practice. The notion of intellectual capital has been developed in the last two decades. No single definition, interpretation, or set of components contained in the concept has been created, either in theory or in practice (Martín-de Castro, 2014). Overall, the notion dates back to the mid-1990s, associated with such factors as the new, knowledge-based economy and the service sector, which remains dominant to date, or the advances in information and communications technology (Alcaniz, Gomez-Bezares, & Roslender, 2011). However, intellectual capital is most commonly discussed in the context of value creation, resource-based competitive advantage, and innovation and economic performance of an enterprise. The interrelations and combinations or configurations of its components are considered less often, but this is the case in the network approach.

Intellectual capital has multiple definitions. It may be understood as a derivative of "capital," which is a fundamental category in economics and related fields, such as finance and accountancy. Though economics and management science use terms such as knowledge assets, intellectual (non-measurable) assets, intangible assets, and so on, in accounting, intangible values and intellectual capital are interchangeable concepts.

For the present discussion, intellectual capital is best viewed from the perspective of value creation, components, and resources, as is the case in the ICBV. The notion of intellectual capital aspires to reflect the entirety of the enterprise, a balanced view comprising both physical and financial resources. It determines capabilities for acting in various circumstances, creating tangible and intangible assets (Sveiby, 1997). The purpose of intellectual capital is to create a framework for the description of all resources in an enterprise and their interrelations that create value (Peppard & Rylander, 2001). Most importantly, however, it is the sum of all knowledge an enterprise has and is capable of using in the course of its operations to obtain competitive advantage (Youndt et al., 2004). Authors of intellectual capital definitions associate it with value creation, competitiveness, and performance (e.g., Bontis, 1999; Hsu & Fang, 2009; Kong & Thomson, 2009; Stewart, 1997; Subramaniam & Youndt, 2005; Sullivan, 2000; Teece, Pisano & Shuen, 1997). Intellectual capital comprises flows of intangible resources and skills that enable the development of the core business processes in an enterprise, producing competitive advantage (Martín-de Castro, 2014). Thus, its components include skills, culture, strategy, processes, intellectual property, and relationship networks that are sources of value or competitive advantage (Hsu & Fang, 2009), in line with the definition of resources by Barney (1991), and Peppard and Rylander (2001). Many authors also view intellectual capital in the context of the relationship between market value and book value (Edvinsson & Malone, 1997; Martínez-Torres, 2006; Sveiby, 1997).

The entirety of intangible resources has been well described within the concept of intellectual capital based on information and knowledge. Its basic components are: human, structural, and relational capital (Figure 2.1). The focus of analysis is the set of information and knowledge, with their various configurations, within these components of intellectual capital.

2.1.2 The Structural Approach to Information, Knowledge, and Intellectual Capital

Brown and Starkey (1994) proposed the notion of information consciousness, created in an organization, related to employees' capability of obtaining information. This concept describes an organization's attitude toward the value of information as a resource, facilitation of organizational learning, and access to knowledge through facilitated transfer and sharing among professionals. Constant access to a communications network and to expert information affects the capability to obtain information. Chong et al. (2011) performed empirical verification of these assumptions and found a positive association between the ability to obtain information and an organization's performance.

Information exchange is a key factor in an organization's competitiveness. It requires free, unobstructed, and ongoing flow of information among the members. Broad availability of information, however, tends to be an exception rather than a rule in organizations (Li & Lin, 2006). SNA is believed to provide an adequate set of instruments for specifying the scope of information exchange between groups in an organization, going beyond a simple description of complex interpersonal interaction systems in organizations, as it illustrates communication both within working groups and between them. Fostering information exchange and positive behaviors increases employee productivity (Hatala & George Lutta, 2009). One desirable aspect of SODNA (SNA, ONA, and DNA) techniques is their versatility related to the fact that the scope of information and knowledge exchange both within and between organizational units is virtually unlimited. These techniques allow one to understand how people create, accept, store, share, and exchange information and knowledge when performing their tasks.

Restricted information flow, both internal and external, prevents organizations from preparing for sudden changes in their environment and adapting to them, creating information gaps (Barua, Ravindran, & Whinston, 2007). Efficiency is increased when new information is constantly distributed to the key individuals in an organization, which effectively means that information is viewed as an economic asset. Such constant transfer of new information to key individuals increases efficiency because current, quality information can support the management in their decision-making processes, shorten product development times, and accelerate customer service by better adaptation to customer needs. The likelihood of seeking information from another person depends on one's knowledge of what the other person knows. So far, however, most researchers have focused on declarative or procedural knowledge, disregarding knowledge on existing interpersonal relations. Perceptions of others are shaped by direct interaction, observation, and third-party comments, and all these factors affect the likelihood of seeking information from a person in the future (Borgatti & Cross, 2003). Of course, the size of a network also affects communication efficiency, which is lower in larger networks with longer paths.

According to Parraguez, Eppinger, and Maier (2015), in an organization, information is the basis for the creation of knowledge for all individuals involved in its acquisition and use. It molds awareness of what happens within the organization and in its environment. It also enables the organization to adapt to the changing reality and to transform this reality in order to operate effectively, as well as to become aware of existing problems and search for solutions. Interestingly, the authors also state that information is subjective by nature, as it must always be considered in the context of its recipient. The same information may elicit various interpretations in different individuals, depending on their knowledge that is derived from the information through integration with their previous knowledge.

Explicit knowledge is formal, systematic, and uniform—similar to information. Tacit knowledge is personalized. It comprises technical skills and know-how, enriched with cognitive dimensions such as covert thought patterns and beliefs that shape an individual's world view. Personal knowledge is typically transformed into organizational knowledge, thus gaining value for the organization as a whole. The popular knowledge spiral model (externalization, combination, internalization, socialization) by Nonaka and Takeuchi (1995), comprising four patterns for knowledge creation in an organization, bears a resemblance to the process view of information. What is interesting about the approach is that knowledge and information are recursive (Bhatt, 2001), which makes knowledge creation and communication a dynamic process. Contrary to tacit knowledge, explicit knowledge is defined as knowledge that can be made uniform, enabling its transfer and sharing.

Multiple types of knowledge exist in an organization, for instance: knowledge regarding a specialized area or process (technical knowledge), design knowledge, knowledge on the environment (competitors, customers). These types of knowledge are not mutually exclusive, which means an organization can have knowledge of various types (technical, design, and many others). The form of knowledge (explicit or tacit) is also important, as it implies the possible ways of knowledge transfer and distribution in the organization. Knowledge can be categorized as knowledge related to tasks (know-what) and knowledge related to the way things are done based on procedures and processes (know-how).

Knowledge is the condition of understanding something through acquired experience, or a state of knowing the truth or the fact through reason and intellect. Previous experience and knowledge are the basis for creating new knowledge (Reid, 2015). Knowledge can be presented as a structure of interrelated concepts, with existing knowledge acting as a filter for selecting and discarding new information and knowledge structures that may or may not change. Conceptual change develops gradually, modifying and transforming the existing knowledge structures. Experience plays a significant role in the understanding of and ability to apply tacit knowledge (Kogut & Zander, 1992). Explicit knowledge can be understood and applied in a relatively simple manner, without necessarily involving experience. As to tacit knowledge, it cannot be shared formally, and requires experience in order to be understood. Thus, the flow of tacit knowledge may be considered only potentially possible.

Knowledge is incorporated in social relationships, especially in communities of practice (Kalafatis, Lemos, Lo, & Frank, 2015), centered around a certain field of knowledge (e.g., law, economics, organizational management), that accumulate expert knowledge in the field over time. Organizational communities develop common practices by their involvement in problem-solving, analyses, and creation of a shared knowledge base (Wenger & Snyder, 2000; Wenger, McDermott, & Snyder, 2002). Effective use of knowledge requires the creation of a network in which employees' knowledge and experience are made available. Networks have a much stronger impact on the creation and sharing of knowledge than collection and storage of data in databases. Thus, barriers to knowledge should be at least decreased, and prominent individuals, knowledge, and resources should be networked to promote knowledge evolution, distribution, and application (Seufert, Von Krogh, & Bach, 1999). Common understanding, and the capability of transforming knowledge into action producing a result, should, therefore, be regarded as a social process, whereby individuals attempt to arrive at a common knowledge on the reality by using various combinations of signs (e.g., language signs, gestures, drawings) and tools (e.g., physical objects, communications technology, thought models).

A significant portion of knowledge is produced and maintained collectively. Such knowledge is created when people work together within a community of practice. Organizational knowledge is social by nature, and organizing knowledge is by far the most difficult aspect for organizations. It is an error to confound information with knowledge, as not all problems can be solved using information technology. New knowledge is formed in the process of continuous development and production by various individuals in an organization (Brown & Duguid, 1998). Network analysis techniques can be effectively used for researching social structures, modeling knowledge networks, and understanding team knowledge. Organizational knowledge is founded on the knowledge of teams (employee groups). It is both a set of tasks and the interrelated (interacting) individual knowledge of the organization's employees (Espinosa & Clark, 2014). Knowledge in an organizational setting is often team knowledge (Espinosa & Clark, 2014). In this case, social knowledge is exchanged through communication and action, creating cognitive relationships that help define the dynamics of a team. Connections between nodes represent knowledge relationships, such as shared knowledge—termed collective knowledge by Spender (1996)—which is the most secure and strategically significant organizational knowledge, illustrating the way knowledge is shared among members. At the levels of nodes, dyads, subgroups, or teams, major characteristics of knowledge can be identified, such as: the proportion of knowledge-based relations to other actors, actors without knowledge relationships, and cliques—subgroups fully connected in a given field of knowledge, useful for performing tasks.

In order to understand the essence of intellectual capital, it is worthwhile to regard its different levels: individual, organizational, and inter-organizational, enabling the identification of its major components. At the individual level (human capital), the most important factor is the knowledge possessed by an employee—their attitudes, behaviors, experience, skills, and capabilities developed by training and formal education (Bontis, 1999; Edvinsson & Malone, 1997; Martín-de-Castro, Delgado-Verde, López-Sáez, & Navas-López, 2010). At the organizational level, intellectual capital takes on the form of structural capital (Chang, Chen & Lai, 2008; Hormiga, Batista-Canino, & Sánchez-Medina, 2010; Hsu & Fang, 2009; Sveiby, 1997), which comprises, for example, infrastructure (including IT systems and management processes), intellectual property, business processes, technological capital, ideas, models, computer systems and architecture, routines, procedures, organizational structures, strategies, business structures, and organizational culture. Its role is to capture (record or codify) human capital as explicit knowledge, that is, documented designs, routines, and procedures. The inter-organizational level is mainly related to such forms of intellectual capital as social capital (Nahapiet & Ghoshal, 1998; Reiche, Harzing, & Kraimer, 2009), relational capital (Hormiga et al., 2010), customers (Edvinsson & Malone, 1997), and market assets (Brooking, 1997), which comprise the brand of a product or service, reputation, and image. It is extraneous to the enterprise and concerns value created within relationships with other entities operating in the environment: partners, customers, suppliers, the society, allies, and labor unions (Bontis, 2001; Hsu & Fang, 2009; Subramaniam & Youndt, 2005). It provides an understanding of how enterprises can create and develop new knowledge and value in collaboration with a broad range of stakeholders.

The components of intellectual capital may provide a template for comparisons against the intellectual capital of competing entities, and for assessing the impact of each component on enterprise performance and customer behaviors. Enterprises can benefit from knowing which components increase their income, attract customers, or enhance business relations. Key differences in the components of each intellectual capital and resource configuration affect the perceived customer value. Knowledge of components that create value for an enterprise enables investors to better allocate their capital and to make investments offering a higher return. Enterprises that understand which of their intellectual capital components are the most important can focus on those specific components, adding, removing, and modifying components deliberately so as to enhance increases of enterprise performance and customer satisfaction.

The value dimension is a result, rather than a component, of the intellectual capital model. Value is created through interaction of the above-mentioned intellectual capital components: human, structural, and relational capital (Hermans & Kauranen, 2005). Financial aspects are increasingly often included in intellectual capital analysis, particularly when the purpose is to comprehensively depict the company's value structure, resource base, and asset monetization. Other than the product of intellectual capital, the financial dimension may also be seen as a burden or even a restriction to its development, in the case of insufficient funds. Intellectual capital is not only a resource, but also an expense, and it competes with other types of investments in an organization within organizational processes such as financial planning or budgeting (Murthy & Mouritsen, 2011).

2.1.3 The Dynamic Approach to Information, Knowledge, and Intellectual Capital

From relations between network actors, information is an object of relationships, as it is transferable and communicable, hence the importance of defining information in the context of activities and relations. Information is an activity and is more often referred to by verbs (e.g., send, transfer, receive) than nouns. As an activity, it occurs among individuals. Davenport and Prusak (2013) define information as a message transferred as a document or in another communication form. Transferred information comprises both the sender's intention and the recipient's expectations. Therefore, it acts as a bridge between subjective and objective knowledge that can be transferred and communicated (Oppenheim, Stenson, & Wilson, 2003a). The definition of information in *Practical Information Policies* (1999) also refers to the cognitive approach, whereby information becomes knowledge when people wish to communicate with others.

Another, equally important, stage of information exchange processes in a network is the use of information, meaning an intellectual activity or cognitive effort performed as an inherent component of action or practice, for example, for estimating the relevance of work-related information. Cognitive processes and internalization of information are associated with the understanding of information and its processing using own intellectual categories, thus transforming information into knowledge (Spink & Cole, 2006). Information is meant to be used in action. This requires not only information exchange, but also a special approach resulting in other individuals also changing their knowledge and their behaviors (Cook & Brown, 1999).

Therefore, information is not an abstract concept, but a relationship between two entities: the carrier of information (actor) and its recipient (interpreter). Such a relationship requires definition. Notably, in this relationship (between network actors), it is the recipient that is key, as they are the one upon whom the affirmation, internalization, and activation of information depend. The relationship is always intentional rather than random, as it comprises the intention (of a person), which in the inter-organizational context is to affect the accomplishment of objectives.

Knowledge has an economic value, both in societies and in organizations (Campbell, Coff, & Kryscynski, 2012; Harris, 2001). The latter appreciate the importance of knowledge as a resource and an asset that can be managed. Currently, when viewing an organization from the perspective of an activity system in the context of activity theory, one leaves behind the classical division into resources or the view of knowledge as an economic asset. Knowledge is essentially linked to human activity. The knowledge-based view, termed the "knowledge-based theory of the firm" by Spender (1996), is a platform allowing one to see an organization as a dynamic, emerging, quasi-autonomous system of knowledge production and application. Here, knowledge is not considered as an organizational resource in the positivist sense, but as a qualitative aspect of the activity system created by the managing staff. Earlier approaches (e.g., by Starbuck, 1992) show expert knowledge as a resource rather than a flow. The intensities (flow frequencies) of knowledge and information are not mutually dependent. Intensified processing of information does not necessarily entail many new applications of knowledge. Arguably, however, intense flows of information result in the creation of new knowledge, if not its use.

Knowledge is often perceived as an object and defined as a "justified true belief" (Dawson, 1981; Hess, 1981). This perspective assumes that knowledge can be codified and separated from the human mind, which means that knowledge sharing would be generally understood as a "transfer of knowledge objects," similarly to the way information is transferred in the "sender-receiver" model (Shannon & Weaver, 2015). From the perspective of knowledge personalization, knowledge can only exist in the human mind, as only people are capable of "knowing," converting knowledge into action or information into knowledge, and creating new knowledge. In this approach, knowledge sharing is typically seen as exchanging information to acquire knowledge.

According to Polanyi (1958), knowledge is an activity better described as a process of knowing. The author defines three levels in the model of knowledge: skills (acting by the rules), know-how (skills and actions in a social context), and expert knowledge (capability of influencing the rules and the domain of knowledge) (see also Tooman, Akinci, & Davies, 2016). His two types of knowledge, explicit and tacit, have gained widespread acceptance, and have later been verified and extended into individual, social, declarative, procedural, incidental, conditional, relational, and pragmatic types of knowledge. Many terms and components are used in reference to the creation of knowledge, including experience, judgment, common sense, practical guidelines, values and beliefs, fundamental truths, context, best practices, emotions, desires, or socialization. Knowledge is a reflective process, whereby information and data are retrieved in a social context, and the above-mentioned components and factors are combined to generate new data, information, and knowledge (Spiegler, 2003).

Knowledge is recognized as important for an organization and its various activities. In the context of network analysis, one can assume that knowledge in an organization is a social construct. Individuals share and exchange knowledge through communication and activities, creating cognitive relationships that help define the dynamics of a team and its coordination and performance. This exchange may be best represented as a network composed of the employees' knowledge and cooperation, as needed for a specific task. Information and knowledge are useful if an individual is capable of applying the information and knowledge in the course of his or her tasks (Grant, 1996). Such an approach enables the application of methods and instruments developed for analyzing complex relationships in social actor systems (Altman, Carley, & Reminga, 2018) to the individual knowledge of team members as network nodes. Among the most popular areas of knowledge research using SNA are: knowledge sharing analysis (Aubke, Woeber, Scott, & Baggio, 2014; Avnet & Weigel, 2013; Martin-Rios, 2014; Tagliaventi, Bertolotti, & Macri, 2010), knowledge diffusion and flow through international patent citations (Chen & Guan, 2016; Ye, Zhang, Liu, & Su, 2015), or knowledge exchange (Diez-Vial & Montoro-Sanchez, 2014; Hsu & Tzeng, 2010; Weiss, Hamann, Kinney, & Marsh, 2012). Here, knowledge is seen as action or activity, rather than something passive—the focus is placed on the use of knowledge in action.

Intellectual capital only creates value in combination and synergy with other assets. It is seen as a driver of value, based on a causal relationship between resources and value creation, which plays a key role in strategy and management, affecting the competitiveness of enterprises. Competitive advantage manifests in improved execution and coordination of activities within the internal value chain and better management in areas of contact between the enterprise and other entities in the value network, that is, vendors, partners, distribution channels, and various coalitions that go beyond the traditional view of enterprise resources (Morris, Schindehutte, & Allen, 2005; Nair, Nisar, Palacios, & Ruiz, 2012). Notably, in the intellectual capital concept, these resources are identified within social, or more broadly relational, capital. The three broad components of intellectual capital are closely associated with the configuration of the value chain (Musteen & Ahsan, 2013). Youndt et al.

(2004) performed empirical verification in enterprises with high levels of human, organizational, and social capital, which were willing to invest in IT and R&D, gaining competitiveness.

In the deductive aspect of the static approach to resources, focus is placed on developing a typology and analyzing associations between resources and enterprise performance. The purpose is to depict the components of intellectual capital and their distribution. On the other hand, the dynamic approach focuses on changes in intellectual capital and its components. An enterprise's capability of knowledge co-creation and transfer in a network seems to be central to the discussion on the creation and continuing development of dynamic intellectual capital. The concept of learning and inter-organizational knowledge transfer become parts of the dynamics, in which the key process is value creation based on knowledge (including inter-organizational knowledge) and its application (Mason & Leek, 2008).

No single definition of intellectual capital nor consensus regarding its classification and major components exist. The identification of elements or components of intellectual capital and understanding of their interrelations is, however, required to explain how value is created for customers and for the enterprise. Thus, the interrelations between components of intellectual capital should be included as an important area of focus in the dynamic approach to intellectual capital.

Such a dynamic approach is by no means essential for the RBV. Ricceri (2011) reviewed various approaches to intellectual capital measurement from two perspectives: stock and flow. The stock perspective measures value associated with intellectual capital, while the flow perspective aims at grasping the process of value creation by intellectual capital. The stock perspective fits into the static approach, and the flow perspective into the dynamic approach. Nonetheless, it is essential to complement the approach with causal analyses (change in intellectual capital components results from changes in the enterprise's resource base) or relation networks. The dynamic approach indicates that various sets and combinations of components and their attributes lead to differences in organizations' ability to deliver a value proposition. But in order to be capable of managing these dynamics, one must measure them within the process of intellectual capital management, which can be divided into three stages: the identification of components, their mapping, and flow (Schiuma, 2009). This measurement, however, remains a challenge, due to the difficulties involved in capturing changes in resources throughout a given time frame and their transformations resulting from causal relationships. Thus, the domain of an enterprise is the unique combination of resources involved in resource creation (Nielsen & Montemari, 2012). Mason and Leek (2008), analyzing intellectual capital from the perspective of networks and flows, identified the following components: network structure, inter-organizational routines, forms of knowledge and their integration into problem-solving. The authors also emphasized the impact of information and knowledge flows within the network and organization structure on the organization's performance.

The above reflections on information, knowledge, and intellectual capital as dynamic resources pertaining to activities, rather than static ones, makes it possible to include these concepts in the respective audit models: information audit, knowledge audit, and intellectual capital audit.

2.2 Information Audit, Knowledge Audit, and Intellectual Capital Audit

2.2.1 Information Audit

The audit consists of an analysis of an organization's operations, performed by independent agents, to verify compliance of these operations with the relevant standards or procedures. It may be viewed in a variety of ways, including as part of the social control mechanism, associated with accountability (Flint, 1988). Most commonly, however, it is viewed as a financial control instrument (Lakis, 2014). Initially, the scope of audit was limited to an analysis of accounting records, and was subsequently gradually extended to comprehensively cover the organization's operations and management processes. Audit is also an assessment of an individual, system, process, project, or product. It is performed in order to ensure the accuracy and reliability of information and to assess the internal control system, using a selection of instruments (e.g., surveys, interviews, observation). This understanding of audit is essentially identical to the notion of "internal audit." Its specific functions in an enterprise, including in particular its control and advisory function, manifest especially in cases where the reality does not comply with the model and the auditor (the person performing the audit in an organizational setting) recommends remedial measures to the managing staff, and thus creates added value for the organization.

Currently, audits are performed to establish the credibility of both financial and non-financial information presented by the management in financial statements. Expectations toward auditors are high, including not only the requirement to conscientiously assess the accuracy of financial statements, but also to provide value-added services, such as reporting on irregularities, identifying business risks, and internal control consultancy (Cosserat, 2009).

This book focuses on intangible resource audit, which is discussed in detail further in the chapter. Here, audit is seen as a management technique that assists the managing staff of an organization in reviewing its current resources (Botha & Boon, 2003). As organizational intangible resource audit is an integrated model comprising information audit, knowledge audit, and intellectual capital audit, the respective audit types should be presented.

Information audit was developed in the 1970s and 1980s, with the advent of enterprise information technology. The notion of auditing mainly information and financial resources has its roots in finance and accounting departments, which were the first to use audits in order to understand how financial resources are used in the enterprise, to improve processes and reduce costs (Raliphada & Botha, 2013). Information audit shares its origins with financial audit and uses it as a basis for analyzing the audited processes from an information manager view (Botha & Boon, 2003; Burk & Horton, 1988). Today, both the quantity and the scope of information grow exponentially. Managing unstructured information and its creation and distribution would be impossible tasks for organizations to accomplish without information audit.

The scope of information audit includes data and information stored in databases or IT systems, as well as document and content analysis. Its purpose is to demonstrate what information employees need in order to do their jobs, and how they use the information.

Until 1990, which is when Orna (1990) proposed her model for information audit, various attempts had been made to provide definitions and models of information audit. All such propositions were rather simple and undeveloped, typically limited to an identification of information resources and needs in an organization (Ellis, Barker, Potter, & Pridgeon, 1993). Buchanan and Gibb (1998) used an audit model to provide a comprehensive and integrated strategic approach to information resources. The authors listed the following objectives of information audit:

- identifying costs and benefits associated with information resources;
- identifying possible use of information resources for creating competitive advantage;
- integrating IT investments with strategic business initiatives;
- identifying information flows and processes;
- developing an integrated information policy;
- raising awareness of the importance of information asset management and determining the role of management;
- monitoring and verifying compliance with information standards, legal regulations, and policy guidelines.

The objectives of information audit have been evolving since the 1980s. Burk and Horton (1988) were the first to propose a complete information audit methodology. Their approach is quite narrow; the premise is to identify information resources as strategic and competitive factors, to understand the value of these resources and improve their management. The work mainly focused on document management, without including the broader context of the audit, for example, organizational culture and structure, as in the concepts by Buchanan and Gibb (2007) and Botha and Boon (2003). A simple, concise definition of information audit was proposed by Dubois (1995), describing it as a useful information management tool concerning the identification, costing, development, and rationalization of information resources and services (Dubois, 1995). The concentration on resources and services means, however, that Dubois does not include information flow and use in an organization.

This gap is filled by Buchanan and Gibb (1998), who added information flow to the scope of their definition of the audit, which describes it as a process of discovering, monitoring and evaluating information flows and resources in order to implement, maintain, or improve the organization's management of information (Buchanan & Gibb, 1998). Besides adding information flow to the scope of information audit, the definition also includes its purpose, that is, improvement of information management in the organization. This is the actual goal of the audit—after an inspection is performed, its results are processed to increase the efficiency and effectiveness of information management.

An even broader definition was provided by Botha and Boon (2003). The authors consider information audit a systematic examination of the information resources, information use, information flows, and information management in an organization. It involves the identification of users' information needs and how effectively (or not) these are being met (Botha & Boon, 2003). By contrast, Buchanan and Gibb (1998) focus specifically on the information users they consider to be key success factors concerning the improvement of information management.

Definitions of audit vary, but the general idea remains the same: to review information resources and to understand ways to improve the management of these resources. According to the cited authors, information audit is based on value. It aims at valuating information, for example, regarding machinery or traditional resources (land, labor, tools), or is based on the effectiveness of the audit that leads to value creation by improvement of information, for example, increasing employee productivity. In summary, the overall objectives of information audit are centered around enhancing knowledge on information resources and their sources, and on ways in which users integrate these information resources in their daily work (Pantry & Griffiths, 2002).

As mentioned above, the information audit definition by Buchanan and Gibb (1998) differs from those of their predecessors. Their approach may offer a tentative indication of a connection between information and knowledge audits. Their notions regarding information audit directed the process toward a more comprehensive and integrated strategic approach, where the audit is seen as a process of discovering, monitoring, and evaluating information flows and resources of an organization in order to implement, maintain, or improve the organization's management of information. This approach was based on an analysis of solutions available at the time, and is more comprehensive and flexible than the previously existing models. Table 2.1 lists the major stages in the three selected[1] information audit models.

Table 2.1 Information audit stages

1. *Buchanan & Gibb (1998)*	2. *Orna (1999)*	3. *Henczel (2001)*
1. Promote 1.1. Communicating benefits 1.2. Ensuring cooperation 1.3. Conducting a preliminary survey	1. Key business objectives 1.1. Organizational needs 1.2. Information needs	1. Planning 1.1. Organization analysis 1.2. Audit scope definition 1.3. Methodology selection 1.4. Communication strategy development 1.5. Support from management
2. Identify 2.1. Identifying the external environment of the organization 2.2. Identifying the organizational structure 2.3. Identifying the organizational culture 2.4. Information flows 2.5. Information resources	2. Support 2.1. Support from management 2.2. Support from employees	2. Data collection 2.1. Collecting data on activities and tasks 2.2. Collecting data on critical issues 2.3. Diagnosing information transfer
3. Analyze 3.1. Evaluating information resources 3.2. Diagram of information flows 3.3. Preliminary report 3.4. Action plan	3. Planning 3.1. Importance of information 3.2. Team selection 3.3. Methodology selection	3. Data analysis 3.1. General analysis 3.2. Detailed analysis 3.3. Information flow mapping
4. Account (cost analysis of organizational resources)	4. Execution 4.1. Identifying information resources 4.2. Identifying stakeholders 4.3. Identifying flows and interactions 4.4. Identifying technology and systems 4.5. Identifying the cost-effectiveness of information	4. Data evaluation 4.1. Identifying issues 4.2. Defining priority issues 4.3. Identifying solutions 4.4. Ranking solutions 4.5. Formulating the list of recommendations
5. Synthesize 5.1. Reporting on the audit 5.2. Developing information strategy	5. Interpreting findings 5.1. Comparison: actual state vs. target state 5.2. Identifying issues	5. Communicating recommendations 5.1. Reporting on the audit 5.2. Presenting findings
	6. Presenting findings 6.1. Reporting on the audit 6.2. Preparing presentation 6.3. Communicating the findings	6. Implementing recommendations
	7. Effects of the audit 7.1. Implementing changes 7.2. Monitoring effects 7.3. Re-auditing	7. Re-auditing

Stage one involves promoting the benefits of information audit and securing management support. Stage two focuses on identifying and defining the organization's environment, mission, structure, culture, and information and resource flow. Stage three concerns the evaluation of information resources, creation of information flow diagrams, and development of the report and recommendations. Stage four (cost/benefit) assigns costs to the organization's information resources and the related services in order to help the organization identify its information-related costs. The final stage, titled "Synthesize," delivers the final information audit report and an information strategy proposal. The main weakness of this audit model is the fact that, as an information control method, it does not include tacit knowledge. This, however, is not essential to information audit, contrary to knowledge audit.

Orna was among the first authors to propose a formal approach to knowledge audit, as early as 1990. In its original form, the model comprised four stages, and was extended with six additional stages in 1999 (Orna, 1999). The author uses a top-down approach and focuses on organizational analysis. The process comprises seven steps investigating both information resources and information flows. Audit scope includes identifying information needs, ensuring management support, planning, execution, interpretation and presentation of findings, developing the report, and repeating the audit. In 2004, Orna (2004) amended her proposition, adding a series of diagnostic questions that direct the development of strategic information policy in the organization.

In turn, Henczel (2001) proposes that the development of a knowledge management strategy should be the first step in finding out the locations of knowledge and the decisions and actions that require it. Thus, she differentiates between information audit and knowledge audit, the latter being a consequence of the former. Knowledge audit identifies knowledge assets, the ways they are created, and the individuals that create them (Henczel, 2001). Henczel places information audit between need analysis and knowledge audit, but only describes information audit in detail. Her model was based on audit methodologies used by librarians and consultants. The author states that the actual information audit must be preceded with a need analysis stage, in which users are asked about the information resources and services they need for the tasks they perform. Only then can one determine the actual uses of information. In her paper, the author describes the major steps of performing an information audit (planning; data collection, analysis, and evaluation; communicating and implementing recommendations), but omits the knowledge needs analysis and knowledge audit procedures. Similarly to Orna's model, the final stage is repeating the audit at an appropriate time.

What Buchanan and Gibb (1998) and Henczel (2001) disregard in their descriptions of information audit is knowledge transfer between individuals, and more specifically the dimension of tacit knowledge and its potential flows. Therefore, information audit should be performed as part of knowledge audit, which comprises both explicit knowledge, equivalent to information (Smith, 2001), and tacit knowledge (based on experience). This conclusion results from the definition of knowledge as information used in a specific context (contextual information). Information audit can involve analyzing the contents of databases and websites, or numbers of files and folders in an organization. Knowledge audit, on the other hand, must incorporate the engagement of people by placing them in the center of activities. This means that knowledge audit, discussed in more detail in Section 2.2.2, may be defined as an investigation of an organization's knowledge needs and the relationships between people and the resources they use (e.g., technology).

2.2.2 Knowledge Audit

Debenham and Clark (1994) are the precursors of knowledge audit, having introduced the term *knowledge audit* in 1994. Earlier, knowledge audit had only been referred to in passing, for example, in 1981 (Adam, Hershauer, & Ruch, 1981), as an administrative process in evaluating the effectiveness of communications policies in a public sector organization (Federal Reserve Bank), or in 1987 (Anderson, 1987) in the context of a model for developing new products and services. Here, knowledge audit is perceived as a *capability model*, whereby the management can discover what knowledge the organization is going to need and how it can be acquired. Debenham and Clark's proposition offers a rather narrow view of knowledge audit, which is understood as a management document. The authors define both the objectives and the outcomes of knowledge audit, but disregard details of its performance and ways of achieving the set objectives. Main activities, leading to the development of a document, include exploring a portion of previously undocumented organizational knowledge, improving existing knowledge, and comparing current and past states of knowledge. In this knowledge audit model, basic concepts include: chunks of knowledge, task sets, knowledge repositories, and audit granularity (level of detail). Their approach is quite limited in the sense that it does not explain how the procedure should be performed—it prescribes the final result of the activities without defining the activities themselves.

Knowledge audit can have various definitions, with authors choosing various focal points. It is typically seen as an instrument supporting organizational leadership in delivering the right information, avoiding risk through better decision-making, and identifying the available, required, and missing knowledge. Cheung, Li, Shek, Lee, and Tsang (2007) describe audit as a process aiming at a comprehensive analysis and investigation of organizational knowledge, its location (where), users (who), and creation (how). Tsui (2005), in turn, defines knowledge audit as a technique allowing the organization to identify what knowledge it has and what knowledge it needs to achieve its goals. A similar definition of knowledge audit is provided by Dalkir and Liebowitz (2011), focusing on identification of key information, knowledge needs, and use in the organization; information and knowledge gaps and duplication; and flows, with regard to achievement of business objectives and improvements. Gourova et al. (2009) highlight similar features. Their knowledge audit model determines the organization's status regarding knowledge availability, needs, flows, sharing, and use in business processes, leading to added value creation. As defined by Jashapara (2004), knowledge audit comprises all the effective processes associated with the exploration (identification, evaluation, management) of knowledge (both explicit and tacit) in a business unit or organization. The approach is thus process based, but places more emphasis on knowledge management,[2] similarly to the one proposed by Pfeffer and Sutton (2000), whose knowledge audit model focuses on evaluating knowledge required at a given time, knowledge carriers, and links between the knowledge carriers and additional connections required. Knowledge audit is an instrument for identifying weaknesses, encouraging improvements, and monitoring existing knowledge management metrics. As emphasized by Dalkir and Liebowitz (2011), successful implementation of knowledge management depends on preliminary and in-depth analyses of knowledge resource availability, flows, and use in an organization, studied in a knowledge audit. The various approaches to knowledge audit typically focus on identifying the current status of organizational knowledge, locating the knowledge, and diagnosing knowledge flows and processes (Gourova, 2010).

Knowledge audit is recurrent in nature and helps determine whether knowledge resources are appropriately managed and what knowledge management strategies, tools, and solutions could maximize benefits for the organization. It is based on a systematic methodology for identifying, analyzing, and measuring the organization's knowledge resources. Audit planning and preparation create a foundation for transparent performance of the knowledge audit.

Most commonly, knowledge audit is a process comprising a sequence of stages, concluding with the development of a report, knowledge (flow) map, or knowledge inventory. Both knowledge audit and knowledge mapping are considered significant in defining and describing organizational knowledge. Audit allows the organization to see what knowledge it has, who exactly has the knowledge, and how the knowledge flows in the organization. As a diagnostic tool, it enables the identification of changes required in the organization, relationships between members, and business processes. In general, knowledge audit should demonstrate valuable knowledge resources, areas for improvement in the existing business processes, and employees who act as brokers or gatekeepers in knowledge proliferation (in a positive or negative sense) (Burnett, Illingworth, & Webster, 2004).

Models for knowledge audit proposed by management researchers or practitioners are too numerous to list here. The selected models are those that comprehensively define both the notion of knowledge audit and the actual stages of the process, and that are recognized in the literature on the subject. The discovery of an organization's knowledge status consists of determining what the organization knows and what it should know in order to achieve its business objectives. Is the organization using its knowledge in an effective manner? What knowledge resources support its business processes? These are some of the questions that knowledge audit attempts to answer.

Knowledge audit seen from the process perspective, that is, comprising a sequence of actions, is described differently by various authors (see Table 2.2). The number of main stages of the knowledge audit process is between three and eight, and each stage usually includes specific steps (activities) of audit performance.

In Ragsdell et al. (2014), the essence of knowledge audit comprises mapping explicit and tacit knowledge flows, and identifying gaps and bottlenecks through a process of analyzing key knowledge for organizational activities. In the audit procedure, the authors mainly use interview methods, with open- and closed-ended questions divided into four categories: knowledge required for performance of employee's tasks, procedures related to information and knowledge and their acquisition for task performance, employees' perceptions of the organization, and organizational culture. Audit is performed in two selected departments and not applied to the entire organization. An analysis of the organizational culture that supports knowledge sharing and open collaboration is a noteworthy component.

The model proposed by Burnett, Williams and Grinnall (2013) and Burnett, Williams, and Illingworth (2013) was developed on the basis of experiences described in the authors' 2004 publication (Burnett et al., 2004). Their first proposition for knowledge audit comprises seven stages. First, employees should receive information on the nature and potential of knowledge management. Then, at the measurement stage, knowledge management process metrics are defined. A six-item scale is used, with scores for each process represented on a radar chart. Result interpretation requires in-depth, semi-structured interviews with employees, subsequently used for knowledge mapping. After the analysis, a meeting is held in order to provide employees with feedback and learning from the organizational knowledge audit process and knowledge management process. The audit concludes with an analysis of expectations and suggested changes, and implementation of the solutions (e.g., expert guide, mentoring and coaching programs, trainings, knowledge maps). In their second model, proposed more than ten years after the first, the same

Table 2.2 Knowledge audit stages

4. *Ragsdell, Probets, Ahmed, and Murray (2014)*	5. *Burnett (2013)*	6. *Chan & Lee (2011)*	7. *Gourova, Antonova, and Todorowa (2009)*	8. *Levantakis et al. (2008)*
1. Mapping of explicit and tacit knowledge flows in the organization 2. Identification of the most important knowledge assets in terms of supporting the organization's activities 3. Identification of knowledge gaps and bottlenecks	1. Knowledge audit process 1.1. Organization's activities supporting knowledge management 1.2. Engaging employees in knowledge management processes 2. Knowledge inventory and maps 2.1. Existing knowledge assets 2.2. Knowledge location 3. Analysis of knowledge needs 3.1. Required knowledge 3.2. Forms of knowledge (explicit, tacit, internal, external) 3.3. Benefits of knowledge 3.4. Impact of knowledge on activities	1. Identification of organizational context 1.1. Definition of priorities and selection of processes 1.2. Analysis of workflows 1.3. Individual interviews 2. Audit findings 2.1. Knowledge inventory 2.2. Stakeholders 2.3. Distribution of explicit and tacit knowledge 2.4. Knowledge map 2.5. Social network analysis 3. Data analysis 3.1. Data validation 4. Identification of intellectual capital metrics 5. Development of value tree and reporting intellectual capital 6. Recommendations for ongoing quality improvement	1. Preparation 1.1. Scope, activities, and schedule planning 1.2. Audit team selection 1.3. Audit methodology 2. Implementation 2.1. Questionnaire adaptation 2.2. Questionnaire distribution 2.3. Result analysis 3. Finalization 3.1. Report development 3.2. Knowledge management roadmap	1. Preparation 1.1. Organization brief 1.2. Observation 1.3. Audit objectives 1.4. Audit scope 2. Promotion 2.1. Management support 2.2. Fostering employee collaboration 3. In-depth investigation 3.1. Core processes 3.2. Key actors 3.3. Knowledge requirements 3.4. Knowledge processes 4. Data collection 4.1. Meeting key actors 4.2. Questionnaires and interviews 5. Data analysis 5.1. Knowledge inventory 5.2. Knowledge map 5.3. Social network analysis 5.4. Knowledge gaps 6. Data evaluation 6.1. Gaps and bottlenecks 6.2. Problem priorities 6.3. Suggested solutions 6.4. Solution ranking 7. Conclusions 7.1. Action plan 7.2. Report 7.3. Presentation of findings 7.4. Action plan approval 8. Re-auditing

9. *Cheung et al. (2007)*	10. *Perez-Soltero et al. (2007)*	11. *Burnett et al. (2004)*	12. *Liebowitz (2000)*
1. Identifying organizational context 1.1. Meeting 1.2. Project plan 2. Knowledge audit 2.1. Organizational culture evaluation 2.2. In-depth investigation 2.3. Knowledge inventory 2.4. Knowledge map 2.4. Knowledge network analysis 2.5. Social network analysis 3. Knowledge management strategy 3.1. Knowledge management strategy recommendation 3.2. Tool implementation 3.3. Cooperation culture building 4. Re-auditing	1. Organization analysis 1.1. Meeting with managers 1.2. Acquiring strategic information 1.3. Identifying organizational processes 2. Analyzing core processes 2.1. Identifying core processes 2.2. Defining measurement criteria 3. Selecting processes for audit 3.1. Prioritizing processes 3.2. Selecting processes 4. Meetings 4.1. Identifying key people 4.2. Meeting key people 4.3. Exploration 5. Analyzing data 5.1. Knowledge inventory 5.2. Knowledge flows 5.3. Knowledge mapping 6. Finalizing audit 6.1. Final report 6.2. Re-auditing	1. Preparation 1.1. Preliminary meetings 1.2. Survey 1.3. Knowledge process identification 2. Learning day 2.1. Workshop (promoting project and collaboration) 2.2. Survey result presentation 3. Measurement criteria 3.1. Encouraging employees to complete the measurement table 3.2. Result analysis 3.3. Identifying main areas for improvement 4. Interviews 4.1. Semi-structured interview 4.2. Initiating process analysis 5. Knowledge map 5.1. Employee knowledge map 5.2. Employee information 6. Feedback 6.1. Informing employees about the audit process 6.2. Summary of conclusions 6.3. Recommendations 7. Implementation plan 7.1. Recommendation priorities 7.2. Knowledge management actions 8. Implementation	1. Identifying existing knowledge 1.1. Identifying existing and potential sources, flows, and restrictions 1.2. Identifying and locating existing explicit and tacit knowledge 1.3. Knowledge mapping 2. Identifying missing knowledge 2.1. Analyzing knowledge gaps 2.2. Determining who needs the missing knowledge 3. Developing the report

authors reduced the knowledge process audit to three essential, much simpler stages. In this case, the knowledge process audit is performed to investigate whether employees know and understand the current knowledge-based practices in an organization.

Explicit and tacit knowledge inventory and map are presented similarly to other solutions. Similarly, knowledge needs identification and analysis allow for demonstrating knowledge asset types and forms that employees must have in order to perform their tasks more effectively.

References to intellectual capital are especially prominent in the knowledge audit concepts by Chan and Lee (2011) and Wang and Xiao (2009), which were not included in Table 2.2 due to lack of details regarding specific audit stages. The authors list human, structural, and relational capital, which are the basic components of intellectual capital, in their description of the knowledge asset analysis stage of the audit, but do not discuss any measurement or evaluation methods. Nonetheless, it is worth mentioning that the proposed model comprises four stages. The first one includes preliminary activities, such as specifying the audit objectives, plan, and team. The next stage, analysis, comprises activities related to investigating the knowledge and intellectual capital management environment, capabilities, and knowledge management effectiveness. The performance stage includes an analysis of knowledge needs (demand), knowledge resources, and knowledge mapping. The final stage involves evaluation of the findings, report on the audit, and re-auditing. However, this is a concept proposition, without discussion of the audit instruments or empirical verification using qualitative and quantitative study methods.

Added value from the Chan and Lee (2011) model consists in a presentation of tools and metrics that can be used for developing the inventory and maps of explicit knowledge (documentation) and tacit knowledge (experience and skills), though they are limited to a simple count of diagnosed knowledge items. As in other proposed models, the explicit and tacit knowledge inventory is the basis for exposing both formal and informal knowledge exchange networks. As for the knowledge resource map, it allows for a visualization of knowledge and document flows in the organization. The authors do not, however, prescribe ways for developing these tools. Similarly to Liebowitz et al. (2000), Gourova et al. (2009) divide the knowledge audit procedure into three main stages: preparation (planning, audit team selection, choice of methodology), performance (questionnaire development, questionnaire distribution, result analysis), and finalization (presenting the report and a roadmap for implementing a knowledge management concept). For each stage, a series of steps are detailed for the systematic performance of the audit.

An interesting knowledge audit model was proposed by Levantakis, Helms, and Spruit (2008) based on other solutions described in literature. The authors, taking heed of the negative connotations associated with audit, emphasize the inclusion of managerial staff and the promotion of the audit among employees to ensure management support, build a positive image of the audit process, and showcase its benefits for the organization.

Cheung et al. (2007) and Shek et al. (2007) describe eight stages in the knowledge audit process. Initial stages focus on learning about the organization, defining the audit scope, and relating documents and employees to specific tasks in the workflow in order to define the business process. Subsequently, workflow and process analyses are used to collect information regarding the process actors (employees), knowledge, and activities in the organization, and to develop a knowledge inventory. The inventory, divided into explicit and tacit knowledge areas, has the following basic components:

- for explicit knowledge—document type, purpose, location, creator, owner, main users, and score (on a scale of 1–5);
- for tacit knowledge—department, owner, scope, communication channel, main recipients (clients), and score (on a scale of 1–5).

These are later used for mapping the organization's knowledge and social network, identifying strengths and weaknesses, and investigating opportunities and threats originating in the environment that may influence the creation and use of knowledge by the organization. Following the analysis of findings, the audit concludes with a presentation of recommendations for increasing process efficiency and improving knowledge management in the organization. Additionally, the Shek et al. (2007) version incorporates an evaluation of organizational culture and collection of feedback regarding the implementation of knowledge management strategies.

Another proposition for knowledge audit, by Perez-Soltero et al. (2007), is based on the concept of core business processes and describes ten audit stages in detail. For each stage, the authors discuss the purpose to be achieved and the methods and instruments that should be used in audit performance.

The classic knowledge audit concept by Liebowitz et al. (2000) is also noteworthy. It comprises three basic processes, essentially aiming at determining the knowledge gap, or the relationship between the knowledge an organization has and the knowledge it lacks. The authors also propose a detailed knowledge gap questionnaire with 17 items related to knowledge needs and 20 items related to missing knowledge. Gap analysis is a business technique for comparing the current situation of the organization with the desired optimal situation. Knowledge audit provides the organization with information regarding the knowledge it has and the knowledge it needs but does not have. Orna (1999) is among the few authors who describe the gap analysis process. By studying the organization's documentation and observing the target area of the audit, the auditing team can learn about the organization's objectives, the knowledge required for fulfillment of these objectives, the knowledge that the organization has, and the individual employees who have the knowledge. These findings are interpreted by the auditors in order to help identify knowledge gaps. Matching of "what is" to "what should be" and the interpretation of these two areas is the essence of gap analysis, according to Orna (1999), as this is the most significant information in terms of achieving the objectives of an organization.

The process approaches to organizational knowledge audit described above differ in a number of ways,[3] including not only the number of specific stages, but also the level of detail of the proposed solutions. As shown in Table 2.2, the number of stages ranges between three and eight, and the stages themselves involve different specific activities. Most authors made attempts at empirical verification of their knowledge audit models using case study methods, but not entirely successfully. First of all, not all stages were verified empirically, as most authors focused on knowledge inventory and mapping—which is reasonable, as these are typically the most important activities in the audit, but does not provide a holistic view of the audit procedure (with all its stages and steps). The lack of such a holistic perspective means that only a fragment of the audit is fully presented, which makes it difficult to analyze the consistency and associations between the proposed stages. Detailed presentation and discussion of instruments (e.g., questionnaires, interview questions) is also missing. Despite the fundamental differences described, some stages are either identical between models or feature similar premises and interpretations. Similarities include focusing on core processes, developing a knowledge inventory, or mapping knowledge flows.

Though no standard terminology or methodology for information and knowledge audit exists, some models can be named as the most comprehensive. These are: the information audit process by Orna (1999), the information audit model by Henczel (2001), the Knowledge Audit (Burnett et al., 2004), the Knowledge Audit Methodology with Emphasis on Core Processes (Perez-Soltero et al., 2007), and the Systematic Knowledge Audit (Cheung et al., 2007). The models are more comprehensive than others listed and prescribe specific actions to be performed in the audit process. Most audit models have a narrow scope and purpose, which restricts their potential for universal adaptation in an organizational setting.

2.2.3 *Intellectual Capital Audit*

Two concepts for intellectual capital audit, which includes knowledge assets that have been extensively discussed and classified in literature (e.g., Martín-de-Castro et al., 2010), have been selected for the present discussion. Similarly to information and knowledge audit, intellectual capital audit is a complex analysis process, and involves a systematic analysis of an organization's intellectual capital against its strategic objectives and external environment (Table 2.3).

The model proposed by Brooking (1996) focuses strictly on intellectual assets, including human-centered assets, market assets, infrastructure assets, and intellectual property. It is iterative in nature, as each principal category of assets is divided into subcategories, for which asset aspects (detailed characteristics subject to measurements) are defined. For instance, the customer base is a market asset, and its aspects include size, returning customers, customer profiles, brand loyalty, and so on. What is questionable about Brooking's concept is the way of assigning values (quantitative and qualitative) to audit aspects, as well as aspect ranking,

Table 2.3 Intellectual capital audit stages

13. *Brooking (1996)*	14. *Mertins et al. (2007)*
1. Identifying audit objectives, domains, and limitations 1.1. Core business areas 1.2. Identifying issues 1.3. Identifying domains and restrictions (assets, aspects, behaviors)	1. Preliminary considerations 1.1. Informing the top management 1.2. Selecting the project team 1.3. Selecting the project leader 1.4. Selecting the moderator
2. Determining the optimal set of asset aspects	2. Business model 2.1. Strategy 2.2. Value creation model 2.3. System limits
3. Assigning value to asset aspects	3. Intellectual capital analysis 3.1. Defining intellectual capital 3.2. QQS assessment 3.3. Allocating weights
4. Selecting audit methodology 4.1. Evaluating market assets 4.2. Evaluating intellectual property 4.3. Evaluating infrastructure assets 4.4. Evaluating human-centered assets	4. Intellectual capital measurement 4.1. Defining metrics 4.2. Measuring factors
5. Auditing asset aspects 5.1. Selecting asset audit methods	5. Strategy and indicators 5.1. Interpreting findings 5.2. Defining the intellectual capital strategy
6. Documenting assets and aspects in an intellectual capital database 6.1. Interpreting audit findings 6.2. Evaluating target levels 6.3. Strengths and weaknesses 6.4. Determining improvement strategies	6. Developing the report 6.1. Structure 6.2. Content 6.3. Interpretation
	7. Final considerations 7.1. Communicating the results 7.2. Taking action
	8. Quality requirements 8.1. Developing the external report 8.2. Applying for formal audit

which is not proportional. For instance, for two aspects of market assets, customer loyalty (scored at 40%) and customer recognition (scored at 60%), the author assigns ranks 2 and 4 (on a scale of 1–5), respectively. However, customer recognition should be ranked at 3, if each 20% of the score is assigned 1 point on the scale—the measurement is not precise. The audit itself is performed using classical methods, such as observation, surveying, interviews, data analysis, market research, competition analysis, and others. Its final stage involves the creation of an intellectual capital database and the development of an improvement strategy to enable the achievement of the target level of intellectual assets.

The Intellectual Capital Statement, or ICS, (Mertins, Wang, & Will, 2007) is an interesting proposition for analyzing intellectual capital against the defined strategic goals of an organization. It is likely the only model that includes quality control (formal audit) as the final stage (though it is not obligatory), verifying whether the measurements performed conform with the requirements. The entire intellectual capital evaluation process (stages 1 through 7) in the ICS is verified by a certified auditor. The ICS also includes a moderator for the workshop sessions during which intellectual capital is assessed. Quantity (Q), quality (Q), and systematic management (S) are assessed, and weights are assigned to intellectual capital components. Within the business model, the organization determines the system boundaries (what is assessed: a business process, a department, a unit, the entire organization), describes how value is created, and identifies added value associated with business processes. For general strategic orientation, the organization sets main strategic objectives, considering the external business environment and success factors. Intellectual capital is analyzed in a workshop format, with three areas of focus: definition of intellectual capital components, QQS assessment, and intellectual capital component weighting. Project participants develop an intellectual capital strategy based on findings and analyses of potential for improvement.

The discussed audits typically investigate what sources of data, information, and knowledge are available, how they are used, and what needs are not met in terms of the analyzed resources. Importantly, audits should be adjusted to the needs of the target organization, should be performed regularly, and should include the entire organization—though the scope of audit may be narrower, limited to a single department, business process, or even a single employee. During audit performance, identifying resources, creators, owners, brokers, and users is a major area of focus. Once resources are identified, it is their managers' task to understand their use and dynamics. Another significant component of audit is relating the analyzed resources to the mission, strategy, and basic capabilities of the organization (see Mearns & Du Toit, 2008).

Table 2.4 lists the discussed information, knowledge, and intellectual capital audit concepts in chronological order. The list is by no means

Table 2.4 A chronological perspective of information audit, knowledge audit, and intellectual capital audit

Information audit		
Authors	*Year*	*Audit features*
Burk and Horton	1988	• Document management as a derivative of financial audit. Identifying information resources as strategic and competitive factors, to understand the value of these resources and improve their management.
Ellis, Barker, Potter, and Pridgeon	1993	• Determining the organization's information resources and needs.
Dubois	1995	• Focus on resources and services. Does not include information flow and use in an organization. An information management tool.
Buchanan and Gibb	1998	• Provides a comprehensive and integrated strategic approach to information resources.
Orna	1999	• Uses a top-down approach and focuses on organizational analysis, including information needs.
Henczel	2001	• Places information audit between need analysis and knowledge audit, but does not include knowledge transfer between individuals.
Pantry and Griffiths	2002	• Enhancing knowledge on information resources and their sources, and on ways in which users integrate these information resources in their daily work.
Botha and Boon	2003	• Information audit associated with a systematic examination of the information resources, information use, information flows, and information management in an organization.
Orna	2004	• Concept expanded with a series of diagnostic questions that direct the development of a strategic information policy in the organization.
Buchanan and Gibb	2007	• Broader context of the audit, including organizational culture and structure.
Knowledge audit		
Adam, Hershauer, and Ruch	1981	• Administrative process in evaluating the effectiveness of communications policies in a public sector organization.
Anderson	1987	• Knowledge audit perceived as a capability model, whereby the management can discover what knowledge the organization is going to need and how it can be acquired.
Debenham and Clark	1994	• Rather narrow view of knowledge audit, understood as a management document.

(*Continued*)

Table 2.4 (Continued)

Information audit		
Authors	*Year*	*Audit features*
Liebowitz, Rubenstein-Montano, McCaw, Buchwalter, Browning, Newman, Rebeck	2000	• Amounts to determining the knowledge gap, or the relationship between the knowledge an organization has and the knowledge it lacks.
Pfeffer and Sutton	2000	• Focuses on evaluating knowledge required at a given time, knowledge carriers, and links between the knowledge carriers and additional connections required.
Jashapara	2004	• Comprises all the effective processes associated with the exploration (identification, evaluation, management) of knowledge (both explicit and tacit) in a business unit or organization.
Burnett, Illingworth, and Webster	2004	• Demonstrates valuable knowledge resources, areas for improvement in the existing business processes, and employees who act as brokers or gatekeepers in knowledge proliferation (in a positive or negative sense).
Tsui	2005	• A technique allowing the organization to identify what knowledge it has and what knowledge it needs to achieve its goals.
Cheung, Li, Shek, Lee, and Tsang	2007	• Process approach to audit, comprising eight specific stages, including explicit and tacit knowledge inventory and investigation of organizational knowledge, its location (where), users (who), and creation (how).
Shek, Cheung, Lee, and Chong	2007	• Eight-stage audit model, additionally incorporating organizational culture assessment and collection of feedback related to knowledge management strategy implementation.
Perez-Soltero, Barcelo-Valenzuela, Sanchez-Schmitz, Martin-Rubio, Palma-Mendez, and Vanti	2007	• Based on the concept of core business processes, describes ten audit stages in detail.
Levantakis, Helms, and Spruit	2008	• Inclusion of managerial staff and promotion of knowledge audit among employees of the organization.
Gourova, Antonova, and Todorova	2009	• Determines the organization's status regarding knowledge availability, needs, flows, sharing, and use in business processes, leading to added value creation.
Wang and Xiao	2009	• Refers to activities related to investigating the knowledge and intellectual capital management environment, capabilities, and knowledge management effectiveness.
Chan and Lee	2011	• Reference to intellectual capital. Presents tools and metrics that can be used for developing the inventory and maps of explicit knowledge (documentation) and tacit knowledge (experience and skills).

(*Continued*)

Dalkir and Liebowitz	2011	• Focus on identification of key information, knowledge needs, and use in the organization; information and knowledge gaps and duplication; and flows, with regard to achievement of business objectives and improvements.
Burnett, Williams, and Grinnall	2013	• Process approach to audit, investigating whether employees know and understand the current knowledge-based practices in an organization.
Burnett, Williams, and Illingworth	2013	
Ragsdell, Probets, Ahmed, and Murray	2014	• The essence of knowledge audit comprises mapping explicit and tacit knowledge flows, and identifying gaps and bottlenecks through a process of analyzing key knowledge for organizational activities.
Intellectual capital audit		
Brooking	1996	• Focuses strictly on intellectual assets, including human-centered assets, market assets, infrastructure assets, and intellectual property. It is iterative in nature, as each principal category of assets is divided into subcategories, for which asset aspects (detailed characteristics subject to measurements) are defined.
Mertins, Wang, and Will	2007	• Analyzing intellectual capital against the defined strategic goals of an organization. Concludes with a non-obligatory quality control process.

Sources: Own work based on sources listed in the table.

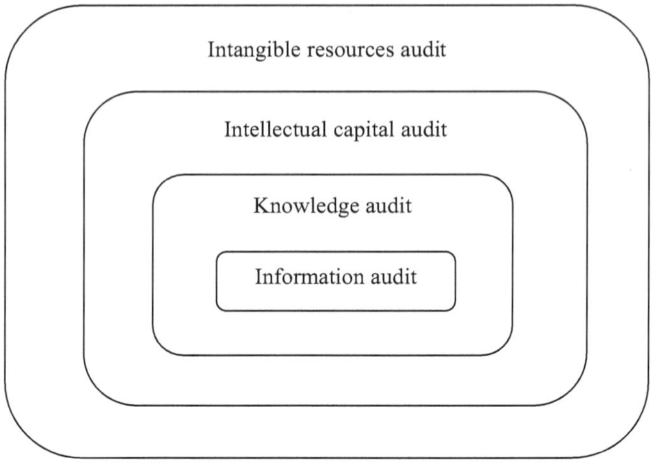

Figure 2.2 Organizational intangible resource audit set against other audit models

exhaustive or complete, but is the first attempt at jointly presenting all three audit types: information, knowledge, and intellectual capital audit, which may later be creatively developed and complemented by other authors.

This discussion of concepts of intangible resources, information audit, knowledge audit, and intellectual capital audit provided a broader context for intangible resource audit, which incorporates solutions from the previous audit models in a new configuration, as shown in Figure 2.2.

The next section provides a detailed description of the organizational intangible resource audit concept.

2.3 Organizational Intangible Resource Audit

2.3.1 Intangible Resource Audit as a Meta-Model

Intangible resource audit is an investigation aiming at identifying and evaluating an organization's key intangible resources and analyzing the dynamics of their relations. It is a complex process involving an analysis of intangible resources, their interrelations, and their use in core business processes. *Intangible resources*, in line with the proposed classification (see Figure 2.1), include information, knowledge, and skills, which are the basis of human, structural, and relational capital, in association with tasks (activities). Employees' knowledge, skills, and resources (structural capital) are used in order to enable the fulfillment of organizational objectives and creation of value through specific business processes. Besides such nodes as human actors (A) seen as carriers of information and knowledge flows, or knowledge and skills (K), organizational network analysis includes resources (R), understood as structural capital including the organization's information and communications infrastructure, which is used as a platform for the flows and relationships that create the organization's relational capital, as well as tasks (T), inherently associated with A, K, and R.

Based on an analysis of information, knowledge, and intellectual capital audit models, an integrated model for organizational intangible resource audit (termed a *meta-model*) was developed, using the formal approach to methodology comparison proposed by Hong, Van den Goor, and Brinkkemper (1993). In line with this approach, the *meta-model* was created out of the least common denominators of all the activities described in the audit processes (stages and steps). This process consists of an analysis of actions and their outcomes, which means that the best portions can be relatively easily selected and integrated with the reference methods. The integrated audit model comprises those stages and activities that are considered by the author to best reflect the overall process of intangible resource audit.

The comparison of existing information, knowledge, and intellectual capital audit methodologies aims at determining activities that should be included in a model for it to be considered complete. As a result, similarities and differences between all the activities will be identified, enabling the creation of the minimum list of consistent activities for all audit stages, making up for an integrated, comprehensive organizational intangible resource audit.

The development of a new intangible resource audit model fulfills two primary objectives. One is the use of Hong et al.'s (1993) approach to comparisons of existing solutions to formulate a *meta-model* for intangible resource audit. The other and far more significant one is the application of new concepts and solutions, namely organizational network analysis with components of dynamic network analysis. Additionally, the proposed model is derived to a much larger extent from the mature information audit models, as the existing knowledge audit models are still at their early concept stages and require further studies. Information audit models mainly focus on explicit knowledge (that is, information), disregarding the tacit knowledge aspect, which may be seen as a weakness of information audit—but one must bear in mind that knowledge audit is the one including analyses of tacit knowledge. The new method includes both explicit knowledge flows and (potential) tacit knowledge flows.

The primary criteria for selection of information, knowledge, and intellectual capital audit models included:

- the full phrase "information audit," "knowledge audit," or "intellectual capital audit" featured in the publication;

- publication of the model in a scientific journal or monograph;
- listing and description of specific audit stages and activities;
- discussion of issues closely related to the specific audit type.

Based on these basic criteria, the following models[4] were selected for analysis, as discussed in Sections 2.2.1, 2.2.2, and 2.2.3, and used as source material for the development of an integrated organizational intangible resource audit model (see Table 2.5).

The comparison table construction procedure proposed by Hong et al. (1993; see also Levantakis et al., 2008) is as follows. Blank fields in the comparison table indicate that the activity shown in the row is absent from the model in the column (1–14). In all other cases, one of three indicators denotes the relationship between the *meta-model* and the other models, and these read as follows:

- the "=" symbol indicates that a similar activity is a part of both the corresponding model and the *meta-model*; additionally, the column includes the number of a specific step of the corresponding model;
- the "<" and ">" symbols indicate that the activity or stage of the corresponding model does more or less than the relevant activity of the *meta-model*;
- the "><" symbol indicates that a part of the activity of the corresponding model overlaps with the activity of the *meta-model*, and the other parts of both activities do not overlap.

The first column lists the stages and steps of intangible resource audit, jointly forming the *meta-model* or integrated organizational intangible resource audit model. This *meta-model* comprises a total of five main stages and their activities or a sequence of 21 steps. Table 2.5 shows that the *meta-model* derives most activities from information audit 2 and intellectual capital audit 14, 9 activities from each (out of 21). Below, the main stages of intangible resource audit are discussed in detail.[5]

2.3.1.1 *The Planning Stage of the Intangible Resource Audit*

Decisions made at this stage affect all the remaining stages of intangible resource audit. Therefore, the first stage comprises three important steps required for the effective and successful performance of the entire audit process: defining audit objectives and scope, selecting the auditing team, and securing support in the organization (Figure 2.3). Similar activities are featured mainly in information audit models by Orna (1999) and Henczel (2001) and in the knowledge audit model by Levantakis et al. (2008). In Orna's model, the first three stages are similar in nature to the planning stage of the *meta-model*, while in Henczel's model (2001), two activities (1.2 and 1.5) correspond to this stage.

Table 2.5 Stages of the intangible resource audit model

Meta-model	Information audit			Knowledge audit									Intellectual capital audit	
	1	*2*	*3*	*4*	*5*	*6*	*7*	*8*	*9*	*10*	*11*	*12*	*13*	*14*
1. Planning stage of the intangible resource audit		<3	=1				><1.1		><1		<1			><1
1.1. Defining audit objectives and scope			>1.2					=1.3 =1.4					<1	
1.2. Selecting the auditing team		=3.2					=1.2							=1.2
1.3. Ensuring support in the organization	=1.1 =1.2	=2 =2.1 =2.2	=1.5		<1.2			=2.1 =2.2		<1.1	<1.1 2.1 =6.1			<1.1
2. Design stage of the intangible resource audit										><1				
2.1. Analyzing the external environment	=2.1					=1			=1					<2.3
2.2. Identifying the organization's main strategic goals		=1 = 1.1												<2.1
2.3. Value creation model														=2 2.2
2.4. Identifying core business processes						<1.1		<3.1		=1.3 >2 =2.1 =3 =3.1 =3.2	<1.3		><1.1	
3. Operationalization stage of the intangible resource audit														
3.1. Selection and development of audit instruments		><3.3	><1.3			><1.3	><1.3 <1.2	<4.2			><3 ><4 =4.1		><4 5.1	

(*Continued*)

Table 2.5 (Continued)

Meta-model	*Information audit*			*Knowledge audit*									*Intellectual capital audit*	
	1	*2*	*3*	*4*	*5*	*6*	*7*	*8*	*9*	*10*	*11*	*12*	*13*	*14*
3.2. Audit metrics						<6								
3.3. Testing the instruments							=2.1							
4. Performance stage of the intangible resource audit		><4												
4.1. Identifying key intangible resources	<2.5	><4.1	<2 <2.1		<2.1							<1		
4.2. Analyzing the dynamics of the organizational intangible resource association network	<2.4 <3.2	><4.3	<2.3 <3.3	<1		<2.4 <2.5		<5.2 <5.3	<2.4 <2.5 <2.6	<5.2 <5.3	<5 <5.1	<1.1 <1.2 <1.3		
4.3. Analyzing the impact of intangible resources on achievement of objectives, value creation, and business processes				<2	<3.4									
4.4. Developing the report	=5.1	=6.1	=5.1			<7	=3.1	=7.2		=6.1		=3		=6 =6.1 =6.2 =6.3 =8.1
5. Implementation stage of the intangible resource audit											<7			
5.1. Developing an organizational intangible resource management strategy	=5.2		>1.4						=3				><6.4	=5 =5.1 ><5.2
5.2. Implementing the strategy	<3.4		>6						=3.2					=7.2
Total	7	9	9	2	3	6	5	6	5	5	6	3	4	9

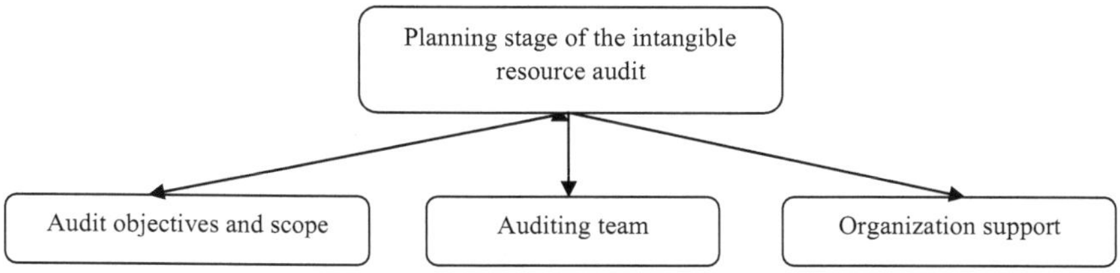

Figure 2.3 The planning stage of the intangible resource audit

Here, the management must define needs and expectations with regard to the audit and the envisaged outcomes of the process. Furthermore, within the planning stage, the lead auditor informs the management of the duration of each audit stage and the proposed tools, methods, and techniques to be used in the process (survey questionnaire, interview, discussion, workshop, observation, documentation analysis, vulnerability analysis, relation network analysis, etc.). As an intangible resource audit is a study, at the planning stage, the auditor and management should jointly formulate the research question and hypotheses that will subsequently be verified using selected research methods and techniques.

For the present methodology, the audit scope includes the entire organization and all its employees. Determination of audit scope is included both in Henczel (2001) and Cheung et al. (2007), and definition of audit objectives is taken from Henczel (2001), where it is best described. The next step in the planning stage is the assembly of a group comprising individuals holding key positions in the organization—with regard to the core business process and the corresponding process actors, and not to departmentalization or functional divisions used in classical structural solutions, such as linear, functional, or divisional structure.

Ensuring support for the intangible resource audit across the organization is essential to the success of the project, since participation from all employees, especially in the questionnaire survey, is indispensable. At this stage, the lead auditor must:

- describe the intangible resource audit concepts in detail;
- present the object of analysis and the research questions and hypotheses;
- discuss the general purpose and premise for the performance of such an investigation in the organization;
- demonstrate the expected outcomes, including an audit report with recommendations for the organization;
- propose an intangible resource strategy;
- outline the implementation conditions for the strategy.

The premise of the planning stage of intangible resource audit is to initiate a preliminary meeting with the managerial staff and to learn about the formal structure of the organization. These activities are included in two models: Cheung et al. (2007) and Perez-Soltero et al. (2007). A similar step features in the model by Burnett et al. (2004), though the purpose of the meeting is to promote benefits of the audit. Before support is sought in the organization, audit objectives and scope must be defined. Important factors include access to data sources, including documentation if required for better understanding of the target area of audit; and observation of the structure and environment. This activity provides open channels of communication not only with the management but with all the involved parties (employees). Securing the involvement and support of employees strengthens the team and prevents misunderstandings (Henczel 2001, Orna 1999). Such suggestions, present in nearly all audit models, should not, therefore, be overlooked by intangible resource audit.

Understanding the organization and its environment is a major step in any audit type. Documentation of the organization and participant observation empowers the audit team in regard to understanding both the organizational culture and the environment in which the study (audit) is to be performed. These activities are in line with the information audit model by Orna (1.1. Organizational needs) and the knowledge audit model by Perez-Soltero et al. (1.2. Acquiring strategic information). Particular activities are given various designations, but share the same purpose—basic learning about the organization.[6]

2.3.1.2 The Design Stage of the Intangible Resource Audit

This stage plays a key role in identifying and defining the organizational context, which is the primary point of reference in the performance of the intangible resource audit (Figure 2.4). Hence the importance of a preliminary analysis of the organization's external (macro- and micro-) environment, including in particular opportunities and risks affecting its functioning, and of the goals the organization must achieve in order to sustain or develop its operation in the long term. Identification of risks and opportunities is the basis for defining the organization's strategic objectives, which may be related to areas of change or development, competitive advantage, customers and partners, markets, product and/or service development, or technology. The defined strategic objectives are a response to the conditions under which the organization operates in its environment. Another component of the intangible resource audit design stage concerns defining the model of value creation for the organization and for the customer (business model).

The proposed analysis of the external environment of the organization is similar to information audit by Buchanan and Gibb (1998) and

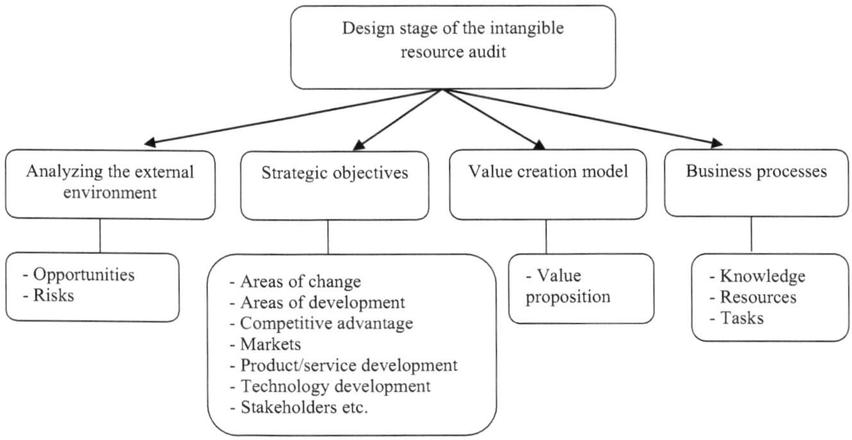

Figure 2.4 The design stage of the intangible resource audit

intellectual capital audit by Mertins et al. (2007). As to defining the organization's strategic objectives, the activity only features in Orna (1999), as step 1. "Key business objectives," and in Mertins et al. (2007) as part of strategy definition. Value creation model, limited to determining proposed value, is included in Mertins et al. (2007). These audit components are quite significant, as intangible resources should be mainly analyzed in the context of achieving strategic objectives and creating value for the customer (or, more broadly, for stakeholders) and for the organization.

When defining the value creation model, auditors also determine the fundamentals of what the enterprise is selling. The created value is what the enterprise offers to its internal and external stakeholders. The question about how value is created is also a question about the enterprise's core business processes, fields of knowledge, tasks, and resources required for the identified business processes. As business processes reflect interactions between individuals, resources, knowledge, and information, they seem to be the most relevant area of analysis for intangible resource audit. They provide insights into the way value is created in the organization, especially since there are a number of stages where the product or service is produced and delivered to the customer. These are typically the most important, fundamental processes in the organization, while all other processes are centered around them, and thus must be defined in detail for each enterprise.

However, the most important aspect of the procedure is the identification of core business processes in the organization, including the performed tasks, and the knowledge and resources used for creating value and achieving the organization's objectives. Value creation is dependent on employees' individual skills and capabilities and especially their transformation into organizational skills and capabilities. Employees with more access to information and knowledge gain more opportunities for their use in the organization's business processes. It is important that the processes be performed based on current information and knowledge. Therefore, an analysis of information and knowledge flows in the organization would help determine the supply of intangible resources and their use in business processes.

In any organization, business processes rely on knowledge available in the entire organization, in specific units, or possessed by individual employees. If, however, the management does not know what knowledge is required for the achievement of objectives, they will not be able to provide it and minimize the knowledge gap. An organization may have several various knowledge resources, but if employees do not know that a specific knowledge resource is available in the organization and where it is located, they will be unable to use it. Unused knowledge, in turn, cannot provide added value in the achievement of organizational objectives. Analysis of specific relationship networks is required in order to understand how they support business processes. Associating the core business processes with employees, knowledge, tasks, and resources contributes to the achievement of strategic goals and value creation, helps avoid repetition of the same tasks, and improves resource use. Intangible resource audit allows for identifying knowledge available in the organization and associated with a specific employee; matching knowledge, tasks, and resources to specific business processes; and analyzing flows of information and knowledge between employees.

With this in mind, another important step in the design stage is analyzing what knowledge and resources are required for the performance of tasks within each business process. The knowledge audit model by Perez-Soltero et al. (2007) attributes much importance to business processes, with significantly more sophisticated identification and selection procedures than in the present audit model. However, as in Levantakis et al. (2008), business process is mainly considered in the context of knowledge content, without including the tasks and resources that are the subject of analyses in the *meta-model*.

2.2.1.3 The Operationalization Stage of the Intangible Resource Audit

This stage focuses on the selection and development of instruments or techniques to be used for performing the intangible resource audit in the specific organization, development of metrics,[7] and testing of these instruments in a pilot study (Figure 2.5).

The preparation of instruments involves developing questions for use in interviews (structured, semi-structured, or unstructured) and survey questionnaires allowing for detailed analysis of relationship networks,

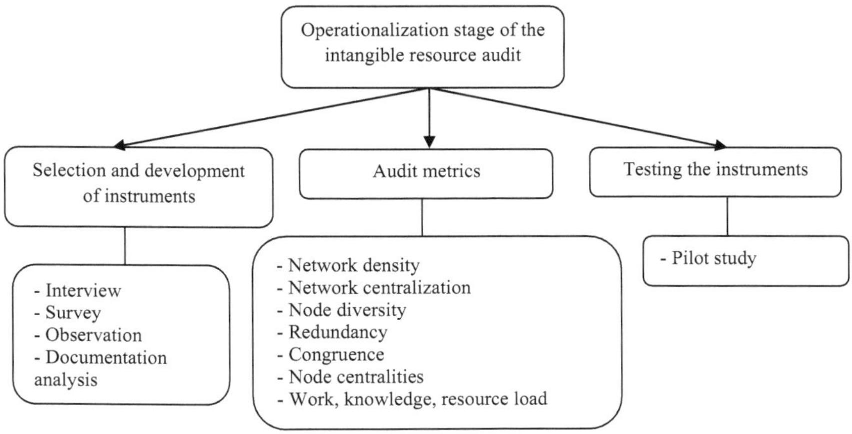

Figure 2.5 The operationalization stage of the intangible resource audit

information and knowledge flows, dynamics, and intangible resource use effectiveness. Table 2.6 lists the basic interview questions categorized into the following areas of interest: external environment, strategic objectives, value creation model, and business processes.

Table 2.6 lists suggested questions, which may be freely adjusted and configured, and may include more or less detail. The next table, 2.7, lists questions used in organizational network analysis. The first four items are based on Cross and Parker (2004). Their purpose is to diagnose the flow of information and tacit knowledge in the organization, and they are also relevant for intangible resource audit metrics, especially those comprising one- and two-mode matrices. Questions can be used with a nominal, ordinal, or interval scale.

The operationalization stage of the intangible resource audit is not listed as such in any audit model but is featured in a different form in some. The step of selecting and developing instruments for audit performance is included in seven models (Orna, 1999; Henczel, 2001; Chan & Lee, 2011; Gourova, 2009; Levantakis et al. (2008; Perez-Soltero et al., 2007; and Burnett et al., 2004), but is only partially consistent with the *meta-model*. Of course, as in the *meta-model*, so in most of the source audit models, interviews and surveys are the primary instruments used for data collection. No model, however, explains how to develop those tools or what questions to include in interviews or surveys, the only exception being Henczel's questionnaire template (2001). As to intangible resource audit metrics, they are not included in any audit model. Though social network analysis is included in knowledge audit models by Chan et al. (2011), Levantakis et al. (2008), and Cheung et al. (2007), the authors do not prescribe specific network metrics or analysis methods.

Table 2.6 Questions for organizational context analysis

External environment	*Strategic objectives*
1. Please name the opportunities in your organization's external environment (macroenvironment) that indirectly affect its functioning. 2. Please name the opportunities in your organization's external environment (microenvironment) that directly affect its functioning. 3. Please name the risks in your organization's external environment (macroenvironment) that indirectly affect its functioning. 4. Please name the risks in your organization's external environment (microenvironment) that directly affect its functioning.	1. What are your organization's major (long-term) objectives?
Value creation model[8]	*Business processes*
1. What is your value proposition for customers? 2. What does your organization offer (in terms of services, products, or combinations thereof)? 3. What problems does your organization solve for its customers?	1. What are your organization's core business processes? 2. What are the key fields of knowledge required for each process? (What do you need to know to complete the business process successfully?) 3. What tasks or activities must be performed for the business process to be successfully completed? 4. What tangible and intangible resources are used within each business process?

2.3.1.4 The Performance Stage of the Intangible Resource Audit

This stage is key to the intangible resource audit process, and includes identifying intangible resources; analyzing the dynamics of the organizational intangible resource relationship network; analyzing the impact of intangible resources on achievement of objectives, value creation, and business processes; and developing the final report (Figure 2.6).

Resources are identified based on the interviews and questionnaires presented in Tables 2.5 and 2.6. This enables the collection of data, which subsequently undergo detailed analysis using network methods. One important activity at this stage is transforming the data into

Table 2.7 Questions (statements) for organizational network analysis

Information	*Knowledge*
1. How often do you provide this person with information directly related to the work performed in the organization? 2. How often do you receive information directly related to the work performed in the organization from this person? 3. How often do you communicate with this person in order to discuss and receive assistance in solving problems related to work? 4. I know the skills and knowledge this person has. This does not mean that I have these skills and this knowledge, but I understand what skills and knowledge this person has.	1. I have knowledge on the subject. 2. I use knowledge on the subject in my work.
Resources	*Tasks*
1. I have access to this resource in my work. 2. I use this resource in my work.	1. I am capable of performing this task. 2. I perform this task in my work.
Knowledge—resources—tasks	
1. Is this knowledge necessary for the performance of this task? 2. Is this resource necessary for the performance of this task?	

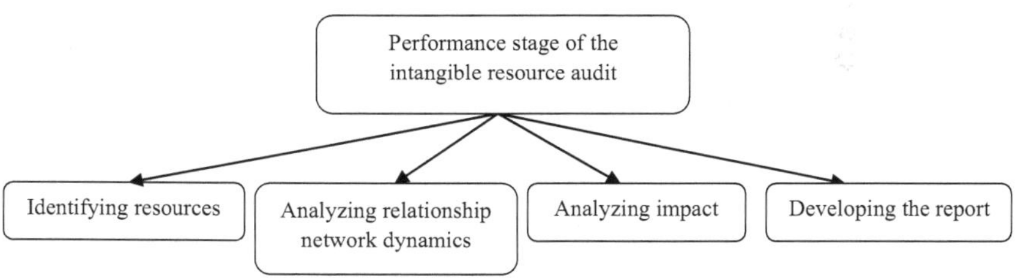

Figure 2.6 The performance stage of the intangible resource audit

a matrix form. The dynamics of the intangible resource network are analyzed based on previously defined network metrics. Each item listed in Table 2.6 creates a specific relationship or network that is subject to measurements using the uni- or multimodal network metrics. These metrics allow for determining the network structure (entire network level), the prominence of specific network nodes (actor, knowledge, resource, task), and the impact of each node on other nodes (dyad level). At the stage of relationship network dynamics analysis, the auditor can perform correlation and regression analyses on the matrices in order to test the research hypotheses. Subsequently, the impact of intangible resources on the organization's strategic objectives, business processes, and value creation is analyzed. Owing to the direct association between intangible resources and these areas, the audit becomes an instrument for measuring competitive advantage based on unique strategic characteristics, value proposition, or effective performance of business processes.

The ultimate important aspect of this stage is the development of the final report, comprising a presentation and analysis of findings, and recommendations for the organization formulated on the basis of the intangible resource audit. The report development activity is mainly derived from Henczel (2001). Typically, all the processed data are summarized and presented in the report, which is a part of the audit summary. Within the discussed audit methodology, the report should comprise the following sections:

1. Introduction, discussing the premise for the intangible resource audit, its objectives and research hypotheses, and the expected outcomes.
2. Definition of the organizational context, discussing the organization's functioning, the opportunities and risks in its macro- and microenvironment, strategic objectives, business model(s), and business processes contributing to value creation for the organization.
3. Audit findings in two areas, on the network, dyad, and node levels:
    a. Intangible resource impact and association matrix.
    b. Intangible resource association dynamics analysis.
4. Analysis of intangible resource audit findings (including the testing of research hypotheses).
5. Summary and conclusions from the intangible resource audit.
6. Recommendations for the organization.
7. References (literature, appendices).

The performance stage of the intangible resource audit differs significantly among the cited audit models, which mainly refer to developing an inventory or a map. For instance, the activity of developing a knowledge inventory is derived from Cheung et al. (2007) and Perez-Soltero et al. (2007). Orna (1999) and Henczel (2001) refer to "identifying information sources," which is similar to the concept of inventory, though their propositions do not indicate a need of developing such an instrument and only cover explicit knowledge. Social network analysis and knowledge network analysis are major steps within data analysis, replacing, in fact, the knowledge-mapping activity. Cheung et al. (2007), Levantakis et al. (2008), and Chan et al. (2011) mention social network analysis in their models but do not explain how it should be performed. As to the identification of missing knowledge, it entails a gap analysis, though only Orna (1999) lists gap analysis as a relevant step in knowledge audit. Identifying knowledge required for the achievement of business objectives is typically difficult, and undoubtedly requires a knowledge inventory and knowledge gap analysis, subsequently used as a basis for developing a system for detecting knowledge needs or for contracting an expert to provide the missing knowledge. However, this portion of the audit process is not particularly emphasized.

In the proposed intangible resource audit model, the performance stage allows for:

- identifying and analyzing incoming and outgoing information flows for all network nodes (animate and inanimate actors);
- identifying and analyzing tacit knowledge flows in the organization;
- identifying and analyzing the information and knowledge network dynamics in the organization, performing simulations, and determining each node's area of influence (e.g., by removing individual nodes from the network);
- identifying and analyzing the dynamics of resource and task networks;
- identifying knowledge and resource needs;
- identifying knowledge and resource waste (mismatch) in the organization;
- identifying prominent and influential network nodes.

2.3.1.5 The Implementation Stage of the Intangible Resource Audit[9]

This stage comprises two steps: developing a strategy for intangible resource management and implementing the strategy (Figure 2.7).

If the intangible resource audit report is well received by the management and employees, the action plan should provide for creating a new intangible resource management strategy aligned with the organizational strategy in order to achieve the envisaged benefits (e.g., Tiwana, 2002) and for implementing the recommendations, which are unique to each audited organization. The strategy describes the overall approach that

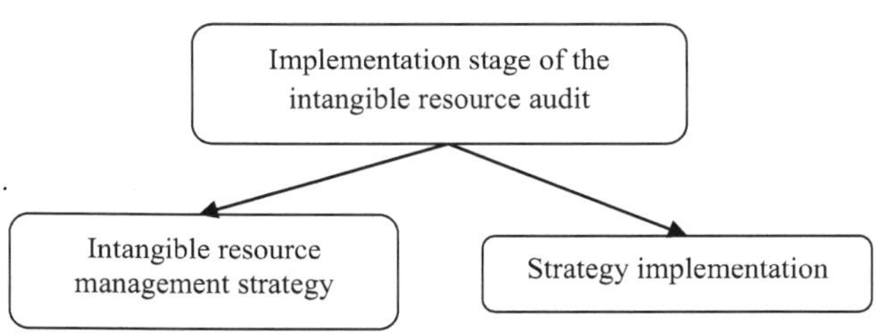

Figure 2.7 The implementation stage of the intangible resource audit

the organization will adopt to adjust its knowledge resources and potential to the intellectual requirements of its organizational strategy (Zack, 1999). The organizational strategy also sets long-term objectives for the competitive development of the organization. Its fulfillment depends on core business processes. If the intangible resource management strategy is to be aligned with organizational strategy, it should ensure an adequate supply of resources for business processes. However, resource management requires additional measures to be implemented, which in turn necessitates careful prioritization to bring about the expected effectiveness and benefits for the organization without excessive use of resources. An organization's business processes exist to support the achievement of its objectives. Some are basic activities that increase value for the organization and are essential to success and competitiveness. When business processes are determined, knowledge required for each process can be identified using qualitative and quantitative analysis methods. The identification of knowledge-based business processes and knowledge gaps within these processes helps define the intangible resource strategy.

Strategy implementation should be accompanied by a detailed consultation of the conditions for implementation of report recommendations, a timetable and financial estimates (to secure the expenses associated with strategy implementation), and implementation control (comparison of the objectives set in the strategy with the actual performance, using relevant metrics). Reporting is included as a step in eight audit models, and development of a resource (information, knowledge, or intellectual capital) strategy in five. Strategy implementation only features as a step in four models (Buchanan and Gibb, 1998; Henczel, 2001; Cheung et al., 2007; and Mertins et al., 2007).

In summary, intangible resource audit comprises the stages shown in Figure 2.8.

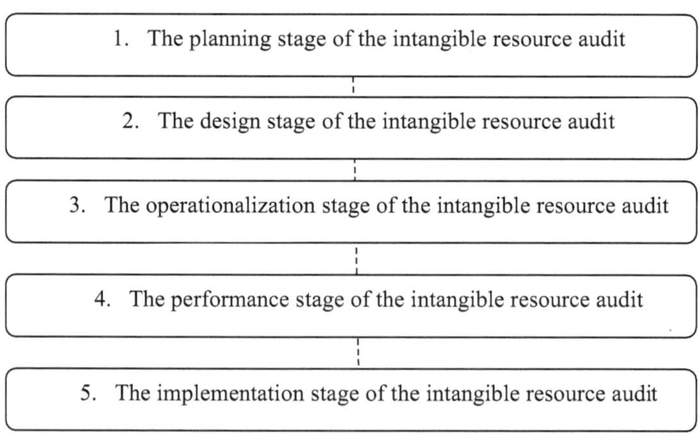

Figure 2.8 Stages of the intangible resource audit

The following section discusses the network metrics used as basic measurement instruments at the performance stage of the intangible resource audit.

2.3.2 Network Metrics in Intangible Resource Audit

Social and organizational network metrics allow for accurate quantification of the positions of network nodes and of the entire network structure. Simple visualization is not sufficient for capturing the essence of a network, and could lead to a misinterpretation of the data (e.g., the significance of a network node in relation to other nodes). The metrics discussed in this section differ in form and character. They can be classified by network dimension (modality) and level, as shown in Figure 2.9.

In intangible resource audit, three dimensions of network techniques are used: one-mode, two-mode, and multimodal. With metrics based on one-mode matrices, network nodes belong to the same category and are not different from one another. For instance, such a matrix could consist only of relationships between (human) network actors, as in the case of the node centrality and network centralization metrics. In these cases, relations refer to relations between people (providing and receiving information, sharing knowledge, knowing the knowledge and skills of other employees in the organization). Two-mode relationship network metrics are based on two types of nodes, with matrix rows representing given network nodes and columns representing nodes of another category. In intangible resource audit, two-mode matrices include relations between: actors and the knowledge they have and use (AK), actors and the resources they have and use (AR), actors and the tasks they can and do perform (AT), knowledge and tasks (KT), and resources and tasks (RT).

Multimodal network metrics are more complex and consist of two or more one- or two-mode matrices. Such a metric is an algebraic measurement of matrix data. In intangible resource audit, the following

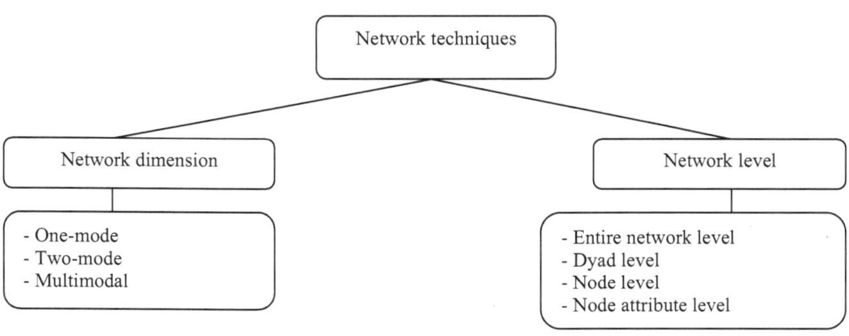

Figure 2.9 Breakdown of network techniques

multimodal metrics are used, based mainly on two-mode matrices: total meta-network density; congruence of an actor's knowledge needs and waste (node level); congruence of an actor's resource needs and waste (node level); and actual work, knowledge, and resource load. Metrics listed in Table 2.8 are divided by level—entire network or individual nodes.

In the book, the following matrix notation and mathematical symbols are used, in accordance with sources used in Table 2.8.

|Matrix| = square matrix size
Matrix (i,j) = the matrix element at the ith row and j^{th} column
Matrix (i,:) = i^{th} row of the matrix (vector)
Matrix (:,j) = j^{th} column of the matrix (vector)
sum(Matrix) = sum of matrix elements
Matrix' = transposed matrix
~Matrix = only for binary matrices, replacing 0 with 1 and 1 with 0
|Set| = set cardinality; for countable and finite sets, this is the number of elements
sgn(x) = 1 if $x \geq 0$, otherwise –1; sign of x
R set of real numbers
Z set of integers
dG(i,j) the shortest path between node i and node j in graph G when $i \neq j$ is $1 \leq dG(i,j) < n$ if there is a connection between i and j (n is the number of nodes in the graph), assuming that dG(i,i) = 0

All metrics listed in Table 2.8 are further discussed below.

2.3.2.1 Network and Meta-Network Density

Network density is a measure of connectivity in the network, defined by the number of possible relations. The value ranges between 0 and 1.0 (0%–100%). When density is close to 1.0, the network is very dense (all possible relations exist in the network). For directed relationships, the maximum possible number of pairs is considered. Classical network density is the number of existing connections in a network divided by the number of possible connections (Freeman, 1978). For square matrices, the algorithm first converts the diagonal to 0 so that self-loops are ignored, and then calculates density D_u (Formula 2.1). The numerator is the number of existing connections, and the denominator is the number of possible connections. Formula 2.2 is used for calculating rectangular (two-mode) network density (D_b) (Freeman, 1978).

$$Du = \frac{sum(M)}{n(n-1)/2} \tag{2.1}$$

Table 2.8 Organizational intangible resource audit metrics

Entire network level			
Metric symbol	*Metrics*	*Definition*	*Input data*
D_u D_b	One-mode and two-mode network density	Network density as the ratio of existing relations to all possible links in the network.	AA, AK, AR, AT, KT, RT
CD^N	Network centralization	Indicates the relative dominance of a single node over other network nodes, measured by the number of direct links this actor has with others.	AA
DK	Knowledge diversity	Distribution of differences in sharing of ideas and knowledge. This is the Herfindahl-Hirschman index applied to normalized sums of AK columns. Describes the network in terms of how (un)equally knowledge is distributed among employees.	AK
DR	Resource diversity	Indicates the distribution of differences in sharing of resources. The Herfindahl-Hirschman index is used (sum of AR columns). Describes the resource network in terms of who has what resources and how (un)equally resources are distributed among employees.	AR
ReK	Knowledge redundancy	Mean number of employees who have access to knowledge already possessed by others.	AK
ReR	Resource redundancy	Mean number of employees who have access to a resource already possessed by others.	AR
ReT	Task redundancy	Mean number of employees who have access to a task already possessed by others.	AT
Node level			
CD^n	Centrality degree	Normalized sum of incoming and outgoing connections. The higher the centrality degree, the more important a node is in the network.	AA
C^{eig}	Eigenvector centrality	A higher value is attributed to a node in relationships with adjacent nodes that play an important role in the network, for example, have key resources or knowledge, perform tasks.	AA
C^b	Betweenness centrality	Measure of indirect connections between nodes, which indicates the node that is best connected with other nodes acts as a broker or gatekeeper and is the most central actor of the entire network. It is the number of indirect connections between nodes that pass through a given node (indicating that the actor is a broker between other nodes).	AA
W^{load}	Actual workload	Here, actual workload indicates the knowledge and resources that an actor uses for performing tasks.	AK, AR, AT, KT, RT

(Continued)

Table 2.8 (Continued)

Entire network level			
Metric symbol	*Metrics*	*Definition*	*Input data*
K^{load}	Actual knowledge load	Knowledge used by an actor for performing tasks to which the knowledge is relevant.	AK, AT, KT
R^{load}	Actual resource load	Resources used by an actor for performing tasks to which the resources are relevant.	AR, AT, RT
CK^{needs}	Actor knowledge needs congruence	Measure of knowledge that an actor lacks for performing the assigned task.	AK, AT, KT
CK^{waste}	Actor knowledge waste congruence	Knowledge that an actor has, but does not need for the performed tasks. Unused knowledge is considered wasted.	AK, AT, KT
CR^{needs}	Actor resource needs congruence	Measure of resources that an actor lacks for performing the assigned task.	AR, AT, RT
CR^{waste}	Actor resource waste congruence	Resources that an actor has, but does not need for the performed tasks. Unused resources are considered wasted.	AR, AT, RT
$C^{(K/A)}$	Row degree centrality of knowledge/actor	For each actor and knowledge node, these are the outgoing connections, that is, connections from the node to other nodes.	AK
$C^{(R/A)}$	Row degree centrality of resources/actor	For each actor and resource node, these are the outgoing connections, that is, connections from the node to other nodes.	AR
$C^{(T/A)}$	Row degree centrality of tasks/actor	For each actor and task node, these are the outgoing connections, that is, connections from the node to other nodes.	AT
$C^{(A/K)}$	Row degree centrality of actor/knowledge	For each knowledge and actor node, these are the outgoing connections, that is, connections from the node to other nodes.	AK'
$C^{(T/K)}$	Row degree centrality of tasks/knowledge	For each task and knowledge node, these are the outgoing connections, that is, connections from the node to other nodes.	KT
$C^{(A/R)}$	Row degree centrality of actor/resources	For each actor and resource node, these are the outgoing connections, that is, connections from the node to other nodes.	AR'
$C^{(K/A)}$	Row degree centrality of tasks/resources	For each task and resource node, these are the outgoing connections, that is, connections from the node to other nodes.	RT
$C^{(A/T)}$	Row degree centrality of actor/tasks	For each actor and task node, these are the outgoing connections, that is, connections from the node to other nodes.	AT'
$C^{(K/T)}$	Row degree centrality of knowledge/tasks	For each knowledge and task node, these are the outgoing connections, that is, connections from the node to other nodes.	KT'
$C^{(R/T)}$	Row degree centrality of resources/tasks	For each resource and task node, these are the outgoing connections, that is, connections from the node to other nodes.	RT'

Source: Own work based on Bonacich (1972, 1987); Borgatti, Everett, & Johnson (2018); Carley (2002); Carley & Yuqing (2001); Freeman (1978); Hirschman (1945); Jiang, Carley, & Eberlein (2012); Prell (2012); Scott (2012); Wasserman & Faust (1994).

$$Db = \frac{sum(M)}{m \cdot n} \quad (2.2)$$

Where:
M—matrix
n—number of nodes
m^*n—two-mode matrix with *m* rows and *n* columns

The density metric compares the existing connections (relations) with all possible connections, for example, in a communications network of employees (Wasserman & Faust, 1994), and reflects the level of social organizational cohesion. It should be interpreted in relation to the size of groups and the type of work performed. What is problematic about the density metric is that it is affected by the number of network nodes and thus cannot be used for comparisons between networks that differ significantly in size. Wang and Gao (2011) suggest that increases in network size may entail a decrease in network density, as maintenance of strong relationships becomes more difficult for actors forming the network. For instance, typical social network density levels range from 5% to 30% in the case of frequent or very frequent information exchanges, and the number of connections varies depending on network size.[10] According to Parise (2007), a minimum social network density of 15%—20% may reflect efficient information and knowledge sharing in a network comprising approximately 100 nodes (e.g., an organization with 100 employees). In the case of meta-network density, all one-mode and two-mode matrices are taken into account, and density is calculated for all networks in the audit. This density measure reflects the interrelatedness and cohesion among the nodes in an organization (actors, knowledge, resources, tasks). The higher the density, the more complete or interconnected the network.

Density is a very popular measure, used in multiple studies, typically as an independent or control variable. A study might concern, for instance, increases in productivity seen with increased group density (Reagans & Zuckerman, 2001) or positive correlations between group performance and the density of relations between coworkers (Mehralian, Rasekh, Akhavan, & Ghatari, 2013). According to Parker, Cross, and Walsh (2001), users in networks with a high relationship density are more likely to access higher-quality information than those in networks with a lower density. A higher density of an actor's network combined with a higher diversity of knowledge and connections may increase knowledge production by a given person, because higher network density promotes trust and reciprocity among the members, encouraging the sharing of diverse knowledge and information (Fleming, Mingo, & Chen, 2007).

Gilsing et al. (2008) also emphasize problems related to low network density. Relatively dense networks favor the creation of new knowledge in the aspect of perceived credibility of knowledge sources, as well as understanding and evaluation of the sources. Knowing what others know is a major factor in knowledge exchange, transfer, and innovation. On the other hand, very dense networks, for example, in a team, can be inefficient, due to a more restricted scope of information (Nahapiet & Ghoshal, 1998). Fragmentation allows for describing looser structures or even cliques, which typically reflect task orientation. The contact itself is not sufficient, as cooperation also matters—it contributes to problem-solving, collaborative projects, and product development. Thanks to cooperation, employees have the opportunity to observe and experience the application of tacit knowledge by others (Droege & Hoobler, 2003).

2.3.2.2 Network Centralization

Centralization at the network level indicates the relative dominance of a single node over other network nodes, measured by the number of direct links this actor has with others, as in Formula 2.3 (Freeman, 1978):

$$\text{Let } \bar{d} = max\{d_1 \mid 1 \le i \le n\}$$

$$\text{then } CD^N = \frac{\sum_{i=1}^{n}\left(\bar{d} - d_i\right)}{n-2} \tag{2.3}$$

Where:
d_i—centrality of node *i*, the number of direct connections between the actor and other actors

Centralization is calculated by dividing the number of connections for each node by the maximum sum possible. It measures the degree to which the network structure is centralized, that is, has multiple links distributed around one or more nodes. A decentralized network, in turn, is characterized by small differences between the number of links each node has. Higher centralization prevents free contact within the organization or with its environment and decreases initiative in forming interdepartmental relations for sharing information and knowledge (Tsai, 2002). Mudambi and Swift (2009) found that network centralization may be a potentially significant factor in knowledge absorption by an organization. Relations between organizational units are often established by leaders, that is, those taking part in decisions about the mutual interactions of the units. For instance, social network centralization of around 0.5 (50%) is considered relatively high (Wasserman & Faust, 1994). If centralization is approximately 0.10 (10%), there is no risk that a central group of (human) actors has power and authority over the entire network. Notably, centralization may have a positive impact on the organization's performance, as the central group or individual typically integrates information for task performance (Scott, 2012). Reports by other researchers (e.g., Wang, Zhao, Li, & Li, 2015) demonstrate that central networks have a positive impact both on innovation and on efficiency in an organization. The impact of network centralization on organizational innovation is even higher in smaller organizations, while in large organizations and in sectors requiring specialized knowledge, centralization affects organizational efficiency.

2.3.2.3 Knowledge and Resource Diversity

The diversity of knowledge (DK) and resources (DR) at the network level reflects their accessibility and equality of distribution among network actors (A). High diversity values (>0.5) may indicate that only some employees have access to knowledge and resources, while others have limited or no access. Knowledge and resource diversity reflects the distribution of differences in knowledge and resource sharing. The Herfindahl-Hirschman index (Hirschman, 1945) is applied to the normalized sums of AK and AR columns (Formulas 5 and 6) (Altman et al., 2018). It describes the network in terms of how (un)equally knowledge and resources are distributed among employees. It is a normalized value between 0 and 1, with 1 indicating a high level of diversity. For instance, 0.97 indicates diverse (or dispersed) knowledge in the knowledge network (AK). People communicate with each other if they know what knowledge others in the organization have ("who knows what") or what tasks they perform ("who does what"). Such cognitive networks define the mutual interactions of actors who make choices based on their own perception of the organization (see Formulas 2.4 and 2.5; Altman et al., 2018):

Let $w_k = \sum_{i=1}^{|A|} AK(i,k) \quad for 1 \le k \le |K|$

and $W = \sum_{k=1}^{|K|} w_k$

then knowledge diversity (DK) is:

$$DK = 1 - \sum_{k=1}^{|K|} (w_k / W)^2 \qquad (2.4)$$

or for resource diversity

$$\text{let } w_k = \sum_{i=1}^{|A|} AR(i,k) \quad for 1 \le k \le |R|$$

$$\text{and } W = \sum_{k=1}^{|K|} w_k$$

then resource diversity (DR) is:

$$DR = 1 - \sum_{k=1}^{|R|} (w_k / W)^2 \tag{2.5}$$

Where:
$|K|$ — number of elements in set K (knowledge)
$|R|$ — number of elements in set R (resources)
$|A|$ — number of elements in set A (actors)

2.3.2.4 *Knowledge, Resource, and Task Redundancy*

In most organizations, knowledge and resources are distributed unequally. The flow of knowledge is key to the organization's efficiency and performance. Though knowledge flow is dynamic by nature, the associated phenomena remain poorly understood, and the existing approaches to their modeling, included in the discussed information and knowledge audits, are predominantly static and vague. Hence the need for a multidimensional view of the process, considering not only the flow of knowledge, but also its use, redundancy, and congruence. Redundancy denotes the extent to which knowledge or skills one person has resemble those of other people in the organization. Network organizations are resistant to employee dismissal, but the loss of redundancy can restrict learning or the flexible and adaptive reactions available to the organization (Carley, 1990).

Knowledge redundancy (ReK) measures the mean number of actors who have redundant knowledge, using a normalized scale ranging from 0 to 1, with 1 indicating that all knowledge is completely redundant for a given actor. For instance, a value of 0.262 indicates the existence of individual redundancy in the organization. This can be associated with the need to mitigate the personal risk of the organization's flexibility being affected if an expert is unavailable. Individual redundancy increases the flexibility of an organization (Ronfeldt & Arquilla, 2001), protecting small network organizations against risk and minimizing the consequences of actor unavailability. If an actor changes its position in the association network, the change may be significant in the aspect of risk management and timely response, if strategic decisions are to be made. For a manager, the understanding of changes in an organizational network is as important as the understanding of its structure at any given time. A complete outlook on the network of relations between actors, knowledge, resources, and tasks allows for strategic interventions aiming at anticipation of changes and reduction of risk, through effective use of redundant knowledge and re-identification of key actors, among other processes.

Redundancy is similar to diversity, as it describes the distribution of knowledge, resources, and tasks in the organization, at the same time indicating the percentage of actors having access to the same resources, tasks, or knowledge (Formulas 2.6, 2.7, 2.8; Carley, 2002).

$$ReK \in \left[0, \left(|A| - 1\right) * |K|\right] \tag{2.6}$$

$$ReR \in \left[0, \left(|A| - 1\right) * |R|\right] \tag{2.7}$$

$$ReT \in \left[0, \left(|A| - 1\right) * |T|\right] \tag{2.8}$$

Where:
$|K|$ — number of elements in set K (knowledge)
$|R|$ — number of elements in set R (resources)
$|A|$ — number of elements in set A (actors)
$|T|$ — number of elements in set T (tasks)

High levels of knowledge (ReK), resource (ReR), and task (ReT) redundancy mean that many actors have the same knowledge, perform the same tasks, or use the same resources. Knowledge specialization can be higher than actually necessary for the performed tasks. Redundancy measures the mean number of employees who have access to knowledge, resources, or tasks already possessed by others (Carley, 2002). Network efficiency can be measured by the number of nodes having access to a large number of diverse nodes (knowledge and information sources) via a relatively small number of relationships. These nodes are considered nonredundant. For instance, networks of identical size, but with more nonredundant contacts than others, have additional benefits, as the benefit of an additional redundant contact (with the same information or knowledge) is minor compared to that of an entirely new contact between actors. Dense networks usually have redundant knowledge (Susskind, Miller, & Johnson, 1998). In accordance with Granovetter's concept of weak and strong ties (1973), the people with whom one has weak ties are the ones with unique experiences and access to new and valuable information. Nonredundant information is, then, more likely to be provided by weak relationships between actors. In this context, non-redundancy is not an attribute of the information (or knowledge), but a consequence of the fact that exchange is limited, which means the information levels of various nodes are more likely to differ. In the aspect of knowledge sharing, Hansen (1999) found that weak ties are not effective in transferring complex information. For the transfer of complex knowledge based on mutual connections, strong ties are required. Therefore, weak ties provide nonredundant knowledge, while strong ties provide incentives for knowledge sharing with others (Droege & Hoobler, 2003).

Successful recombination of existing knowledge in novel ways through the network is an example of effective knowledge "morphology." It can, however, prove ineffective, if actions or organizations have equivalent knowledge due to similar knowledge profiles—leading to redundancy (Cowan & Jonard, 2004). A network consisting of nonredundant ties favors better use of limited resources and is more effective in terms of timeliness and access to information (Soda, Usai, & Zaheer, 2004). Knowledge transfer as such is facilitated by knowledge redundancy and duplication (Nonaka & Takeuchi, 1995) among actors, and by common interpretations of knowledge; when the knowledge gap between actors decreases, benefits of transfer are eliminated.

2.3.2.5 Centrality Degree

A node's centrality degree is a normalized sum of its rows and columns (Formula 2.9). This value indicates the number of direct incoming and outgoing relationships of this node and its influence over other nodes (Mizruchi & Bunting, 1981; Wasserman & Faust, 1994):

$$\mathrm{CD}^{\mathrm{n}} = node\,i = \frac{1}{2(n-1)} \sum_{i=1}^{n} \sum_{\substack{j=1 \\ i \neq 1}}^{n} X(i,j) \tag{2.9}$$

Where:
X—the matrix representing the network

Actors with numerous connections are considered prominent or prestigious in the network (others seek to form ties with this actor), which may indicate their importance. Centrality is an important characteristic of an actor's position in the network, used in numerous studies (e.g., Bright, Greenhill, Reynolds, Ritter, & Morselli, 2015; Mizruchi & Potts, 1998; Young, Wang, & Lewis, 2016). Actors with many direct contacts (high centrality degree) are active in the network and have access to many behaviors (e.g., knowledge sharing) that make them more efficient and less dependent on others. From knowledge and innovation sharing, different network positions represent different possibilities a person or an organization has. Entities that are more central can have better access to knowledge and resources (Tsai, 2001).

2.3.2.6 In-Degree

The in-degree (C^{in}) indicates a node's centrality based on the number of incoming relations directed to this node from other nodes and the impact of direct links, understood as the possibility of being directly influenced. The higher the incoming relation count, the more central a node is to the network (Formula 2.10, Carley 2002).

$$C^{in} = column\,j = \frac{1}{m}\sum_{i=1}^{m} X(i,j) \tag{2.10}$$

Where:
m —number of all incoming links

2.3.2.7 Out-Degree

The out-degree (C^{out}) indicates a node's centrality based on the number of outgoing relations directed from this node to other nodes and the impact of direct links, understood as the possibility of directly influencing other nodes. The higher the outgoing relation count, the more influential (due to its expert knowledge and information) a node is in the network (Formula 2.11, Carley 2002).

$$C^{out} = row\,i = \frac{1}{n}\sum_{j=1}^{n} X(i,j) \tag{2.11}$$

Where:
n—number of all outgoing links

2.3.2.8 Eigenvector Centrality

A higher value is attributed to a node (e.g., actor) in relationships with adjacent nodes that play a significant role in the network, for example, have key resources or knowledge, or perform tasks. This value identifies nodes that are connected to nodes with large numbers of connections. Thus, in a given group, the node that is best connected with other nodes in own and other groups may be the most prominent (e.g., important or influential) node in the network (Formula 2.12, Bonacich, 1987):

$$C^{eig} = \lambda \sum_{j=1}^{N} a_{ij} * e_j \; for(i \neq j) \quad (2.12)$$

Where:
e_i—eigenvector centrality of the analyzed node i
λ —eigenvalue, a scalar that can be calculated using the matrix equation $Ae = \lambda e$
e_j—eigenvector centrality of node j

Borgatti (2005) considers eigenvector centrality perfectly suited for analysis of influence processes, especially in the case of information-based influence. Nodes with high eigenvector centralities are more likely to act as brokers in the exchange of information, gaining more influence in the process. People largely rely on their own social networks for information and problem solutions. The more extensive information and knowledge exchange is, the more individual knowledge is transformed into collective knowledge. Direct interaction should also increase knowledge sharing (Cross, Borgatti, & Parker, 2002). An actor's position in the network affects the knowledge outcomes. Individuals in more central positions have quicker access to larger amounts of richer and more diversified information, which increases the learning level of actors in the network, as well as their potential for synthesizing and recombining this information into new ideas (Phelps, Heidl, & Wadhwa, 2012). People become more creative when their networks comprise many connections between individuals or organizations, as the peripheral connections ensure access to diverse information. Each individual's position in the network determines their access to resources (information and knowledge) and the support they can receive from other network members (Hortoványi, Szabó, and Szabó, 2006).

2.3.2.9 *Betweenness Centrality*

Betweenness is a measure of indirect connections between nodes, which indicates the node that is best connected with other nodes, acts as a broker or gatekeeper, and is the most central node of the entire network, potentially having significant influence over other nodes. An information or knowledge broker can act as an important communications link between subgroups of people in the network, mediating and coordinating information exchange, or interfering with information flow. Network positions reveal who controls, facilitates, or inhibits information flow, and who has similar information needs (Lai, 2016).

Betweenness is measured by the number of indirect connections between nodes that pass through a given node (e.g., indicating that the actor is a broker between the other nodes) (Formula 2.13; Freeman, 1978):

$$C^b = \sum \frac{C_{u,i} * C_{i,v}}{C_{u,v}} for(u,v), where D_{u,v} = D_{u,i} + D_{i,v} \tag{2.13}$$

Where:

D—distance network for the input network; *D*(*i*,*j*) = the shortest path from *i* to *j*, or zero if no path exists

C—network of shortest path counts for the input network; *C*(*i*,*j*) = the number of shortest paths from *i* to *j*, or zero if no path exists

Actors that often act as bridges based on the shortest paths between other entities (have high betweenness centrality) are strong, key actors capable of isolating, influencing, or even preventing contact between teams or departments. This demonstrates the extent to which a node passes information to others when acting as a bridge between the communicating parties. A node with a low centrality degree can have a high betweenness centrality value, as it acts as a link to other nodes. A node with a high betweenness centrality can facilitate or restrict interactions between nodes (Freeman, 1978). Actor positions show, for instance, to what extent an actor is capable of transferring information or exchanging it selectively, and of influencing others. Network positions often correspond with specific social roles, functions, or tasks in the social network.

2.3.2.10 *Work, Knowledge, and Resource Load*

Due to the increasing complexity of production and development of multiple products and services, demand arises for people specializing in a specific field of knowledge, depending on the particular division of labor. Contact with specialists becomes indispensable. The nature of the knowledge-sharing process depends on the involved actors. The dependency level of actors in the organization or team determines whether knowledge is transferred. Knowing *who knows what* is a form of knowledge in itself. It helps locate knowledge among the many potential sources inside the organization and successfully transfer all the elements required to solve problems and support decisions (Mentzas, Apostolou, Kafentzis, & Georgolios, 2006). The transfer of knowledge is also affected by its articulation, or the extent to which it can be verbalized or codified in any form (physical or electronic). The tacit aspect of knowledge results in uncertainty regarding its applicability in a given problem situation, as it is not always possible to use tacit knowledge to solve a specific problem at a specific time. Internalization of knowledge within one's own reasoning framework and its application requires time.

The work, knowledge (Formula 2.14), and resource (Formula 2.15) load indicates assignment of knowledge and resources to tasks performed by a specific person. Individuals or organizations with high values of these metrics are those who perform more complex tasks and have both the knowledge and the resources these tasks require. Task complexity increases with the scope of knowledge and resources required (Carley 2002):

$$K^{load} = [\mathrm{AK} * KT * AT'](i,\mathrm{j}) \ / \ \mathrm{sum}\ (KT) \tag{2.14}$$

or

$$R^{load} = [\mathrm{AR} * RT * AT'](i,\mathrm{j}) \ / \ \mathrm{sum}(RT) \tag{2.15}$$

Actual workload (W^{load}) is calculated based on K^{load}, by replacing network AK with combined networks [AK and AR], and KT with combined networks [KT; RT].

2.3.2.11 Actor Knowledge Needs (waste) Congruence—Actor Resource Needs(waste) Congruence

Here, congruence is a relation of equivalence between the organization's design (the way it is organized) and its capability of performing tasks. The metrics indicate the amount of knowledge or resources that an agent lacks for performing the assigned task, and are calculated as a percentage showing the relation between the knowledge or resources required to perform a task and the total amount of knowledge or resources an agent has (Formulas 2.16 and 2.17). This is a sum of knowledge that is needed, but not available. Full congruence exists when the agent has exactly the knowledge or resources required for performing the task (Jiang et al., 2012; Altman, Carley, & Reminga, 2018):

$$CK^{\mathrm{needs}} = \mathrm{actor}\ i = sum\big(NK(i,:)\ .*\sim AK(i,:)\big) / sum\big(NK(i,:)\big) \tag{2.16}$$

Where:
NK = AT*KT'—knowledge needed by the actor to perform the task

$$CR^{\mathrm{needs}} = \mathrm{actor}\ i = sum\big(NR(i,:)\ .*\sim AR(i,:)\big) / sum\big(NR(i,:)\big) \tag{2.17}$$

Where:
NR = AT*RT'—resources needed by the actor to perform the task

In the opposite case, the metrics indicate knowledge or resources that an actor has, but does not need for the performed tasks. Unused knowledge or resources are considered wasted (Formulas 2.18 and 2.19; Jiang et al., 2012; Altman, Carley, & Reminga, 2018):

$$CK^{\text{waste}} = \text{actor } i = sum\left(\sim NK(i,:)\ .\ {}^{*}AK(i,:)\right) / \, sum\left(NK(i,:)\right) \quad (2.18)$$

Where:
NK = AT*KT'—wasted knowledge, that is, knowledge not needed by the actor to perform the task

$$CR^{\text{waste}} = \text{actor } i = sum\left(\sim NR(i,:)\ .\ {}^{*}AR(i,:)\right) / \, sum\left(NR(i,:)\right) \quad (2.19)$$

Where:
NR = AT*RT'—wasted resources, that is, resources not needed by the actor to perform the task

2.3.3 Knowledge and Information Resource and Flow Mapping as an Essential Audit Tool

Information or knowledge mapping[11] techniques are used in nearly all the audit methods discussed here. The Intellectual Capital Statement proposes a slightly different form of this instrument, called an intellectual capital management portfolio, which uses a two-dimensional chart mapping intellectual capital components according to their weights and QQS (quantity, quality, systematic management) scores. The matrix features four intervention areas: analysis, development, stabilization, and "action not required," associated with the highest mean QQS score and lowest weighted measure. Brooking's model (1996) does not include a map but does include an intellectual asset inventory. Some authors' descriptions of information audit (e.g., Buchanan and Gibb, 1998; Henczel, 2001) omit transfer of knowledge between people, and specifically the tacit aspect of knowledge, which is also a significant component of the map. This section discusses connections between knowledge (information) mapping, knowledge (information) flows, and SNA and ONA in the context of mapping.

Nearly every audit model features its own definition and interpretation of information or knowledge maps. Many definitions of these maps and techniques for their creation exist. Regardless of the differences, the primary purpose is to visualize information and knowledge resources and flows. Vail (1999) defines the knowledge map as a visualization of captured information and relationships. Knowledge map items are called "intellectual capital," which can take the form of text, stories, images, models, or numbers. Connections denote knowledge sources, including in particular relationships with experts capable of interpreting intellectual capital components. Kim et al. (2003) define the knowledge map as a visual representation of corporate knowledge, where nodes represent knowledge, and connections (links) are associated with knowledge, its profile, or parameters. Davenport and Prusak (2013), in turn, state that knowledge mapping consists of locating relevant knowledge in the organization and subsequently publishing information (e.g., a list of experts) on where knowledge can be found. They also name expert registries, databases, or actual representations of knowledge flows between employees as forms of knowledge maps, which is, in fact, closer to knowledge inventory.

Nonetheless, the authors consider the map a guide to knowledge resources rather than a knowledge repository. Ebener et al. (2006) view the knowledge map as a set of connected items of information, preferably visual, that creates new, practical information. A similar view is proposed by Vail (1999), stating that knowledge maps enable the visualization of both explicit and tacit knowledge and its flow in an organization. The author defines knowledge mapping as the process of associating items of information or knowledge in such a way that the mapping itself also contributes to the creation of additional knowledge. The mapping process[12] may create value from intellectual capital by developing new knowledge through the discovery of previously unknown relations. Effective knowledge mapping can bring about economic, structural, and organizational benefits (Wexler, 2001).

The definitions cited above demonstrate that no single definition of the knowledge map exists and that it is sometimes erroneously associated with a knowledge inventory. The map is created on the basis of an inventory, and not the other way around. In this case, the map is static, and depicts the resources and their distribution in an organization. It becomes dynamic when connections, relations, and flows of information and knowledge resources are identified, and changes can be simulated. Most authors view the knowledge map as a visualization of knowledge flows (e.g., Vail, 1999; Kim et al., 2003; Hansen and Kautz, 2004). In this book, the knowledge map is seen as a tool for visualizing organizational knowledge (in the static approach) and its flows (in the dynamic approach). Such a map only identifies knowledge and its aspects, without including the multifaceted view of intangible resources (comprising, e.g., human actors and the tasks they perform using knowledge and other resources).

Knowledge inventory, knowledge mapping, and knowledge gap analysis are the primary data processing tools in knowledge audit. Knowledge inventory is listed as an important stage of audit performance by Cheung et al. (2007) and Perez-Soltero et al. (2007). The authors do not, however, provide sufficient guidance for its performance, similarly to Wiig et al. (1997) and Choy et al. (2004). The knowledge inventory is a snapshot of the status quo, thus reflecting the state of resources in the target area—in this case, explicit and tacit knowledge—at a given time, which can be used in knowledge mapping (Cheung et al., 2007; Wiig et al., 1997; Choy et al., 2004). As stated by Wiig et al. (1997), when performing a knowledge inventory, one should answer basic questions regarding the field of knowledge, identification of knowledge assets, time and location, and the organizational roles (employees) or artifacts (systems, documents) related to the objects or subjects providing the knowledge. Choy et al. (2004) propose a similar interpretation of knowledge inventory, which should determine who is responsible for what process in which department, what knowledge they have, and how knowledge items are ranked.

Organizational network analysis and knowledge network analysis (KNA) are more sophisticated ways of visualizing the flows of information, knowledge, resources, and tasks. KNA is a technique allowing for demonstrating knowledge flows and bottlenecks within an organization in a structured way based on the network perspective (Helms & Buijsrogge, 2005). The technique is based on SNA, and uses network graphs of knowledge for visualizing the flows of specific knowledge between entities (employees, systems). Thus, the network graph of knowledge replaces the notion of a knowledge map in knowledge audit. Helms and Buijsrogge (2005) define three basic concepts used in network knowledge graph modeling:

- the knowledge area, which determines the scope of the network knowledge graph;
- knowledge actors, including either employees or systems that create, use, or share knowledge in the specified knowledge area;
- knowledge flows, or regular transfers of knowledge between members identified in a study (e.g., survey).

Authors increasingly notice the importance of SNA in knowledge auditing (e.g., Cheung et al., 2007; Tsui & Liebowitz, 2005). Network diagrams can be seen as knowledge maps, as they show how knowledge flows in the organization—and, as suggested by Hansen and Kautz (2004), actors and flows are basic elements of the knowledge map and knowledge network. For Zhuge (2002), knowledge map contents include knowledge flows understood as the process of knowledge transfer between individuals or systems, having three critical attributes: direction, content, and link. Another common point with SNA is Hansen and Kautz's (2004) view of knowledge flows as a notion related to knowledge exchange. It is also clear that the knowledge map does not determine the effectiveness of knowledge flows. As rightfully remarked by Tsui and Liebowitz (2005), SNA compensates for this weakness by providing measurement techniques and mathematical instruments. SNA and KNA allow for identifying bottlenecks, gaps, and barriers to knowledge flow, and thus, SNA and KNA play an important role in the development of a new intangible resource audit model. Not all audits discussed in this chapter apply classical SNA and KNA: out of the 14 methods, only four incorporate network analysis, including Cheung et al. (2007), who do not explain what KNA is or how it can be performed.

Effective knowledge transfer and sharing, both in terms of explicit and tacit knowledge, is an important knowledge management process contributing to improved organizational performance and innovation (Chong et al., 2011; Becerra-Fernandez et al., 2004). Knowledge and information transfer and sharing are also key elements in mapping (development of a resource flow map). The purpose of knowledge transfer is to support and facilitate knowledge sharing, collaboration, and networking, which in turn enhances decision-making and problem-solving. Organizations represent various interrelation scenarios (e.g., between technology and environment), and every such scenario involves various forms of knowledge (e.g., know-who, know-what, know-how) and requires various activities aimed at improving the knowledge exchange. Knowledge sharing is understood as a process combining various organizational interrelations associated with the current operations of the organization (Christensen, 2007). As emphasized by Thompson (2007), organizations are dominated by processes rather than formal structures. Knowledge sharing is often viewed as a separate process, somewhat distant from the current operations. But rather than seeing it as an isolated part of an organization's activities, concerning the transfer of knowledge resources, one should rather recognize that it is inherent in the daily tasks of the organization, as shown by the present work. Personal, intra-organizational, and inter-organizational networks play an important role in accessing and sharing knowledge. Without networks, there would be no access to resources, which can be maintained by formal or informal relations or by organizational infrastructure (intranet, Wikis, communities of practice, and many other modern communications and information solutions).

The flow of resources within an organization and between organizations intensifies due to the increasingly common access to technology and communication tools. A map enables the visualization of resources and their relations, but not the measurement of these elements and relations. As stated above, SNA and ONA techniques complement the maps by providing a range of metrics that can be used to measure the properties of a network and its components (nodes or vertices). Their calculated values (at the network and node levels) can be used to identify employees acting as information and knowledge sources and those who are isolated in terms of the analyzed relationships.

Intangible resource mapping takes a different form when using ONA. Mapping is a process of examining and analyzing networks of relations and interactions among intangible resources and visualizing them in a network of relations among information, knowledge, resources (structural capital), and their complementary tasks. Thus, ONA depicts information and knowledge exchanges in the organization, the use of knowledge and resources in tasks, and providers and recipients of information and knowledge. This produces an organizational intangible resource map, which is a visual representation of resources and their flows. It identifies relationships of resources within business processes and the entire organization, which provides insights as to improvements that should be introduced at all organizational levels (node, dyad, entire network).

Organizational intangible resources contribute significantly to value creation, and are static until activated (by identification of their relations with other resources used for creating value or increasing performance for the organization). One can identify actors, components of knowledge, resources, and tasks, as well as their potential direct or indirect impact on value creation. Thus understood, resources and their flows are key factors in the achievement of business objectives and include the components of human capital, such as expertise, capabilities, skills, and capabilities (Cricelli & Grimaldi, 2008). Based on dynamic capabilities theory (Barreto, 2010; Chatterji & Patro, 2014; Chiou, 2011; Eisenhardt & Martin, 2000; Teece, Pisano, & Shuen, 1997; Zollo & Winter, 2002), the proposed intangible resource audit methodology aims at identifying resources, as contributors to value creation, and resource flows, seen in the context of interrelations between the identified resources (Nissen, 2002). This approach, based on resource flows and relationships, extends beyond quantitative or qualitative valuation of intangible resources and allows for assessing the significance of resources and their direct or indirect impact on value creation and effective management. Therefore, the audit does not focus on intangible resource classification (though it is incorporated), but on the nature of connections of these resources.

In the proposed intangible resource audit methodology, ONA replaces the notion of knowledge and information mapping, as it is a more mature and multidimensional instrument for identifying, analyzing, and measuring the flows of organizational intangible resources. This entails the need for defining a new map type—the intangible resource map. *The intangible resource map* is an instrument for multidimensional analysis of intangible resources and their interactions (flows of information, knowledge, resources, and tasks) in an organization, using graphs and matrices. It is developed with the use of social, organizational, and dynamic network analysis techniques, including but not limited to visualization. These techniques are an integral part of the interactive intangible resource map, which makes the map dynamic—the auditor can simulate changes in the network by creating positive and negative scenarios and examining changes in the visualization of the network and its nodes (intangible resources).

Notes

1. All 14 audit models (including 3 information audits, 9 knowledge audits, and 2 intellectual capital audits) were selected out of the 38 incomplete literature descriptions published in the years 1990–2014, based on criteria listed in Section 2.3.1.
2. Knowledge management is not the focus of the present book. Knowledge audit is usually a preliminary investigation, potentially aiming at or resulting in an implementation of a knowledge management strategy in an organization.
3. The fundamental differences between the proposed *meta-model* for intangible resource audit and the models listed here are discussed in detail in Section 5.1.
4. All 14 information, knowledge, and intellectual capital audit models, with their respective numbers, are listed in Tables 2.1, 2.2, and 2.3.
5. This concept of intangible resource audit was presented by the author at the 17th European Conference on Knowledge Management, which took place on September 1–2, 2016, at Ulster University, Belfast, UK (Ujwary-Gil, 2016).
6. In the intangible resource audit model proposed here, especially at the design stage, more emphasis is placed on the external context of the organization.
7. Intangible resource audit metrics are listed and discussed in the following section (2.3.2).
8. These questions concern a portion of the business model template according to Osterwalder and Pigneur (2010). Of course, the business model may be analyzed in more detail within the intangible resource audit, but for the present discussion, it is justified to focus mainly on determining the value proposition offered by the organization to its customers.
9. The performance stage of the intangible resource audit is the primary focus of the present book. It is discussed in Chapter 4, which presents an analysis of network structure and dynamics of associations between network nodes. The implementation stage is only outlined, and will be presented in detail in a separate publication, as the extensive analyses required are beyond the scope of the present book.
10. The ranges are not applicable to organizational network analysis, as such studies have not yet been performed at a large scale in the IT sector, in which the studied case operates. Hence the need for more extensive quantitative studies that would demonstrate the ranges applicable to the specific field, sector, environment, and operating conditions of the organization. It is, however, worth familiarizing the reader with interpretations of social network density found in literature, as such networks are also included in the present book.
11. Knowledge and information maps are similar concepts, with similar functions, as shown in this section. The primary difference between them is the scope of each map, that is, explicit and tacit knowledge for knowledge audit, and information for information audit, respectively, bearing in mind that explicit knowledge in knowledge audit also includes information, as explained in Section 2.1.
12. A "map" is an instrument used for visualizing organizational knowledge and information resources, which are often dispersed. "Mapping" is a process of creating a map by visualizing flows and relations.

References

Adam, E. E., Hershauer, J. C., & Ruch, W. A. (1981). Developing quality productivity ratios for public sector personnel services. *Public Productivity Review*, *5*(1), 45–61. https://doi.org/10.2307/3380165

Alcaniz, L., Gomez-Bezares, F., & Roslender, R. (2011). Theoretical perspectives on intellectual capital: A backward look and a proposal for going forward. *Accounting Forum*, *35*(2), 104–117. https://doi.org/10.1016/j.accfor.2011.03.004

Altman, N., Carley, K. M., & Reminga, J. (2018). *ORA user's guide 2018*. Technical Report CMU-ISR-18–103. Pittsburgh, Pennsylvania: Carnegie Mellon University, School of Computer Science, Institute for Software Research.

Anderson, J. V. (1987). Technology and mindset: A model for generating new product and service ideas. *National Productivity Review*, *6*(2), 111–124. https://doi.org/10.1002/npr.4040060203

Aubke, F., Woeber, K., Scott, N., & Baggio, R. (2014). Knowledge sharing in revenue management teams: Antecedents and consequences of group cohesion. *International Journal of Hospitality Management*, *41*, 149–157. https://doi.org/10.1016/j.ijhm.2014.05.010

Avnet, M. S., & Weigel, A. L. (2013). The structural approach to shared knowledge: An application to engineering design teams. *Human Factors*, *55*(3), 581–594. https://doi.org/10.1177/0018720812462388

Barney, J. (1991). Firm resources and sustained competitive advantage. *Journal of Management*, *17*(1), 99–120. https://doi.org/10.1177/014920639101700108

Barreto, I. (2010). Dynamic capabilities: A review of past research and an agenda for the future. *Journal of Management*, *36*(1), 256–280. https://doi.org/10.1177/0149206309350776

Barua, A., Ravindran, S., & Whinston, A. B. (2007). Enabling information sharing within organizations. *Information Technology and Management*, *8*(1), 31–45.

Becerra-Fernandez, I., González, A. J., & Sabherwal, R. (2004). *Knowledge management: Challenges, solutions, and technologies*. Englewood Cliffs, NJ: Pearson/Prentice Hall.

Bhatt, G. D. (2001). Knowledge management in organizations: Examining the interaction between technologies, techniques, and people. *Journal of Knowledge Management*, *5*(1), 68–75.

Bierly III, P. E., Kessler, E. H., & Christensen, E. W. (2000). Organizational learning, knowledge and wisdom. *Journal of Organizational Change Management*, *13*(6), 595–618.

Bock, G. W., Zmud, R. W., Kim, Y. G., & Lee, J. N. (2005). Behavioral intention formation in knowledge sharing: Examining the roles of extrinsic motivators, social-psychological forces, and organizational climate. *MIS Quarterly*, *29*(1), 87–111.

Boisot, M., & Canals, A. (2004). Data, information and knowledge: Have we got it right? *Journal of Evolutionary Economics*, *14*(1), 43–67.

Bollinger, A. S., & Smith, R. D. (2001). Managing organizational knowledge as a strategic asset. *Journal of Knowledge Management*, *5*(1), 8–18.

Bonacich, P. (1972). Factoring and weighting approaches to status scores and clique identification. *Journal of Mathematical Sociology*, *2*(1), 113–120.

Bonacich, P. (1987). Power and centrality: A family of measures. *American Journal of Sociology*, *92*(5), 1170–1182.

Bontis, N. (1999). Managing organizational knowledge by diagnosing intellectual capital: Framing and advancing the state of the field. *International Journal of Technology Management*, *18*(5–8), 433.

Bontis, N. (2001). Assessing knowledge assets: A review of the models used to measure intellectual capital. *International Journal of Management Reviews*, *3*(1), 41–60. https://doi.org/10.1111/1468-2370.00053

Borgatti, S. P. (2005). Centrality and network flow. *Social Networks*, *27*(1), 55–71. https://doi.org/10.1016/j.socnet.2004.11.008

Borgatti, S. P., & Cross, R. (2003). A relational view of information seeking and learning in social networks. *Management Science*, *49*(4), 432–445.

Borgatti, S.P., Everett, M. G., & Johnson, J. C. (2018). *Analyzing social networks* (2nd ed.). London: Sage Publications.

Botha, H., & Boon, J. A. (2003). The information audit: Principles and guidelines. *Libri*, *53*(1), 23–38.

Braman, S. (1989). Defining information: An approach for policymakers. *Telecommunications Policy*, *13*(3), 233–242.

Bright, D. A., Greenhill, C., Reynolds, M., Ritter, A., & Morselli, C. (2015). The use of actor-level attributes and centrality measures to identify key actors: A case study of an Australian drug trafficking network. *Journal of Contemporary Criminal Justice*, *31*(3), 262–278. https://doi.org/10.1177/1043986214553378

Brooking, A. (1996). *Intellectual capital: Core asset for the third millennium* (1st ed.). London: International Thomas Business Press.

Brooking, A. (1997). The management of intellectual capital. *Long Range Planning*, *30*(3), 364–365.

Brown, A. D., & Starkey, K. (1994). The effect of organizational culture on communication and information. *Journal of Management Studies*, *31*(6), 807–828. https://doi.org/10.1111/j.1467-6486.1994.tb00640.x

Brown, J. S., & Duguid, P. (1998). Organizing knowledge. *California Management Review*, *40*(3), 90–111.

Buchanan, S., & Gibb, F. (1998). The information audit: An integrated strategic approach. *International Journal of Information Management*, *18*(1), 29–47. https://doi.org/10.1016/S0268-4012(97)00038-8

Buchanan, S., & Gibb, F. (2007). The information audit: Role and scope. *International Journal of Information Management*, *27*(3), 159–172. https://doi.org/10.1016/j.ijinfomgt.2007.01.002

Burk, C. F., & Horton, F. W. (1988). *Infomap: A complete guide to discovering corporate information resources*. Englewood Cliffs, NJ: Prentice Hall.

Burnett, S., Illingworth, L., & Webster, L. (2004). Knowledge auditing and mapping: A pragmatic approach. *Knowledge and Process Management*, *11*(1), 25–37. https://doi.org/10.1002/kpm.194

Burnett, S., Williams, D., & Grinnall, A. (2013). The strategic role of knowledge auditing and mapping: An organisational case study. *Knowledge and Process Management*, *20*(3), 161–176. https://doi.org/10.1002/kpm.1416

Burnett, S., Williams, D., & Illingworth, L. (2013). Reconsidering the knowledge audit process: Methodological revisions in practice. *Knowledge and Process Management*, *20*(3), 141–153.

Campbell, B. A., Coff, R., & Kryscynski, D. (2012). Rethinking sustained competitive advantage from human capital. *Academy of Management Review*, *37*(3), 376–395.

Carley, K. M. (1990). Coordinating the success: Trading information redundancy for task simplicity. *Proceedings of the Twenty-Third Annual Hawaii International Conference on Systems Sciences*, *4*, 261–270. Retrieved from http://ieeexplore.ieee.org/abstract/document/205265/

Carley, K. M. (2002). Summary of key network measures for characterizing organizational architectures. *Computational Analysis of Social and Organizational Systems Working Paper*. Pittsburgh, PA: Carnegie Mellon University.

Carley, K. M., & Ren, Y. (2001). Tradeoffs between performance and adaptability for C3I architectures. *Proceedings of the 6th International Command and Control Research and Technology Symposium*. Vienna: Command and Control Research Program.

Carlsson, S. A. (2003). Knowledge managing and knowledge management systems in inter-organizational networks. *Knowledge and Process Management*, *10*(3), 194–206.

Chan, P. C. W., & Lee, W. B. (2011). Knowledge audit with intellectual capital in the quality management process: An empirical study in an electronics company. *The Electronic Journal of Knowledge Management*, *9*(2), 98–116.

Chang, S. C., Chen, S. S., & Lai, J. H. (2008). The effect of alliance experience and intellectual capital on the value creation of international strategic alliances. *Omega-International Journal of Management Science*, *36*(2), 298–316. https://doi.org/10.1016/j.omega.2006.06.010

Chatterji, A., & Patro, A. (2014). Dynamic capabilities and managing human capital. *Academy of Management Perspectives*, *28*(4), 395–408. https://doi.org/10.5465/amp.2013.0111

Chan, P. C. W., & Lee, W. B. (2011). Knowledge audit with intellectual capital in the quality management process: An empirical study in an electronics company. *The Electronic Journal of Knowledge Management*, *9*(2), 98–116.

Chen, Z., & Guan, J. (2016). The core-peripheral structure of international knowledge flows: Evidence from patent citation data. *R&D Management*, *46*(1), 62–79. https://doi.org/10.1111/radm.12119

Cheung, C. F., Li, M. L., Shek, W. Y., Lee, W. B., & Tsang, T. S. (2007). A systematic approach for knowledge auditing: A case study in transportation sector. *Journal of Knowledge Management*, *11*(4), 140–158.

Chiou, C. H. (2011). Dynamic capabilities, collaborative network and business model: An empirical analysis of Taiwan HTC corporation. *African Journal of Business Management*, *5*(2), 294–305.

Chong, S. C., Salleh, K., Noh Syed Ahmad, S., & Syed Omar Sharifuddin, S. I. (2011). KM implementation in a public sector accounting organization: An empirical investigation. *Journal of Knowledge Management*, *15*(3), 497–512.

Choy, S. Y., Lee, W. B., & Cheung, C. F. (2004). A systematic approach for knowledge audit analysis: Integration of knowledge inventory, mapping and knowledge flow analysis. *Journal of Universal Computer Science*, *10*(6), 674–682.

Christensen, P. H. (2007). Knowledge sharing: Moving away from the obsession with best practices. *Journal of Knowledge Management*, *11*(1), 36–47. https://doi.org/10.1108/13673270710728222

Cook, S. D. N., & Brown, J. S. (1999). Bridging epistemologies: The generative dance between organizational knowledge and organizational knowing. *Organization Science*, *10*(4), 381–400. https://doi.org/10.1287/orsc.10.4.381

Cosserat. (2009). *Modern auditing* (3rd ed.). New York: John Wiley & Sons.

Cowan, R., & Jonard, N. (2004). Network structure and the diffusion of knowledge. *Journal of Economic Dynamics and Control*, *28*(8), 1557–1575.

Cricelli, L., & Grimaldi, M. (2008). A dynamic view of knowledge and information: A stock and flow based methodology. *International Journal of Management and Decision Making*, *9*(6), 686. https://doi.org/10.1504/IJMDM.2008.021221

Cross, R. L., Borgatti, S. P., & Parker, A. (2002). Making invisible work visible: Using social network analysis to support strategic collaboration. *California Management Review*, *44*(2), 25–46.

Cross, R. L., & Parker, A. (2004). *The hidden power of social networks: Understanding how work really gets done in organizations*. Boston: Harvard Business Press.

Dalkir, K., & Liebowitz, J. (2011). *Knowledge management in theory and practice* (2nd ed.). Cambridge, MA: The MIT Press.

Davenport, T. H., & Prusak, L. (2013). *Working knowledge: How organizations manage what they know*. Boston: Harvard Business Press.

Dawson, G. (1981). Justified true belief is knowledge. *Philosophical Quarterly*, *31*(125), 315–329. https://doi.org/10.2307/2219402

Debenham, J., & Clark, J. (1994). The knowledge audit. *Robotics and Computer-Integrated Manufacturing*, *11*(3), 201–211.

Diez-Vial, I., & Montoro-Sanchez, A. (2014). Social capital as a driver of local knowledge exchange: A social network analysis. *Knowledge Management Research & Practice*, *12*(3), 276–288. https://doi.org/10.1057/kmrp.2014.7

Droege, S. B., & Hoobler, J. M. (2003). Employee turnover and tacit knowledge diffusion: A network perspective. *Journal of Managerial Issues*, 50–64.

Dubois, C. P. R. (1995). The information audit: Its contribution to decision making. *Library Management*, *16*(7), 20–24. https://doi.org/10.1108/01435129510093746

Eaton, J. J., & Bawden, D. (1991). What kind of resource is information? *International Journal of Information Management*, *11*(2), 156–165.

Ebener, S., Khan, A., Shademani, R., Compernolle, L., Beltran, M., Lansang, M., & Lippman, M. (2006). Knowledge mapping as a technique to support knowledge translation. *Bulletin of the World Health Organization*, *84*(8), 636–642.

Edvinsson, L., & Malone, M. S. (1997). *Intellectual capital: Realizing your company's true value by finding its hidden brainpower* (1st ed). New York: HarperBusiness.

Eisenhardt, K. M., & Martin, J. A. (2000). Dynamic capabilities: What are they? *Strategic Management Journal*, *21*(10–11), 1105–1121. https://doi.org/10.1002/1097-0266(200010/11)21:10/11<1105::AID-SMJ133>3.0.CO;2-E

Ellis, D., Barker, R., Potter, S., & Pridgeon, C. (1993). Information audits, communication audits and information mapping: A review and survey. *International Journal of Information Management*, *13*(2), 134–151.

Espinosa, J. A., & Clark, M. A. (2014). Team knowledge representation a network perspective. *Human Factors: The Journal of the Human Factors and Ergonomics Society*, *56*(2), 333–348. https://doi.org/10.1177/0018720813494093

Fleming, L., Mingo, S., & Chen, D. (2007). Collaborative brokerage, generative creativity, and creative success. *Administrative Science Quarterly*, *52*(3), 443–475.

Flint, D. (1988). *Philosophy and principles of auditing: An introduction*. London, UK: Palgrave Macmillan.

Freeman, L. C. (1978). Centrality in social networks conceptual clarification. *Social Networks*, *1*(3), 215–239. https://doi.org/10.1016/0378-8733(78)90021-7

Gilsing, V., Nooteboom, B., Vanhaverbeke, W., Duysters, G., & van den Oord, A. (2008). Network embeddedness and the exploration of novel technologies: Technological distance, betweenness centrality and density. *Research Policy*, *37*(10), 1717–1731.

Gourova, E. (2010). Knowledge management strategy for small and medium enterprises. In N. Deo, M. Demiralp, M. Stork, E. Milkova, H. Wakamatsu, & K. Tchizawa (Eds.), *Recent advances in circuits, systems and signals* (pp. 19–19). Malta: Applied Computer Science (ACS).

Gourova, E., Antonova, A., & Todorova, Y. (2009). Knowledge audit concepts, processes and practice. *WSEAS Transactions on Business and Economics*, *12*(6), 605–619.

Grant, R. M. (1996). Toward a knowledge-based theory of the firm. *Strategic Management Journal*, *17*(S2), 109–122. https://doi.org/10.1002/smj.4250171110

Granovetter, M. S. (1973). The strength of weak ties. *American Journal of Sociology*, 1360–1380.

Hansen, M. T. (1999). The search-transfer problem: The role of weak ties in sharing knowledge across organization subunits. *Administrative Science Quarterly*, *44*(1), 82–111.

Hansen, B. H., & Kautz, K. (2004). Knowledge mapping: A technique for identifying knowledge flows in software organisations. In T. Dingsøyr (Ed.), *Software process improvement* (Vol. 3281, pp. 126–137). Berlin, Heidelberg: Springer Berlin Heidelberg.

Harris, R. G. (2001). The knowledge-based economy: Intellectual origins and new economic perspectives. *International Journal of Management Reviews*, *3*(1), 21–40.

Hatala, J. P., & George Lutta, J. (2009). Managing information sharing within an organizational setting: A social network perspective. *Performance Improvement Quarterly*, *21*(4), 5–33. https://doi.org/10.1002/piq.20036

Helms, R., & Buijsrogge, K. (2005). Knowledge network analysis: A technique to analyze knowledge management bottlenecks in organizations. *Database and Expert Systems Applications. Proceedings. Sixteenth International Workshop*, 410–414. Retrieved from http://ieeexplore.ieee.org/abstract/document/1508307/

Henczel, S. (2001). *The information audit: A practical guide*. Munich: K.G. Saur.

Hermans, R., & Kauranen, K. (2005). Value creation potential of intellectual capital in biotechnology—Empirical evidence from Finland. *R&D Management*, *35*(2), 171–185. https://doi.org/10.1111/j.1467-9310.2005.00381.x

Hess, P. (1981). Justified true belief is knowledge. *Dialogue-Canadian Philosophical Review*, *20*(4), 665–673.

Hirschman, A. O. (1945). *National power and the structure of foreign trade*. Berkeley, Los Angeles: University of California Press.

Hong, S., Van den Goor, G., & Brinkkemper, S. (1993). A formal approach to the comparison of object-oriented analysis and design methodologies. *Proceeding of the Twenty-Sixth Hawaii International Conference on System

Sciences, *4*, 689–698. Retrieved from http://ieeexplore.ieee.org/xpls/abs_all.jsp?arnumber=284253

Hormiga, E., Batista-Canino, R. M., & Sánchez-Medina, A. (2010). The role of intellectual capital in the success of new ventures. *International Entrepreneurship and Management Journal*, *7*(1), 71–92. https://doi.org/10.1007/s11365-010-0139-y

Hortoványi, L., Szabó, R. Z., & Szabó, R. Z. (2006). Knowledge and organization: A network perspective. *Society and Economy*, *28*(2), 165–179.

Hsu, S. H., & Tzeng, S. F. (2010). A dyadic perspective on knowledge exchange. *International Journal of Technology Management*, *49*(4), 370–383.

Hsu, Y. H., & Fang, W. (2009). Intellectual capital and new product development performance: The mediating role of organizational learning capability. *Technological Forecasting and Social Change*, *76*(5), 664–677. https://doi.org/10.1016/j.techfore.2008.03.012

Jashapara, A. (2004). *Knowledge management: An integral approach*. London, UK: Pearson Education.

Jiang, L., Carley, K. M., & Eberlein, A. (2012, June). Assessing team performance from a socio-technical congruence perspective. *International Conference on Software and System Process* (pp. 160–169). Retrieved from https://doi.org/10.1109/ICSSP.2012.6225961

Kalafatis, S. E., Lemos, M. C., Lo, Y. J., & Frank, K. A. (2015). Increasing information usability for climate adaptation: The role of knowledge networks and communities of practice. *Global Environmental Change*, *32*, 30–39.

Knight, L., & Harland, C. (2005). Managing supply networks: Organizational roles in network management. *European Management Journal*, *23*(3), 281–292.

Kogut, B., & Zander, U. (1992). Knowledge of the firm, combinative capabilities, and the replication of technology. *Organization Science*, *3*(3), 383–397. https://doi.org/10.1287/orsc.3.3.383

Kong, E., & Thomson, S. B. (2009). An intellectual capital perspective of human resource strategies and practices. *Knowledge Management Research & Practice*, *7*(4), 356–364. https://doi.org/10.1057/kmrp.2009.27

Lai, H. C. (2016). When is betweenness centrality useful to firms pursuing technological diversity? An internal-resources view. *Technology Analysis & Strategic Management*, *28*(5), 507–523. https://doi.org/10.1080/09537325.2015.1105949

Lakis, V. (2014). Financial audit under conditions of global economic crisis. *Argumenta Oeconomica*, *32*(1), 5–13.

Levantakis, T., Helms, R., & Spruit, M. (2008). Developing a reference method for knowledge auditing. In T. Yamaguchi (Ed.), *Practical aspects of knowledge management* (Vol. 5345, pp. 147–159). Retrieved from http://link.springer.com/10.1007/978-3-540-89447-6_15

Li, S., & Lin, B. (2006). Accessing information sharing and information quality in supply chain management. *Decision Support Systems*, *42*(3), 1641–1656. https://doi.org/10.1016/j.dss.2006.02.011

Liebowitz, J., Rubenstein-Montano, B., McCaw, D., Buchwalter, J., Browning, C., Newman, B., & Rebeck, K. (2000). The knowledge audit. *Knowledge and Process Management*, *7*(1), 3–10.

Lillrank, P. (2003). The quality of information. *International Journal of Quality & Reliability Management*, *20*(6), 691–703. https://doi.org/10.1108/02656710310482131

Machlup, F. (1984). *The study of information: Interdisciplinary messages* (1st ed.). New York: Wiley-Interscience.

Martín-de Castro, G. (2014). Intellectual capital and the firm: Some remaining questions and prospects. *Knowledge Management Research & Practice*, *12*(3), 239–245. https://doi.org/10.1057/kmrp.2014.13

Martín-de-Castro, G., Delgado-Verde, M., López-Sáez, P., & Navas-López, J. E. (2010). Towards "an intellectual capital-based view of the firm": Origins and nature. *Journal of Business Ethics*, *98*(4), 649–662. https://doi.org/10.1007/s10551-010-0644-5

Martínez-Torres, M. R. (2006). A procedure to design a structural and measurement model of intellectual capital: An exploratory study. *Information & Management*, *43*(5), 617–626. https://doi.org/10.1016/j.im.2006.03.002

Martin-Rios, C. (2014). Why do firms seek to share human resource management knowledge? The importance of inter-firm networks. *Journal of Business Research*, *67*(2), 190–199. https://doi.org/10.1016/j.jbusres.2012.10.004

Mason, K. J., & Leek, S. (2008). Learning to build a supply network: An exploration of dynamic business models. *Journal of Management Studies*, *45*(4), 774–799. https://doi.org/10.1111/j.1467-6486.2008.00769.x

Mearns, M. A., & Du Toit, A. S. A. (2008). Knowledge audit: Tools of the trade transmitted to tools for tradition. *International Journal of Information Management*, *28*(3), 161–167.

Mehralian, G., Rasekh, H. R., Akhavan, P., & Ghatari, A. R. (2013). Prioritization of intellectual capital indicators in knowledge-based industries: Evidence from pharmaceutical industry. *International Journal of Information Management*, *33*(1), 209–216. https://doi.org/10.1016/j.ijinfomgt.2012.10.002

Mentzas, G., Apostolou, D., Kafentzis, K., & Georgolios, P. (2006). Inter-organizational networks for knowledge sharing and trading. *Information Technology and Management*, *7*(4), 259–276.

Mertins, K., Wang, W. H., & Will, M. (2007). How to ensure the quality and reliability of intellectual capital statements? *Electronic Journal of Knowledge Management*, *5*(4), 437–447.

Mizruchi, M. S., & Bunting, D. (1981). Influence in corporate networks: An examination of four measures. *Administrative Science Quarterly*, *26*(3), 475–489.

Mizruchi, M. S., & Potts, B. B. (1998). Centrality and power revisited: Actor success in group decision making. *Social Networks*, *20*(4), 353–387. https://doi.org/10.1016/S0378-8733(98)00009-4

Morris, M., Schindehutte, M., & Allen, J. (2005). The entrepreneur's business model: Toward a unified perspective. *Journal of Business Research*, *58*(6), 726–735. https://doi.org/10.1016/j.jbusres.2003.11.001

Mudambi, R., & Swift, T. (2009). Professional guilds, tension and knowledge management. *Research Policy*, *38*(5), 736–745.

Murthy, V., & Mouritsen, J. (2011). The performance of intellectual capital. *Accounting, Auditing & Accountability Journal*, *24*(5), 622–646. https://doi.org/10.1108/09513571111139120

Musteen, M., & Ahsan, M. (2013). Beyond cost: The role of intellectual capital in offshoring and innovation in young firms. *Entrepreneurship Theory and Practice*, *37*(2), 421–434. https://doi.org/10.1111/j.1540-6520.2011.00477.x

Nahapiet, J., & Ghoshal, S. (1998). Social capital, intellectual capital, and the organizational advantage. *The Academy of Management Review*, *23*(2), 242–266. https://doi.org/10.2307/259373

Nair, S., Nisar, A., Palacios, M., & Ruiz, F. (2012). Impact of knowledge brokering on performance heterogeneity among business models. *Management Decision*, *50*(9), 1649–1660. https://doi.org/10.1108/00251741211266732

Nielsen, Ch., & Montemari, M. (2012). The role of human resources in business model performance: The case of network-based companies. *Journal of Human Resource Costing & Accounting*, *16*(2), 142–164. https://doi.org/10.1108/14013381211284254

Nissen, M. E. (2002). An extended model of knowledge-flow dynamics. *Communications of the Association for Information Systems*, *8*(1), 251–266.

Nonaka, I. (1994). A dynamic theory of organizational knowledge creation. *Organization Science*, *5*(1), 14–37.

Nonaka, I., & Takeuchi, H. (1995). *The knowledge-creating company: How Japanese companies create the dynamics of innovation.* Oxford, UK: Oxford University Press.

Nonaka, I., vonKrogh, G., & Voelpel, S. (2006). Organizational knowledge creation theory: Evolutionary paths and future advances. *Organization Studies*, *27*(8), 1179–1208. https://doi.org/10.1177/0170840606066312

Oppenheim, C., Stenson, J., & Wilson, R. M. S. (2003a). Studies on information as an asset I: Definitions. *Journal of Information Science*, *29*(3), 159–166. https://doi.org/10.1177/01655515030293003

Oppenheim, C., Stenson, J., & Wilson, R. M. S. (2003b). Studies on information as an asset II: Repertory grid. *Journal of Information Science*, *29*(5), 419–432. https://doi.org/10.1177/01655515030295007

Orna, E. (1999). *Practical information policies* (2nd ed.). Aldershot, Hampshire, England, Brookfield, USA: Gower.

Orna, E. (2004). *Information strategy in practice.* Aldershot, Hampshire, England, Brookfield, USA: Gower.

Orna, E., & Orna, E. (1990). *Practical information policies: How to manage information flow in organizations.* Aldershot: Gower.

Osterwalder, A., & Pigneur, Y. (2010). *Business model generation: A handbook for visionaries, game changers, and challengers.* Hoboken, NJ: John Wiley & Sons.

Pantry, S., & Griffiths, P. (2002). The internal information audit: Conducting the audit and implementing the results. *Business Information Review*, *19*(1), 43–54. https://doi.org/10.1177/0266382024238284

Parise, S. (2007). Knowledge management and human resource development: An application in social network analysis methods. *Advances in Developing Human Resources*, 9(3), 359–383. https://doi.org/10.1177/1523422307304106

Parker, A., Cross, R., & Walsh, D. (2001). Improving collaboration with social network analysis. *Knowledge Management Review*, 4, 24–29.

Parraguez, P., Eppinger, S. D., & Maier, A. M. (2015). Information flow through stages of complex engineering design projects: A dynamic network analysis approach. *Engineering Management, IEEE Transactions On*, 62(4), 604–617.

Peppard, J., & Rylander, A. (2001). Using an intellectual capital perspective to design and implement a growth strategy: The case of APiON. *European Management Journal*, *19*(5), 510–525. https://doi.org/10.1016/S0263-2373(01)00065-2

Perez-Soltero, A., Barcelo-Valenzuela, M., Sanchez-Schmitz, G., Martin-Rubio, F., Palma-Mendez, J. T., Vanti, A. A., & others. (2007). A model and methodology to knowledge auditing considering core processes. *ICFAI Journal of Knowledge Management*, *5*(1), 7–23.

Pfeffer, J., & Sutton, R. I. (2000). *The knowing-doing gap: How smart companies turn knowledge into action* (1st ed.). Boston: Harvard Business School Press.

Phelps, C., Heidl, R., & Wadhwa, A. (2012). Knowledge, networks, and knowledge networks a review and research agenda. *Journal of Management*, *38*(4), 1115–1166.

Polanyi, M. (1958). *Personal knowledge*. London: Routledge.

Porter, M. E., & Millar, V. E. (1985). *How information gives you competitive advantage*. Retrieved from http://faculty.yu.edu.jo/iaad/Lists/Taught%20Courses/Attachments/5/Reading%205-How%20Information%20Gives%20You%20Comp-Fall2015.pdf

Prell, C. (2012). *Social network analysis: History, theory and methodology*. London: Sage Publications.

Prescott, M. E. (2016). Big data: Innovation and competitive advantage in an information media analytics company. *Journal of Innovation Management*, *4*(1), 92–113.

Ragsdell, G., Probets, S., Ahmed, G., & Murray, I. (2014). Knowledge audit: Findings from the energy sector. *Knowledge and Process Management*, *21*(4), 270–279. https://doi.org/10.1002/kpm.1435

Raliphada, L., & Botha, D. (2013). Testing the viability of Henczel's information audit methodology in practice. *South African Journal of Libraries and Information Science*, *72*(3). https://doi.org/10.7553/72-3-1121

Reagans, R., & Zuckerman, E. W. (2001). Networks, diversity, and productivity: The social capital of corporate R&D teams. *Organization Science*, *12*(4), 502–517. https://doi.org/10.1287/orsc.12.4.502.10637

Reiche, B. S., Harzing, A. W., & Kraimer, M. L. (2009). The role of international assignees' social capital in creating inter-unit intellectual capital: A cross-level model. *Journal of International Business Studies*, *40*(3), 509–526. https://doi.org/10.1057/jibs.2008.86

Reid, L. A. (2015). *Ways of knowledge and experience*. London: Routledge.

Ricceri, F. (2011). *Intellectual capital and knowledge management: Strategic management of knowledge resources* (1st ed.). London: Routledge.

Ronfeldt, D., & Arquilla, J. (2001). Networks, netwars and the fight for the future. *First Monday*, *6*(10). Retrieved from http://ojphi.org/ojs/index.php/fm/article/view/889

Schiuma, G. (2009). The managerial foundations of knowledge assets dynamics. *Knowledge Management Research & Practice*, *7*(4), 290–299. https://doi.org/10.1057/kmrp.2009.21

Scott, J. (2012). *Social network analysis*. London: Sage Publications.

Seufert, A., Von Krogh, G., & Bach, A. (1999). Towards knowledge networking. *Journal of Knowledge Management*, *3*(3), 180–190.

Shannon, C. E., & Weaver, W. (2015). *The mathematical theory of communication*. Urbana, IL: University of Illinois Press.

Shek, W. Y., Cheung, C. F., Lee, W. B., & Chong, Y. Y. (2007). Systematic knowledge auditing: A case study in a power utility company. *Journal of Information & Knowledge Management*, *06*(04), 231–239. https://doi.org/10.1142/S0219649207001809

Smith, E. A. (2001). The role of tacit and explicit knowledge in the workplace. *Journal of Knowledge Management*, *5*(4), 311–321.

Soda, G., Usai, A., & Zaheer, A. (2004). Network memory: The influence of past and current networks on performance. *Academy of Management Journal*, *47*(6), 893–906.

Spender, J. C. (1996). Making knowledge the basis of a dynamic theory of the firm. *Strategic Management Journal*, *17*(S2), 45–62.

Spiegler, I. (2003). Technology and knowledge: Bridging a "generating" gap. *Information & Management*, *40*(6), 533–539. https://doi.org/10.1016/S0378-7206(02)00069-1

Spink, A., & Cole, C. (2006). Human information behavior: Integrating diverse approaches and information use. *Journal of the American Society for Information Science and Technology*, *57*(1), 25–35.

Starbuck, W. H. (1992). Learning by knowledge-intensive firms. *Journal of Management Studies*, *29*(6), 713–740. https://doi.org/10.1111/j.1467-6486.1992.tb00686.x

Stewart, T. A. (1997). *Intellectual capital: The new wealth of organizations*. London: Doubleday/Currency.

Subramaniam, M., & Youndt, M. A. (2005). The influence of intellectual capital on the types of innovative capabilities. *The Academy of Management Journal*, *48*(3), 450–463. https://doi.org/10.2307/20159670

Sullivan, P. H. (2000). *Value driven intellectual capital: How to convert intangible corporate assets into market value* (1st ed). New York: Wiley.

Susskind, A. M., Miller, V. D., & Johnson, J. D. (1998). Downsizing and structural holes their impact on layoff survivors' perceptions of organizational chaos and openness to change. *Communication Research*, *25*(1), 30–65.

Sveiby, K. E. (1997). *The new organizational wealth: Managing & measuring knowledge-based assets*. San Francisco: Berrett-Koehler Publishers.

Swash, G. D. (1997). The information audit. *Journal of Managerial Psychology*, *12*(5), 312–318.

Tagliaventi, M. R., Bertolotti, F., & Macri, D. M. (2010). A perspective on practice in interunit knowledge sharing. *European Management Journal*, *28*(5), 331–345. https://doi.org/10.1016/j.emj.2010.04.001

Teece, D. J., Pisano, G., & Shuen, A. (1997). Dynamic capabilities and strategic management. *Strategic Management Journal*, *18*(7), 509–533. https://onlinelibrary.wiley.com/doi/abs/10.1002/%28SICI%291097-0266%28199708%2918%3A7%3C509%3A%3AAID-SMJ882%3E3.0.CO%3B2-Z

Thompson, J. D. (2007). *Organizations in action: Social science bases of administrative theory* (5th ed.). London: Transaction Publishers.

Tiwana, A. (2002). *The knowledge management toolkit: Orchestrating IT. Strategy, and knowledge platforms*. Delhi, India: Pearson Education India.

Tooman, T., Akinci, C., & Davies, H. (2016). Understanding knowledge and knowing. In K. Orr, S. Nutley, S. Russell, R. Bain, B. Hacking, & C. Moran

(Eds.), *Knowledge and practice in business and organisations* (pp. 17–29). New York, London: Routledge.

Tsai, W. (2001). Knowledge transfer in intraorganizational networks: Effects of network position and absorptive capacity on business unit innovation and performance. *Academy of Management Journal*, *44*(5), 996–1004.

Tsai, W. (2002). Social structure of "coopetition" within a multiunit organization: Coordination, competition, and intraorganizational knowledge sharing. *Organization Science*, *13*(2), 179–190.

Tsui, E. (2005). The role of IT in KM: Where are we now and where are we heading? *Journal of Knowledge Management*, *9*(1), 3–6. https://doi.org/10.1108/13673270510584198

Tsui, E., & Liebowitz, J. (2005). Linking social network analysis with the analytic hierarchy process for knowledge mapping in organizations. *Journal of Knowledge Management*, *9*(1), 76–86.

Ujwary-Gil, A. (2016). The concept and stages of the audit of intangible resources: A network approach. In S. Moffett & B. Galbraith (Eds.), *Proceedings of the 17th European Conference on Knowledge Management* (pp. 916–925). Belfast, UK: Ulster University.

Vail, E. F. (1999). Knowledge mapping: Getting started with knowledge management. *Information Systems Management*, *16*(4), 16–23. https://doi.org/10.1201/1078/43189.16.4.19990901/31199.3

Vives, X. (1990). Information and competitive advantage. *International Journal of Industrial Organization*, *8*(1), 17–35.

Wang, H., Zhao, J., Li, Y., & Li, C. (2015). Network centrality, organizational innovation, and performance: A meta-analysis. *Canadian Journal of Administrative Sciences-Revue Canadienne Des Sciences De L Administration*, *32*(3), 146–159. https://doi.org/10.1002/cjas.1316

Wang, J., & Xiao, J. (2009). Knowledge management audit framework and methodology based on processes. *Journal of Technology Management in China*, *4*(3), 239–249. https://doi.org/10.1108/17468770911013546

Wang, Q., & Gao, S. (2011). Network architecture and firm performance: A resources-based view. *Frontiers of Business Research in China*, *5*(4), 559–579. http://dx.doi.org/10.1007/s11782-011-0145-0

Wasserman, S., & Faust, K. (1994). *Social network analysis: Methods and applications*. Cambridge, UK: Cambridge University Press.

Weiss, K., Hamann, M., Kinney, M., & Marsh, H. (2012). Knowledge exchange and policy influence in a marine resource governance network. *Global Environmental Change-Human and Policy Dimensions*, *22*(1), 178–188. https://doi.org/10.1016/j.gloenvcha.2011.09.007

Wenger, E. C., McDermott, R. A., & Snyder, W. (2002). *Cultivating communities of practice: A guide to managing knowledge*. Cambridge, MA: Harvard Business School Press.

Wenger, E. C., & Snyder, W. M. (2000). Communities of practice: The organizational frontier. *Harvard Business Review*, *78*(1), 139–146.

Wexler, M. N. (2001). The who, what and why of knowledge mapping. *Journal of Knowledge Management*, *5*(3), 249–264. https://doi.org/10.1108/EUM0000000005868

Wiig, K. M., de Hoog, R., & van der Spek, R. (1997). Supporting knowledge management: A selection of methods and techniques. *Expert Systems with Applications*, *13*(1), 15–27. https://doi.org/10.1016/S0957-4174(97)00019-5

Ye, X., Zhang, J., Liu, Y., & Su, J. (2015). Study on the measurement of international knowledge flow based on the patent citation network. *International Journal of Technology Management*, *69*(3–4), 229–245. https://doi.org/10.1504/IJTM.2015.072971

Youndt, M. A., Subramaniam, M., & Snell, S. A. (2004). Intellectual capital profiles: An examination of investments and returns. *Journal of Management Studies*, *41*(2), 335–361. https://doi.org/10.1111/j.1467-6486.2004.00435.x

Young, T. V., Wang, Y., & Lewis, W. D. (2016). Explaining how political actors gain strategic positions: Predictors of centrality in state reading policy issue networks. *Educational Policy*, *30*(6), 799–819. https://doi.org/10.1177/0895904814552896

Zack, M. H. (1999). Developing a knowledge strategy. *California Management Review*, *41*(3), 125–134.

Zhuge, H. (2002). A knowledge flow model for peer-to-peer team knowledge sharing and management. *Expert Systems with Applications*, *23*(1), 23–30. https://doi.org/10.1016/S0957-4174(02)00024-6

Zins, C. (2007). Conceptual approaches for defining data, information, and knowledge. *Journal of the American Society for Information Science and Technology*, *58*(4), 479–493.

Zollo, M., & Winter, S. G. (2002). Deliberate learning and the evolution of dynamic capabilities. *Organization Science*, *13*(3), 339–351. https://doi.org/10.1287/orsc.13.3.339.2780

3 Research Methodology

The proposed own research methodology is complex and multidimensional, and regards two main areas: 1) developing a methodology for intangible resource audit and 2) exemplifying the intangible resource audit, which is a study in itself. The main purpose of the audit includes the identification of intangible resources and their diagnosis within the framework of specific relations (information, knowledge, task, and resource networks). These networks (one- and two-mode matrices) are accompanied by metrics that allow one to measure intangible resources from the perspective of an association network. Analysis techniques were selected to measure the organizational network structure, pairs of nodes (dyads), and individual nodes and their interconnectedness.

The formulated research problem is followed by research questions, objectives, and assumptions regarding a multistage process of creating a methodology of intangible resource audit, as well as the study methods and network techniques used in this process. Notably, the organization of the study and the own study methodology presented, broken down into quantitative, qualitative, and network-based methods, serve to exemplify the intangible resource audit process. It is not possible, though, to empirically verify the methodology of intangible resource audit based on a single case. Intangible resource audit is in itself a research process, within which the auditor (in collaboration with the management) defines the goals and the scope of the audit, as well as research assumptions and hypotheses, which are then verified using selected methods and network analysis techniques. In sociological research, a social network is frequently composed of a small number of people, which enables collection of data from all members of the organization (see Borgatti, Everett, & Johnson, 2018). In this case, the number of people was N = 45, with 1980 relations established in a single matrix, and a total of 19,800 observations were made for all ten matrices, which were then subjected to correlation and regression analyses. The fact that the observations are not independent of one another makes for an important distinction between network research and traditional social research. The subjects of observation are not isolated (social) actors, but relations, which are interdependent in the organizational context.

The aims and scope of the audit, as well as its research assumptions, are affected by the specific nature of an organization, determined by its external environment, business model, business processes, strategic goals, and types of intangible resources. These elements differentiate organizations operating in different sectors, as they will be different for organizations operating in the IT, medical, and higher education sectors, and still different for the manufacturing sector, where tangible resources might dominate. For instance, knowledge and skills (K) such as *analytical thinking* will be applied in a different context in an IT enterprise than in a medical enterprise. The skill might even not be identified within the business processes specific to an organization at all. What is common when identifying intangible resources are their types (components): actors (A) as carriers of information and knowledge, knowledge and skills (K), tasks (T), and resources (R).

3.1 Research Focus, Problems, Aims, and Assumptions

For over 20 years, we have been observing the increasing importance of information and knowledge resources, as well as of their application for creating competitive advantage in an organization and boosting its value (Bontis, Dragonetti, Jacobsen, & Roos, 1999). In the knowledge-based economy, information and knowledge are the dominant intangible resources that determine growth and competitiveness (Cricelli & Grimaldi, 2008). In the late 20th century, more attention was paid to studying and mapping knowledge, which allows one to identify and visualize organizational knowledge (Burnett, Williams, & Illingworth, 2013). Organizations recognize the growing importance of knowledge, which is prerequisite for innovation, efficiency, and product or service quality, with constant updating of knowledge minimizing the risk of it being lost due to high staff mobility (Alavi & Leidner, 2001; Greiner, Böhmann, & Krcmar, 2007). The association between knowledge and economic success is commonly accepted. However, scholars and practitioners disagree on what constitutes useful knowledge and how it should be managed (Handzic, Lagumdzija, & Celjo, 2008). The iterative cycle of intangible resource audit entails consideration of the changing environment of the organization and the required modifications of the resource base, also taking dynamic capabilities into account. The network perspective on organizations (including the intra-organizational and inter-organizational approach) is valuable in the dynamically changing environment, as it promotes the generation of many desired responses to change.

Knowledge, both tacit and explicit (Nonaka & Takeuchi, 1995; Sveiby, 1997), is a fundamental element of intangible resources and is applied in all core business processes (Potoczek, 2018). Knowledge cannot only be considered as something static (a repository of documentation, procedures, etc.)—it also has a dynamic aspect, manifesting in knowledge transfer, flows, and application in the organization. The static form of knowledge and its identification are reflected in the definition of knowledge-based intellectual capital. The dynamic form refers to the management and application of knowledge resources within the defined business processes.

At the initial stage of intangible resource audit development, the identification of business processes is a critical step in designing the audit (see Section 2.4), allowing one to avoid processing an overwhelming amount of data, only concentrating on the knowledge, skills, tasks, and resources (structural capital) supporting the core business processes.

The study does not aim at analyzing business processes, even though their identification makes it possible to define the key knowledge, skills, resources, and tasks, which are the core of an organization's intangible resources. Such an analysis would considerably exceed the scope of the present study, which mainly concentrates on the network approach to intangible resources and their efficient application in an organization. Limitations of this study will be further discussed in Section 5.3. This intangible resource audit allows for diagnosing information and knowledge flows in the organization; determining what skills, knowledge, and resources employees have and use in the organization; what tasks they can and do perform; what knowledge and resources are used for what tasks; and, finally, what the efficiency of their application and their configuration is in the relationship network.

Employees (actors) are seen here in a simplified form as repositories of tacit knowledge (carriers of this knowledge, which is inherently associated with a human being), which can be potentially transferred via direct interpersonal relations. Two complementary approaches to knowledge are present here (Cook & Brown, 1999): epistemology of possession and epistemology of practice, emphasizing the distinction between the possession of knowledge and knowledge that is a part of action (*knowing*). This study refers to epistemology of practice, in the sense that respondents answer questions about the knowledge they use at work, previously defined and assigned to business processes. The authors call the interaction between acquiring and using knowledge "a dynamic affordance," which is applied in the analysis of knowledge transfer and application. Since it is very difficult to clearly distinguish between explicit and tacit knowledge, the undertaken activities (tasks) with their complexity and connection to professional work become more meaningful when it is possible to assess the application of this knowledge and its usefulness for the organization (Levin & Cross, 2004).

The study comprises two parts. In the first part, the aim is to develop a methodology of intangible resource audit and, as a result, an integrated *meta-model* of organizational intangible resources (see Section 2.3).

Despite the importance of intangible resource auditing, literature on this subject is very scarce. Two aspects of the audit are outlined: one oriented toward results (report), and another oriented toward the auditing process. If we assume that intangible resource audit has an iterative character, then the processes[1] (stages) of the audit and the dynamic approach to audit, understood as interactions between individual stages, gain importance. The dynamics of the audit are enhanced by the inclusion of organizational network analysis instruments, which allow for diagnosing the interrelations between various elements that are the subject of analysis (here: information, knowledge, tasks, and resources).

In the second part, the intangible resource audit is exemplified by applying organizational network analysis techniques to diagnose resources, particularly knowledge, within the network approach. Intangible resource audit with the use of ONA can be configured in many different ways, as there is a wide range of metrics that can be applied. By default, the suggested scope of analyses must be limited. Metrics used in intangible resource audit must allow for measuring relations and interactions associated with information, knowledge, resources (structural capital), and tasks, inherently connected to the other elements. Table 3.1 presents the main metrics used in the audit, discussed in detail in Section 2.3.2 (except for the QAP and MRQAP techniques, described in Section 3.2).

Table 3.1 Intangible resource audit metrics—a multilevel approach

Entire network level
Network and meta-network density (AA, AK, AR, AT, KT, RT)
Network centralization (AA)
Knowledge (AK) and resource (AR) diversity
Knowledge (AK), resource (AR), and task (AT) redundancy
Dyad level
Correlation of information (AA) and knowledge (AA) networks, knowledge networks (AK), resource networks (AR), and task networks (AT) following the transformation of two-mode networks into one-mode networks (QAP)
Regression of a dependent variable (knowledge network AK) and independent variables in the form of information (AA), knowledge (AA), task (AT), and resource (AR) networks following the transformation of two-mode networks into one-mode networks (MRQAP)
Node level
Centrality degree of actors (A), knowledge (K), resources (R), and tasks (T)
Eigenvector centrality (AA)
Betweenness centrality (AA)
Work (AK, AR, AT, KT, RT), knowledge (AK, AT, KT), and resource (AR, AT, RT) load
Knowledge and resource (AK, AR, AT, KT, RT) needs and waste congruence

The scope of intangible resource audit and the accompanying metrics at the level of the entire network (organization) will make it possible to:

- measure the information-, knowledge-, resource-, and task-related connectivity in the organization;
- assess the extent of network centralization and existence of any dominant node(s) in the network;
- assess knowledge and resource distribution in the organization;
- assess the extent of redundancy (overlap) of knowledge, resources, and tasks in the organization.

As for intangible resource audit at the dyad level (pairs of relations in the network), it will make it possible to:

- assess the correlations between information, knowledge, resource, and task networks;
- assess any causal relationships between the discussed networks.

Intangible resource audit at the level of individual nodes will make it possible to:

- analyze information and knowledge flows between the organization's employees, as well as the prominence of actors, knowledge, resources, and tasks;
- identify knowledge, tasks, and resources available in the organization, and their relation to individual employees;
- assign knowledge, tasks, and resources to specific business processes;
- determine the work, knowledge, and resource load of each employee;
- assess the level of congruence, that is, knowledge and resource needs, and available knowledge and resources that are not used by each employee.

For this study, the main focus has been placed on:

- Identifying intangible resources in the organization: knowledge and skills (K), resources (R, structural capital of the organization), and tasks (T). Identification of tasks (activities) is inherently related to knowledge and resources (R), which are used in the performance of these tasks. Without defining tasks, there would be no reference point for identifying knowledge and resources. Therefore, this approach gives intangible resources a more dynamic character, rather than defining the *status quo* of these resources in a given time frame and only presenting their static snapshot, as it happens in many information, knowledge, and intellectual capital audit models.

- Presenting the information network (AA), in which the key role is played by human network actors and the process of information exchange. Information network analysis allows for identifying the actors' relations and their prominence (the most exposed position in the network in terms of incoming and outgoing relations).
- Presenting the knowledge network. It is assumed that knowledge networks include network AA (in which actors seek assistance and support when solving problems related to their professional work and know what knowledge and skills their colleagues have—with possible flow of tacit knowledge), and network AK (in which one can see what knowledge actors have and what knowledge they use at work).
- Presenting the resource network (AR), which allows for defining the resources[2] (structural capital) that actors can access and the resources they use at work.
- Presenting the task network (AT), which allows one to identify what tasks actors can perform and what tasks they perform in an organization.
- Presenting the knowledge–task network (KT), which makes it possible to define what knowledge is critical when performing particular tasks. Knowledge load, congruence, and centrality metrics were used to define the efficiency of knowledge application in the organization.
- Presenting the resource–task network (RT), which makes it possible to define what resources are critical when performing particular tasks. Resource load, congruence, and centrality metrics were used to define the efficiency of resource use in the organization.
- Indicating potential risks related to the flow of intangible resources in the organization, in particular when a prominent node in the network is removed. Relations between these elements, their concentration (density), and prominence imply the efficiency of knowledge generation, knowledge and resource use, and task performance in an organization.

The primary research problem was formulated as a question: How can one identify an organization's intangible resources and their relations in the information network, knowledge network, task network, and resource network? This gives rise to the following specific research questions:

1. How, in light of network and management theories, should one develop a methodology for organizational intangible resource audit, bearing in mind the uniqueness both of the intangible resources and their relations, and of the organization itself?
2. What prerequisites should be met by an organization for intangible resource audit to be feasible and effective?
3. Can organizational intangible resource audit be considered a valuable management technique in the modern knowledge-based economy?

4. How can intangible resources be measured, evaluated, and included in audit planning and performance using the network-based view?

At the empirical stage of the study, more detailed research questions can be formulated, resulting from the use of ONA techniques.

1. How dense are the networks of intangible resource relations in the organization?
2. What is the level of network centralization and knowledge and resource diversity in the organization?
3. What is the level of knowledge, resource, and task redundancy in the organization?
4. What are the correlations and causal relationships among information, knowledge, resource, and task networks?
5. Who provides information to whom in the information network?
6. Who receives information from whom in the information network?
7. Who discusses and solves complex work-related problems with whom?
8. Who knows what knowledge and skills other employees in the organization have?
9. Which nodes (actors, knowledge, resources, tasks) are the most prominent in the network?
10. Which actors have the highest work, knowledge, and resource loads?
11. What is the level of knowledge and resource needs congruence (match) and waste (mismatch) among employees?
12. What knowledge and skills do the organization's employees have?
13. What knowledge and skills do the organization's employees use?
14. Who has access to what resources at work?
15. Who uses what resources at work?
16. What tasks can each employee perform in the organization?
17. What tasks does each employee perform in the organization?
18. What knowledge and skills are critical for performing a given task?
19. What resources are critical for performing a given task?
20. How intangible resource (information and knowledge) networks change following the disappearance of a prominent node in the network?

With the general goal in mind, that is, to develop a methodology for organizational intangible resource audit based on the network approach and organizational network analysis tools (as discussed in the introduction to this book), the specific objectives included:

1. Developing a concept for organizational intangible resource audit, based on an exploration of theoretical precepts, where the author shall creatively combine own and other researchers' concepts.

2. Creating a methodology for organizational intangible resource audit based on approaches developed by Hong, Van den Goor, and Brinkkemper (1993) and Brinkkemper (1996).
3. Identifying and analyzing the dynamics of associations and relations between intangible resources on the basis of network and resource theories.
4. Providing an empirical basis for intangible resource audit, and in particular for its key stage, that is, performance, using organizational network analysis techniques.
5. Testing selected instruments indispensable for the diagnosis and operationalization of the relations of intangible resources in an organization.
6. Formulating the findings from the organizational intangible resource audit, highlighting study limitations and areas for further investigation.
7. The developed intangible resource audit may become another important component of the *meta-model* and *meta-process* approach to audit for other authors' future research.

Based on a literature review and the innovative combination of the intangible resource audit *meta-model* with the network-based view, the author has formulated the following assumptions:

- Organizational network analysis is an instrument in intangible resource auditing, allowing one to view the resources from the perspective of a network of relations and interconnections.

- Understanding of information, knowledge, and intellectual capital audit concepts, and of organizational network analysis techniques, is a prerequisite for designing an integrated intangible resource audit model.
- The network-based view, in the form of organizational network analysis, is a comprehensive instrument for intangible resource audit, enabling the auditing of relations and dynamics of the resources and thus going beyond the standard methodology of simply measuring the resources themselves.
- Developing and implementing a measurement system comprising metrics of intangible resource relations and dynamics assists in organizational intangible resource auditing in the aspect of interrelatedness of the resources.
- Simulating changes of each resource in the relationship network allows for shaping conditions optimal for an organization's performance.

3.2 Research Organization and Discussion of Research Methods

3.2.1 *Qualitative Research*

The qualitative part involved a case study, documentation analysis, and semi-structured interviews conducted in order to understand the organization and the conditions of its operation, and also as a foundation for developing the study questionnaire. In the case of network analysis, it is important to organize the study well, decide what the boundaries of the network are, and develop a strategy for sample selection. Network analysis provides a complete set of instruments for measuring the structure and individual nodes in the network using selected metrics available, for example, in the ORA and UCINET software. In quantitative research, besides descriptive statistics, the QAP and MRQAP techniques were also used. They will be further discussed in this chapter.

3.2.1.1 Case Study

Case study is a method used in research strategy to provide a full description of a single case existing in a specific context, which offers insight into an actual situation. This method is particularly popular, because it allows for investigating the processes and problems related to organizational management, in order to understand and describe them in full and to improve management practices through in-depth insight and analysis. Qualitative analyses provide a comprehensive understanding of non-numerical data acquired from interviews, stressing the *how* and *why* questions (Myers, 2013). The case study method is used for formulating and testing theories when the existing theoretical and conceptual frameworks are insufficient (Eisenhardt, 1989; Yin, 2013). Case study use is justified (based on criteria listed in Benbasat, Goldstein, & Mead, 1987; Ponelis, 2015) by the fact that the development of an integrated organizational intangible resource audit methodology:

- cannot be studied outside of its natural (organizational) setting;
- focuses on current events (conditions of organizational functioning);
- control or manipulation of objects, people, and events is not possible; and
- theoretical knowledge of the studied problem is still limited and immature.

The choice of the case study method is motivated by the complexity of the issue and the scarcity of research on the subject. It allows for the explanation of causal relationships that are too complex for survey-based research and impossible to analyze in experiments, with a detailed description of the context of the focus of research (intangible resources). In total, three case studies were used in this research—as explained in the introduction, the first two were pilot studies, and the third was the main study. Nevertheless, in network research, the scope of analysis usually comprises one case (e.g., de Oliveira Maciel & Chaves, 2016; Tsai & Ghoshal, 1998), which defines the boundaries of the network (the entire organization). Selection of cases for analysis was based primarily on the prominence (intensity) of intangible resources in the functioning of each organization. An organization operating in the IT sector is undoubtedly a suitable case. The main motivation for case selection was the criterion related to the significance of knowledge and the strategic maturity of the organization, enhancing the likelihood of identifying the intangible resources sought and their association with value and strategy creation. The basic principle for selecting cases is the abundance of information concerning the topics investigated—the use of targeted sampling is therefore justified. Additionally, the accessibility criterion was used (Czakon, 2015; (Creswell & Poth, 2017). The credibility of findings from the case study was enhanced by triangulation (secondary data analysis, survey, and interview) and the proper processing of results.

Case studies support research validity, as they are considered more persuasive for managers than theoretical discussions. The selection of the case study was based on the interpretivist paradigm, in which, from an epistemological point of view, our knowledge of the reality is a social construct of human actors. It is characterized by the need to understand the world from a subjective point of view, seeking explanations in the reference system of a given individual involved in the events rather than an impartial observer. The resulting nature of the study aiming at developing and testing a methodology of organizational intangible resource audit in a small organization seems to be most suitable in the interpretative approach, which brings an understanding of core issues by reducing the distance between the researcher and the key manager. Technical and social aspects, as well as their interactions in an organization, are taken into consideration.

3.2.1.2 Interview

Interviews were carried out in three organizations. In all cases, the CEO and managing directors, who usually have the most substantial knowledge concerning the workings of the organization, were asked for an interview (Tsai & Ghoshal, 1998). The dates, times, and locations for meetings with each of the interviewees were arranged by e-mail or phone. The interviewees knew about the aims of the audit and interviews, to be able to prepare adequately. The aims were also discussed at the beginning of each interview. The semi-structured interview format was selected, as a less formal type of interview, so that each interviewee could feel at ease, while constructively contributing to the discussion in line with the aims of the interview. The interviews focused on:

1. Discussing the opportunities and risks present in the external macro- and micro-environment of the organization.
2. Identifying the organization's main strategic goals.
3. Discussing the business model.
4. Identifying the most important (core) business processes from the point of view of strategic goal implementation.
5. Identifying the knowledge, tasks, and resources critical for the business processes.

Methodologies of knowledge audit based on the identification of core business processes had already been suggested by Gourova, Antonova, and Todorova (2009) and Perez-Soltero et al. (2007, 2006). Similarly, in organizational intangible resource audit, the main criteria for selecting core processes are: direct impact on the organization's mission and vision, income generation, and overall success; added value creation for the organization, satisfying customers' needs; and reliance on valuable human, technological, and information resources. Interviews allowed for enhanced understanding of business processes, the knowledge required in these processes and created by them, resources needed and used in these processes, and the performed tasks. Findings from the interviews enabled the categorization of typical knowledge, skills, resources, and tasks associated with the identified business processes, which were then used as response options in the surveys.

First, two pilot studies were performed. The first one was conducted in a public organization from the higher education sector, from April to December 2015. In total, 82 members of the organization took part in the pilot study. The second pilot study took place from April to May 2015 in a joint-stock company from the medical sector. In total, 30 employees took part in the study, constituting 100% of the studied population.

The two studies resulted in a simplification of the survey and selection of the matrix (multigrid) method for presenting questions and answers instead of a repeated roster, which significantly reduced the time needed to complete the survey and reduced the involvement of respondents, as suggested by Borgatti et al. (2018). Interviews were transcribed and coded using descriptive codes (Miles & Huberman, 1994).

Information collected from the interviews was used for developing a research questionnaire, based on the glossary of own terms of the studied organizations. The questionnaire was composed of two main parts. The first one included a limited set of questions to collect general information concerning each respondent (name and surname,[3] location, professional experience, gender, etc.). The second part included four questions already used by Cross and Parker (2004), in a slightly changed form, and two questions each for knowledge, tasks, and resources. Their purpose was to collect data crucial for organizational network analysis. The questionnaire was piloted on a sample of two employees. After reducing complexity and time needed for completion, the final version was ready. The date of the study was set and the employees were invited to participate by e-mail. In the case of the higher education organization, in the first week, the survey was completed by 76 people. After this period, a reminder was sent by the head of unit, and another 6 people completed the survey, resulting in a total of 82 completed surveys. The response rate was 93%, which can be considered highly satisfying for network research (Ferrin, Dirks, & Shah, 2006). In the case of the enterprise from the medical sector, two reminders were sent. The pilot study was concluded with the development of a dedicated study report, presented to the management and employees. Table 3.2 shows the basic information on the data collection process.

In most organizations, the number of respondents is between 50 and 100. Many network studies are also performed in very small organizations, with as few as 22 (Maciel & Chaves, 2017) or 29 employees

Table 3.2 Data collection process

	Pilot study	*Pilot study*	*Main study*
Sector in which the organization operates	higher education	medical	IT
Research method	interview	interview	interview
Number of interviews	1	1	1
Person	Head of unit	CEO	Member of the board (head of the Implementation Department)
Interview date	May 7, 2015	May 10, 2015	Jan 6, 2017
Interview duration (hours)	7	4	8
Number of respondents	82	30	45
Number of people testing the questionnaire	2	2	2
Survey start date	Nov 17, 2015	Aug 25, 2015	Feb 6, 2017
Survey end date	Dec 4, 2015	Nov 22, 2015	Feb 27, 2017
Duration of study, including data analysis	April—December 2015	May—December 2015	January—March 2017
Presentation of the study report	Dec 8, 2015	Dec 15, 2015	Sep 30, 2017

(Gibbons, 2004). However, it is not the number of an organization's employees (respondents) that matters, but the number of observed relations.

3.2.2 *Quantitative Research*

In the quantitative analyses, measurements were made based on the metrics discussed in Section 2.3.2. In order to measure the values of metrics described in Table 2.7, the ORA (Organizational Risk Analyzer) software, version ORA-NetScenes 3.0.9.9.38, was used (Carley, Pfeffer, Reminga, Storrick, & Columbus, 2013). Additionally, the UCINET 6 software was used (Windows version 6.627) (Borgatti, Everett, & Freeman, 2002) with two tools: quadratic assignment procedure (QAP) and the matrix regression testing tool (MRQAP), discussed in more detail later in the chapter.

For the purpose of ORA and UCINET analyses, a total of 12 matrices were created, which included all the responses collected in the study (Table 3.3)

The first four matrices represent actor × actor (AA) networks in terms of four different relations: receiving information (AA^1), providing information (AA^2), joint problem-solving (AA^3), and knowing others' knowledge and skills (AA^4).[4] The validity of these relations has already been verified by authors (e.g., Borgatti & Cross, 2003; Cross, Borgatti, & Parker, 2002). As proposed by Nonino (2013), a four-item qualitative scale was used, dichotomized as follows: answers 0 (never) and 1 (at least once a month) were considered weak relations and marked 0 in the matrix; answers 3 (at least once a week) and 4 (at least once a day) were considered strong relations and marked 1. Strong ties, which provide more frequent and richer communication, offer more opportunities for explanation and feedback between the actors, leading to mutual understanding (Tenkasi & Chesmore, 2003). Each of these matrices was analyzed separately based on the research questions that defined the relation.

In order to calculate the reliability of the scales in the questionnaire, in-degree and out-degree centrality metrics were used for ten matrices, and Cronbach's alpha was calculated (see Hsu & Tzeng, 2010) at $\alpha = 0.886$, which confirmed high correlations between the matrices.

The next matrices represent actor × knowledge (AK) networks, divided into two relations: the actor has knowledge/skills (AK^1), and the actor uses knowledge/skills (AK^2) at work. Here, a five-item Likert scale was used (5—definitely yes; 1—definitely no), dichotomized as follows: scores 4 and 5 were marked 1; scores 1–3 were considered to denote weak relations and marked 0. The remaining matrices were processed the same way (AR^1, AR^2, AT^1, AT^2). For further analysis, in particular matrix correlation and regression, it was necessary to transform two-mode matrices into one-mode matrices using the folding operation.[5] As a result, matrices

Table 3.3 Questions/statements used in organizational network analysis

No.	*Question/statement*	*Scale*	*Matrix*	*α*
One-mode network: actor x actor				
1.	How often do you receive information directly related to the work performed in the organization from this person?	0—never 1—at least once a month 2—at least once a week 4—at least once a day	AA_receives (AA^1)—information network (1)	.881 .881
2.	How often do you provide this person with information directly related to the work performed in the organization?		AA_provides (AA^2)—information network (2)	.883 .883
3.	How often do you communicate with this person for assistance in solving work-related problems?		AA_solves (AA^3)—knowledge network (1)	
4.	I know the skills and knowledge this person has. This does not mean that I have these skills and this knowledge, but I understand what skills and knowledge this person has.	1—definitely no 5—definitely yes	AA_knows (AA^4)—knowledge network (2)	
Two-mode network: actor x knowledge				
5.	I have knowledge and skills related to the subject.	1—definitely no 5—definitely yes	AK_has_knowledge (AK^1)—knowledge network (3)	.869 .870
6.	I use this knowledge or skill in my work.		AK_uses_knowledge (AK^2)—knowledge network (4)	
Two-mode network: actor x resource				
7.	I have access to this resource in my work.	1—definitely no	AR_has_access (AR^1)—resource network (1)	.867
8.	I use this resource in my work.	5—definitely yes	AR_uses_resource (AR^2)—resource network (2)	.862
Two-mode network: actor x task				
9.	I know how to perform this task in my work.	1—definitely no	AT_can_perform (AT^1)—task network (1)	.874
10.	I perform this task in my work.	5—definitely yes	AT_performs_task (AT^2)—task network (2)	.870
Knowledge and resources assigned to tasks				
11.	Is this knowledge/skill necessary for performing this task?	0—no	KT_knowledge_tasks	-
12.	Is this resource necessary for performing this task?	1—yes	RT_resource_tasks	-

AK^1 and AK^2 are marked AK^{1_shared} and AK^{2_shared}, and the same goes for the remaining matrices (AR^{1_shared}; AR^{2_shared}; AT^{1_shared}; AT^{2_shared}).

The last two matrices represent knowledge × task (KT) and resource × task (RT) networks, which are the basis for evaluating congruence levels, resource loads, and row degree centralities of intangible resources (knowledge, resources, and tasks).

All the matrices were introduced into the ORA software, which then calculated centrality degrees (incoming and outgoing), betweenness centralities, eigenvector centralities, and other factors for which descriptive statistics were generated.

3.2.2.1 QAP/MRQAP

In typical network studies, every dependent and independent variable is measured using a question concerning a relation in one network (Ibarra, 1995). It is important to bear in mind that the analysis unit in the study assumes a relationship between pairs of individuals. Hence, all variables are dyadic. These data are cross-sectional, which means that all variables were collected at the same time point. A cross-sectional study justifies the selection of ONA rather than DNA techniques, as DNA studies are longitudinal in nature. Nevertheless, elements of DNA are also present here, in particular with regard to simulating changes and positions of nodes in the network.

Analysis methods and concepts applied in SNA, ONA, and DNA are entirely different from those commonly used in traditional statistics and data analysis (Prell, 2012). The procedures of network analysis are particularly problematic when they are used in statistical reasoning and hypothesis testing. Nonetheless, descriptive techniques can be used successfully, as they offer crucial information on how nodes are connected in the network. Descriptive statistics and statistical reasoning were produced using networks and statistics generated by ORA and UCINET. Beside basic quantitative statistics, such as standard deviations, means, and minimum and maximum values, the quadratic assignment procedure and multiple regression of quadratic assignment procedure were used, which are not limited to social network analysis. In the literature, scarce publication can be found using these tools in ONA based on organizational and management theories. Therefore, a more detailed analysis is justified here.

QAP is a non-parametric test measuring correlations between two variables with the same matrix size, using, for example, Pearson's correlation coefficient. The QAP test is a two-stage procedure, in which data in the form of matrices are extended into a vector of observations, and an ordinary multiple regression is performed on them, providing a traditional beta coefficient estimated for every independent variable. The problem is that traditional estimates of standard errors of those coefficients are very sensitive to auto-correlation in the data, and thus may not be used as the basis for significance testing for these coefficients. Therefore, the second step involves generating a null hypothesis from the reference distribution, against which the observed coefficient can be compared to verify its statistical significance. This distribution is created by multiple random permutations of the dependent variable matrix, each time calculating the regression coefficient for each independent variable, predicting the permuted dependent variable (Hinds, Carley, Krackhardt, & Wholey, 2000). *P*-values are determined based on relative frequency of a statistical value in the reference distribution obtained by permutation, which is larger than or equal to the empirically observed value (Dekker, Krackhardt, & Snijders, 2007). The QAP technique generates significant levels of independent variables and pseudo R^2, which can be interpreted similarly to R^2 statistics in traditional ordinary least squares (OLS) regression.

QAP and MRQAP are used in numerous studies. Hubert and Schultz (1976) are credited with the first use of the term "quadratic assignment procedure." Mantel (1967) is considered the author of MRQAP, first developed for identifying geographically concentrated disease clusters using distance matrices. Krackhardt (1988) developed QAP in order to solve the structural problem of auto-correlation of data in a network and to compare data at the matrix level. The author calls the critical condition in correlation analysis resulting from the lack of independence of observations "structural auto-correlation."

In the case of QAP, investigation typically concerns informal relations in organizations (e.g., D'Errico, Stefani, & Torriero, 2014; Rank, 2008). MRQAP is more commonly used to analyze inter-organizational knowledge exchange networks (e.g., Diez-Vial & Montoro-Sanchez, 2014) or knowledge networks related to human resource management (Martin-Rios, 2014). MRQAP is also applied when examining intra-organizational relations and organizational management. There are also studies concerning knowledge exchange (Hsu & Tzeng, 2010), knowledge flow (Marouf & Doreian, 2010), knowledge sharing (Maciel & Chaves, 2017), knowledge transfer (Kaše, Paauwe, & Zupan, 2009), product development program management (Kratzer, Leenders, & van Engelen, 2009), social capital (Nonino, 2013; Tsai & Ghoshal, 1998), or trust (Ferrin et al., 2006; Gupta, Ho, Pollack, & Lai, 2016; Rašković & Makovec-Brenčič, 2015; Zagenczyk, Purvis, Shoss, Scott, & Cruz, 2015). MRQAP can be treated as a statistical approach to recognizing structural dependencies between relational data. In MRQAP analysis, the dependent variable is a one-mode matrix, not a vector, as is usually the case in regression analysis. MRQAP is associated with a logarithmic regression or OLS model, which includes relational variables and takes into consideration their interrelations when assessing their statistical significance (Broekel, Balland, Burger, & van Oort, 2014). In the first stage, the regression coefficient is calculated using OLS, ignoring the diagonals. Then, the dependent variable matrix rows and columns are permuted to create a new, random matrix. OLS regression is repeated with the new, permuted matrix, producing different beta (β) coefficients. The procedure is repeated, generating a distribution of the beta value based on the matrix permutations, which then becomes a reference distribution against which the observed coefficients are compared (Hinds et al., 2000).

In order to test the statistical correlation model, the networks were subjected to regression, with significance tests constructed using the permutation/randomization technique. The significance values for correlation and regression are based on the distribution generated in 50,000 random permutations. The selection of random permutations is significant, as it affects the accuracy of standard error estimation and stabilizes the p values and significance. The larger the number of permutations, the less the p-value variability (Borgatti et al., 2018). It is impossible to test hypotheses in which the variable takes the form of a matrix representing a relation using classical statistical regression, as the observations are not independent, which justifies the use of MRQAP to test for the existence or absence of a given relation.

3.2.3 Network Research

In ONA, there are various methods and strategies both for collecting data and for measuring relations between actors. In this study, the realistic strategy (Laumann, Marsden, & Prensky, 1989) and the full network strategy were selected. In the latter, relations between all members of the networks are studied, and the scope is limited by the organization's boundaries. Network analysis requires complete data to capture the entire network of relations in the organization. Therefore, nearly all members of the organization were studied, which made it possible to acquire comprehensive information concerning interactions and relations in the network. The main study was carried out in early 2017.

The selection of the sampling method in a study requiring peripheral network specification is, to a large extent, determined by the existence of certain actors. A full list of organization members (employees) allows for defining relations of every node with all the others, which makes it possible to present the structure (topography) and positions of individual nodes in the network (Sparrowe & Liden, 2005). This method of population selection can enhance the credibility of network data (Marsden, 1990).

The network of relations was created based on responses from the survey questionnaire; then, network visualization and statistical analysis were performed. The results were entered into ORA and UCINET for further analysis. ORA was used to understand better the dynamics existing among network actors and the available knowledge, resources, and tasks. ONA was performed to determine the importance of intangible resource management with regard to the business processes of the organization. Data related to the flows of work-related information, knowledge, skills, resources, and tasks in the organization operating in the IT sector were collected. Then, network visualization was performed, to present the relations and flows of intangible resources in the organization in the form of graphs.[6] Network analysis required the creation of a matrix for each question, with the use of applicable response scales. Matrix creation allowed for discovering the nature of interactions in the target population and identifying prominent (central) network nodes, which can be presented using networks and quantitative results.

The way in which data were collected significantly contributed to the elimination of the missing data issue, which is quite problematic in network research (e.g., Kossinets, 2006). Therefore, a survey (closed, password-locked) was distributed online through the "Ankieta Plus" service (www.ankietaplus.pl/) only to a selected population of employees in the given organization. Additional settings of the survey eliminated the risk of missing data, as, without all the required data, the respondent would not be able to continue the survey. As a data collection tool, a survey has both advantages and disadvantages (Borgatti et al., 2018). Advantages include limiting errors related to data collection and data sensitivity in the case of direct contact between the respondent and the researcher. Incomplete data cause problems in statistical reasoning. Lack of associations between actors interferes with the ability to formulate conclusions based on the data and misguides the researcher.

Confidentiality remains an important ethical aspect of network research (Everton, 2012). Providing anonymity is difficult, as in this type of network research, relations among all participants are examined, and respondents should say with whom they communicate when performing their work. In order to maintain the confidentiality of the obtained data, each respondent was assigned a special identification number (e.g., A01), and the identity behind the number was only known to the researcher. The respondents were assured of data confidentiality and informed that the results would be sent to an entirely external server, beyond the control of managerial staff.

Table 3.4 shows a summary of study methods, techniques, and tools; data sources used; and the obtained results.

3.3 Presentation of the Selected Case Study and the Studied Population, Broken Down by Intangible Resource Audit Model Stages

In order to exemplify the developed methodology of integrated intangible resource audit, an enterprise operating in the IT sector was invited to take part in the study. Special attention was paid to illustrating the tools (metrics) of organizational network analysis. The planning, design,

Table 3.4 Research methodology

Literature study						
Literature review	Resource-based view	Knowledge-based view	Intellectual capital-based view	Network theory	Actor–network theory	Activity theory
	Information	Knowledge	Intellectual capital	Social network analysis		
	Information audit	Knowledge audit	Intellectual capital audit	Organizational network analysis	Dynamic network analysis	
Data sources	Web of Science; Scopus; Scimago; Google Scholar					
Result	Integrated organizational intangible resource audit			Instruments for organizational network analysis		
Qualitative research						
Methods	Interviews and data coding	Documentation analysis		Case study		
Data sources	Managing directors	Organizational documentation		Documentation, interview		
Result	Survey development			Examining the organizational context		
Quantitative research						
	Data collection	Survey results		Data analysis		
Tools and techniques	Survey ORA	ORA, SPSS		UCINET: QAP/MRQAP		
Result	Development of matrices	Interpretation of findings		Correlation and regression		
Network research						
	Metrics of organizational network analysis	Network visualization		Hypothesis testing		
Tools and techniques	ORA	ORA		UCINET: QAP/MRQAP		
Research results						
	Conclusions	Theoretical and practical recommendations		Limitations and directions for further research		

and operationalization stages of intangible resource audit are briefly presented, in accordance with Table 2.5. The performance stage is discussed in more detail, and its results are presented in Chapter 4. The implementation stage, due to its size and complexity, including the need to develop an intangible resource management strategy, requires a separate publication.

Connecto Sp. z o.o. is a company established in 2005, localized in Silesia, Poland. At the end of 2016, the enterprise employed 47 people. Connecto offers comprehensive IT solutions for streamlining enterprise operations in all sectors. It implements enterprise resource planning (ERP) systems by Comarch S.A., with whom they have been cooperating for over 12 years, and develops data management system (DMS) software, assisting in enterprise management and customer relationship management using computers and/or mobile devices. These solutions allow for constant monitoring of tasks in the enterprise and increasing the efficiency of particular departments. Connecto provides services to companies operating in production, retail, service, construction, and many other sectors. Since 2011, Connecto has been a partner of the Silesian Construction Chamber. Their services involve supporting customers at every stage of their project—from defining the needs, to system implementation, to training and ongoing support. Connecto approaches each client individually and selects the right IT tools to help companies achieve tangible financial benefits. In 2016, the Microsoft company selected Connecto as a "Gold Partner."

3.3.1 The Planning Stage of the Intangible Resource Audit in Connecto

At the planning stage of the intangible resource audit, a presentation of the Connecto enterprise was made by the managing director, and the auditor was introduced to the staff. The most important steps at this stage included defining the goals and scope of intangible resource audit, as well as the research assumptions and hypotheses, in cooperation with the managing staff. Both the aims and assumptions of intangible resource audit were adjusted to the needs of Connecto. The aim of the audit was to identify and analyze intangible resources from the point of view of the network of relations. Research hypotheses (see Section 4.2) concerned correlations existing among specific information, knowledge, task, and resource networks. Techniques of organizational network analysis were presented. The study was planned to analyze the dynamics of the network of relations, and dependencies existing among employees, information, knowledge, tasks (actions), and resources (tools) the employees use or perform at work. Network metrics were discussed, broken down into the entire network, dyad, and individual node levels. Owing to the support of the managing director, almost all employees took part in the study. During the study, one person left the enterprise and one was on a long-term health leave, which brought the total number of surveys to 45 (98%). Employees engaged in the novel study with eagerness and were curious about the results.

3.3.2 The Design Stage of the Intangible Resource Audit in Connecto

The stage was preparatory in nature, in the sense that its primary goal was to examine the organizational context of the Connecto enterprise. The first step involved identifying the opportunities and risks present in the enterprise's external environment. The last two years prove that there is increasing demand for IT products and, consequently, for implementation services—both specialties of Connecto, establishing the enterprise's competitive position in the market. The achievement of the company's goals depends to a large extent on macroeconomic conditions, in particular the level of IT investment in large and medium enterprises, the level of competition in the IT sector, and the labor market. The labor market is dynamic, and there is a high demand for qualified IT specialists. However, the supply does not satisfy the demand, which creates pressure to raise salaries, resulting in increased costs. In the long term, the pressure to increase salaries in the IT sector offers an opportunity to attract qualified employees.

On the other hand, staff turnover and shortages of qualified employees in IT entail the risk of slower growth and development of companies operating in the sector, particularly since the educational market in Poland is characterized by a smaller number of students graduating from technical faculties. IT companies are sensitive to customers' increasing requirements related to IT solutions. As a company operating in the B2B system, Connecto uses the latest achievements and technological advances offered by the Comarch company. The increasing importance of technology is further enhanced by the implementation of services offered by Connecto in the market. These include software for construction and property development (the specialty of the studied enterprise), IT systems for production, a unique approach to Business Intelligence, software for the services and maintenance sectors, production planning and execution, mobile business solutions, and effective e-Commerce and B2B solutions.

Changes in the external environment also have a growing impact on transformation of the business model itself. Changes related to technical advances and economic development create demand for new IT systems, and the growing competition between IT companies drives down profit margins. New technologies are applied in automation and robotics—which is the field where Connecto recognizes potential for future growth as part of the planned diversification of development. Global companies could gradually withdraw from the IT market in Poland due to salary-related pressure and limited flexibility compared to smaller companies that operate closer to the end customer. Polish IT sector and IT systems offer very high quality, hence the growing trend for international expansion into the United States, Canada, Saudi Arabia, and many other markets.

Risks are mostly related to politics and legislation, as changes in these areas can result in decreased investment, changing organizational cost structure, and higher tax costs. In this market, there are no technical barriers to globalization of activity. In Poland, the demand for IT and implementation services is high, and Connecto performs excellently in this market, for now having no plans of expanding their business geographically. The risk of losing the main vendor is also low, as the cooperation is mutually beneficial, based on a relationship with partners who generate income for the vendor.

The opportunities and risks presented above shape the strategic goals of Connecto, which include:

- increase in subject matter knowledge (on IT and new technologies),
- intra-organizational knowledge transfer,
- further professionalization,
- diversification of income,
- generation of profit and company value.

Considering these opportunities and risks associated with the external environment, which determine Connecto's goals and directions for development, identification of the business model is essentially a response to seizing opportunities and minimizing risks in the context of value generation for customers and for Connecto. The business model is seen from the point of view of generating and delivering value for customers (Morris, Schindehutte, & Allen, 2005; Zott, Amit, & Massa, 2011). For the purpose of this book, the definition of the business model according to Johnson, Christensen, and Kagermann (2008) was adopted. According to this definition, the business model comprises a value proposition for the customer, a profit formula, key resources, and core processes, associated with creating and delivering value for customers and the organization. An important role is played by business processes, within which one can analyze how value is created for the organization. The business model is also often defined in the context of conceptualization of associations between the organization and its stakeholders, in particular the customers (Baden-Fuller & Morgan, 2010), cooperation, partnership, and joint value creation, acknowledging the interrelations of performed actions as the essence of the business model (Zott & Amit, 2010). In the intra-organizational view of the business model, the information network (information flow) plays an important part, as it makes the model dynamic and affects all its components (see Zhang, Zhao, & Xu, 2016).

The components of Connecto's business model are as follows (see Table 3.5). *Key resources* and *key activities* were not taken into consideration, as they will be listed in Table 3.6 in the context of core business processes.

The above elements related to the analysis of Connecto's external environment and business model constitute the design stage of intangible resource audit, which plays an important part in identifying and defining the organizational context. Business model definition is accompanied by the identification of business processes, which allowed the auditor to understand how value is created in the Connecto company. These include (Table 3.6) the commercial process (including advertising, telemarketing,

Table 3.5 The components of Connecto business model

Business model components	*Attributes*
Value proposition	- satisfying a wide range of customers' IT and IT-related needs; - long-lasting customer attachment through the professional character of services; - competing on quality, not price; - long-lasting cooperation with customers; - handling customers' issues that they need not be burdened with.
Customer groups	- B2B, - SMEs (small and medium enterprises), - large enterprises.
Distribution channels	- website, - Internet, - e-mail, - personal contact.
Customer relationships	- personal contact, - contact by telephone.
Partners	- vendors: Comarch, Microsoft, Dell, IBM, Lenovo; - ABC Data; - DevExpress; - Team Viewer; - Cristal Reports (SAP).
Sources of income	- implementation process, - sale of licenses and services.
Sources of costs	- remunerations (personal costs), - maintenance of infrastructure.

Sources: Author's own work based on Osterwalder and Pigneur (2010) and the interviews performed.

Table 3.6 Connecto business processes and the relevant knowledge, skills, tasks, and resources

Business processes	*Knowledge and skills*	*Tasks/actions/activities*	*Resources/tools/ structural capital*
1. Commercial process			
a. Advertising	Copywriting	Developing specialized portals	Google Adwords
	Communication and creativity	Recording and/or finding customers in the database	MS Office
	Knowledge of the Connecto product group	Handling the company blogs	Website traffic tracking software
	Knowledge of SEO principles	Monitoring competitors' activities	Phone
	Knowledge of Web portal construction	Connecto brand image building	Computer
		Search engine optimization for the Connecto website	
b. Telemarketing	Verbal (communication) skills	Developing prospective customer databases	The DMS system
	General knowledge of the product group	Preliminary customer classification by product	MS Office
	Product targeting (matching products to customers and their business processes)	Contacting customers by phone	Phone
	Knowledge of references	Referring interested customers to the sales division	Computer
c. Sales	Knowledge of Connecto DMS	Customer needs analysis	MS Office
	Knowledge of project management	Preparing presentation points	The DMS system
	Knowledge of document flows	Preparing an offer	Company car
	Knowledge of customer relationship management (CRM)	Providing references	Conference room
	Knowledge of BI	Drawing up contracts	Projector
	Knowledge of Comarch Optima	Negotiating sales terms	Phone
	Knowledge of Comarch XL	Delivering presentations for customers	Computer
	Knowledge of the operations of Connecto	Selling the service	

(*Continued*)

	Knowledge of the IT industry	Renewing contracts	
	Knowledge of hardware infrastructure	Selling customer warranties/assistance	
	Knowledge of competitors' products	Issuing invoices	
	Knowledge of references	(Re)negotiating contract terms	
	Communication	Reporting	
	Knowledge of customers (their size, organizational structure, business processes, etc.)		
	Knowledge of the customer's industry (e.g., construction)		
	Product targeting (matching products to customers and their business processes)		
	Negotiation skills		
2. Implementation process	Knowledge of enterprise operation	Visiting customers	Car
	Knowledge of implementation methods	Developing pre-implementation documents	Team Viewer
	Implementation progress reporting skills	Adjusting the system to the customer's needs (e.g., configuration and/or reconfiguration)	MS Office
		Providing training in the implementation process	The DMS system
		Customer system maintenance	Help desk
	Detailed product knowledge	Hardware maintenance	Microsoft SQL
	Knowledge of customers' business processes	Network maintenance (servers, domains)	Cristal Reports
	Knowledge in specific areas (accounting, HR, logistics, production)	Customer service (customer retention)	Phone
	Technical (IT) knowledge		Computer
	Analytical thinking		
	Assertiveness (being able to make one's case)		
	Knowledge of SQL databases		

(Continued)

Table 3.6 (Continued)

Business processes	*Knowledge and skills*	*Tasks/actions/activities*	*Resources/tools/ structural capital*
3. Customer retention (service) process	Knowledge of past customer implementations (what has been implemented)	Handling customer requests	Car
	Knowledge of current licenses	Communication with customers (remote/ personal)	Team Viewer
	Knowing people involved in the project	Fulfilling service requests (repairs)	MS Office
	Knowledge of customers' technical parameters (e.g., servers, platforms, login processes, IP addresses)	Initiating processes, e.g., development	The DMS system
	Knowledge in specific areas (accounting, HR, logistics, production)	Closing service requests	Help desk
	Technical (IT) knowledge		Microsoft SQL
	Knowledge of SQL databases		Phone
			Computer
4. Production process	Object-oriented programming	Recording specifications	Team Viewer
	Knowledge of SQL databases	Delegating tasks	MS Office
	Mathematical thinking	Writing source code	The DMS system
	Creatively solving complex problems	Software testing	Help desk
		Installing software	Visual Studio
		Software development	Programming libraries
			Microsoft SQL
			Computer

(*Continued*)

5. Administrative process	Accounting	Customer billing	The financial and accounting system
	Debt collection	Matching contracts to billing documents	The DMS system
	Organizational activities of Connecto	Employee payroll services	MS Office
	Organizational structure of Connecto	Technical services for company events (e.g., training, conferences)	E-mail
	Personnel and legal services	Regulatory reporting	"Płatnik"—the social security document submission system
	Mail management	Customer service for the accounting company (Consigno)	Phone
	Insurance and lease document management		Computer
	Organizational document management		

Source: Own work based on the interviews.

sales), the implementation process, the customer retention (service) process, the production process, and the administrative process. The defined business processes were matched with the knowledge and skills, tasks (actions), and resources (tools) required in their execution, which are the basis for identifying the intangible resources of an enterprise and performing the audit (Table 2.4, stage 4.1). The performance stage is described in Chapter 4.

3.3.3 Operationalization Stage of the Intangible Resource Audit

At this stage, the tools for audit execution were selected and developed. In the audit, ONA was the principal technique, comprising metrics discussed in detail in Sections 2.3.2 and 3.2 (discussion of study methods). The discussed network techniques were tested in pilot studies, performed in two organizations, one from the higher education sector (Ujwary-Gil, 2019), and one from the medical sector. As a result of the pilot studies, the questionnaire was simplified and its completion time was shortened, as discussed in the previous section (3.2).

3.4 Studied Population

In total, 45 Connecto employees took part in the study, constituting 98% of the population. Seven were female (15%), and 38 were male (85%). Basic descriptive statistics are shown in Table 3.7.

The participants had 10 years of experience on average, the oldest employee (62 years) having the most experience (32 years). The mean time of employment in Connecto was 4 years and was the longest, 13 years, for the founders of the company. The vast majority of employees (78%) had a university degree, out of which 20% had an MSc, 36%—MA, 16%—BSc, and 7%—BA.

Table 3.7 Descriptive statistics of the population

	M	*SD*	*Minimum*	*Maximum*
Women	15%	-	-	-
Men	85%	-	-	-
Total years of experience	10.20	7.14	1	35
Years of work at Connecto	4.28	3.46	1	13
Education	4.24	1.44	2	6
Age	32.91	7.49	23	62

Key: M—mean; SD—standard deviation.

Notes

1. This refers to the stages and steps of the audit, and not business processes to which the audit can be applied. Business processes provide a framework for analyzing information, knowledge, tasks, or resources that make up the essence of a business process.
2. Resources (R) comprise tools and structural capital in the form of information and communications infrastructure (in the Connecto enterprise, this is mainly specialized production and sales software). A few resources (e.g., telephone, computer, conference room, or company car) are physical, which shows that intangible and tangible resources may be complementary, and their separation may be pointless.
3. Respondents in all studies were assured that the data are confidential and that, after the study, each participant would be coded with a unique identification number, for example, A01. It was impossible to provide anonymity due to the researcher's need to identify relations between individual employees in the organization. Use of another form of name coding would have been too complex and time consuming.
4. A five-degree Likert scale was used for this and the following questions (5–10).
5. This is part of a linear algebra operation called the inner-dot product of the first row vector and column vector, in which the network (matrix) is multiplied by transposition.
6. The number of graphs (network visualizations) that could be presented here exceeds 60. As it is not possible to show all of them, only several examples have been selected for demonstration.

References

Alavi, M., & Leidner, D. E. (2001). Review: Knowledge management and knowledge management systems: Conceptual foundations and research issues. *MIS Quarterly*, 107–136.

Baden-Fuller, C., & Morgan, M. S. (2010). Business models as models. *Long Range Planning*, *43*(2–3), 156–171. https://doi.org/10.1016/j.lrp.2010.02.005

Benbasat, I., Goldstein, D. K., & Mead, M. (1987). The case research strategy in studies of information systems. *MIS Quarterly*, 369–386.

Bontis, N., Dragonetti, N. C., Jacobsen, K., & Roos, G. (1999). The knowledge toolbox: A review of the tools available to measure and manage intangible resources. *European Management Journal*, *17*(4), 391–402. https://doi.org/10.1016/S0263-2373(99)00019-5

Borgatti, S. P., & Cross, R. (2003). A relational view of information seeking and learning in social networks. *Management Science*, *49*(4), 432–445.

Borgatti, S. P., Everett, M. G., & Freeman, L. C. (2002). *UCINET 6 for windows: Software for social network analysis user's guide*. Harvard, MA: Analytic Technologies.

Borgatti, S. P., Everett, M. G., & Johnson, J. C. (2018). *Analyzing social networks*. London: Sage Publications.

Brinkkemper, S. (1996). Method engineering: Engineering of information systems development methods and tools. *Information and Software Technology*, *38*(4), 275–280.

Broekel, T., Balland, P. A., Burger, M., & van Oort, F. (2014). Modeling knowledge networks in economic geography: A discussion of four methods. *The Annals of Regional Science*, *53*(2), 423–452.

Burnett, S., Williams, D., & Illingworth, L. (2013). Reconsidering the knowledge audit process: Methodological revisions in practice. *Knowledge and Process Management*, *20*(3), 141–153.

Carley, K. M., Pfeffer, J., Reminga, J., Storrick, J., & Columbus, D. (2013). ORA user's guide 2013. Technical Report, CMU-ISR-13–108. Pittsburgh: Carnegie Mellon University, School of Computer Science, Institute for Software Research.

Cook, S. D. N., & Brown, J. S. (1999). Bridging epistemologies: The generative dance between organizational knowledge and organizational knowing. *Organization Science*, *10*(4), 381–400. https://doi.org/10.1287/orsc.10.4.381

Creswell, J. W., & Poth, C. N. (2017). *Qualitative inquiry and research design: Choosing among five approaches*. London: Sage Publications.

Cricelli, L., & Grimaldi, M. (2008). A dynamic view of knowledge and information: A stock and flow based methodology. *International Journal of Management and Decision Making*, *9*(6), 686. https://doi.org/10.1504/IJMDM.2008.021221

Cross, R. L., Borgatti, S. P., & Parker, A. (2002). Making invisible work visible: Using social network analysis to support strategic collaboration. *California Management Review*, *44*(2), 25–46.

Cross, R. L., & Parker, A. (2004). *The hidden power of social networks: Understanding how work really gets done in organizations*. Brighton, MA: Harvard Business Press.

Czakon, W. (2015). Zastosowanie studiów przypadku w badaniach nauk o zarządzaniu. In W. Czakon (Ed.), *Podstawy metodologii badań w naukach o zarządzaniu* (pp. 189–210). Warsaw: Wydawnictwo Nieoczywiste.

D'Errico, M., Stefani, S., & Torriero, A. (2014). Informal ties in organizations: A case study. *Quality & Quantity*, *48*(4), 1929–1943.

Dekker, D., Krackhardt, D., & Snijders, T. A. (2007). Sensitivity of MRQAP tests to collinearity and autocorrelation conditions. *Psychometrika*, *72*(4), 563–581.

Diez-Vial, I., & Montoro-Sanchez, A. (2014). Social capital as a driver of local knowledge exchange: A social network analysis. *Knowledge Management Research & Practice*, *12*(3), 276–288. https://doi.org/10.1057/kmrp.2014.7

Eisenhardt, K. M. (1989). Building theories from case study research. *Academy of Management Review*, *14*(4), 532–550.

Everton, S. F. (2012). *Disrupting dark networks*. Cambridge, UK: Cambridge University Press.

Ferrin, D. L., Dirks, K. T., & Shah, P. P. (2006). Direct and indirect effects of third-party relationships on interpersonal trust. *Journal of Applied Psychology*, *91*(4), 870–883. https://doi.org/10.1037/0021-9010.91.4.870

Gibbons, D. E. (2004). Friendship and advice networks in the context of changing professional values. *Administrative Science Quarterly*, *49*(2), 238–262.

Gourova, E., Antonova, A., & Todorova, Y. (2009). Knowledge audit concepts, processes and practice. *WSEAS Transactions on Business and Economics*, *12*(6), 605–619.

Greiner, M. E., Böhmann, T., & Krcmar, H. (2007). A strategy for knowledge management. *Journal of Knowledge Management*, *11*(6), 3–15. https://doi.org/10.1108/13673270710832127

Gupta, N., Ho, V., Pollack, J. M., & Lai, L. (2016). A multilevel perspective of interpersonal trust: Individual, dyadic, and cross-level predictors of performance. *Journal of Organizational Behavior*, *37*(8), 1271–1292.

Handzic, M., Lagumdzija, A., & Celjo, A. (2008). Auditing knowledge management practices: model and application. *Knowledge Management Research & Practice*, *6*(1), 90–99. https://doi.org/10.1057/palgrave.kmrp.8500163

Hinds, P. J., Carley, K. M., Krackhardt, D., & Wholey, D. (2000). Choosing work group members: Balancing similarity, competence, and familiarity. *Organizational Behavior and Human Decision Processes*, *81*(2), 226–251.

Hong, S., Van den Goor, G., & Brinkkemper, S. (1993). A formal approach to the comparison of object-oriented analysis and design methodologies. *Proceeding of the Twenty-Sixth Hawaii International Conference on System Sciences*, *4*, 689–698. Retrieved from http://ieeexplore.ieee.org/xpls/abs_all.jsp?arnumber=284253

Hsu, S. H., & Tzeng, S. F. (2010). A dyadic perspective on knowledge exchange. *International Journal of Technology Management*, *49*(4), 370–383.

Hubert, L., & Schultz, J. (1976). Quadratic assignment as a general data analysis strategy. *British Journal of Mathematical and Statistical Psychology*, *29*(2), 190–241.

Ibarra, H. (1995). Race, opportunity, and diversity of social circles in managerial networks. *Academy of Management Journal*, *38*(3), 673–703.

Johnson, M. W., Christensen, C. M., & Kagermann, H. (2008). Reinventing your business model. (cover story). *Harvard Business Review*, *86*(12), 50–59.

Kaše, R., Paauwe, J., & Zupan, N. (2009). HR practices, interpersonal relations, and intrafirm knowledge transfer in knowledge-intensive firms: A social network perspective. *Human Resource Management*, *48*(4), 615–639.

Kossinets, G. (2006). Effects of missing data in social networks. *Social Networks*, *28*(3), 247–268.

Krackhardt, D. (1988). Predicting with networks: Nonparametric multiple regression analysis of dyadic data. *Social Networks*, *10*(4), 359–381.

Kratzer, J., Leenders, R. Th. A. J., & van Engelen, J. M. L. (2009). A social network perspective on the management of product development programs. *The Journal of High Technology Management Research*, *20*(2), 169–181. https://doi.org/10.1016/j.hitech.2009.09.005

Laumann, E. O., Marsden, P. V., & Prensky, D. (1989). The boundary specification problem in network analysis. In R. S. Burt & M. J. Minor (Eds.), *Applied network analysis: A methodological introduction* (pp. 18–34). Beverly Hills, CA: Sage Publications.

Levin, D. Z., & Cross, R. (2004). The strength of weak ties you can trust: The mediating role of trust in effective knowledge transfer. *Management Science*, *50*(11), 1477–1490.

Maciel, C. de O., & Chaves, C. E. L. (2017). Informational status in intra-organizational networks: The role of knowledge sharing and structural holes. *Revista de Administração*, *52*(2), 189–198. https://doi.org/10.1016/j.rausp.2016.12.008

Mantel, N. (1967). The detection of disease clustering and a generalized regression approach. *Cancer Research*, *27*(2 Part 1), 209–220.

Marouf, L., & Doreian, P. (2010). Understanding information and knowledge flows as network processes in an oil company. *Journal of Information & Knowledge Management*, *9*(02), 105–118.

Marsden, P. V. (1990). Network data and measurement. *Annual Review of Sociology*, *16*(1), 435–463.

Martin-Rios, C. (2014). Why do firms seek to share human resource management knowledge? The importance of inter-firm networks. *Journal of Business Research*, *67*(2), 190–199. https://doi.org/10.1016/j.jbusres.2012.10.004

Miles, M. B., & Huberman, A. M. (1994). *Qualitative data analysis: An expanded sourcebook*. London: Sage Publications.

Morris, M., Schindehutte, M., & Allen, J. (2005). The entrepreneur's business model: Toward a unified perspective. *Journal of Business Research*, *58*(6), 726–735. https://doi.org/10.1016/j.jbusres.2003.11.001

Myers, M. D. (2013). *Qualitative research in business and management*. London: Sage Publications.

Nonaka, I., & Takeuchi, H. (1995). *The knowledge-creating company: How Japanese companies create the dynamics of innovation*. Oxford, UK: Oxford University Press.

Nonino, F. (2013). The network dimensions of intra-organizational social capital. *Journal of Management & Organization*, *19*(04), 454–477.

Osterwalder, A., & Pigneur, Y. (2010). *Business model generation: A handbook for visionaries, game changers, and challengers*. Hoboken, NJ: John Wiley & Sons.

Perez-Soltero, A., Barcelo-Valenzuela, M., Sanchez-Schmitz, G., Martin-Rubio, F., & Palma-Mendez, J. T. (2006). Knowledge audit methodology with emphasis on core processes. *European and Mediterranean Conference on Information Systems*, 1–10. Retrieved from http://aperez.mx/KAMCP_EMCIS2006.pdf

Perez-Soltero, A., Barcelo-Valenzuela, M., Sanchez-Schmitz, G., Martin-Rubio, F., Palma-Mendez, J. T., Vanti, A. A., & others. (2007). A model and methodology to knowledge auditing considering core processes. *ICFAI Journal of Knowledge Management*, *5*(1), 7–23.

Ponelis, S. R. (2015). Using interpretive qualitative case studies for exploratory research in doctoral studies: A case of information systems research in small and medium enterprises. *International Journal of Doctoral Studies*, *10*. Retrieved from www.informingscience.com/ijds/Volume10/IJDSv10p535-550 Ponelis0624.pdf

Potoczek, N. (2018). *Zarządzanie zasobami ludzkimi w organizacji zorientowanej procesowo*. Warsaw: Wydawnictwo Naukowe PWN.

Prell, C. (2012). *Social network analysis: History, theory and methodology*. London: Sage Publications.

Rank, O. N. (2008). Formal structures and informal networks: Structural analysis in organizations. *Scandinavian Journal of Management*, *24*(2), 145–161. https://doi.org/10.1016/j.scaman.2008.02.005

Rašković, M., Makovec-Brenčič, M., & others. (2015). The trust-commitment-flexibility link in transnational buyer-supplier relationships: A network perspective. *Market/Tržište*, *27*(1), 7–19.

Sparrowe, R. T., & Liden, R. C. (2005). Two routes to influence: Integrating leader-member exchange and social network perspectives. *Administrative Science Quarterly*, *50*(4), 505–535.

Sveiby, K. E. (1997). *The new organizational wealth: Managing & measuring knowledge-based assets*. San Francisco: Berrett-Koehler Publishers.

Tenkasi, R. V., & Chesmore, M. C. (2003). Social networks and planned organizational change: The impact of strong network ties on effective change implementation and use. *The Journal of Applied Behavioral Science*, *39*(3), 281–300.

Tsai, W., & Ghoshal, S. (1998). Social capital and value creation: The role of intrafirm networks. *Academy of Management Journal*, *41*(4), 464–476.

Ujwary-Gil, A. (2019). Organizational network analysis: A study of a university library from a network efficiency perspective. *Library & Information Science Research*, *41*(1), 48–57. https://doi.org/10.1016/j.lisr.2019.02.007

Yin, R. K. (2013). *Case study research: Design and methods*. London: Sage Publications.

Zagenczyk, T. J., Purvis, R. L., Shoss, M. K., Scott, K. L., & Cruz, K. S. (2015). Social influence and leader perceptions: Multiplex social network ties and similarity in leader—Member exchange. *Journal of Business and Psychology*, *30*(1), 105–117.

Zhang, Y., Zhao, S., & Xu, X. (2016). Business model innovation: An integrated approach based on elements and functions. *Information Technology & Management*, *17*(3), 303–310. https://doi.org/10.1007/s10799-015-0225-5

Zott, C., & Amit, R. (2010). Business model design: An activity system perspective. *Long Range Planning*, *43*(2–3), 216–226. https://doi.org/10.1016/j.lrp.2009.07.004

Zott, C., Amit, R., & Massa, L. (2011). The business model: Recent developments and future research. *Journal of Management*, *37*(4), 1019–1042. https://doi.org/10.1177/0149206311406265

4 Organizational Intangible Resource Audit Findings—A Case Study

The presented intangible resource audit findings are broken down into three areas, reflecting the multitiered view of the organization: the network level, the dyad level, and the node level. Findings at the network level provide understanding of the network structure (density, centralization) and present intangible resources in the context of network effectiveness (diversity and redundancy). The dyad perspective is also useful for network analysis, enabling the study of correlations between specific relationships, which take the form of matrices. At the node level, analysis results show prominent actors (both human and nonhuman) that can become targets for organizational policy instruments and the influence of these prominent actors on the creation of an intangible resource management strategy. The chapter also discusses the process and significance of network node simulation (in this case, based on identification and removal of prominent nodes) in the context of modeling intangible resource flows and changes in network structure. Change simulation and network modeling merit consideration as the distinctive features of the dynamic approach to networks.

4.1 Intangible Resource Audit Findings at the Network Level

This chapter exemplifies the performance stage of intangible resource audit. As indicated in Table 2.4 in Chapter 2, performance is the fourth stage of the audit process, comprising four steps: identifying key intangible resources; analyzing the dynamics of the organizational intangible resource relationship network; analyzing the impact of intangible resources on achievement of objectives, value creation, and business processes; and developing the audit report. Intangible resources were identified based on the core business processes diagnosed in interviews: the commercial process (including advertising, telemarketing, sales), the implementation process, the customer retention (service) process, the production process, and the administrative process. These processes were used as the basis for defining intangible resources, broken down into knowledge and skills (K), resources understood as structural capital (R), and tasks or activities (T) inherently associated with the former—shown in Table 4.1.

Table 4.1 The intangible resources of Connecto

	Knowledge and skills		*Resources*		*Tasks*
K01	Analytical thinking	R01	Programming libraries	T01	(Re)negotiating contract terms
K02	Assertiveness (being able to make one's case)	R02	Cristal Reports	T02	Customer needs analysis
K03	Copywriting	R03	Google Adwords	T03	Delegating tasks
K04	Organizational activities of Connecto	R04	Help desk	T04	Initiating processes, for example, development
K05	Creatively solving complex problems	R05	Microsoft SQL	T05	Installing software
K06	Accounting	R06	MS Office	T06	Matching contracts to billing documents
K07	Mathematical thinking	R07	Website traffic tracking software	T07	Connecto brand image building
K08	Personnel and legal services	R08	E-mail	T08	Monitoring competitors' activity
K09	General knowledge on the Connecto product group	R09	Projector	T09	Negotiating sales terms
K10	Organizational structure of Connecto	R10	Conference room	T10	Customer service for the accounting company
K11	Detailed knowledge on Connecto products	R11	Car	T11	Employee payroll services
K12	Verbal (communication) skills	R12	"Płatnik"—the social security document submission system	T12	Customer service (customer retention)
K13	Negotiation skills	R13	The DMS system	T13	Network maintenance (servers, domains)
K14	Implementation progress reporting skills	R14	The financial and accounting system	T14	Hardware maintenance
K15	Product targeting (matching products to customers and their business processes)	R15	Team Viewer	T15	Developing pre-implementation documents
K16	Knowledge of BI	R16	Phone	T16	Developing specialized portals
K17	Knowledge of the IT industry	R17	Visual Studio	T17	Preparing presentation points

(*Continued*)

Table 4.1 (Continued)

	Knowledge and skills		*Resources*		*Tasks*
K18	Knowledge of the customer's industry (e.g., construction)	R18	Computer	T18	Drawing up contracts
K19	Knowledge of Comarch Optima			T19	Handling customer requests
K20	Knowledge of Comarch XL			T20	Search engine optimization for the Connecto website
K21	Knowledge of Connecto DMS			T21	Handling the company blogs
K22	Knowledge of CRM			T22	Renewing contracts
K23	Knowledge of the operations of Connecto			T23	Providing references
K24	Knowledge of hardware infrastructure			T24	Referring interested customers to the sales division
K25	Knowledge of customers (their size, organizational structure, business processes, etc.)			T25	Providing training in the implementation process
K26	Knowledge of document flows			T26	Developing prospective customer databases
K27	Knowledge of customers' business processes			T27	Preparing an offer
K28	Knowledge of competitors' products			T28	Reporting
K29	Knowledge of past customer implementations (what has been implemented)			T29	Fulfilling service requests (repairs)
K30	Knowledge of project management			T30	Customer billing
K31	Knowledge of current licenses			T31	Software development
K32	Technical (IT) knowledge			T32	Communication with customers (remote/personal)
K33	Subject matter knowledge (logistics)			T33	Adjusting the system to the customer's needs (e.g., configuration and/or reconfiguration)

	Knowledge and skills	*Resources*		*Tasks*
K34	Subject matter knowledge (production)		T34	Recording specifications
K35	Debt collection		T35	Regulatory reporting
K36	Organizational document management		T36	Selling customer warranties/ assistance
K37	Mail management		T37	Selling the service
K38	Insurance and lease document management		T38	Technical services for company events (e.g., training, conferences)
K39	Object-oriented programming		T39	Contacting customers by phone
K40	Knowledge of SQL databases		T40	Software testing
K41	Knowledge of customers' technical parameters (e.g., servers, platforms, login processes, IP addresses)		T41	Writing source code
K42	Knowledge of implementation methods		T42	Customer system maintenance
K43	Knowing people involved in the project		T43	Visiting customers
K44	Knowledge of references		T44	Recording and/or finding customers in the database
K45	Knowledge of Web portal construction		T45	Preliminary customer classification by product
K46	Knowledge of enterprise operation		T46	Delivering presentations for customers
K47	Knowledge of SEO principles		T47	Issuing invoices
			T48	Closing service requests

Key: K (knowledge and skills); R (resources, tools, structural capital); T (tasks).

Figure 4.1 shows a visualization of a group of nodes identified in the studied organization.[1] As shown in Table 4.1, the number of actors (employees) was A = 45, knowledge and skills—K = 47, resources—R = 18, and tasks—T = 48.

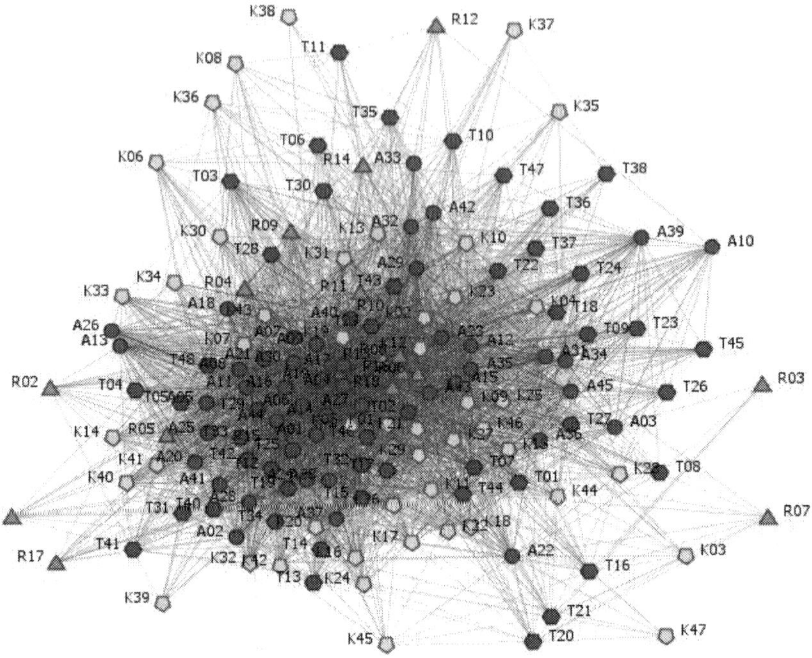

Figure 4.1 Visualization of major network nodes in the studied organization

The illustration begins with a presentation of network metrics' values at the network (organization) level, including network density and centralization; knowledge and resource diversity; and knowledge, resource, and task redundancy. Network density scores, denoting the ratio of all existing links (relations) in a network to all potential links, are shown in Table 4.2. The highest density was found for network AR^1 (0.642), then for AA^4 (0.618), AR^2 (0.570), and AK^1 (0.538), representing the existence of 64%, 62%, 57%, and 54% of possible relations, respectively. In other words, more than half of the relations possible in each network exist. Slightly lower densities (of approximately 46%) were found for networks AT^1 (0.462) and AK^2 (0.455). Densities of approximately 33% were found for networks AT^2 (0.327), KT (0.334), and RT (0.361). The lowest relative network density, 20% or lower, was found in networks AA^3 (0.172), AA^1 (0.193), and AA^2 (0.207). The total density of all the discussed networks (also termed "complexity") was 0.387.

Considering connections related to the department in which employees work, Tables 4.3 and 4.4 show densities of information (AA^1, AA^2) and knowledge networks (AA^3, AA^4) by department, as well as the number of internal and external relations. Internal relations are links connecting a node with another node in the same group. External relations are links

Table 4.2 Network-level metrics

	AA^1	AA^2	AA^3	AA^4	AK^1	AK^2	AR^1	AR^2	AT^1	AT^2	KT	RT
Row no.	45	45	45	45	45	45	45	45	45	45	47	18
Column no.	45	45	45	45	47	47	18	18	48	48	48	48
Links	383	410	341	1224	1138	963	520	462	999	708	754	312
Density	0.193	0.207	0.172	0.618	0.538	0.455	0.642	0.570	0.462	0.327	0.334	0.361
CD^N	0.368	0.354	0.391	0.316	—	—	—	—	—		—	—
DK	—	—	—	—	0.996	0.995	—	—	—		—	—
DR	—	—	—	—	—	—	0.983	0.978	—		—	—
ReK	—	—	—	—	0.528	0.443	—	—	—		—	—
ReR	—	—	—	—	—	—	0.324	0.324	—		—	—
ReT	—	—	—	—	—	—	—	—	0.450	0.312	—	—

Key: AA^1—receiving information; AA^2—providing information; AA^3—joint problem-solving; AA^4—knowing the knowledge and skills of others; AK^1—having knowledge; AK^2—using knowledge; AR^1—having access to a resource; AR^2—using a resource; AT^1—being able to perform a task; AT^2—performing a task; KT—task-related knowledge; RT—task-related resources; CD^N—network centralization; DK—knowledge diversity; DR—resource diversity; ReK—knowledge redundancy; ReR—resource redundancy; ReT—task redundancy.

connecting a node in the group with another node outside the group. The E/I (external to internal relations) index ranges between –1 (all links are internal, and communication silos exist in the group; that is, communication and knowledge sharing only occur within the group, work station, location, etc.) and +1 (all links are external), with 0 denoting an equal number of internal and external links.

Table 4.3 shows that external relations dominate, as demonstrated by a positive E/I index. One hundred percent external (outgoing) relations were found for the Marketing Department and the Sales Department Head, which is understandable, considering their size (one person). Over 90% of external relations were found in the Maintenance Department, Implementation Department (Board), and Administration Department, with slightly lower indices in the Sales Department (87%) and Programming Department (73%). A balanced ratio of internal and external relations was found in the Implementation Department (excluding the Board). Table 4.4 shows row-normalized connection values, or relation network densities, for each department. Row normalization was performed by weighting a single link against the node's number of links, using the formula: x_ij/(sum *i*).

Network density enables the measurement of connectivity in information and knowledge networks existing in each location (department). Information and knowledge flow between departments ranged from 0 to 0.230. The highest normalized density (0.230) was found for relations

Table 4.3 Internal and external relations by department

Group	*Size*	*Density*	*Internal links (I)*	*External links (E)*	*Percentage of internal links*	*E/I index*
Implementation Department	17	0.754	205	593	25.689	0.486
Programming Department	8	0.911	51	330	13.386	0.732
Telemarketing Department	5	1	20	114	14.925	0.701
Sales Department	5	0.800	16	241	6.226	0.875
Administration Department	4	0.917	11	240	4.382	0.912
Maintenance Department	2	1	2	144	1.370	0.973
Implementation Department/Board	2	1	2	144	1.370	0.973
Marketing Department	1	0	0	33	0	1
Sales Department/ Head	1	0	0	65	0	1

Table 4.4 Normalized network density by department

Group	*1*	*2*	*3*	*4*	*5*	*6*	*7*	*8*	*9*
1. Implementation Department	0.131	0.127	0.039	0.086	0.146	0.154	0.154	0.051	0.113
2. Programming Department	0.170	0.209	0.011	0.057	0.093	0.186	0.158	0.000	0.115
3. Telemarketing Department	0.023	0.022	0.215	0.138	0.151	0.086	0.108	0.129	0.129
4. Sales Department	0.099	0.078	0.083	0.118	0.118	0.118	0.148	0.089	0.148
5. Administration Department	0.106	0.086	0.079	0.108	0.132	0.144	0.126	0.108	0.108
6. Maintenance Department	0.124	0.115	0.066	0.105	0.131	0.131	0.131	0.131	0.066
7. Implementation Department/ Board	0.130	0.122	0.026	0.104	0.130	0.098	0.130	0.130	0.130
8. Marketing Department	0.027	0.029	0.000	0.138	0.230	0.230	0.115	0.000	0.230
9. Sales Department/ Head	0.129	0.055	0.087	0.146	0.146	0.146	0.146	0.146	0.000

between the Telemarketing Department on the one hand and the Administration Department, the Maintenance Department, and the Sales Department Head on the other. No strong relationships (providing or receiving information at least once a week or once daily, joint problem-solving, knowing others' knowledge and skills) were found between the Marketing Department and the Telemarketing and Programming Departments. Relationship density between the Programming and Telemarketing Departments was among the lowest found (0.011). Mean normalized density was 0.117, and standard deviation was 0.047.

Table 4.2 also shows structural characteristics of the organization that may affect its decision-making and planning activities. Total centralization in the four AA networks ranged between 0.391 and 0.316, potentially indicating unequally distributed communication. Were all employees connected to a central (principal) node, the score would be 1, while a score above 0.5 would indicate a centralized network. Knowledge (DK) and resource (DR) diversity values denote their distribution in the organization in terms of how (un)equally they are distributed among network actors (A). Diversity scores are very high (>0.9). Redundancy is a similar measure, related to knowledge and resource distribution, but denotes the percentage of actors who have access to the same resources or tasks or use the same knowledge. Knowledge (ReK), resource (ReR), and task (ReT) redundancy values differ among the two-mode networks. The scores are relatively high for networks AK^1 = 0.528, AT^1 = 0.450, and $AK^2 = 0.443$; and lower for network $AT^2 = 0.312$ and for networks AR^1 and $AR^2 = 0.324$.

4.2 Intangible Resource Audit Findings at the Dyad Level

Providing and receiving information related to one's work constitutes an information network, in which information flows occur. Knowledge flows (including tacit knowledge flows) occur in a network where actors seek assistance in solving problems related to their work, provided that they know what knowledge and skills their colleagues have. The quality and intensity of these relations in an organization are viewed as a significant determinant of value creation (Marouf & Doreian, 2010). It is impossible to understand the flow of information and knowledge in contemporary organizations without identifying and analyzing the diverse networks of relations between human actors (individuals) and/or nonhuman actors (knowledge, resources, tasks). Typically, in information networks, there is an information flow called communication, which gives a dynamic dimension to tacit knowledge sharing among an organization's employees (Swan, Newell, Scarbrough, & Hislop, 1999). Knowledge is sought within intra-organizational relation networks. Information and knowledge are transferred in the social network by direct contact and/or indirectly, through communications and information infrastructure (structural capital).

Resource audit findings at the dyad level were analyzed using matrix correlations (QAP) and regression (MRQAP), in order to demonstrate the interrelations and mutual impact of specific associations found. As in Kaše, Paauwe, and Zupan (2009, p. 626), the *Double-Dekker* and *semi-partialling* procedures were used, as they account well for collinearity of relational variables.

In line with the assumptions made at the planning stage, for the dyadic hypotheses listed below, it is expected that a given pair of actors A having one type of relationship is more likely to also have other types of relationships. Two network instruments, QAP and MRQAP, were used, similarly to studies by Ferrin, Dirks, and Shah (2006); Marouf and Doreian (2010); Hsu and Tzeng (2010); Zagenczyk, Gibney, Few, and Purvis (2013); Zagenczyk, Purvis, Shoss, Scott, and Cruz (2015); Maciel and Chaves (2017); Leon, Rodríguez-Rodríguez, Gómez-Gasquet, and Mula (2017); and D'Errico, Stefani, and Torriero (2014), where hypotheses were tested based on a single specifically selected case (organization or enterprise). In another study, Kaše, Paauwe, and Zupan (2009) analyzed four Slovenian knowledge-intensive firms (KIFs).

Below, example hypotheses are listed, with dependent and independent variables, illustrating ways in which networks may be correlated and regressed—which is particularly significant, seeing as scarce studies in the field of management have yet used these instruments, and thus Polish readers can benefit from their presentation. Considering the above, example hypotheses regarding the case may be as follows.

4.2.1 Having Knowledge and Skills

H1a. There is a connection between knowledge network 3 and information network 1, indicating that possession of shared knowledge by actors favors providing information among actors in the network.

H1b. There is a connection between knowledge network 3 and information network 2, indicating that possession of shared knowledge by actors favors receiving information from actors in the network.

H1c. There is a connection between knowledge network 3 and knowledge network 1, indicating that possession of shared knowledge by actors favors joint problem-solving.

H1d. There is a connection between knowledge network 3 and knowledge network 2, indicating that possession of shared knowledge by actors favors knowing what knowledge and skills other network actors have.

H2a. There is a connection between knowledge network 3 and resource network 1, indicating that possession of shared knowledge by actors favors shared access to resources in the workplace.

H2b. There is a connection between knowledge network 3 and resource network 2, indicating that possession of shared knowledge by actors favors shared use of resources in the workplace.

H3a. There is a connection between knowledge network 3 and task network 1, indicating that possession of shared knowledge by actors favors the actors' ability to perform tasks jointly.

H3a. There is a connection between knowledge network 3 and task network 2, indicating that possession of shared knowledge by actors favors the joint performance of tasks by the actors.

4.2.2 Using Knowledge and Skills

H1a. There is a connection between knowledge network 3 and information network 1, indicating that use of shared knowledge by actors favors providing information among actors in the network.

H1b. There is a connection between knowledge network 3 and information network 2, indicating that use of shared knowledge by actors favors receiving information from actors in the network.

H1c. There is a connection between knowledge network 3 and knowledge network 1, indicating that use of shared knowledge by actors favors joint problem-solving.

H1d. There is a connection between knowledge network 3 and knowledge network 2, indicating that use of shared knowledge by actors favors knowing what knowledge and skills other actors have.

H2a. There is a connection between knowledge network 3 and resource network 1, indicating that use of shared knowledge by actors favors shared access to resources in the workplace.

H2b. There is a connection between knowledge network 3 and resource network 2, indicating that use of shared knowledge by actors favors shared use of resources in the workplace.

H3a. There is a connection between knowledge network 3 and task network 1, indicating that use of shared knowledge by actors favors the actors' ability to perform tasks jointly.

H3a. There is a connection between knowledge network 3 and task network 2, indicating that use of shared knowledge by actors favors the joint performance of tasks by the actors.

First, entire matrices were correlated using QAP (Table 4.5), and statistical correlations were calculated using Pearson's r, an ordinary measure. Then, p values were constructed by calculating the proportion of correlations between independent matrices that were as large as the observed correlations. As suggested by Borgatti et al. (2018), a large number of permutations (50,000, random number seed 20,602) were used to stabilize the p values—this way, the node order changed randomly, but the network structure did not. The generated distribution enabled the calculation of a variable's statistical significance. Data were analyzed using UCINET 6 (Borgatti, Everett, & Freeman, 2002). Hypotheses were tested using QAP correlations and MRQAP regression (Table 4.6). To test hypotheses, dependent variable matrices were subjected to regression using independent variable matrices. Unlike standard OLS regression, QAP does not allow for calculating degrees of freedom, statistical power, or effect size. R^2 values can be lower than p values at .01, which means that 1% of the permutations show a higher correlation than that observed (Gibbons, 2004).

The strongest correlations were found between information networks AA^1 and AA^2 ($r = .895$, $p < .001$), and between knowledge network AA^3 and information networks AA^1 ($r = .877$, $p < .001$) and AA^2 ($r = .817$, $p < .001$), thus confirming the positive association between these organizational networks. A strong, statistically significant positive correlation exists between knowledge networks AK^{1_shared} and AK^{2_shared} (r = .811, $p < .001$), in line with the rather obvious assumption that actors having shared knowledge and skills are more likely to use them. The weakest correlations were found between resource network AR^{1_shared} and information network AA^2 ($r = .143$, $p < .001$), and between knowledge network AA^3 and knowledge network AK^{2_shared} ($r = .138$, $p < .01$).

Table 4.6 shows MRQAP regression results for dependent and independent variables. MRQAP was used to model the values of dyadic dependent variables (knowledge networks 3 and 4). The number of observations was 1980 pairs for each matrix (N * [N – 1]), 19,800 pairs in total for all ten matrices. Standardized coefficients with p values were

Table 4.5 QAP correlation results for the organizational networks*

Variable	*1*	*2*	*3*	*4*	*5*	*6*	*7*	*8*	*9*	*10*
1. AA_receives (AA^1)—information network (1)	1.000	.895	.877	.343	.153**	.223	.226	.236	.185	.215
2. AA_provides (AA^2)—information network (2)	.895	1.000	.817	.312	.148**	.197	.234	.243	.192	.212
3. AA_solves (AA^3)—knowledge network (1)	.877	.817	1.000	.342	.138**	.203	.210	.219	.168	.214
4. AA_knows (AA^4)—knowledge network (2)	.343	.312	.342	1.000	.265	.259	.383	.328	.255	.264
5. AK_has_knowledge (AK^{1_shared})—knowledge network (3)	.153**	.148**	.138**	.265	1.000	.811	.549	.594	.634	.464
6. AK_uses_knowledge (AK^{2_shared})—knowledge network (4)	.223	.197	.203	.259	.811	1.000	.507	.596	.556	.572
7. AR_has_access (AR^{1_shared})—resource network (1)	.226	.234	.210	.383	.549	.507	1.000	.862	.523	.521
8. AR_uses_resource (AR^{1_shared})—resource network (2)	.236	.243	.219	.328	.594	.596	.862	1.000	.561	.677
9. AT_can_perform (AT^{1_shared})—task network (1)	.185	.192	.168	.255	.634	.556	.523	.561	1.000	.696
10. AT_performs_task (AT^{1_shared})—task network (2)	.215	.212	.214	.264	.464	.572	.521	.677	.696	1.000

Key: * $p < .001$ for all networks, except ** $p < .01$

Table 4.6 MRQAP regression analysis for dyadic dependent variables: having knowledge and using knowledge

Networks		*Knowledge network (3)*		*Knowledge network (4)*	
		AK_has_knowledge (AK^{1_shared})		*AK_uses_knowledge (AK^{2_shared})*	
	Independent variable	*Model 1*	*Model 2*	*Model 3*	*Model 4*
Information network (1)	AA_receives (AA^1)	.050		.172*	
Information network (2)	AA_provides (AA^2)	.055		–.019	
Knowledge network (1)	AA_solves (AA^3)	–.033		–.003	
Knowledge network (2)	AA_knows (AA^4)	.242 ***		.207***	
Resource network (1)	AR_has_access (AR^{1_shared})		.017		–.027
Resource network (2)	AR_uses_resource (AR^{1_shared})		.413**		.370*
Task network (1)	AT_can_perform (AT^{1_shared})		.527***		.250*
Task network (2)	AT_perform_task (AT^{1_shared})		–.192*		.161
	Adj R^2 ($p < 0.001$)	.073	.499	.086	.437
	Random seed:	367	590	77	325

Key: * $p < .05$, ** $p < .01$, *** $p < .001$.

obtained using 50,000 permutations. MRQAP determines the relevance of predictor (explanatory) relationships for predicting knowledge-based behaviors. In the context of standardized coefficients, dependent variables are very important for work-related resource and task flows.

Four models were developed to test the hypotheses. Models 1 and 3 comprise four independent variables and account for 7.3% (Adj. $R^2 = 0.073$, $p < .001$) and 8.6% of variance in the dependent variable (Adj. $R^2 = .086$, $p < .001$), respectively, which suggests that neither information networks 1 and 2 nor knowledge network 1 are major factors for possessed knowledge and skills. Models 2 and 4 included the remaining variables, which increased their explanatory power to 49.9% (Adj. $R^2 = 0.499$, $p < .001$) and 43.6% (Adj. $R^2 = .436$, $p < .001$), respectively. Hypothesis H1d was confirmed ($\beta = .243$, $p < .001$), indicating a similarity between actors' having the same knowledge and actors' knowing the knowledge and skills of others in the organization. Hypotheses H2b ($\beta = .413$, $p < .01$), H3a ($\beta = .527$, $p < .001$), and H3b ($\beta = -.192$, $p < .05$) were also confirmed, indicating that having knowledge has an impact on resource and task networks, as highlighted in Model 2. For hypothesis H3b, the increase of one variable is associated with the decrease of the other. For the second dependent variable in Model 3 (knowledge network 4), there is an impact of the use of shared knowledge on information network AA^1 and knowledge network AA^4. Hypotheses H1a ($\beta = .172$, $p < .05$), H1d ($\beta = .2017$, $p < .001$), H2b ($\beta = .370$, $p < .05$), and H3b ($\beta = .250$, $p < .05$) were confirmed.

Overall, the hypothesis testing results highlight the significant impact of information, resource, and knowledge networks on variance in having and using knowledge and skills. Even though statistical generalization is not possible, one important theoretical or analytical generalization is that these networks create alternative pathways for shaping knowledge networks in an organization. Results show that social networks are a source of social inequality in an organization, which means that changing and balancing these inequalities is the domain of organizational actors, who are the foundation of all the discussed relationships.

4.3 Intangible Resource Audit Findings at the Node Level

Table 2.7 listed metrics describing the positions of network actors (the most important individuals in terms of prominence, position in the information and knowledge networks, and their impact on the network and its other members). Table 4.7 shows prominence scores for the top ten actors in information networks AA^1 and AA^2 and knowledge networks AA^3 and AA^4. Nodes with values higher than normal (more than 1 standard deviation from the mean) are listed in regular type, and nodes within 1 standard deviation from the mean are listed in italics. No scores in the

Table 4.7 Information and knowledge network centrality metrics

Network		*AA_receives (AA[1])*				*AA_provides (AA[2])*				*AA_solves (AA[3])*				*AA_knows (AA[4])*			
Metric	*R*	*A*	*V*	*US*	*Context**	*A*	*V*	*US*	*Context**	*A*	*V*	*US*	*Context**	*A*	*V*	*US*	*Context**
CD^n	1	A19	0.545	48	5.978	A19	0.545	48	5.602	A19	0.545	48	6.631	A19	0.920	81	4.174
	2	A29	0.352	31	2.698	A42	0.420	37	3.533	A29	0.318	28	2.593	A32	0.920	81	4.174
	3	A31	0.341	30	2.505	A29	0.398	35	3.156	A31	0.318	28	2.593	A29	0.886	78	3.703
	4	A11	0.330	29	2.312	A11	0.375	33	2.780	A11	0.307	27	2.391	A43	0.864	76	3.389
	5	A23	0.330	29	2.312	A17	0.341	30	2.216	A06	0.284	25	1.988	A27	0.841	74	3.075
	6	A44	0.318	28	2.119	A31	0.341	30	2.216	A44	0.284	25	1.988	A06	0.830	73	2.918
	7	A17	0.307	27	1.926	A44	0.341	30	2.216	*A27*	*0.261*	*23*	1.584	*A14*	*0.795*	*70*	2.448
	8	*A06*	*0.295*	*26*	1.733	A23	0.330	29	2.028	*A04*	*0.250*	*22*	1.382	*A40*	*0.795*	*70*	2.448
	9	*A43*	*0.295*	*26*	1.733	A27	0.330	29	2.028	*A23*	*0.250*	*22*	1.382	*A15*	*0.784*	*69*	2.291
	10	*A27*	*0.284*	*25*	1.540	A06	0.318	28	1.839	*A39*	*0.239*	*21*	1180	*A38*	*0.773*	*68*	2.133
		Min:	0.034	Max:	0.545	Min:	0.034	Max:	0.545	Min:	0.045	Max:	0.545	Min:	0.125	Max:	0.920
		M:	0.193	SD:	0.105	M:	0.207	SD:	0.110	M:	0.172	SD:	0.094	M:	0.618	SD:	0.179
		M in random network:			0.193	M in random network:			0.207	M in random network:			0.172	M in random network:			0.618
		SD in random network:			0.059	SD in random network:			0.060	SD in random network:			0.056	SD in random network:			0.072
Network		*AA_receives (AA[1])*				*AA_provides (AA[2])*				*AA_solves (AA[3])*				*AA_knows (AA[4])*			
Metric	*R*	*A*	*V*	*US*		*A*	*V*	*US*		*A*	*V*	*US*		*A*	*V*	*US*	
C^{in}	1	A17	0.386	17		A17	0.409	18		A19	0.386	17		A19	0.886	39	
	2	A19	0.386	17		A11	0.386	17		A17	0.318	17		A27	0.864	38	
	3	A32	0.386	17		A19	0.386	17		A27	0.318	14		A17	0.841	37	
	4	A27	0.364	16		A27	0.341	15		A32	0.295	13		A32	0.841	37	
	5	A31	0.318	14		A14	0.318	14		A06	0.250	11		A41	0.818	36	
	6	A42	0.318	14		A29	0.318	14		A11	0.250	11		A43	0.818	36	
	7	A11	0.295	13		A31	0.318	14		A14	0.250	11		*A06*	*0.773*	*34*	
	8	A14	0.295	13		A42	0.318	14		A23	0.250	11		*A29*	*0.773*	*34*	
	9	*A23*	*0.273*	*12*		A44	0.318	14		A31	0.250	11		*A30*	*0.773*	*34*	
	10	*A29*	*0.273*	*12*		*A06*	*0.295*	*13*		A41	0.250	11		*A40*	*0.773*	*34*	
		Min:	0.045	M:	0.193	Min:	0.045	M:	0.207	Min:	0.045	M:	0.172	Min:	0.159	M:	0.618
		Max:	0.386	SD:	0.092	Max:	0.409	SD:	0.093	Max:	0.386	SD:	0.077	Max:	0.886	SD:	0.182

(*Continued*)

Network		AA_receives (AA^1)			AA_provides (AA^2)			AA_solves (AA^3)			AA_knows (AA^4)		
Metric	*R*	*A*	*V*	*US*	*A*	*V*	*US*	*A*	*V*	*US*	*A*	*V*	*US*
C^{out}	1	A19	0.705	31	A19	0.705	31	A19	0.705	31	A29	1	44
	2	A29	0.432	19	A42	0.523	23	A29	0.432	19	A32	1	44
	3	A43	0.432	19	A29	0.477	21	A31	0.386	17	A19	0.955	42
	4	A23	0.386	17	A23	0.409	18	A11	0.364	16	A15	0.909	40
	5	A11	0.364	16	A11	0.364	16	A44	0.364	16	A43	0.909	40
	6	A21	0.364	16	A31	0.364	16	A21	0.341	15	A06	0.886	39
	7	A31	0.364	16	A44	0.364	16	A06	0.318	14	A14	0.886	39
	8	A44	0.364	16	*A06*	*0.341*	*15*	A43	0.318	14	A38	0.864	38
	9	*A06*	*0.341*	*15*	*A40*	*0.341*	*15*	*A04*	*0.295*	*13*	*A27*	*0.818*	*36*
	10	*A20*	*0.318*	*14*	*A20*	*0.318*	*14*	*A35*	*0.295*	*13*	*A40*	*0.818*	*36*
		Min: 0	M: 0.193		Min: 0	M: 0.207		Min: 0	M: 0.172		Min: 0.068	M: 0.618	
		Max: 0.705	SD: 0.147		Max: 0.705	SD: 0.151		Max: 0.705	SD: 0.140		Max: 1	SD: 0.229	

Network		AA_receives (AA^1)				AA_provides (AA^2)				AA_solves (AA^3)				AA_knows (AA^4)			
Metric	*R*	*A*	*V*	*US*	*Context**	*A*	*V*	*US*	*Context**	*A*	*V*	*US*	*Context**	*A*	*V*	*US*	*Context**
C^{eig}	1	A19	0.454	0.321	−0.346	A19	0.449	0.318	−0.404	A19	0.501	0.354	−0.106	A29	0.257	0.182	−1.790
	2	A29	0.348	0.246	−0.725	A42	0.360	0.254	−0.721	A29	0.358	0.253	−0.629	A32	0.257	0.182	−1.790
	3	A17	0.343	0.243	−0.743	A17	0.352	0.249	−0.750	A11	0.329	0.233	−0.732	A19	0.254	0.180	−1.799
	4	A43	0.326	0.231	−0.804	A29	0.336	0.237	−0.807	A27	0.322	0.227	−0.761	A43	0.254	0.180	−1.799
	5	A27	0.312	0.220	−0.856	A11	0.324	0.229	−0.849	A17	0.321	0.227	−0.765	*A27*	*0.250*	*0.177*	−1.812
	6	A11	0.309	0.218	−0.867	A27	0.318	0.225	−0.869	A44	0.320	0.226	−0.767	*A15*	*0.248*	*0.175*	−1.821
	7	A32	0.297	0.210	−0.910	A44	0.303	0.215	−0.921	A06	0.304	0.215	−0.824	*A31*	*0.248*	*0.175*	−1.821
	8	A31	0.295	0.209	−0.914	A06	0.293	0.207	−0.958	A31	0.299	0.211	−0.844	*A14*	*0.246*	*0.174*	−1.826
	9	*A44*	*0.285*	*0.202*	−0.951	*A31*	*0.279*	*0.197*	−1.007	*A43*	*0.277*	*0.196*	−0.925	*A06*	*0.246*	*0.174*	−1.828
	10	*A14*	*0.279*	*0.197*	−0.974	*A23*	*0.263*	*0.186*	−1.065	*A21*	*0.266*	*0.188*	−0.963	*A40*	*0.245*	*0.174*	−1.828
		Min: 0.013		Max:	0.454	Min: 0.012		Max:	0.449	Min: 0.013		Max:	0.501	Min: 0.044		Max:	0.257
		M: 0.183		SD:	0.104	M: 0.184		SD:	0.102	M: 0.182		SD:	0.106	M: 0.206		SD:	0.047
		M in random network:			0.550	M in random network:			0.564	M in random network:			0.530	M in random network:			0.804
		SD in random network:			0.279	SD in random network:			0.283	SD in random network:			0.273	SD in random network:			0.305

(*Continued*)

Table 4.7 (Continued)

Network		*AA_receives (AA¹)*				*AA_provides (AA²)*				*AA_solves (AA³)*				*AA_knows (AA⁴)*			
Metric	R	*A*	*V*	*US*	*Context**	*A*	*V*	*US*	*Context**	*A*	*V*	*US*	*Context**	*A*	*V*	*US*	*Context**
C^b	1	A19	0.164	310.448	6.403	A19	0.125	236.118	4.845	A19	0.217	411.013	8.146	A32	0.044	83.946	44.233
	2	A44	0.126	238.656	4.570	A39	0.106	200.404	3.878	A39	0.140	264.526	4.712	A29	0.040	75.782	38.874
	3	A39	0.118	224.171	4.200	A42	0.084	159.567	2.771	A31	0.093	176.416	2.647	A19	0.027	51.972	23.244
	4	A23	0.082	155.627	2.449	A29	0.083	156.797	2.696	A29	0.090	169.366	2.482	A43	0.020	37.012	13.424
	5	A29	0.063	119.896	1.537	A44	0.082	155.002	2.648	A23	0.073	137.891	1.744	A15	0.020	36.953	13.386
	6	*A31*	*0.055*	*103.523*	1.119	A23	0.071	134.564	2.094	*A04*	*0.061*	*115.382*	1.216	*A34*	*0.017*	*31.716*	9.947
	7	*A04*	*0.041*	*77.005*	0.441	A27	0.064	120.370	1.709	*A27*	*0.059*	*110.714*	1.107	*A27*	*0.016*	*29.388*	8.419
	8	*A35*	*0.040*	*75.966*	0.415	A11	0.063	118.402	1.656	*A32*	*0.052*	*98.871*	0.829	*A35*	*0.015*	*29.138*	8.255
	9	*A27*	*0.039*	*73.123*	0.342	*A06*	*0.041*	*77.881*	0.558	*A44*	*0.050*	*94.401*	0.724	*A06*	*0.015*	*27.626*	7.262
	10	*A01*	*0.038*	*71.018*	0.288	*A04*	*0.037*	*69.636*	0.334	*A06*	*0.047*	*88.016*	0.575	*A40*	*0.014*	*25.870*	6.110
		Min:	0	Max:	0.164	Min:	0	Max:	0.125	Min:	0	Max:	0.217	Min:	0.000	Max:	0.044
		M:	0.026	SD:	0.035	M:	0.025	SD:	0.031	M:	0.026	SD:	0.042	M:	0.009	SD:	0.009
		M in random network:			0.032	M in random network:			0.030	M in random network:			0.034	M in random network:			0.009
		SD in random network:			0.021	SD in random network:			0.020	SD in random network:			0.023	SD in random network:			0.001

Key: A—actor; V—standardized value; US—unscaled score; CD^n—centrality degree; C^{in}—in-degree; C^{out}—out-degree; C^{eig}—eigenvector centrality; C^b—betweenness centrality; Min—minimum value; Max—maximum value; M—mean; SD—standard deviation.

* number of standard deviations from the mean for a random network of the same size and density.

tables are below normal (1 standard deviation below the mean), as the scope is limited to the top ten actors (A).

Considering the three metrics: centrality degree (in-degree and out-degree), eigenvector centrality, and betweenness centrality, actor A19 is the most prominent individual in the information and knowledge networks. Individuals central to the network are those who have links with many others and whose position provides access to the information, knowledge, ideas, thoughts, and beliefs of many others. Individuals in high positions have more links to others in the same network. In- and out-degree centrality values differ in each network. Centrality degree values allowed for identifying the most connected individuals in the networks with regard to information and knowledge flows. Besides actor A19, prominent positions are occupied by actors: A29 and A31 (AA^1), A42 and A29 (AA^2), A29 and A31 (AA^3), and A32 and A29 (AA^4). These individuals can quickly send information, share knowledge, and control information and knowledge flows in the organization. In networks AA^1, AA^2, and AA^3, employee A19 has incoming and outgoing connections with 54% of network actors, the majority (70%) being outgoing relations. Employees in the top ten positions tend to know what knowledge and skills their colleagues have, though some do not, which restricts information and knowledge sharing. For instance, eight people know what knowledge and skills actor A10 has (reflected in the centrality degree of 0.182), while actor A10 only knows the knowledge and skills of three people (0.068). Many employees do not participate in information and knowledge flows: as many as 44% have incoming relations with five or fewer people; for outgoing relations, the percentage is 40%. Some employees (e.g., A15, A25, and A33) only have one person with whom they communicate on a daily or weekly basis.

Eigenvector centrality (C^{eig}) helps identify people connected to those who have many connections with others. In other words, in a given group, the person having the most connections with others in the same and other groups may be the group leader. People connected to many isolated individuals have much lower eigenvector centralities than those linked with well-connected groups. Thus, eigenvector centrality reflects the fact that not all connections are equal, and that actors with fewer contacts could be more important in a network than actors with more contacts. Again, based on eigenvector centrality, actor A19 is prominent in three networks—all except network AA^4. Compared to the random network mean, scores are considerably lower: the mean values are approximately 18% (0.182, 0.183, 0.184), compared to 55% (0.550, 0.564, 0.530) in the random network. Slightly higher C^{eig} values were found in network AA^4, with a mean of 20% (0.206)—compared to 80% (0.804) for the random network.

The betweenness centrality of a network node was defined as the percentage of information flow between network actors that allows for identifying information and knowledge flow brokers or gatekeepers. Potentially influential individuals are brokers for connections between groups and can regulate the influence of one group over the other or act as gatekeepers between groups. Individuals with high betweenness centrality are located on many of the shortest paths between other individuals. A person with low centrality degree and high betweenness and eigenvector centralities typically links two dense networks without participating actively in either of them. Again, actor A19 dominates as the broker in all networks except AA^4 (A32). In percentage terms, 16%, 12%, and 22% of information and knowledge flows occurred between A19 and others. This value also reflects the degree of control over the flow that a person has. Here, the scores did not differ from the random network mean.

Table 4.8 shows scores for total workload (W^{load}) and knowledge (K^{load}) and resource (R^{load}) loads. Actual workload indicates the knowledge and resources used by the actor to perform tasks to which the knowledge and resources have been assigned. Individuals with higher loads perform more complex tasks and have the resources, knowledge, and experience required for their performance. Tasks are considered more complex if they require more knowledge and/or resources. Knowledge and resource loads indicate the knowledge and resources used by the actor to perform tasks. Table 4.8 shows that actors A09 and A19 have the highest work, knowledge, and resource loads, followed by actors A04 and A40. Mean values were: W^{load} = 0.238, K^{load} = 0.22, and R^{load} = 0.284.

The next discussed metric is congruence (see Table 4.9), indicating the match between the way an organization is organized and its ability to perform tasks. Congruence values indicate the knowledge and resources an actor needs, but does not have, and knowledge and resources an actor

Table 4.8 Work, knowledge, and resource load values for actors

Rank	*Actual workload (W^{load})*		*Knowledge load (K^{load})*		*Resource load (R^{load})*	
	Actor	*Result*	*Actor*	*Result*	*Actor*	*Result*
1.	A09	0.643	A09	0.63	A09	0.673
2.	A19	0.497	A04	0.505	A19	0.503
3.	A04	0.492	A19	0.495	A40	0.481
4.	A40	0.47	A40	0.466	A30	0.465
5.	A17	0.431	A17	0.419	A04	0.458
6.	A06	0.386	A06	0.37	A17	0.458
7.	A23	0.386	A23	0.369	A23	0.429
8.	A01	0.376	A01	0.363	A06	0.423
9.	A30	0.374	A30	0.337	A01	0.407
10.	A31	0.33	A31	0.332	A16	0.404
	Min: 0.031	M: 0.238	Min: 0.019	M: 0.22	Min: 0.048	M: 0.284
	Max: 0.643	SD: 0.142	Max: 0.63	SD: 0.146	Max: 0.673	SD: 0.14

Key: Min—minimum value; Max—maximum value; M—mean; SD—standard deviation.

Table 4.9 Network node congruence

	Actor knowledge needs congruence (CK^{needs})		*Actor knowledge waste congruence (Ck^{waste})*		*Actor resource needs congruence (CR^{needs})*		*Actor resource waste congruence (CR^{waste})*	
Rank	*Actor*	*Result*	*Actor*	*Result*	*Actor*	*Result*	*Actor*	*Result*
1.	A26	0.802	A29	0.238	A10	0.429	A10	0.2
2.	A39	0.693	A10	0.222	A22	0.309	A11	0.111
3.	A33	0.682	A02	0.214	A36	0.28	A29	0.111
4.	A13	0.644	A42	0.214	A34	0.259	A13	0.1
5.	A20	0.615	A32	0.208	A03	0.25	A32	0.1
6.	A02	0.606	A05	0.105	A02	0.237	A42	0.1
7.	A10	0.582	A28	0.100	A24	0.22	A28	0.091
8.	A42	0.579	A33	0.100	A20	0.204	A35	0.083
9.	A03	0.547	A36	0.087	A07	0.2	A19	0.077
10.	A27	0.535	A40	0.081	A01	0.186	A21	0.071
	Min:	0.063	Min:	0	Min:	0.007	Min:	0
	Max:	0.802	Max:	0.238	Max:	0.429	Max:	0.2
	M:	0.389	M:	0.048	M:	0.113	M:	0.023
	SD:	0.183	SD:	0.069	SD:	0.085	SD:	0.046

Key: Result—unscaled score; Min—minimum value; Max—maximum value; M—mean; SD—standard deviation.

has, but does not use, and are calculated as a percentage showing the relation between the knowledge or resources required to perform a task, and the total amount of knowledge or resources. This is a sum of knowledge that is needed, but not available. Full congruence exists when the actor has exactly the knowledge or resources required for performing the task. In the opposite case, the metrics indicate knowledge or resources that an actor has, but does not need for the performed tasks. Unused knowledge or resources are considered wasted.

Actor A26 has the largest knowledge needs associated with the performed tasks—80% (0.802). Actor A39 is missing 69% (0.693) of knowledge, which means that knowledge is not assigned to the actor even though it should be, based on the tasks this actor performs. A similarly high level of knowledge needs congruence was found for actor A33 (0.682). The mean for the entire organization is 39% (0.389). Actor A09's knowledge is best suited for the tasks performed, with a knowledge needs congruence value of 0.063, or 6%, followed by actors A43, A40, and A31, with a score of 10% (0.100, 0.101, and 0.102, respectively). Knowledge waste congruence denotes knowledge that an actor has, but does not need for the tasks performed. The five highest values (for actors A29, A10, A02, A42, and A32) range between 24% and 21%. The organizational mean is rather low, just below 5% (0.048). In the case of resources, actor A10 does not have 43% of resources (0.429) assigned to the performed tasks. Slightly lower resource needs percentages are found for actors A22 (31%, 0.309), A36 (28%, 0.28), and A34 (26%, 0.259). The best match of resources to tasks is found for actor A45, with a resource needs congruence score of 8% (0.078). Resource waste congruence values are lower than the analogous scores for knowledge—20% (0.2) and 11% (0.111) for actors A10, A11, and A29, respectively. Mean resource waste congruence, or mismatch between resources and tasks, is 2% for the entire organization.

Centrality measures are the most popular metrics in organizational network analysis, allowing the identification of individuals who use the most knowledge and resources, and perform the most tasks. Table 4.10 shows scores for actors having the most knowledge and resources and performing the most tasks. For each actor, knowledge, resource, and task node, the outgoing connections are connections from the node to other nodes. In the knowledge use (AK), resource use (AR), and task performance (AT) networks, the outgoing connection count for an actor is the number of items of knowledge, resources, or tasks associated with the actor. Individuals or organizations that are rich in knowledge (resources, tasks) have more expert knowledge (resources, tasks) or more types of knowledge (resources, tasks) than others.

Row degree centrality shows that actor A09 (0.872) is the person having nearly all out of the 47 available knowledge types, followed by actors: A04, A40 (0.787), and A23 (0.723). Actors: A17, A19, and A43 use 31 types of knowledge in their work (0.660). Regarding the use of resources by actors, the highest score is obtained by actor A09 (89%) who used nearly all out of the 18 available resource types. Also in the top ten are actors: A21 (0.778), A17, A19, and A24, using 72% of the available resources (0.722). Row degree centrality values in the "task performance" network are also the highest for actor A09, who performed 67% (0.667) of tasks associated with the identified business processes. Mean knowledge and skills use percentage is 44% (0.445), resource use—57% (0.57), task performance—33% (0.328).

In order to determine what knowledge, resources, and tasks are key in the network, the row degree centrality metrics were applied to transposed matrices, as shown in Table 4.11. Row degree centralities (outgoing connection counts) for knowledge, resources, and tasks were used to identify the most important network nodes. The table shows row degree centralities, or outgoing connections to other network nodes, broken down into knowledge, resources, and tasks. Actor/knowledge row centrality shows that 43 out of 45 employees (96%) use the knowledge item K12 (verbal communication skills)—the score was 0.956. Thirty-five tasks (73%, 0.729) are associated with the knowledge item K09 (general knowledge of the Connecto product group). As for key resources in the organization, these are R08 (e-mail), R16 (phone), and R18 (computer), used by all

Table 4.10 Row degree centralities of knowledge, resources, and tasks for network actors

Rank	*Row degree centrality knowledge/actor* ($C^{K/A}$)			*Row degree centrality resource/actor* ($C^{R/A}$)			*Row degree centrality task/actor* ($C^{T/A}$)		
	A	*Result*	*K*	*A*	*Result*	*R*	*A*	*Result*	*T*
1.	A09	0.872	41	A09	0.889	16	A09	0.667	32
2.	A04	0.787	37	A21	0.778	14	A19	0.521	25
3.	A40	0.787	37	A17	0.722	13	A04	0.479	23
4.	A23	0.723	34	A19	0.722	13	A30	0.479	23
5.	A17	0.660	31	A24	0.722	13	A40	0.479	23
6.	A19	0.660	31	A25	0.722	13	*A01*	*0.458*	*22*
7.	A43	0.660	31	A40	0.722	13	*A06*	*0.458*	*22*
8.	A15	0.638	30	A44	0.722	13	*A17*	*0.458*	*22*
9.	*A44*	*0.596*	*28*	*A04*	*0.667*	*12*	*A23*	*0.458*	*22*
10.	*A12*	*0.574*	*27*	*A05*	*0.667*	*12*	*A16*	*0.438*	*21*
	Min: 0.149 M: 0.445 Max: 0.872 SD: 0.173			Min: 0.278 M: 0.57 Max: 0.889 SD:0.13			Min: 0.063 M: 0.328 Max: 0.667 SD: 0.131		

Key: Result—unscaled score; Min—minimum value; Max—maximum value; M—mean; SD—standard deviation; A—actor; K—knowledge and skills; R—resources, structural capital; T—tasks.

employees. In the context of task performance, resource R18 (computer) is used in 81% of tasks. Mean percentage of knowledge and resources assigned to tasks is 33% (0.334) and 36% (0.361), respectively, which means that not all resources are assigned to specific tasks, as indicated by the KT and RT network densities. With regard to task performance, 96% of employees (0.956) perform task T39 (contacting customers by phone), 80% (0.800) perform task T32 (remote or personal communication with customers), and 69% (0.689) perform task T07 (Connecto brand image building). The mean for network AT (I perform this task in my work) was 0.323.

Knowledge is associated with various tasks. Sixty-eight percent (0.681) of knowledge is used for task T46 (delivering presentations for customers) and 64% (0.638) for task T25 (providing training in the implementation process). Associations between task performance and resources are less extensive. Tasks T12 (customer service/retention), T31 (software development), and T46 (delivering presentations for customers) use 61% of the available resources (0.611), and tasks T02 (customer need analysis), T17 (preparing presentation points), and T33 (adjusting the system to the customer's needs, e.g., configuration and/or reconfiguration) 56% (0.556).

Knowledge items K37 (mail management) and K39 (object-oriented programming) are associated with the fewest tasks (0.042). On the other hand, this knowledge or these skills may turn out to be highly

Table 4.11 Row degree centralities of knowledge, resources, and tasks in the network

	Row centrality degree actor/knowledge ($C^{A/K}$)			*Row centrality degree task/knowledge ($C^{T/K}$)*			*Row centrality degree actor/resource ($C^{A/R}$)*		
Rank	*K*	*Result*	*A*	*K*	*Result*	*T*	*R*	*Result*	*A*
1.	K12	0.956	43	K09	0.729	35	R08	1	45
2.	K01	0.911	41	K01	0.708	34	R16	1	45
3.	K05	0.889	40	K23	0.688	33	R18	1	45
4.	K02	0.778	35	K11	0.583	28	R13	0.956	43
5.	K19	0.756	34	K04	0.563	27	R06	0.933	42
6.	K07	0.733	33	K21	0.563	27	*R15*	*0.822*	*37*
7.	K21	0.733	33	K29	0.563	27	*R04*	*0.756*	*34*
8.	*K09*	*0.667*	*30*	K05	0.542	26	*R05*	*0.711*	*32*
9.	*K26*	*0.667*	*30*	K25	0.542	26	*R10*	*0.689*	*31*
10.	*K20*	*0.644*	*29*	*K27*	*0.521*	*25*	*R11*	*0.644*	*29*
	Min: 0.044	M: 0.455		Min: 0.021	M: 0.334		Min: 0	M: 0.57	
	Max: 0.956	SD:0.222		Max: 0.729	SD:0.188		Max: 1	SD:0.345	

	Row centrality degree task/resource ($C^{T/R}$)			*Row centrality degree actor/task ($C^{A/T}$)*			*Row centrality degree knowledge/task ($C^{K/T}$)*		
Rank	*R*	*Result*	*T*	*T*	*Result*	*A*	*T*	*Result*	*K*
1.	R18	0.813	39	T39	0.956	43	T46	0.681	32
2.	R06	0.792	38	T32	0.800	36	T25	0.638	30
3.	R08	0.792	38	T07	0.689	31	T17	0.617	29
4.	R16	0.771	37	T02	0.667	30	T12	0.596	28
5.	R13	0.750	36	T19	0.644	29	T42	0.596	28
6.	*R11*	*0.417*	*20*	T44	0.644	29	T33	0.574	27
7.	*R15*	*0.354*	*17*	T48	0.622	28	T15	0.553	26
8.	*R05*	*0.271*	*13*	T43	0.600	27	T29	0.553	26
9.	*R10*	*0.271*	*13*	T05	0.578	26	T01	0.511	24
10.	*R04*	*0.250*	*12*	T24	0.556	25	*T02*	*0.489*	*23*
	Min: 0.063	M: 0.361		Min: 0.061	M: 0.323		Min: 0.085	M: 0.334	
	Max: 0.813	SD: 0.278		Max: 0.841	SD: 0.213		Max: 0.681	SD: 0.157	

	Row centrality degree resource/task ($C^{R/T}$)		
Rank	*T*	*Result*	*R*
1.	T12	0.611	11
2.	T31	0.611	11
3.	T46	0.611	11
4.	T02	0.556	10
5.	T17	0.556	10
6.	T33	0.556	10
7.	T15	0.500	9
8.	T22	0.500	9
9.	T25	0.500	9
10.	T29	0.500	9
	Min: 0.111	M: 0.361	
	Max: 0.611	SD: 0.135	

Key: Result—unscaled score; Min—minimum value; Max—maximum value; M—mean; SD—standard deviation; A—actor; K—knowledge and skills; R—resources, structural capital; T—tasks.

specialized, as few people are capable of using them in their work. The least used resource is R12 (the "Płatnik" system), associated with three tasks (0.063).

Tasks, relying on the relevant knowledge and resources, differ in centrality for an organization. It is worth comparing knowledge and resources in terms of their importance for specific tasks. For instance, 13% of knowledge (0.128) is used in tasks T06 (matching contracts to billing documents), T45 (preliminary customer classification by product), and T47 (issuing invoices), and 9% (four items each) is used in tasks T11 (employee payroll services) and T44 (recording and/or finding customers in the database). In the case of resources, the ranking is different. Tasks T26 (developing prospective customer databases), T34 (recording specifications), T38 (technical services for company events, e.g., training, conferences), and T44 (recording and/or finding customers in the database) are associated with three resources each (0.167). Neither knowledge nor resources are fully used in tasks, based on the relations identified in networks KT and RT.

4.4 Simulation of Node Position Changes in the Network

Change dynamics in the network are an important factor in organizational intangible resource management, allowing for creating positive and negative scenarios, used for simulating changes in network structure in order to verify the impact of these changes on value creation and/or performance. The total density of all networks listed in Table 4.2 (Chapter 4) changed from 0.384 to 0.377 (meta-network density decreased by 1.79%). The density of information network AA^1 also decreased, by 8.46%, and that of network AA^2 decreased by 7.60%. The largest density drop (by 10.08%) was seen in knowledge network AA^3 (joint problem-solving), the least in knowledge network AA^4 (2.27%). For the purposes of demonstrating network change dynamics, the above information networks (AA^1, AA^2) and knowledge networks (AA^3, AA^4) were selected for analysis. A strategy proposed by Valente (2012) was used, involving the identification of actors based on their centrality degree. In this case, the ORA *Key entities* report was used to identify the most prominent individual in the networks (AA^1, AA^2, AA^3, AA^4)—actor A19. Figure 4.2 shows the incoming links, providing insights about the nodes that influence the ego-node (actor A19), and the outgoing links (on the right), indicating actors directly influenced by actor A19. Figure 4.3 shows knowledge networks—joint problem-solving (AA^3) and knowing what knowledge and skills one's colleagues have (AA^4).

Subsequently, the node was removed in order to simulate changes in the remaining nodes' centralities (Tables 4.12 and 4.13). The one-mode matrices for the information and knowledge networks determine the mutual influence of actors. An area of influence exists around each node

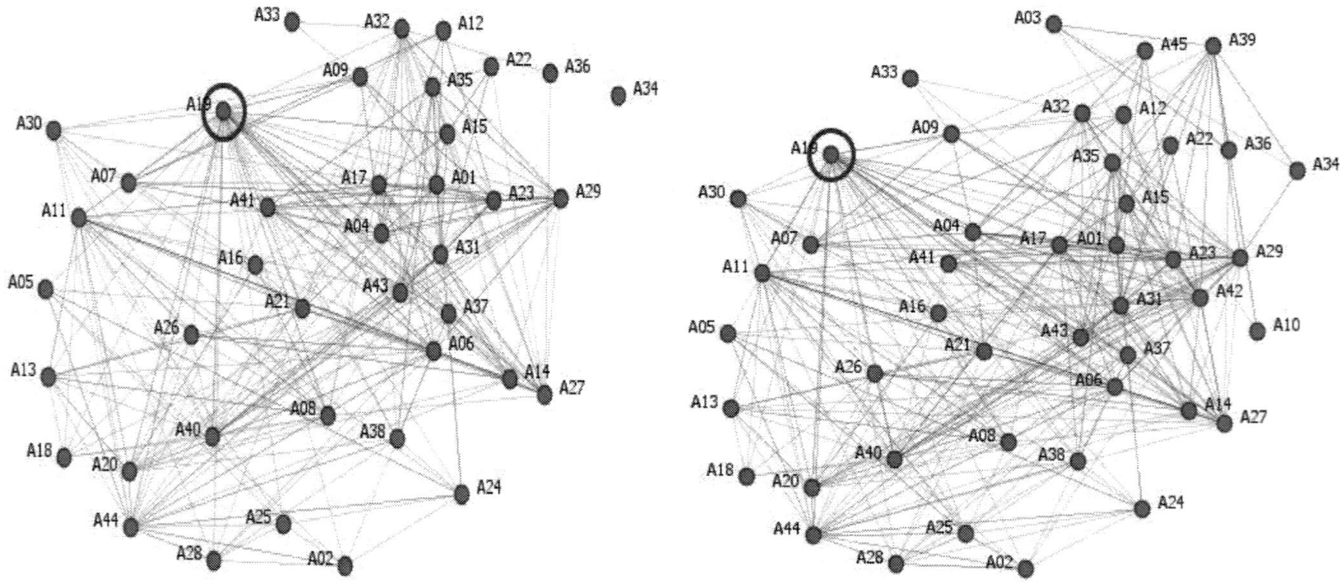

Figure 4.2 Links between actor A19 and other actors in information networks AA^1 and AA^2

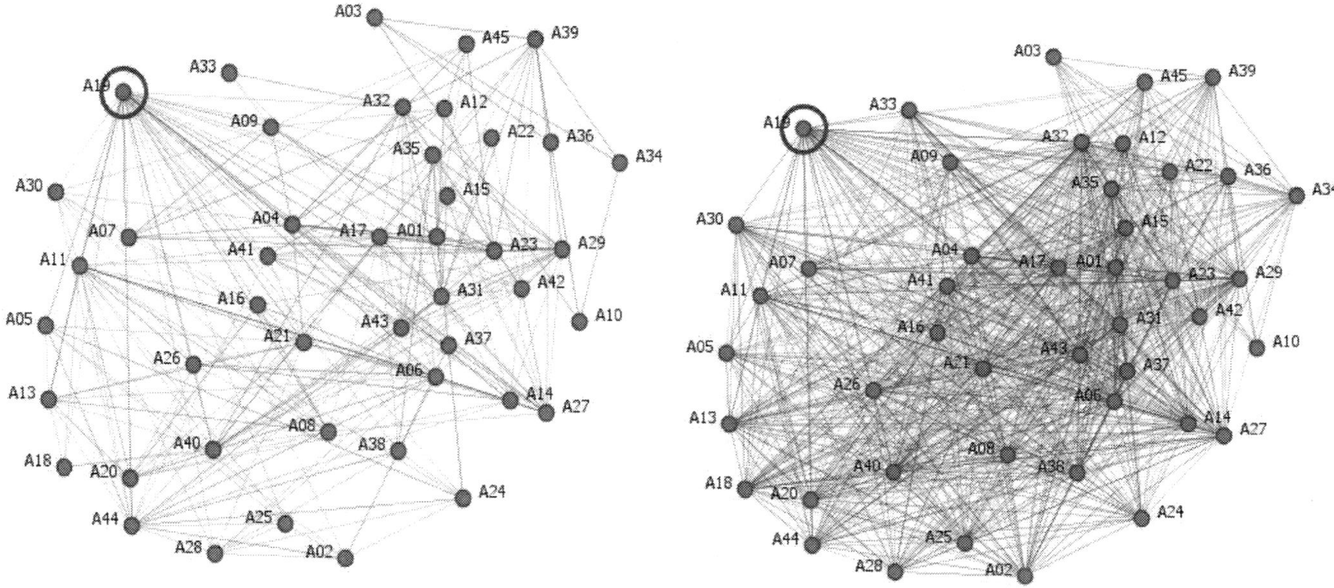

Figure 4.3 Links between actor A19 and other actors in knowledge networks AA^3 and AA^4

Table 4.12 Change dynamics—area of influence in a one-mode information network

Information network (AA_receives; AA[1])						*Information network (AA_provides; AA[2])*					
A	*R-1*	*V-1*	*R-2*	*V-2*	*Ch-%*	*A*	*R-1*	*V-1*	*R-2*	*V-2*	*Ch-%*
A19	1	0.545	Removed actor			A19	1	0.545	Removed actor		
A29	2	0.352	1	0.349	–0.98%	A42	2	0.420	1	0.419	–0.44%
A31	3	0.341	3	0.326	–4.50%	A29	3	0.398	2	0.395	–0.60%
A11	4	0.330	4	0.314	–4.73%	A11	4	0.375	3	0.360	–3.88%
A23	5	0.330	2	0.326	–1.20%	A17	5	0.341	4	0.326	–4.50%
A44	6	0.318	5	0.302	–4.98%	A31	6	0.341	6	0.326	–4.50%
A17	7	0.307	6	0.291	–5.25%	A44	7	0.341	7	0.326	–4.50%
A06	8	0.295	7	0.279	–5.55%	A23	8	0.330	5	0.326	–1.20%
A43	9	0.295	8	0.279	–5.55%	A27	9	0.330	8	0.314	–4.73%
A27	10	0.284	9	0.267	–5.86%	A06	10	0.318	9	0.302	–4.98%
A04	11	0.261	11	0.244	–6.57%	A15	11	0.273	10	0.256	–6.20%
A39	12	0.261	10	0.267	+2.33%	A04	12	0.261	12	0.244	–6.57%
A32	13	0.250	12	0.244	–2.33%	A14	13	0.250	13	0.233	–6.98%
A14	14	0.239	15	0.221	–7.42%	A20	14	0.250	14	0.233	–6.98%
A20	15	0.239	16	0.221	–7.42%	A39	15	0.250	11	0.256	+2.33%
A21	16	0.239	17	0.221	–7.42%	A40	16	0.250	15	0.233	–6.98%
A35	17	0.239	13	0.244	+2.33%	A43	17	0.227	17	0.209	–7.91%
A42	18	0.239	14	0.233	–2.55%	A21	18	0.216	18	0.198	–8.45%
A40	19	0.227	18	0.209	–7.91%	A35	19	0.216	16	0.221	+2.33%
A15	20	0.216	20	0.198	–8.45%	A26	20	0.193	20	0.186	–3.69%
A01	21	0.193	19	0.198	+2.33%	A41	21	0.193	21	0.186	–3.69%
A08	22	0.193	22	0.174	–9.71%	A01	22	0.182	19	0.186	+2.33%
A41	23	0.193	21	0.186	–3.69%	A25	23	0.182	22	0.174	–4.07%
A26	24	0.170	23	0.163	–4.50%	A32	24	0.182	23	0.174	–4.07%
A09	25	0.159	25	0.140	–12.29%	A08	25	0.170	25	0.151	–11.32%
A13	26	0.159	24	0.151	–4.98%	A09	26	0.170	26	0.151	–11.32%
A37	27	0.148	26	0.140	–5.55%	A13	27	0.170	24	0.163	–4.50%
A24	28	0.136	28	0.128	–6.20%	A28	28	0.159	27	0.151	–4.98%
A38	29	0.136	29	0.128	–6.20%	A38	29	0.159	28	0.151	–4.98%
A07	30	0.125	30	0.116	–6.98%	A16	30	0.148	30	0.140	–5.55%
A12	31	0.125	27	0.128	+2.33%	A24	31	0.148	31	0.140	–5.55%
A16	32	0.125	31	0.116	–6.98%	A30	32	0.148	32	0.140	–5.55%
A28	33	0.114	33	0.105	–7.91%	A07	33	0.136	33	0.128	–6.20%
A30	34	0.114	34	0.105	–7.91%	A12	34	0.136	29	0.140	+2.33%
A45	35	0.114	32	0.116	+2.33%	A37	35	0.136	34	0.128	–6.20%
A02	36	0.091	35	0.081	–10.47%	A02	36	0.125	35	0.116	–6.98%
A05	37	0.091	37	0.081	–10.47%	A05	37	0.114	37	0.105	–7.91%
A03	38	0.080	36	0.081	+2.33%	A45	38	0.114	36	0.116	+2.33%
A18	39	0.080	39	0.070	–12.29%	A22	39	0.080	38	0.081	+2.33%
A25	40	0.080	41	0.070	–12.29%	A03	40	0.068	39	0.070	+2.33%
A36	41	0.080	38	0.081	+2.33%	A18	41	0.068	41	0.058	–14.73%
A22	42	0.068	40	0.070	+2.33%	A36	42	0.068	40	0.070	+2.33%
A10	43	0.057	42	0.058	+2.33%	A34	43	0.057	42	0.058	+2.33%
A33	44	0.034	43	0.035	+2.33%	A10	44	0.045	43	0.047	+2.33%
A34	45	0.034	44	0.035	+2.33%	A33	45	0.034	44	0.035	+2.33%

Key: A—actor; R-1—rank before the removal of actor A19; V-1—centrality degree before the removal of actor A19; R-2—rank after the removal of actor A19; V-2—centrality degree after the removal of actor A19; Ch-%—change percentage.

Table 4.13 Change dynamics—area of influence in a one-mode knowledge network

Knowledge network (AA_solves; AA³)						*Knowledge network (AA_knows; AA⁴)*					
A	*R-1*	*V-1*	*R-2*	*V-2*	*Ch-%*	*A*	*R-1*	*V-1*	*R-2*	*V-2*	*Ch-%*
A19	1	0.545	Removed actor			A19	1	0.920	Removed actor		
A29	2	0.318	1	0.314	−1.33%	A32	2	0.920	1	0.919	−0.20%
A31	3	0.318	2	0.302	−4.98%	A29	3	0.886	2	0.884	−0.30%
A11	4	0.307	3	0.291	−5.25%	A43	4	0.864	3	0.860	−0.37%
A06	5	0.284	4	0.267	−5.86%	A27	5	0.841	4	0.837	−0.44%
A44	6	0.284	5	0.267	−5.86%	A06	6	0.830	5	0.826	−0.48%
A27	7	0.261	7	0.244	−6.57%	A14	7	0.795	6	0.791	−0.60%
A04	8	0.250	9	0.233	−6.98%	A40	8	0.795	7	0.791	−0.60%
A23	9	0.250	6	0.256	+2.33%	A15	9	0.784	8	0.779	−0.64%
A39	10	0.239	8	0.244	+2.33%	A38	10	0.773	9	0.767	−0.68%
A21	11	0.227	10	0.209	−7.91%	A31	11	0.750	10	0.744	−0.78%
A17	12	0.216	13	0.198	−8.45%	A13	12	0.727	11	0.721	−0.87%
A32	13	0.216	11	0.209	−3.06%	A21	13	0.716	12	0.709	−0.92%
A35	14	0.216	12	0.209	−3.06%	A23	14	0.716	13	0.709	−0.92%
A43	15	0.216	14	0.198	−8.45%	A02	15	0.705	14	0.698	−0.98%
A40	16	0.205	15	0.186	−9.04%	A08	16	0.705	15	0.698	−0.98%
A14	17	0.193	16	0.174	−9.71%	A18	17	0.705	16	0.698	−0.98%
A13	18	0.182	17	0.163	−10.47%	A41	18	0.693	17	0.686	−1.03%
A08	19	0.170	20	0.151	−11.32%	A35	19	0.682	18	0.674	−1.09%
A20	20	0.170	18	0.163	−4.50%	A20	20	0.659	19	0.651	−1.20%
A09	21	0.159	22	0.140	−12.29%	A26	21	0.659	20	0.651	−1.20%
A26	22	0.159	21	0.151	−4.98%	A11	22	0.636	21	0.628	−1.33%
A01	23	0.148	19	0.151	+2.33%	A01	23	0.625	22	0.616	−1.40%
A41	24	0.148	23	0.140	−5.55%	A16	24	0.614	23	0.605	−1.46%
A42	25	0.148	24	0.140	−5.55%	A17	25	0.614	24	0.605	−1.46%
A24	26	0.136	26	0.128	−6.20%	A25	26	0.614	25	0.605	−1.46%
A07	27	0.125	27	0.116	−6.98%	A44	27	0.614	26	0.605	−1.46%
A12	28	0.125	25	0.128	+2.33%	A04	28	0.602	27	0.593	−1.54%
A16	29	0.125	28	0.116	−6.98%	A24	29	0.602	28	0.593	−1.54%
A37	30	0.125	29	0.116	−6.98%	A30	30	0.602	29	0.593	−1.54%
A05	31	0.114	35	0.093	−18.14%	A37	31	0.591	30	0.581	−1.61%
A28	32	0.114	30	0.105	−7.91%	A28	32	0.523	31	0.512	−2.12%
A38	33	0.114	31	0.105	−7.91%	A33	33	0.523	32	0.512	−2.12%
A02	34	0.102	33	0.093	−9.04%	A34	34	0.489	33	0.477	−2.43%
A15	35	0.102	36	0.093	−9.04%	A09	35	0.455	35	0.442	−2.79%
A30	36	0.102	37	0.093	−9.04%	A39	36	0.455	34	0.453	−0.23%
A45	37	0.102	32	0.105	+2.33%	A12	37	0.432	36	0.419	−3.06%
A03	38	0.091	34	0.093	+2.33%	A36	38	0.432	37	0.419	−3.06%
A10	39	0.080	38	0.081	+2.33%	A42	39	0.398	38	0.395	−0.60%
A25	40	0.068	42	0.058	−14.73%	A45	40	0.398	39	0.395	−0.60%
A34	41	0.068	39	0.070	+2.33%	A05	41	0.386	40	0.372	−3.69%
A36	42	0.068	40	0.070	+2.33%	A07	42	0.386	41	0.372	−3.69%
A18	43	0.057	43	0.047	−18.14%	A22	43	0.375	42	0.360	−3.88%
A22	44	0.057	41	0.058	+2.33%	A03	44	0.205	43	0.209	+2.33%
A33	45	0.045	44	0.047	+2.33%	A10	45	0.125	44	0.128	+2.33%

Key: A—actor; R-1—rank before the removal of actor A19; V-1—centrality degree before the removal of actor A19; R-2—rank after the removal of actor A19; V-2—centrality degree after the removal of actor A19; Ch-%—change percentage.

(Carley, Diesner, Reminga, & Tsvetovat, 2007) containing nodes influencing the node or influenced by it. In a standard social network of relations between network actors, the area of influence is simply an actor's ego network. A central node's ego network comprises direct connections with network actors and connections between these actors. It is, then, worth investigating how the removal of actor A19 from the network would affect other actors. The selected actor is removed, and the effect is measured by comparing total centrality degrees before and after the removal. The portion of the network that is "near" the selected actor is defined by all nodes located within two path lengths. For instance, if actor A19 is selected, the network comprises all other actors directly linked to actor A19 or to another actor that is directly linked to A19.

Actor centralities changed by different percentages. A positive percentage change occurred for actor A39 in information network AA^1, who moved into the tenth position (increase by 2.33%). Most actors moved down in the ranking after actor A19 was removed (their importance and potential impact decreased), and the change percentages ranged between 0.98% and 12.29%. In information network AA^2, the largest centrality decrease occurred for actor A18 (–14.73%), though the actor's rank remained unchanged (41). In knowledge network AA^3, the centrality degree of actor A05 decreased by 18.14%, while the centrality of 11 actors, including A23 and A29, increased by 2.33%. Knowledge network AA^4 was the least affected, with change percentages ranging between –0.20% and –3.88% for nearly all actors, except for A03 and A10 (+2.33%).

Following the removal of prominent intangible resources: actor A19, knowledge/skill K09 (general knowledge on the Connecto product group), resource R18 (computer), and task T39 (contacting customers by phone), the basic metrics were as follows (Tables 4.14, 4.15, and 4.16).

At the entire network level, the relation density in all two-mode networks decreased between 1.20% (KT) and 6.09% (RT). Knowledge (DK) and resource (DR) diversity metrics changed slightly, by –0.10% and –0.20%, respectively; with an unchanged DK value in network AK^1. The largest drops were seen in resource redundancy values (–8.02%) in networks AR^1 and AR^2 (having access to resources and using resources). Task redundancy dropped by 5.77% in network AT^2 (performing tasks).

In the case of workload (W^{load}) and knowledge (K^{load}) and resource (R^{load}) loads, the situation was different. The removal of actor A19 caused minor changes in ranks among the top ten actors with the highest work, knowledge, and resource loads (who typically moved one or two ranks up), but the removal of prominent resources (K09, R18, and T39) did affect the metrics. For instance, there was a sharp drop in the minimum value of W^{load} (–25.81%), and the mean (M) decreased by 4.62%. Interestingly, the minimum value of K^{load} increased by 5.26%; its maximum value increased by 0.16, while M decreased by 5%. In the case of

Table 4.14 Change dynamics after the removal of prominent intangible resources (A19, K09, R18, T39)—entire network level

	AK[1]	*After*	*AK*[2]	*After*	*AR*[1]	*After*	*AR*[2]	*After*	*AT*[1]	*After*	*AT*[2]	*After*	*KT*	*After*	*RT*	*After*
Number of rows	45	44	45	44	45	44	45	44	45	44	45	44	47	46	18	17
Number of columns	47	46	47	46	18	17	18	17	48	47	48	47	48	47	48	47
Links	1138	1068	963	903	520	463	462	405	999	930	708	641	754	713	312	271
Density	0.538	0.528	0.455	0.446	0.642	0.619	0.570	0.541	0.462	0.449	0.327	0.310	0.334	0.330	0.361	0.339
DK	0.996	0.996	0.995	0.994	—		—		—		—		—		—	
DR	—		—		0.983	0.981	0.978	0.976	—		—		—		—	
ReK	0.528	0.517	0.443	0.433	—		—		—		—		—		—	
ReR	—		—		0.324	0.298	0.324	0.298	—		—		—		—	
ReT	—		—		—		—		0.450	0.437	0.312	0.294	—		—	

Key: AK[1]—having knowledge; AK[2]—using knowledge; AR[1]—having access to a resource; AR[2]—using a resource; AT[1]—being able to perform a task; AT[2]—performing a task; KT—task-related knowledge; RT—task-related resources; DK—knowledge diversity; DR—resource diversity; ReK—knowledge redundancy; ReR—resource redundancy; ReT—task redundancy.

Table 4.15 Actors' work, knowledge, and resource loads after the removal of prominent intangible resources (A19, K09, R18, T39)—node level

Rank	*Actual workload (W^{load})*		*Value after removing node(s)*		*Knowledge load (K^{load})*		*Value after removing node(s)*		*Resource load (R^{load})*		*Value after removing node(s)*	
	Actor	*Result*	*Actor*	*Result*	*Actor*	*Result*	*Actor*	*Result*	*Actor*	*Result*	*Actor*	*Result*
1.	A09	0.643	A09	0.642	A09	0.63	A09	0.631	A09	0.673	A09	0.672
2.	A19	0.497	A04	0.49	A04	0.505	A04	0.502	A19	0.503	A40	0.48
3.	A04	0.492	A40	0.465	A19	0.495	A40	0.46	A40	0.481	A30	0.465
4.	A40	0.47	A17	0.428	A40	0.466	A17	0.415	A30	0.465	A17	0.461
5.	A17	0.431	A06	0.394	A17	0.419	A06	0.384	A04	0.458	A04	0.458
6.	A06	0.386	A23	0.376	A06	0.37	A01	0.358	A17	0.458	A23	0.428
7.	A23	0.386	A01	0.37	A23	0.369	A23	0.356	A23	0.429	A06	0.421
8.	A01	0.376	A30	0.367	A01	0.363	A30	0.33	A06	0.423	A01	0.402
9.	A30	0.374	A08	0.328	A30	0.337	A31	0.318	A01	0.407	A16	0.399
10.	A31	0.33	A31	0.318	A31	0.332	A43	0.316	A16	0.404	A08	0.395
	Min:	0.031	Min:	0.023	Min:	0.019	Min:	0.02	Min:	0.048	Min:	0.033
	Max:	0.643	Max:	0.642	Max:	0.630	Max:	0.631	Max:	0.673	Max:	0.672
	M:	0.238	M:	0.227	M:	0.22	M:	0.209	M:	0.284	M:	0.273
	SD:	0.142	SD:	0.14	SD:	0.146	SD:	0.142	SD:	0.14	SD:	0.141

Key: R—actors' rank; Min—minimum value; Max—maximum value; M—mean; SD—standard deviation.

Table 4.16 Network node congruence after the removal of prominent intangible resources (A19, K09, R18, T39)—node level

Rank	*Actor knowledge needs congruence* (CK^{needs})		*Value after removing node(s)*		*Actor knowledge waste congruence* (Ck^{waste})		*Value after removing node(s)*		*Actor resource needs congruence* (CR^{needs})		*Value after removing node(s)*		*Actor resource waste congruence* (CR^{waste})		*Value after removing node(s)*	
	Actor	*Result*	*Actor*	*Result*	*Actor*	*Result*	*Actor*	*Result*	*Actor*	*Result*	*Actor*	*Result*	*Actor*	*Result*	*Actor*	*Result*
1.	A26	0.802	A26	0.79	A29	0.238	A42	0.308	A10	0.429	A10	0.571	A10	0.2	A10	0.25
2.	A39	0.693	A39	0.753	A10	0.222	A29	0.3	A22	0.309	A03	0.357	A11	0.111	A11	0.125
3.	A33	0.682	A03	0.667	A02	0.214	A32	0.261	A36	0.28	A22	0.354	A29	0.111	A29	0.125
4.	A13	0.644	A10	0.667	A42	0.214	A10	0.25	A34	0.259	A34	0.35	A13	0.1	A13	0.111
5.	A20	0.615	A33	0.667	A32	0.208	A02	0.214	A03	0.25	A36	0.341	A32	0.1	A32	0.111
6.	A02	0.606	A42	0.631	A05	0.105	A05	0.105	A02	0.237	A02	0.277	A42	0.1	A42	0.111
7.	A10	0.582	A13	0.617	A28	0.100	A28	0.105	A24	0.22	A24	0.25	A28	0.091	A28	0.1
8.	A42	0.579	A20	0.6	A33	0.100	A33	0.1	A20	0.204	A20	0.237	A35	0.083	A35	0.091
9.	A03	0.547	A34	0.6	A36	0.087	A36	0.091	A07	0.2	A07	0.229	A19	0.077	A21	0.077
10.	A27	0.535	A02	0.594	A40	0.081	A40	0.083	A01	0.186	A01	0.21	A21	0.071	A01	0
	Min:	0.063	Min:	0.064	Min:	0	Min:	0	Min:	0.007	Min:	0.008	Min:	0	Min:	0
	Max:	0.802	Max:	0.79	Max:	0.238	Max:	0.308	Max:	0.429	Max:	0.571	Max:	0.2	Max:	0.25
	M:	0.389	M:	0.405	M:	0.048	M:	0.055	M:	0.113	M:	0.157	M:	0.023	M:	0.025
	SD:	0.183	SD:	0.187	SD:	0.069	SD:	0.084	SD:	0.085	SD:	0.11	SD:	0.046	SD:	0.054

Key: Rank—actors' rank; Min—minimum value; Max—maximum value; M—mean; SD—standard deviation.

R^{load}, removal of resource R18 (computer) effected a –31.25% change in the minimum value, -0.15% in the maximum value, and –3.87% in the mean.

For knowledge needs congruence (CK^{needs}), the minimum value increased by 1.59%, the maximum value decreased by 1.50%, and the mean increased by 4.11%. Considerably greater changes occurred in the knowledge waste congruence metric (CK^{waste}), where the maximum value increased by nearly 30% (29.41) and the mean by 14.58%. Following the removal of resource R18 (computer), resource needs (CR^{needs}) increased by 14.28% (minimum), 33.10% (maximum), and 38.94% (mean). The maximum value of CR^{waste} increased by 25% and its mean by 8.69%, as shown in Table 4.16.

The purpose of the above analysis was solely to illustrate how changes in information and knowledge network structure (communication load) and node positions may be simulated, as the simulation requires a more sophisticated approach. Such studies depict scenarios (positive and/or negative) of changes in network structure and actor positions following the removal of the most prominent node or the loss of strategic resources. Of course, the analysis is not exhaustive, as only a minor portion of the possible configurations of intangible resources has been presented. Based on these results, more detailed analyses can be performed for each actor, knowledge/skill, resource, and task in the network (randomly selected nodes can also be simulated). Certainly, each actor will have a different influence network and area of influence, comprising both incoming and outgoing connections. This, however, should be the subject of more detailed analysis, with a comprehensive view of the network and its actors.

Note

1. For clarity of illustration, one matrix for each of the following relation types was selected for presentation: AA (joint problem-solving), AK (actor using knowledge and skills), AT (actor performing a task), AR (actor using a resource), KT (task-related knowledge), and RT (task-related resource).

References

Borgatti, S. P., Everett, M. G., & Freeman, L. C. (2002). *UCINET 6 for windows: Software for social network analysis*. Harvard, MA: Analytic Technologies.

Borgatti, S. P., Everett, M. G., & Johnson, J. C. (2018). *Analyzing social networks*. London: Sage Publications.

Carley, K. M., Diesner, J., Reminga, J., & Tsvetovat, M. (2007). Toward an interoperable dynamic network analysis toolkit. *Decision Support Systems*, *43*(4), 1324–1347. https://doi.org/10.1016/j.dss.2006.04.003

D'Errico, M., Stefani, S., & Torriero, A. (2014). Informal ties in organizations: A case study. *Quality & Quantity*, *48*(4), 1929–1943.

Ferrin, D. L., Dirks, K. T., & Shah, P. P. (2006). Direct and indirect effects of third-party relationships on interpersonal trust. *Journal of Applied Psychology*, *91*(4), 870–883. https://doi.org/10.1037/0021-9010.91.4.870

Gibbons, D. E. (2004). Friendship and advice networks in the context of changing professional values. *Administrative Science Quarterly*, *49*(2), 238–262.

Hsu, S. H., & Tzeng, S. F. (2010). A dyadic perspective on knowledge exchange. *International Journal of Technology Management*, *49*(4), 370–383.

Kaše, R., Paauwe, J., & Zupan, N. (2009). HR practices, interpersonal relations, and intrafirm knowledge transfer in knowledge-intensive firms: A social network perspective. *Human Resource Management*, *48*(4), 615–639.

Leon, R. D., Rodríguez-Rodríguez, R., Gómez-Gasquet, P., & Mula, J. (2017). Social network analysis: A tool for evaluating and predicting future knowledge flows from an insurance organization. *Technological Forecasting and Social Change*, *114*, 103–118. https://doi.org/10.1016/j.techfore.2016.07.032

Maciel, C. O., & Chaves, C. E. L. (2017). Informational status in intra-organizational networks: The role of knowledge sharing and structural holes. *Revista de Administração*, *52*(2), 189–198.

Marouf, L., & Doreian, P. (2010). Understanding information and knowledge flows as network processes in an oil company. *Journal of Information & Knowledge Management*, *9*(02), 105–118.

Swan, J., Newell, S., Scarbrough, H., & Hislop, D. (1999). Knowledge management and innovation: Networks and networking. *Journal of Knowledge Management*, *3*(4), 262–275.

Valente, T. W. (2012). Network interventions. *Science*, *337*(6090), 49–53.

Zagenczyk, T. J., Gibney, R., Few, W. T., & Purvis, R. L. (2013). The ties that influence: A social network analysis of prototypical employees' effects on job attitudes among coworkers. *Journal of Management Policy and Practice*, *14*(4), 26.

Zagenczyk, T. J., Purvis, R. L., Shoss, M. K., Scott, K. L., & Cruz, K. S. (2015). Social influence and leader perceptions: Multiplex social network ties and similarity in leader—Member exchange. *Journal of Business and Psychology*, *30*(1), 105–117.

5 Discussion of Findings and Conclusions From the Intangible Resource Audit

Chapter 5 is devoted to presenting conclusions and discussing findings from the audit. First, the process of developing the intangible resource audit methodology will be discussed. Figure 5.1 presents the theoretical sources used to list and define the concepts of the proposed intangible resource management theory. The second part of the chapter discusses the exemplification of intangible resource audit, performed in an IT company. The case study provided rich and interesting empirical material. Its analysis in the context of the presented theoretical sources allows for developing the existing knowledge on intra-organizational networks, their formation and structure, prominent actors, and the network approach to managing intangible resources. Network creation is based on identifying intangible resources and the relations that define their connections and interdependencies. Activities performed to achieve the strategic goals in the organization are the reason for the creation of intra-organizational networks. Social networks, in which respondents identified existing and/or missing relations, play a prominent role. Network structuring involves the shaping of its structure, e.g., by the analysis of network efficiency metrics, which include network density, network centralization, diversity, redundancy, and congruence. Network modeling to eliminate weaknesses—resulting from intangible resource overload, incompatibility, excessive centralization, or network density—may play an important role in network structuring. The amount of empirical material is substantial and thus impossible to present in full in this publication. Therefore, only the findings concerning the top ten most prominent human and nonhuman actors are presented.

5.1 Organizational Intangible Resource Audit Methodology

An integrated model of organizational intangible resource audit was created using the network-based view, which allowed for identifying intangible resources and diagnosing their relations. The intangible resource audit model was developed through identification, analysis, and creative

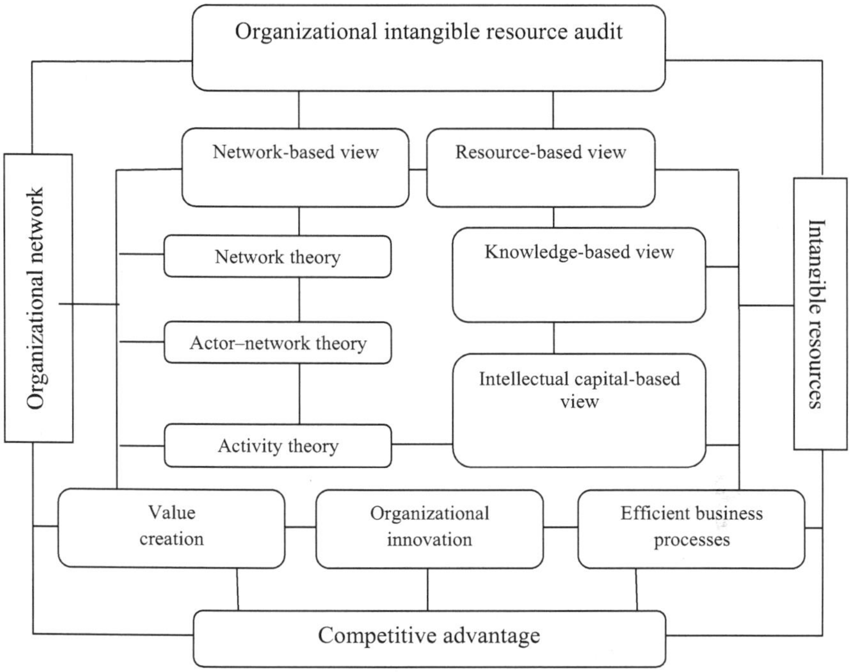

Figure 5.1 Theoretical foundations of the organizational intangible resource audit concept

integration of the existing qualitative audit models, which include information, knowledge, and intellectual capital audits. An innovative combination of intangible resources with their identification and diagnosis was performed based on organizational network analysis, which resulted in the creation of a whole new approach to auditing resources from the point of view of their relationship network. So far, no similar examination of the structure of the audits (information, knowledge, and intellectual capital) has been carried out in such a comprehensive way, with reference to network and resource theories, either in Polish or English literature. Figure 5.1. shows how these concepts are combined into the theoretical foundation of organizational intangible resource audit.

The inclusion of the emerging "network-based view" in the discussion of organizational intangible resources and their dynamics from the point of view of the network of relations was justified, as it allowed for defining network approaches in an entirely new context and introducing them into the area of organizations and management. This resulted in the development and definition of a number of notions, presented below as a contribution to the theory of management science.

The essence of the network-based view lies in identifying and exploring complex structures and behaviors existing among animate (human) and inanimate actors (knowledge and skills; structural capital—resources, tools; activities—tasks), as is the case in the proposed intangible resource audit. It is justified to combine the concepts of social network, organizational network, and dynamic network analysis in order to identify and explore the relations of intangible resources, since the intentionality of actions, related to the social network created by employees, is an important factor in any organization.

Actor–network theory and activity theory are useful theoretical perspectives for formulating the premise of intangible resource audit and the actual audit model. Intangible resource audit, including the perspective of actors (human), knowledge, tasks, and resources, can be described by translation in actor–network theory. If the main actor is human, the way intangible resource relations are formed allows one to describe this process both in the collective and in the individual context. The selection of the actant or actor whose point of view is used to analyze specific actions affects how other actors are involved in taking on the assigned roles (using specific knowledge or a specific resource to perform a specific task), which can be shaped anew. Thus, the dynamics of the relation building process are reflected in terms of network formation and degradation. Actor–network theory offers a different way of thinking about relations in an organization, whereby resources are configured in many different ways. In the resource-based view, resources are usually considered static. In actor–network theory, resources cannot be considered static, as the structure of ties between people and technologies can change, resulting in changes in resources and their interrelations with other elements in the organization (Law, 1992). Law calls the actor-networks "resources." This concept of resources as stabilized actor-networks refers to Penrose's view of a company as a comprehensive set of heterogeneous resources, which comprises interactions between tangible resources and human resources (Penrose, 1995). However, the option of viewing resources as dynamic remains open for discussion.

If actor-networks are resources, and the stability of interactions and translations cannot be taken for granted, resources are liable to change in the process of translation and regulation. The diversity of actor-networks makes networks heterogeneous, which in turn fits in with the material and semiotic nature of relations between subjects and notions. In the context of intangible resource audit, many material and semiotic relations are observed. For instance, the creation or co-creation of business processes requires the participation of people, their knowledge, resources, and tools, which comprise the elements acting jointly in a specific network. At the same time, each of these elements is defined as an actor-network, which is analyzed depending on the adopted level of iteration. This, in turn, demonstrates that no actor acts just for itself, but is affected by a complex material and semiotic network.

Application of activity theory to the problem of intangible resource audit provides new insights, for example, into the construction of actions, tools, and resources available to network members, and the internal conflicts within the analyzed activity (Blackler & Regan, 2009). Activity theory enables one to identify the need to explore conflicts, instabilities, and insecurities, which are inherently related to practice (Hemetsberger & Reinhardt, 2009). The theory is thus suitable for exploring complex and diverse interactions affecting value creation within intangible resources. It allows for explaining how potential conflicts (dilemmas) related to created organizational value affect changes in network structure, and how activities related to knowledge, tasks, and resources are distributed in a complex activity system. Activity theory also enables one to conceptualize intangible resource audit as a developing and evolving activity system, which is dynamically processed by collective engagement and negotiations (intangible resources are increasingly related to the co-creation of value by a complex network of relations).

Despite its potential, activity theory enjoys moderate interest among scholars in organizational and management theory. In this discussion, when combined with organizational network analysis, it can become a consistent theoretical basis for verifying the existing relations and conflicts between specific elements of the activity system. For instance, in activity theory, knowledge and learning have a potential for development within a broader network of interactions. Hansen (1999) claims that weak ties (relations) between individuals foster seeking of useful knowledge in a project team, but hamper the transfer of complex knowledge, which requires strong ties (direct relations) between the parties to the transfer. Although knowledge is not a separate category (element) in the activity system, it pervades all its components and relations. In this approach, an activity can be thought of as a dispersed system, a unit of analysis that makes it possible to describe and explain cognitive properties of the activity system composed of the involved individuals and their communication and information environment. Taking the activity system as the unit of analysis means that activity theory does not need to identify simple causes of knowledge transfer (Boer, Van Baalen, and Kumar, 2002), and instead describes organizational conditions as a set of many systematically interacting elements (e.g., social rules, mediating artifacts, and labor division). The process of knowledge sharing is described, along with its limitations. This description also includes the way in which knowledge sharing occurs within activity systems or between them, which provides an opportunity to explore the dynamics of knowledge transfer within and between actions.

In the context of intangible resources, activity theory offers a number of analysis instruments, including the perception of the activity system and the associated actions as units of analysis. In this case, the activity system may be a business process, which becomes a basis for identifying knowledge, tasks, and resources used in value creation by particular actors. The activity can be seen from the point of view of the involved human, material, or capital resources used in achieving a certain objective. Correlations between particular activities are the key concept in the activity system. They are usually shaped by people in charge (managers, entrepreneurs) who create organizational activities, and by associations, which turn the activities into a system. Despite the complexity of the activity system, activities can be defined at various aggregation levels, such as activity, actions, operations, and their hierarchy (Kuutti, 1996).

Intangible resource audit defines the individual and unique shape of relations among intangible resources in an organization, seen from information, knowledge, structural capital, and performed task networks. These networks create specific configurations that are intentionally modeled to achieve the best possible outcomes for the organization, such as value creation, effective business processes, innovation, or competitive advantage. In intangible resource audit, the object of modeling is a single node in the network (or a group of nodes) and the relevant relations, which create scenarios desirable from the point of view of effective intangible resource management. Network resource modeling becomes an important element of the dynamic approach, which forces managers to manage intangible resources flexibly, taking into consideration organizational changes and environment.

Apart from the already mentioned network-based view, in order to develop the intangible resource audit concept and, as a result, to learn how to manage intangible resources and create management strategies, it was necessary to include resource-based approaches: the resource-based view, the knowledge-based view, and the intellectual capital-based view. The *resource-based view* includes an extremely useful assumption that resources (both tangible and intangible) and actions are not independent from one another, but they are a part of the organization and can be specialized and combined in various configurations. Resource-based competitiveness of the organization depends on how unique this configuration is. Unique configurations result from the diversity of *intangible resources*, based on unlimited combinations of information and knowledge, which are at the core of human, structural, and relational capital. The main premise of the *knowledge-based view*, which echoes throughout this book, is viewing knowledge as an action included in social relations. In turn, in the *intellectual capital-based view*, intellectual capital creates a structure and the entirety of intangible resources, allowing one to look at the organization from the point of view of relations between the intellectual capital components that create value. It is a framework for understanding intangible resources in the organization and the dynamics of their associations.

The resource-based approaches were then used to define information, knowledge, and intellectual capital using three perspectives: static, structural, and dynamic. The *static approach to intangible resources* is a well-known concept of a resource as something static that can be managed (e.g., information and knowledge included in databases or repositories; recognizing competence gaps in the organization and recommending the required training). The *structural approach to intangible resources* entails looking at information, knowledge, and intellectual capital at three levels: individual, organizational, and network. Individual and organizational perspectives have been well presented in literature (see Chapter 2), but the network perspective provides entirely new insight into intangible resources. It allows one to see intangible resources as a network of their relations. What is more, it makes it possible to operationalize flows, understand how they are used in the organization, and, last but not least, model them using the identified techniques of social, organizational, and dynamic network analysis. Resource modeling is a part of the *dynamic approach to intangible resources*, where they are viewed from the perspective of actions and relations. Therefore, intangible resources are defined as intellectual capital with a specific structure of relations, complementary to other resources. These dynamics are also reflected by the use of intangible resources (information and knowledge) in action.

In literature, no similar review and comparison of information, knowledge, and intellectual capital audits can be found. Owing to literature review and carefully selected sources, it was possible to critically analyze the listed audit models (14 in total) and to develop an own concept.

The intangible resource audit methodology was developed based on a formal approach to methodology comparisons by Hong, Van den Goor, and Brinkkemper (1993), discussed in detail in Section 2.3.1. The selection of information, knowledge, and intellectual capital audit models that inspired the development of the proposed intangible resource audit model was substantiated. Also, the criteria for defining the main stages and steps of intangible resource audit (its components) were presented in a way that enables the reader to follow the whole process. The author refers to the developed audit model as a *meta-model*, since it has been developed on the basis of existing models. Some verified assumptions (audit stages) were used in the said audit, which by no means implies that the existing models have simply been copied. On the contrary—the selection of audit stages and steps, and their contents, allowed the author to develop an own model of organizational intangible resource audit, which provides a holistic view of intangible resources.

The methodology of organizational intangible resource audit comprises five main stages and their respective steps, as shown in Figure 5.2. *Intangible resource audit:*

- is a study conducted with the use of specific research methods, data collection, and data analysis based on network techniques;

1. Planning stage of the intangible resource audit
1.1. Defining audit objectives and scope
1.2. Selecting the auditing team
1.3. Ensuring support in the organization

2. Design stage of the intangible resource audit
2.1. Analyzing the external environment
2.2. Identifying the organization's main strategic goals
2.3. Value creation model
2.4. Identifying core business processes

3. Operationalization stage of the intangible resource audit
3.1. Selection and development of audit instruments
3.2. Intangible resource audit metrics
3.3. Testing the instruments

4. Performance stage of the intangible resource audit
4.1. Identifying intangible resources
4.2. Analyzing the dynamics of the organizational intangible resource association network
4.3. Analyzing the impact of intangible resources on achievement of objectives, value creation, and business processes
4.4. Developing the report

5. Implementation stage of the intangible resource audit
5.1. Developing an intangible resource management strategy
5.2. Strategy implementation

Figure 5.2 Stages and steps of intangible resource audit

- comprises five main stages (planning, design, operationalization, performance, and implementation);
- comprises between two and four steps per stage;
- uses interviews, surveys, observations, and documentation analysis as the basic research methods;
- precisely defines what questions should be included in the survey questionnaire and interview questionnaire;
- is the only audit model that specifies and defines network metrics used to measure the efficiency of intangible resources and their networks of relations;

- is the only audit model that presents advanced network analysis techniques (QAP and MRQAP), which make it possible to explore correlations between intangible resources in the organization;
- allows for identifying intangible resources in four areas: information and knowledge flows, knowledge and skills, tasks, and resources (structural capital), in association with business processes;
- defines a map of intangible resources, its functions and capabilities in the organization following the network-based view (in particular, it emphasizes networks of relations among intangible resources, their visualization in the form of matrices and graphs, and the interactive character of the map).
- fills the gap identified in other audits related to the modeling of intangible resource association networks by simulating changes in the network (addition or removal of nodes and/or relations), which enables the creation of positive or negative scenarios related, for example, to loss or excess of intangible resources. Therefore, it is an instrument for identifying risks related to organizational intangible resources;
- is an instrument for managing intangible resources and creating intangible resource strategies in the organization.

A literature review allowed for presenting the theoretical foundations of the intangible resource audit concept, as shown in Figure 5.1. Thus, the most important terms related to organizations and intangible resources in the network-based view were listed and defined here, dismissing the classical, atomistic perspective of organizations. The most important notions are:

- *Actor* (animate, human), as a carrier of information and knowledge (including tacit knowledge) and their flows (employee, person).
- *Social network analysis* in the organizational context aims at understanding the formal and informal relations and interdependencies in the workplace, but omits non-social networks, for example, interrelations between knowledge and tasks, or between resources and tasks, in an organization. Thus, it has been indispensable to incorporate elements of social, *organizational*, and *dynamic* network analysis to provide a comprehensive view of the organization and the problem of intangible resource management, including both social and nonsocial networks, as well as network modeling and configuration, which form the foundation of *dynamic network analysis*. This model is called *SODNA* (combination of *S*NA, *O*NA, and *D*NA) and applies well-known network techniques to intangible resource management.
- *Intangible resource audit* is a study performed to identify and analyze the dynamics of relations and evaluate the intangible resources crucial for an organization's operation (information; knowledge;

tasks—activities; structural capital—resources, tools) in the context of a relation network.

- One important assumption of *(organizational) activity theory* is that value mainly depends on actions and behaviors of managers and other people in the organization. By delving into the organization and its strategies and processes, it is possible to examine what actions employees perform and how efficiently, what resources employees can access and how they use them, and what knowledge and skills they have and use.
- *Actions* (tasks, activities) are essentially the work performed in an organization. This entails transforming knowledge and skills and the available resources into a result (expected outcome). The dynamics of actions are reflected in relations between people that constantly intertwine, emerge, and fade out, and that are the basic element of the socio-technical system. Actions cannot be analyzed without their context, that is, the organizational environment. The scope of actions here is very broad, covering all essential organizational activity (determined by business processes) that directly or indirectly results in value creation. These actions are humanistic, intentional, and causal in nature, as they concern people. In every action, a person uses the available information, knowledge, and resources to perform the assigned task.
- *Organizational network efficiency* is assessed in the light of knowledge, resource, and task diversity, redundancy, congruence, and load among employees.
- *Homophily* is the rate of organizational relation similarity concerning the following attributes: experience, location (e.g., the same department), professional qualifications, education, age, and gender, which shape the organizational network structure. They are the basic elements describing the work environment and the efficiency of information and knowledge flows.
- The *intangible resource map* is an instrument for multidimensional analysis of intangible resources and their interactions (flows of information, knowledge, resources, and tasks) in an organization using graphs and matrices. It is developed with the use of social, organizational, and dynamic network analysis techniques, including but not limited to visualization. These techniques are an integral part of the interactive intangible resource map, which makes the map dynamic—the auditor can simulate changes in the network by creating positive and negative scenarios and examining changes in the visualization of the network and its nodes (intangible resources).
- The *SODNA model* is an integral part of intangible resource audit. It can be used to identify the most efficient employees and to develop modern incentive systems taking into account the relational network (bonuses could be awarded to employees who have central positions

in the network and work toward increasing the flow of information and knowledge, use of resources or performing tasks, activating peripheral employees, and using their knowledge and experience for the benefit of the whole organization). Owing to this model, *intangible resource management* is based on:

- identification of intangible resources and their distribution in the organization;
- assessment of transfers and flows of the available intangible resources;
- network models, which determine capabilities and limitations of individual and collective action in the organization;
- evaluation of intangible resource management efficiency (opportunities and risks) and areas for improvement;
- designing and modeling the best strategy of intangible resource management considering organizational goals;
- developing an intangible resource management strategy.

- *Network models* constitute representations of a given phenomenon (organization, intangible resources) within the network concept, with the help of network data and observations, which are not independent from one another.
- *Organization*—the essence of an organization lies primarily in relations and interactions, that is, an ongoing knowledge and information transfer between people undertaking joint actions. It is thus composed of interdependent actions (activities, tasks) implemented by people who are connected with one another and use their knowledge and resources in these actions. The organization is seen here as the internal networking of actors, including knowledge, resources, and tasks, in which an important role is played by the modeling of networks, flows, transfers, and exchanges. An *organization* is, therefore, a collection of connected actors (animate and inanimate) who collaborate or interact in various, unlimited constellations (combinations of connections), thus creating a socio-technical system.
- *Organizational social capital* refers to embedded knowledge, available as a result of interactions between people and their network of relations in the organization. It provides access to new sources of knowledge and enables the creation of new knowledge by the use of resources (tangible and intangible) in action. In network theory, in the context of social capital, the efficiency of actors' actions is determined by the character of the organizational community network, and not the benefits for an individual in the network of relations.
- Similarly to organizational network theory, in *(organizational) activity theory*, there is a socio-technical system composed of interacting animate (subject, community) and inanimate elements (object, labor division, rules, tools, result) that make up the activity system

in a given organization. In this theory, knowledge is dependent on subjects and tasks, and is the result of discourse and interpersonal communication, which is particularly highlighted in the process of auditing intangible resources using knowledge, task, and resource networks, which are defined and configured in many different ways.

- *Relations* are the associations between elements of the socio-technical system (sociogram and technogram) that are mutually dependent.
- *Network*—a group or a system of interconnected people or things based on specific types of relations between them. The observed organizational reality can be represented (modeled) based on animate and inanimate nodes and a relationship between at least one pair of nodes (dyad), which create a network structure.
- *Dynamic network*—refers to the process of designing and modeling relations, complexities, and interactions in the multimodal network comprising human and nonhuman actors (knowledge and skills, tasks, and resources) used in the organization, which are constantly intermingling and changing their shape. It includes configuring, modeling, simulating, and combining nodes and networks in order to create positive and negative scenarios for the organization (analysis of risks related to intangible resources). Modeling of information, knowledge, task, and resource networks allows one to measure and diagnose how tasks are carried out, how knowledge and information are shared, and how resources are used, which contributes to the optimization of the planned and performed activities.
- *Information network*—a one-mode network comprising human actors contributing (or not) to the transfer of information and knowledge, labor division, and resource control. In information networks, information flow occurs, and information can be transformed into knowledge by joint problem-solving and information transfer. The more coordination there is in the network based on informal relations, the more opportunities there are for joint problem-solving.
- *Organizational network*—a system of connections between people or organizational units created to exchange information, knowledge, resources, and performed tasks, with a view to creating or proposing value. It is a form of informal cooperation between a number of actors, based on labor division and value creation through synergy.
- *Knowledge network*—includes human and nonhuman (knowledge and skills) actors. In a one-mode knowledge network, actors discuss and/or solve complex problems in the workplace, and know the knowledge and skills of their colleagues. A two-mode knowledge network defines what skills and knowledge employees have and what skills and knowledge they actually use at work.
- *Task network*—defines what tasks (actions) employees can perform and what tasks they actually perform at work.

- *Resource network*—defines what resources are available to employees in the workplace and what resources are actually used to perform tasks at work.
- *Intangible resource network*—the identification and analysis of information and knowledge flows in an organization provides an incomplete picture of its functioning. It is necessary to include task and resource networks as complementary to information and knowledge networks, thus making it possible to assess the functioning of the organization from intangible resources, and their associations and relations view.
- *Structure*—the arrangement of and relations between parts or elements of something complex.
- *System*—a complex whole comprising a set of things (elements) working together as parts of a mechanism or an interconnecting network.
- *Socio-technical system*—comprises social and technical factors. Social factors include people, their behaviors, attitudes, organizational norms, principles, and culture. Technical factors include the processes, tasks, techniques, knowledge, and resources used for value creation and proposition. The complexity of the socio-technical system depends on the diversity of its components, their dynamics (inclusion and exclusion), and evolution. All the elements of the socio-technical system (organization) equally affect the shaping of organizational reality and cannot be examined separately.
- *(Organizational) activity theory*—provides a comprehensive view of the organization, because it takes into consideration the internal and external conditions of its functioning, its history, and its culture, as well as the role of artifacts, motivations, and the complexity of the actual human activity. Objects of study include interactions; conflicts; changes; and past, present, and future actions, in line with the precepts of the emerging organizational network theory, in which the network enables the modeling of actors' behaviors and actions.
- *Network theory*—its general assumption is that the position of actors (both animate and inanimate) in the network determines their limitations and capabilities in terms of their achievements, behaviors, beliefs, development, and use. What happens between identified actors is a function of the structure of connections between them.
- *Organizational network theory*—a conceptualization of an organization as a network in which individual socio-technical elements are connected and, as a result, form a system.
- *Value in (organizational) activity theory*—actions generate connectivity between resources and create value through communication activities, in which information and knowledge are constantly moving.

- *Knowledge in actor–network theory*—knowledge is not static, but is constructed within the network. Knowledge-generating processes are based on dynamic connections between heterogeneous actors (human and nonhuman).
- *Intangible resource management* is embedded in a dynamic and complex socio-technical system.
- *Intangible resources* are a dynamic combination of information, knowledge, structural capital (information and communications infrastructure), and performed tasks (actions), which constantly intermingle in a live network of relations, interactions, and flows, creating or destroying value for the organization. Intangible resources include networks of relations among human and nonhuman actors, as perceived in actor–network theory, creating dynamic affordance, which involves constant acquisition and use of resources in action.

In this study, the focal point was organizational intangible resource audit, seen from the point of view of these resources' relations and associations. Therefore:

1. A comprehensive review of English literature on the subject was conducted. English literature dominates, due to the scarcity of research on the subject by Polish researchers and the shortage of Polish publications in the major databases (Web of Science, Scopus), which were the main sources for the literature review.
2. Definitions of the following terms were developed: actor, social network analysis, organizational network analysis, dynamic network analysis, SODNA model, intangible resource audit, (organizational) activity theory, actions, organizational network efficiency, intangible resource map, intangible resource management, network models, organization, organizational social capital, relations, network, dynamic network, information network, organizational network, structure, system, socio-technical system, network theory, organization network theory, value in (organizational) activity theory, knowledge in actor–network theory, intangible resources.
3. Based on literature on the subject (the discussed information, knowledge, intellectual capital audits, and network and resource theories), an organizational intangible resource methodology was developed, which comprises five main stages: planning, design, operationalization, performance, and implementation.
4. In total, 14 audit models were reviewed and subsequently used to develop an original *meta-model* for organizational intangible resource audit.
5. The *meta-model* and its interpretation can be used both by management theorists and practitioners The proposed *meta-model* is

innovative and allows for auditing, mapping, and visualizing intangible resources and their network of relations and associations, which makes this approach much more dynamic than the existing traditional solutions.

6. The new model can be valuable for business and academia alike. On the one hand, it can be used as a normalized first step for all new initiatives in intangible resource management. On the other hand, it can be another model to be analyzed when modeling the processes of selected audits. The new audit model can also be easily broken down into smaller parts, which allows the auditing team to select parts of the model that suit the needs and the available financial resources of an organization.
7. The *meta-model* of organizational intangible resource audit was based on the perspective of the network of relations, which can be freely modeled to achieve the expected outcome for the organization.
8. The network metrics used, which emphasize effective intangible resource management, allow for interventions in areas where this efficiency is low or at risk. Network metrics were selected so as to include the measurement of information, knowledge, resources (structural capital), and task networks. This study uses a unique and multitiered approach (entire network level, dyad level, node level), which is rarely used in network research, as most researchers concentrate on one of the levels.
9. The network-based view allows for identifying both the most prominent (central) intangible resources in the organization and the peripheral ones. It is up to the management to recognize the role of these resources in business processes and value creation. The set of instruments for organizational and dynamic network analysis is one of the most interesting tools for managing intangible resources from a relation dynamics view.
10. Among many approaches related to intangible resources requiring ontological and epistemological identification, the network-based view seems to be the fundamental one with regard to resource dynamics. These dynamics are demonstrated not only in the combination of resources that can result in the creation of new value, but also in the configuration of mutually dependent relations.
11. This holistic approach to intangible resource management also comprises tangible resources that contribute to the creation of value for the organization and stakeholders. In the studied organization, intangible resources dominated. Structural capital, mainly including communication and information infrastructure, is based on complementary material resources, such as computers, phones, access to a multimedia projector, a conference room, and even a company car.
12. Value creation for internal and external stakeholders is the core of management. This study did not attempt to measure value, but

pointed to the sources of value creation for the organization through efficient intangible resource management.

13. In this study, detailed identification of intangible resources associated with business processes and tasks was performed to examine the organization's operation. Network structure and intangible resource position modeling allows for dynamically influencing management processes meant to create value. By simulating specific nodes and relations (e.g., removing or adding nodes or relations), this process delineates the so-called areas of influence of each node. Change simulation is performed as a result of the analysis of changes in the centralities of the remaining nodes and in network density.
14. The dynamics of organizational management should relate to intangible resources, as they are the most important element shaping popular business models in the process of organizational value creation.
15. Currently, intangible resources configured into a specific business model are what determine the strength and competitive advantage of an organization. Measuring and monitoring the variables that describe resource networks and their configurations demonstrates where value is created and where it is destroyed in the organization. This also requires measuring the created value and identifying the dynamics of changes resulting from a specific network configuration.
16. Analyses of intangible resources should include a multitude of issues associated with value creation, innovation, and creation of business models, thus providing synergy and comprehensively depicting the impact of intangible resources on broadly understood organizational success.
17. Organizational management should concentrate on intangible resources that dominate in the contemporary reality and that lie at the core of the major management concepts such as strategic management, value management, or knowledge management. Identifying the role of intangible resources complementary to tangible resources, with their mutual associations, increases an organization's flexibility in its evolving environment.

The findings from the present study make it possible to address the primary research questions in the following way:

1. *How, in the light of network and management theories, should one develop a methodology for organizational intangible resource audit, bearing in mind the uniqueness both of the intangible resources and their relations and of the organization itself?*
   The integrated organizational intangible resource audit methodology (*meta-model*) was developed based on three principal network-based approaches: network theory, actor–network theory, and activity theory. These theoretical approaches made it possible to understand how human and nonhuman actors (knowledge, resources, tasks) can

interact and create networks of associations and relations. Resource-based approaches were also used, including the resource-based view, the knowledge-based view, and the intellectual-capital based view, strongly emphasizing the dynamic character of resources, reflected in their actions, flows, and use in the organization. The unique nature of resources is strictly connected with business processes of a given organization and the context in which an organization operates (including its external environment).

2. *What prerequisites should be met by an organization for intangible resource audit to be feasible and effective?*
   Effective organizational resource audit requires the conditions of the initial, planning stage of the audit to be fulfilled. Employee participation in the study (questionnaire) is crucial and should be no lower than 85%. This depends solely on the management and their engagement, as exemplified by the author's experience. In several cases, it was impossible to complete the audit due to low survey return rates resulting from the lack of support on the part of management.
3. *Can organizational intangible resource audit be considered a valuable management technique in the modern knowledge-based economy?*
   In the modern network-based economy, organizational intangible resource audit provides a comprehensive view of the resource network, taking into consideration the multitiered nature of analyses. The full potential of organizational and dynamic network analysis is reflected particularly when used in the process of organizational management, analysis of business processes, and even business model creation, in which the key role is played by the configuration of intangible resources.
4. *How can intangible resources be measured, evaluated, and included in audit planning and performance using the network-based view?*
   The proposed *meta-model* does not focus on measuring the resources themselves, as is the case in (quantitative) measurement and (qualitative) assessment of organizational intellectual capital. This form of auditing concentrates mainly on measuring relation networks, flows, interactions, and, last but not least, the prominence of network nodes. Relations are measured using matrices (adjacency, affiliation), which are created based on questions that help one explore: who provides information to whom, who receives information from whom, who solves complex work-related problems with whom, if employees know the knowledge and skills of their colleagues, who has what knowledge and skills and how they use them, who has access to resources and which resources are used at work, and who can perform what tasks and which tasks are actually performed. These relations were presented at the operationalization stage of the audit. Notably, the presented network study questionnaire seems to be universal and suitable for use in virtually any organization, regardless of sector.

5.2 Exemplification of Organizational Intangible Resource Audit

The empirical material from the organizational intangible resource audit was collected in an enterprise operating in the IT sector. Planning, design, operationalization, and performance stages of the intangible resource audit were included in the exemplification. Due to the complexity involved and the need to develop an intangible resource management strategy, the implementation stage will be presented in a separate publication by the author.

The intangible resource audit was founded on information audit, among other sources. The key difference is that the information audit scope includes auditing information, understood as the content of documentation, and valuating information. In intangible resource audit, what is audited is the flow of information (provided and received) between employees, in line with the approach to information audit according to Buchanan and Gibb (1998), who concentrate on information users. The goals of information and intangible resource audits seem to be partially convergent. Information audit concentrates on knowledge regarding information (what the information is), its sources (both external and internal), and the way it is used at work. In intangible resource audit, we do not know what exact information employees use and to what sources of information they have access. What is known is the flow of information, creation of tacit knowledge by joint problem-solving, and the potential for knowledge and information sharing due to knowing what knowledge and experience others have. In turn, knowledge and skills are known (having been identified as a resource category). The purpose of information audit is to improve information resource management—to inspect resources to transform the results of this inspection into efficient and successful information management.

Similarly, intangible resource audit aims at improving the management of these resources (which go beyond the flow of information and include knowledge, structural capital, and actions), which is preceded by identification of resources based on the organization's core business processes. In both, the goal is the efficient and successful management: of information resources (information audit) or of intangible resources (intangible resource audit). Intangible resource audit does not aim at valuating these resources, though, as proposed by Buchanan and Gibb (1998), or analyzing the cost-effectiveness of information, as proposed by Orna and Orna (1999). In those two models, the main focus is placed on control, as opposed to intangible resource audit, which emphasizes improvement rather than compliance with procedures. According to Henczel (2001), the identification of problems and solutions using information is a valuable element of information audit. Inclusion of these elements in intangible resource audit may be worth consideration. At present, the proposed audit strongly emphasizes actions (tasks) performed by employees in their workplace, including knowledge and resources relevant to these tasks. If these actions were combined with identifying and solving problems that arise or might arise in the workplace, the improvements brought by the audit would be even more accentuated.

Another component of the proposed intangible resource audit model is knowledge audit. The first concepts of knowledge audit according to Adam, Hershauer, and Ruch (1981), Anderson (1987), and Debenham and Clark (1994) differ from more contemporary propositions. Information and knowledge audits are static, and show information and knowledge only as manageable resources. Hence the concepts of knowledge audit as a management document (Debenham & Clark, 1994), an administrative process (Adam, Hershauer, & Ruch, 1981), or a capability model (Anderson, 1987. Intangible resource audit relies on solutions from information and knowledge audits, but to a much larger extent emphasizes the engagement of employees (social dimension, relations), as well as information and (tacit) knowledge flows (potential for sharing). Almost every knowledge audit model emphasizes the need to identify the knowledge gap by confronting the existing knowledge with missing knowledge. In intangible resource audit, the knowledge gap can be measured based on network metrics such as employees' knowledge and resource needs and waste congruence. One shortcoming of this tool is that it only indicates the percentage of missing knowledge and resources, without specifying what knowledge and resources are missing. In this respect, the knowledge gap analysis featured in knowledge audits provides the management with more information. The case of knowledge reproduction and access to the same knowledge, tasks, or resources is similar. This is measured by the redundancy metrics, which do not specify (as in the case of congruence) which resources exactly are redundant.

Knowledge audit is a tool or basis for knowledge management in an organization. Intangible resource audit has a much larger scope, as it includes not only knowledge, but also broadly understood intangible resources. It is also seen as a management instrument and a tool for diagnosing intangible resources and ensuring their effective use in the organization. Knowledge audit concentrates mainly on areas of knowledge and their identification, and therefore strongly emphasizes the concept of knowledge repositories and inventories as the knowledge bases used by employees. It disregards or downplays the aspect of knowledge auditing based on organizational social capital, whereby knowledge is created in collaboration and various other interpersonal interactions. Of course, the concept of the knowledge map exists in the discussed knowledge audit models, but due to the static perspective (reflecting knowledge as a resource), it does not reflect the dynamics of knowledge flow in the organization, even though it includes the mapped relations. The intangible resource map is presented based on graphs generated through organizational network analysis, with the option of modeling visualizations depending on behaviors and goals of the auditor (addition/removal of a node or a group of nodes, addition or removal of a relation), which makes this map considerably more dynamic and interactive. Possibilities are even broader if one adds the time factor. A longitudinal study with the metrics used would allow for more rigorous analysis of intangible resources and their causal aspects.

None of the listed knowledge audits included metrics to measure the efficiency of these resources, as is the case in the proposed audit (with its redundancy, diversity, congruence metrics discussed above). For example, it remains unclear what the discovery of bottlenecks involves in the knowledge audit, even though these are also related to organizational activities. In intangible resource audit, betweenness centrality is used to identify the employee or employees that act as brokers or gatekeepers in knowledge and information flows. Identification of key knowledge is also problematic—and subjective—in the existing knowledge audit models. The problem does not exist in intangible resource audit, as prominent nodes (resources) are selected using precise measurements (of incoming and outgoing relations), which allow for identifying their centrality (exposure of the most crucial resources in the network in terms of the influence of a given resource on other resources). Few knowledge audit models include survey questionnaires or details regarding the collection, analysis, and interpretation of data—while the proposed intangible resource audit does. Similarly to the other audits discussed, it was impossible to exemplify all audit stages in a case study—this concerns the implementation stage of the intangible resource audit, as has already been mentioned. The most prominent stage of the intangible resource audit model is the performance stage, including in particular the measurement of the results using the defined metrics, graph visualization (intangible resource mapping), and the simulation of changes in the network (modeling).

The final component of the proposed intangible resource audit model is intellectual capital audit. Two models were used: the Technology Broker (Brooking, 1996) and the Intellectual Capital Statement (Mertins, Wang, & Will, 2007). The inclusion of intellectual capital audit is justified in the holistic, structured approach to organizational intangible resources (this concerns the classification of intellectual capital components, which in intangible resource audit was narrowed down to three general elements: human, structural, and relational capital, all founded on information and knowledge flows and on specific knowledge and skills). In the two models, the primary element is the measurement of intellectual capital components, which is not the subject of intangible resource audit, where resources are measured, but from an entirely different perspective—the perspective of relations, not of evaluation or valuation of a resource. Still, the concept of intellectual capital was found useful, as it made it possible to view intangible resources from the perspective of their various configurations and interactions resulting in value creation, competitive advantage, and the achievement of strategic goals.

The intangible resource audit process (the *meta-model*) begins with the planning stage, which is quite similar to the discussed literature propositions. Its scope might even be more narrow than, for example, the planning stage according to Orna and Orna (1990), which gives more freedom to those planning the audit. Here, it was limited to three basic steps: defining the objectives and the scope of the audit, selecting the team, and gaining support in the organization. In the author's experience, the most important element of this stage is ensuring the support and engagement of all employees, which is impossible without the support of the top management. Some audits, though, do not feature a planning stage (e.g., Ragsdell, Probets, Ahmed, & Murray, 2014; Burnett, Williams, & Grinnall, 2013; Liebowitz et al., 2000; and Brooking, 1996). This is quite a significant shortcoming, considering the need to outline the actions to be performed and to obtain the answer to the basic questions: Why and how the audit is to be performed in the organization?

The design stage of intangible resource audit includes four steps: analyzing the external environment, and defining the strategic goals of the organization, its model of value creation, and its core business processes. Interestingly, the analysis of the external environment is only mentioned in audits by Buchanan and Gibb (1998), Chan and Lee (2011), Cheung et al. (2007), and partially in Mertins et al. (2007). It is quite surprising, as the findings of any audit need a reference point. In this case, the identification and analysis of intangible resources refers both to the strategic goals of the organization and to value creation. What is even more surprising is the lack of reference to the strategic goals of an organization in the discussed audits, only mentioned by Orna and Orna (1999) and Mertins et al. (2007). As to the model of value creation, it is only featured in Mertins et al. (2007). The model of value creation (business model) has recently gained in popularity owing to Osterwalder and Pigneur (2010).

Similarly to the concept of intellectual capital, which considers intangible resources holistically, the business model organizes the main resources and actions that have an impact on value creation and proposition. In the intangible resource model proposed here, one very important step involves the identification of core business processes to provide a framework for identifying intangible resources. This differs somewhat from the approaches suggested in other audits (Chan & Lee, 2011; Levantakis et al., 2008; Perez-Soltero et al., 2007; Burnett et al., 2004; Brooking 1996), where it is the business process or the knowledge processes that are audited. In the proposed model, the analysis of business processes is not the objective. Certain prospects for further research arise here, which are discussed in the conclusion.

Another important stage of intangible resource audit is the operationalization stage, in which the audit tools and metrics are developed and tested. Half of the audits analyzed (i.e., seven; see Table 2.4) feature tools (mainly in the form of a survey, interview, or observation), but without providing the details of these tools. Even if authors mention an example questionnaire, it is usually of minor significance (they provide just a few questions, without analysis of all questions or findings, or present results without including the questionnaire). Undoubtedly, the proposed intangible resource audit stands out in this respect, as the survey and interview questionnaires were presented and discussed as the foundation for creating the relation matrices. Only one audit, by Chan and Lee (2011), refers to audit metrics. However, it only features very basic indicators, for example, the number of documents—and how is it important whether the number of documents increased or decreased in a given period? Such an audit overlooks a fundamental issue—associating intangible resources with actions. It does not mention any more advanced network metrics or instrument testing, as is the case in the proposed audit. Testing tools is only included as one of the audit stages in the work of Levantakis et al. (2008).

The next stage is the performance stage, and again, the lack of identification of the information, knowledge, or intellectual capital being the subject of each audit is surprising. It is elementary—one needs to identify something to be able to audit it. In this respect, the audits that stand out are the previously mentioned information audits, and the knowledge audits according to Burnett, Williams, & Illingworth (2013) and Brooking (1996). In the case of information audits, the identification is performed based on an analysis of the organization's external environment, culture, structure, and needs, as well as on collected data regarding activities, tasks, and problems. In the knowledge audit, the identification is performed using knowledge inventory, and in the intellectual capital audit, based on the identification of problems, domains, and limitations. Intangible resource audit deals with resource identification in an entirely different way—taking core business processes as a reference, as has been mentioned several times before.

The most important step that clearly distinguishes intangible resource audit from other audits is analyzing the dynamics of the network of associations between organizational intangible resources. None of the audits discussed incorporated network metrics, which are techniques of organizational and dynamic network analysis, to an extent similar to that presented in this case study. Even if a concept of social network analysis appears (only in Chan & Lee, 2007; Levantakis et al., 2008; and Cheung et al. 2007), it is presented in a very elementary context of node centrality and knowledge flow. Information audits only include information flows, illustrated with an information map, and in intellectual capital audits, the concept is altogether absent. Knowledge audit is based on knowledge maps, which are very limited and static.

The results of this stage concern a specific case study, and are acquired using the relevant organizational network analysis techniques with elements of dynamic network analysis. The obtained results allow for investigating intangible resource networks in line with the research questions posed in the methodological part of the book (Section 3.1.), also presented below. Results were obtained through the following actions:

- One case study was used for the main portion of the study, and two were used as pilot studies. The cases were selected due to the high prominence and intensity of intangible resources in the functioning of these organizations and in the achievement of their strategic goals.
- The study was broken down into three levels: the entire network, dyads, and individual nodes. At the level of the entire network, a total of 47 types of knowledge and skills were identified, as well as 18 resources (structural capital of the organization, including a few tangible resources) and 48 tasks (actions) in which knowledge, skills, and resources were used. Forty-five actors (employees) took part in the study.
- As there were four distinct groups of nodes: (1) (human) actors, (2) knowledge and skills, (3) resources—structural capital, and (4) tasks, the following types of networks were identified: information networks (providing and receiving information), one-mode knowledge networks (joint problem-solving, knowing what skills and knowledge others have), two-mode knowledge networks (having and using knowledge and skills), resource networks (having access to and using resources), task networks (being able to perform a task and actually performing it), and knowledge–task and resource–task networks.

Interpretation of the findings collected based on the defined metrics is quite a difficult task, due to the lack of similar studies using organizational network analysis. The proposed ranges and their interpretation (see Table 5.1) require empirical verification based on further case studies. The values of the metrics are bound to be affected by many variables, including the size of the organization, employees' location, type of work performed, and even the sector in which the company operates. In this study, the findings concern strong relations, as only those were marked 1 in the binary relational matrices. Therefore, the ranges are liable to be different if all relations are considered.

5.2.1 Network-Level Results

Research question 1—How dense are the networks of intangible resource relations in the organization?

Table 5.1 Proposed interpretation of the organizational network metrics' scores

Metric	*Range*	*Interpretation*
Network and meta-network density	0.000–0.250	Relatively low network density
	0.251–0.500	Moderate network density
	0.501–0.750	Dense network
	0.751–1.000	Very dense network
Network centralization	0.000–0.250	Relatively decentralized network
	0.251–0.500	Relatively centralized network
	0.501–0.750	Centralized network
	0.751–1.000	Very centralized network
Knowledge and resource diversity	0.000–0.250	Relatively equal distribution of knowledge or resources
	0.251–0.500	Relatively unequal distribution of knowledge or resources
	0.501–0.750	Unequal distribution of knowledge or resources
	0.751–1.000	Very unequal distribution of knowledge or resources
Knowledge, resource, and task redundancy	0.000–0.250	Relatively low knowledge, resource, and task redundancy
	0.251–0.500	Moderate knowledge, resource, and task redundancy
	0.501–0.750	High knowledge, resource, and task redundancy
	0.751–1.000	Very high knowledge, resource, and task redundancy
Centrality degree, eigenvector centrality, betweenness centrality	0.000–0.250	Relatively low node centrality
	0.251–0.500	Moderate node centrality
	0.501–0.750	High node centrality
	0.751–1.000	Very high node centrality
Actual work, knowledge, and resource load	0.000–0.250	Relatively low work, knowledge, or resource load
	0.251–0.500	Moderate work, knowledge, or resource load
	0.501–0.750	High work, knowledge, or resource load
	0.751–1.000	Very high work, knowledge, or resource load
Actor knowledge needs (waste) congruence	0.000–0.250	Relatively low resource or knowledge needs
	0.251–0.500	Moderate resource or knowledge needs
	0.501–0.750	High resource or knowledge needs
	0.751–1.000	Very high resource or knowledge needs
Actor resource needs (waste) congruence	0.000–0.250	Relatively low mismatch of knowledge or resources to the actor
	0.251–0.500	Moderate mismatch of knowledge or resources to the actor
	0.501–0.750	High mismatch of knowledge or resources to the actor
	0.751–1.000	Very high mismatch of knowledge or resources to the actor

Considering the size of the organization, the relation density in the meta-network (0.384) including all the intangible resource networks listed reflects a certain level of interdependency and consistency between the identified nodes in the organization. Employees with more intense relations in the organization are more likely to have access to higher-quality information. Relatively low density of the information (providing and receiving information) and knowledge networks (joint problem-solving) denotes a low level of connectivity between (human) actors, which means that access to information and knowledge in the studied organization might be relatively difficult.

A dense network of relations (>0.5%) fosters the achievement of better organizational outcomes and increased productivity, as members of the organization can coordinate their actions better. Dense relation networks promote trust and reciprocity when sharing information and knowledge in the organization. In Connecto, the densest networks were: the "knowing what knowledge and skills others have" knowledge network (0.618) and the "having access to resources" resource network (0.620). The "knowing what skills and knowledge other employees have" network demonstrates the potential for sharing knowledge and experience. The denser the network of relations, the more options exist for seeking advice or assistance when solving problems (Cummings, 2004; Cummings & Cross, 2003). Knowing what others know facilitates working on projects or product development. By cooperating in joint problem-solving (knowledge network), Connecto employees have an opportunity to observe and experience the application of tacit knowledge by their colleagues (see Droege & Hoobler, 2003).

Research question 2—What is the level of network centralization and knowledge and resource diversity in the organization?

The "providing and receiving information" network and the knowledge networks (joint problem-solving, knowing what knowledge and skills others have) are moderately centralized, which means that in these networks, there is a slight dominance of one node over others. The scores are below 0.5, so there is no considerable risk that a central group of actors will have power and influence over the whole network. However, network centralization can prevent free contacts inside the organization.

Knowledge and resource diversity scores are high (>0.9), which may indicate that only some employees have access to knowledge and resources, while others have limited or no access. In the studied organization, knowledge and resource diversity metrics indicated unequal allocation of both knowledge and resources (very unequal distribution of knowledge and resources in the organization). There is a risk that work and task performance rely on a handful of people with the most knowledge and access to resources. High levels of diversity most likely mean that the allocation is unequal and that work may be dependent on a few people having the most knowledge or using the most resources, which means that some people or groups might be excessively loaded.

Research question 3—What is the level of knowledge, resource, and task redundancy in the organization?

Knowledge redundancy is high (0.528), indicating that over 52% of employees have knowledge and skills similar to those of other people in the organization. Slightly fewer employees, 44% (0.0443), use the same knowledge and skills, and 45% (0.450) can perform the same tasks. Resource redundancy (in terms of access and use) and performed task redundancy are rather high (30%) considering the relatively small size of the Connecto company. The optimum level of redundancy in IT enterprises is not known, so it impossible to tell whether the Connecto company has sufficient knowledge, resource, and task redundancy for it to act as a protective means against personal risks related to employee unavailability. It can, however, be assumed that access to redundant knowledge, resources, and tasks offers a certain flexibility to Connecto in case one or more employees leave the company. One must also consider the option of replacing absent employees in specific positions by others who have similar knowledge, use similar resources, or perform the same tasks. At this point, however, it is impossible to prescribe a target level of redundancy that would ensure efficient organizational functioning, since the level of redundancy in similar organizations or organizations operating in the same sector is not known. Redundancy defines the level of the required specialization (related to knowledge, resources, and tasks). When knowledge, resources, and tasks are highly specialized, a relation redundant in terms of knowledge, resources, or tasks will not be useful, as opposed to an entirely new relation. Many employees have the same knowledge, perform the same tasks, or use the same resources. Knowledge specialization can be higher than actually necessary for the performed tasks. In the Connecto company, redundancy exists, but it is difficult to tell whether its level is optimal. If we agree with Susskind, Miller, and Johnson (1998) that knowledge is redundant in dense relations, there is a risk that redundant (similar) knowledge exists in the case of the "joint problem-solving" knowledge network, which might affect the creation of new knowledge and innovation.

5.2.2 Findings at the Dyad Level

Research question 4—What are the correlations and causal relationships between information, knowledge, resource, and task networks?

In order to verify correlations between intangible resource networks at the dyad level, two statistical network tools were presented and applied: QAP and MRQAP. The results showed a high correlation between one-mode information and knowledge networks, and between two-mode knowledge, resource, and task networks (transformed into one-mdoe networks). In the study, the overall hypothesis testing results highlight the significant impact of information, resource, and knowledge networks on variance in having and using knowledge and skills by the employees of the Connecto company. The hypotheses presented in Section 3.1. assumed that a pair of actors having one type of relationship is more likely to also have other types of relationships. In total, 16 hypotheses were verified, and half of them proved to be true. Of course, this study also has significant limitations. As the data are cross-sectional, one can only test the existence of a statistical relationship between the variables, but it is impossible to draw conclusions related to the direction of causality.

5.2.3 Findings at the Node Level

Research question 5—Who provides information to whom in the information network?
Research question 6—Who receives information from whom in the information network?
Research question 7—Who discusses and solves complex work-related problems with whom?
Research question 8—Who knows what knowledge and skills other employees in the organization have?

The research questions above concern one-mode networks, in which more or less intense communication takes place (providing and receiving information, joint problem-solving, and knowing other people's knowledge and skills as a potential for tacit knowledge flow and sharing). The use of adjacency matrices makes the analysis of these relations quite an easy task. Figure 5.3. shows relations in the four networks. Relations are directional, but directions are unmarked for the sake of clarity.

The network has no isolated nodes (human actors). The relation density of each of these networks is discussed above. The managerial staff can examine the informal relations in the organization and the areas where interventions are necessary in order to improve information and knowledge flows and see how individual nodes behave, if relations between network actors are reciprocal, and how it affects other members and the entire organization. Each node has a certain position in the network, and each node is analyzed using the advanced network metrics referred to in research question 9.

Detailed analysis of each information, knowledge, resource, and task network enables one to accurately determine who provides information

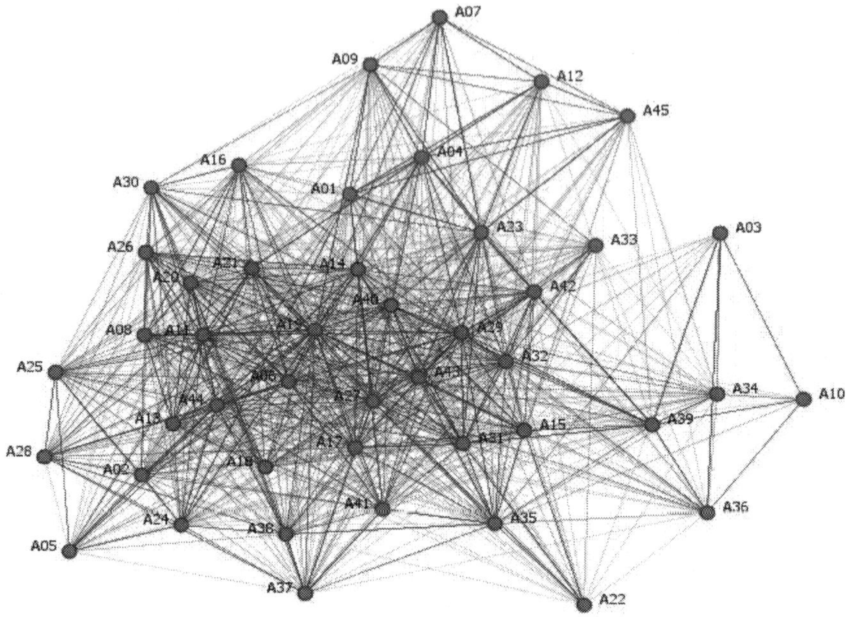

Figure 5.3 One-mode information and knowledge networks in the Connecto company

to whom and who receives work-related information. This is quite an important issue, allowing for identifying individuals who solely receive and who solely provide information. Furthermore, it is possible to determine who asks whom for assistance in solving work-related problems, who plays the role of an expert and is appreciated as such in the network, and who knows the knowledge and skills of their coworkers. In the case of information and knowledge networks, the more extensive the information and knowledge transfer is, the more individual knowledge sharing occurs owing to direct interactions. Understanding the flow of information is an important factor in transforming information into knowledge. Increased knowledge flow based on joint problem-solving and information transfer occurring across the functional divisions in the organization will affect overall efficiency or value creation. In the studied organization, the mean centrality degree is quite low (<0.250), which might not contribute to the increase in efficiency or value creation.

Due to the increasing complexity of services offered by the Connecto company, demand arises for people specializing in a specific field of knowledge, depending on the particular division of labor. Contact with specialists becomes indispensable. The nature of the knowledge sharing process depends on the involved actors. The dependency level of actors in the organization or team determines whether knowledge is transferred.

> *Research question 9—Which nodes (actors, knowledge, resources, tasks) are the most prominent in the network?*

Prominence of individual network nodes was assessed using centrality metrics. Each of the metrics plays a slightly different role. In-degree and out-degree centrality, based on direct relations, identified the most influential employees in the network and those who remain under the influence of others in the knowledge and information networks. Mean centrality degrees were as follows. In the one-mode information networks: providing information—0.192, receiving information—0.207; in the "joint problem-solving" knowledge network—0.172; in the "knowing what knowledge and skills others have" knowledge network—0.618, the highest. Only a few actors had prominent positions, and employee A19 was the most prominent. This actor plays an active role in the network, shares knowledge and resources, and participates in accessing knowledge and resources, which makes them less dependent on other employees in the organization. Individuals in more central positions have quicker access to larger amounts of more diversified information, which increases the learning level of employees in the network, as well as their potential for synthesizing and recombining this information into new ideas (Phelps, Heidl, and Wadhwa, 2012). In Connecto, the most central employees had centrality degrees between 0.251 and 0.920. Each individual's position in the network determines their access to resources and support they can receive from other network members. It is also worth analyzing in-degree and out-degree centralities separately, to verify whether the process is mutual, which fosters reciprocity. There are many employees who provide more information than they receive from their co-workers.

The highest betweenness centrality, 0.217, was found in the "joint problem-solving" knowledge network. The mean value was relatively low (<0.250). It is difficult to identify a person who plays the role of a broker and facilitates the flow of knowledge and information between others or interferes with it.

Borgatti (2005) considers eigenvector centrality perfectly suited for analysis of influence processes, especially in the case of information-based influence. Connecto employees with high eigenvector centralities (A19 and A29) are more likely to act as brokers in the exchange of information, gaining more influence in the process. The results clearly show that the most central person in nearly all the networks is actor A19. This does not mean that the management should only concentrate on prominent nodes in the network. Peripheral nodes (with a smaller number of relations) or those with low values of centrality metrics can be a source of additional specialized knowledge, and their potential may not be fully used by the organization. In order to fully grasp the importance of these nodes in the network, node analysis cannot be performed in separation from the organizational structure, hierarchical position, and critical knowledge protection policies.

In the networks listed, employees have various positions, which determine various opportunities of accessing new information and knowledge, potentially affecting task performance. The remaining in-degree and out-degree centrality metrics allow for evaluating the prominence of knowledge, resources, and tasks, indicating which intangible resources have the largest impact on other resources and are the most significant in their utilization.

Research question 10—Which actors have the highest work, knowledge, and resource loads?
Research question 11—What is the level of knowledge and resource needs congruence (match) and waste (mismatch) among employees?

Actual work, knowledge, and resource load metrics were used to assess whether knowledge and resources are optimally used by the organization and its employees. "Actual" workload corresponds to the amount of knowledge, skills, and resources that each employee can use for performing their current tasks. This metric can be very effective in identifying employees who were assigned tasks that do not match the knowledge they have and the available resources. Interestingly, the findings showed that the person with the highest work, knowledge, and resource load was actor A09, who was not the most prominent one in the network. The values of this particular metric for the top ten employees range between 0.330 and 0.673, denoting moderate to high work, knowledge, and resource loads.

Congruence metrics allowed for assessing the knowledge and resource needs, as well as the percentage of available knowledge and resources that are not used by each employee. It is one of many metrics applicable to measuring the effectiveness of intangible resource use in an organization. It is difficult to estimate whether the levels observed are optimum levels, as in the case of redundancy metric. The top ten knowledge need scores among Connecto employees range between 0.535 and 0.802, indicating moderate to high knowledge needs; this is higher than the resource need scores, which ranged between 0.186 and 0.429 for the top ten employees. This range suggests (according to Table 5.1) that the level of resource needs is relatively low or moderate. It is the role of the management to verify the values of these metrics (knowledge and resource needs) and provide access to the required resources.

The metrics of knowledge and resource mismatch to employees look slightly better. The range is 0.071–0.238, which indicates low to moderate mismatch of knowledge and resources to employees. It can be concluded that the level of unused knowledge and resources is not high and that the organization is efficient in this aspect.

Each of these metrics should be subjected to methodological rigor criteria, in particular in terms of measure validity and reliability, in order to establish whether the metrics measure what they are supposed to measure. For this purpose, in empirical studies, convergent and discriminant validity should be applied (e.g., Fornale-Larcker criterion) (Maciel & Chaves, 2017).

Research question 12—What knowledge and skills do the organization's employees have?
Research question 13—What knowledge and skills do the organization's employees use?
Research question 14—Who has access to what resources at work?
Research question 15—Who uses what resources at work?
Research question 16—What tasks can each employee perform in the organization?
Research question 17—What tasks does each employee perform in the organization?

These questions make it possible to analyze the knowledge and skills that employees have and use at work, their access to and use of resources, and their task-related capabilities and task performance. In the study, relation density showed that more people have knowledge, have access to resources, and know how to perform tasks than use knowledge, skills, and resources in the organization or perform tasks. These types of networks indicate possibilities for utilizing knowledge and skills that are not currently used by employees, or tasks that an employee could perform. Figures 5.4 and 5.5 show the networks of knowledge possession and use.

It was examined who declares having what knowledge and skills, and whether there is any difference between the "having knowledge" network and "using knowledge" network. Similar analyses were performed in resource networks (access, use—Figures 5.6 and 5.7) and task networks (I can/do perform the task—Figures 5.8 and 5.9). It is quite an important issue, as the number of people who declare they have knowledge, access to resources, or the ability to perform tasks was found to be higher that the number of those who use knowledge and resources or perform tasks. This demonstrates that unused knowledge and skills could be managed better by the directors or more efficiently matched to the existing needs in terms of knowledge, resources, and tasks. Additionally, the informal knowledge, resource, and task networks should be confronted with the formal organizational structure, the scopes of competence, or organizational hierarchy. Interestingly, the *Google Adwords* resource is not used

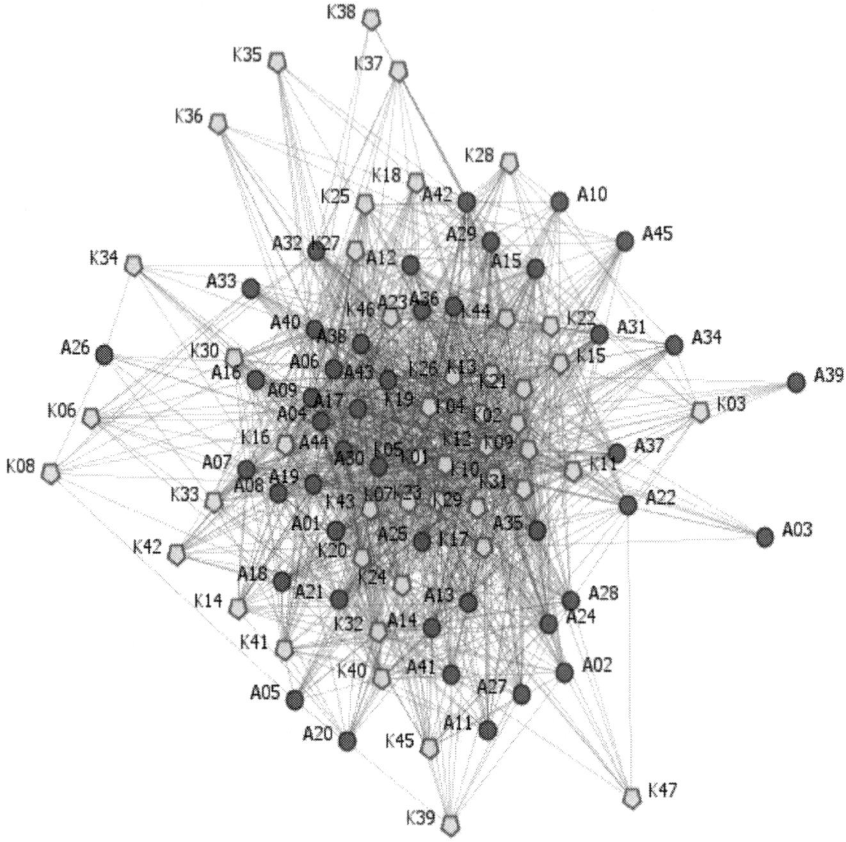

Figure 5.4 Knowledge network (having)

by employees—no strong relations were found between this resource and any employees, as shown in Figure 5.7.

A comprehensive view and understanding of the complexity of information, knowledge, and task flows among employees allows for defining methods for improving these resources' accessibility and use, to increase efficiency and value creation.

> *Research question 18—What knowledge and skills are critical for performing a given task?*
> *Research question 19—What resources are critical for performing a given task?*

Relevance of knowledge and resources to tasks is a basic element of the actual knowledge and resource load and congruence metrics. For example, the task: "*recording and/or finding customers in the database*" relies

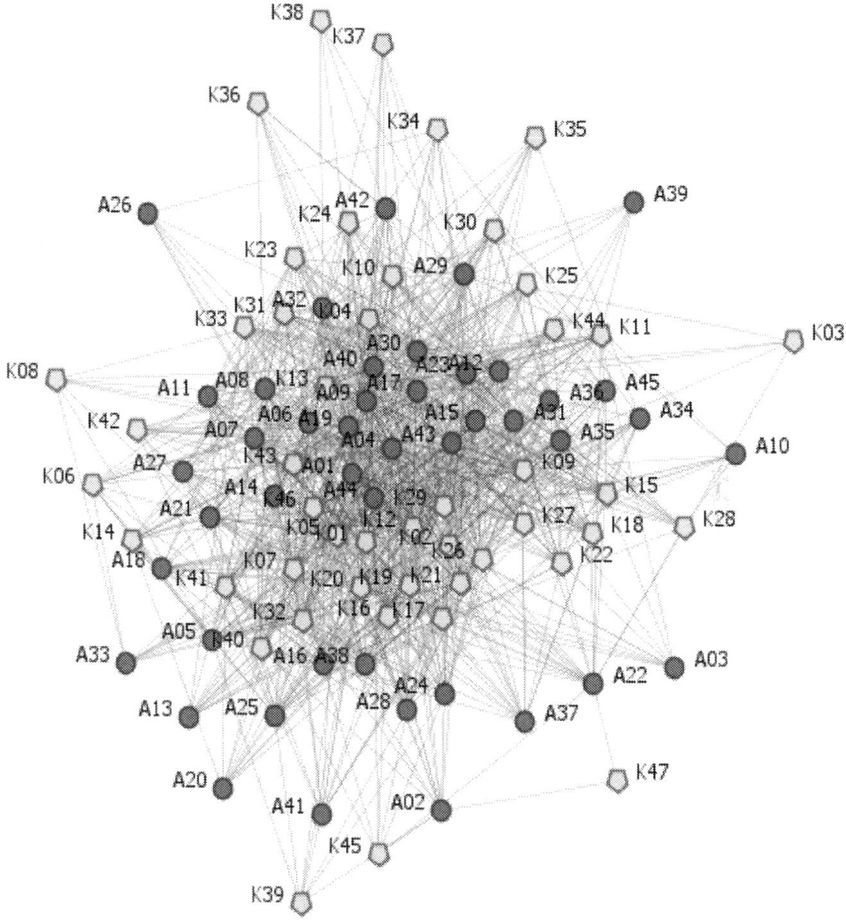

Figure 5.5 Knowledge network (use)

on the following knowledge and skills: general knowledge of the Connecto product group, knowledge of Connecto DMS, knowledge of the operations of Connecto, and knowledge of customers (their size, organizational structure, business processes, etc.). In order to perform this task, one needs three resources: a computer, MS Office, and the DMS system. Associations between knowledge or resources and tasks provide basic information on how the knowledge, resource, and task networks should be modeled so as to optimize congruence (optimally match employees to tasks) as well as work, knowledge, and resource loads.

Research question 20—How do intangible resource networks change following the disappearance of a prominent node in the network?

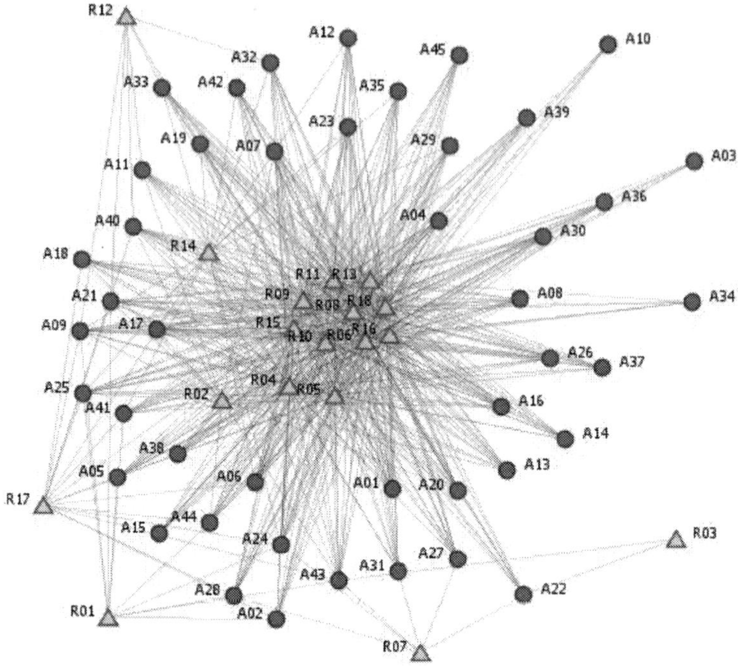

Figure 5.6 Resource network (access)

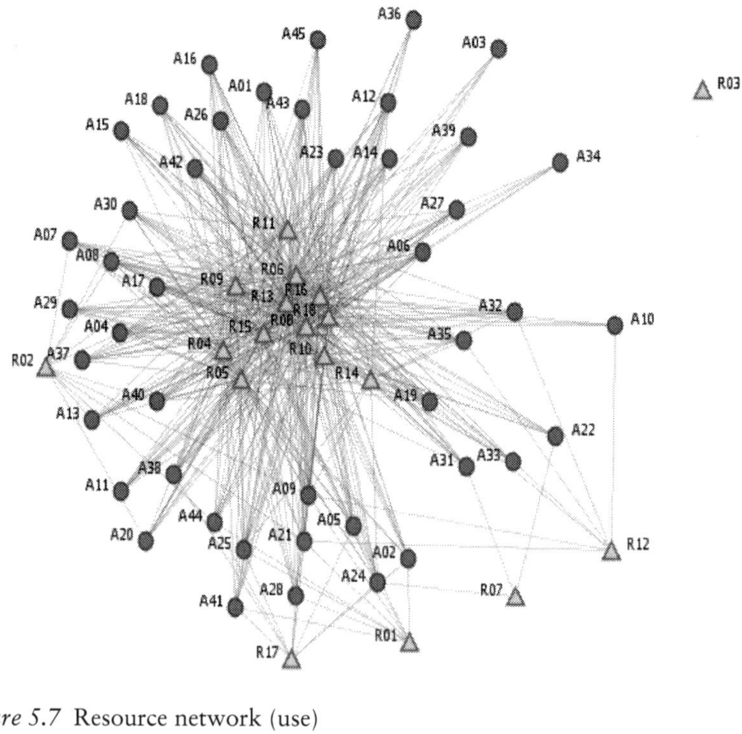

Figure 5.7 Resource network (use)

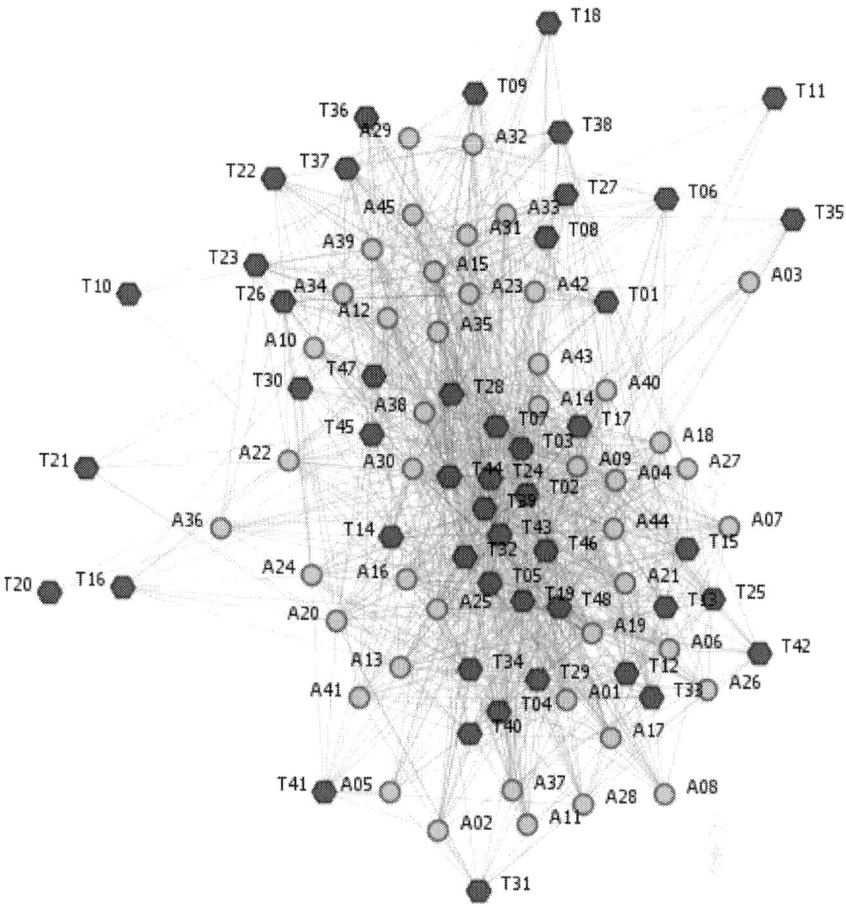

Figure 5.8 Task network (ability)

The removal of the most prominent employee (A19) from the one-mode information and knowledge networks was simulated in order to show how positions of specific nodes and network densities would change. The results showed that actors' positions change in various directions (up or down). For the studied organization, the simulation did not show a large risk related to the loss of actor A19, but not all variants and scenarios were taken into consideration. Such analyses become crucial when simulating the loss of key employees, knowledge, skills, resources, or tasks. They show how the network changes as a result of intentional intervention in the network of relations and correlations. The removal of other nodes was also simulated: general knowledge of the Connecto

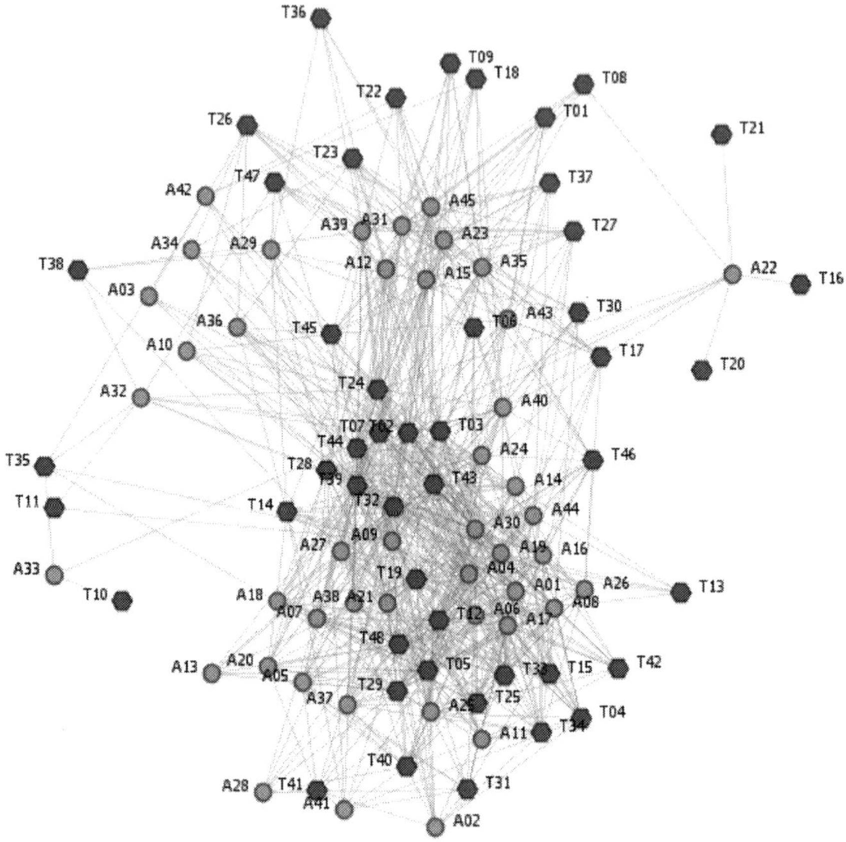

Figure 5.9 Task network (performance)

product group, the "computer" resource, and the "contacting customers by phone" task. Changes in the values of network density, centralization, diversity, redundancy, load, and congruence metrics were analyzed. Even though the removal of these nodes does not pose a significant organizational risk for the continuity and efficiency of organizational functioning, the study offers valuable input in the process of optimally modeling the network structure. Designing this type of change dynamics is a unique approach in intangible resource audit, which had not been included in a similar form in the other discussed audits.

The analysis of the impact of intangible resources on the achievement of strategic objectives, value proposition, and business processes (Table 5.2) is an important part of the performance stage of intangible resource audit (besides the development of a report, submitted to the organizations—see Table 3.2).

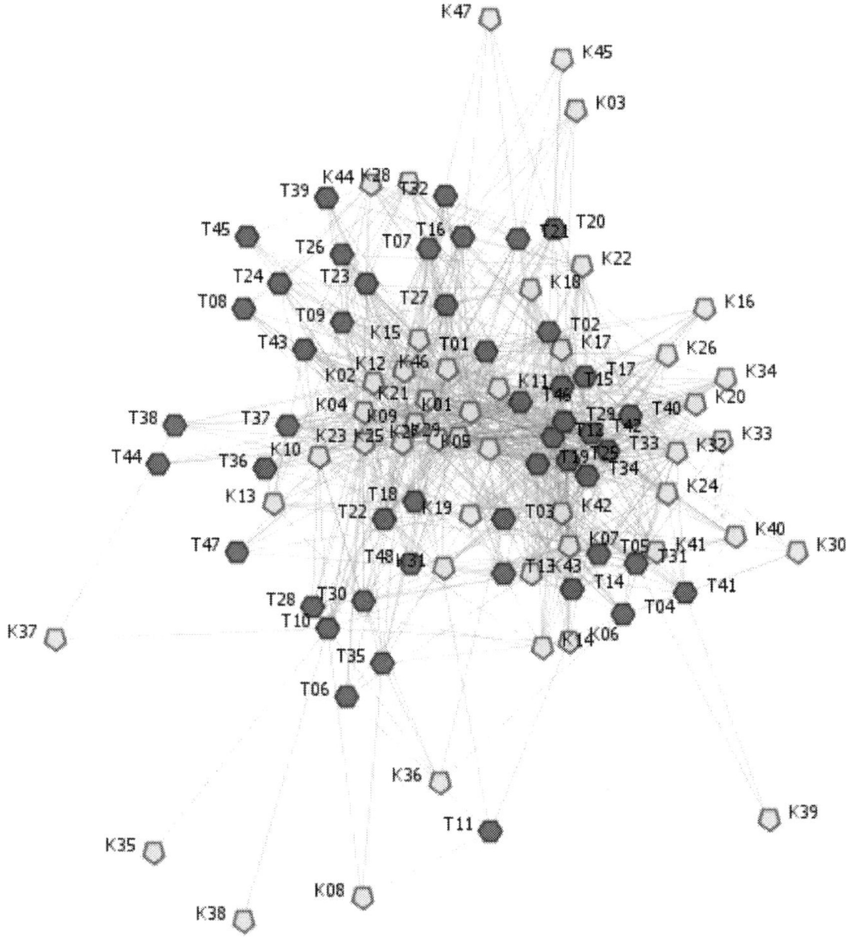

Figure 5.10 Knowledge–task network

The presented strategic objectives and value proposition are affected both by intra-organizational and inter-organizational relations (or, more broadly, relations with the organization's stakeholders, for example, in terms of acquiring new knowledge or external training); however, the latter are beyond the scope of this book. The metrics that have been extensively presented and discussed in intangible resource audit allow for assessing the potential for cooperation, information and knowledge transfer, and, last but not least, the efficiency of knowledge and resource use and of the tasks performed. The efficiency of all these relations affects the performance of work and its outcomes such as achieving the set objectives or proposing value to the customers. The presented goals

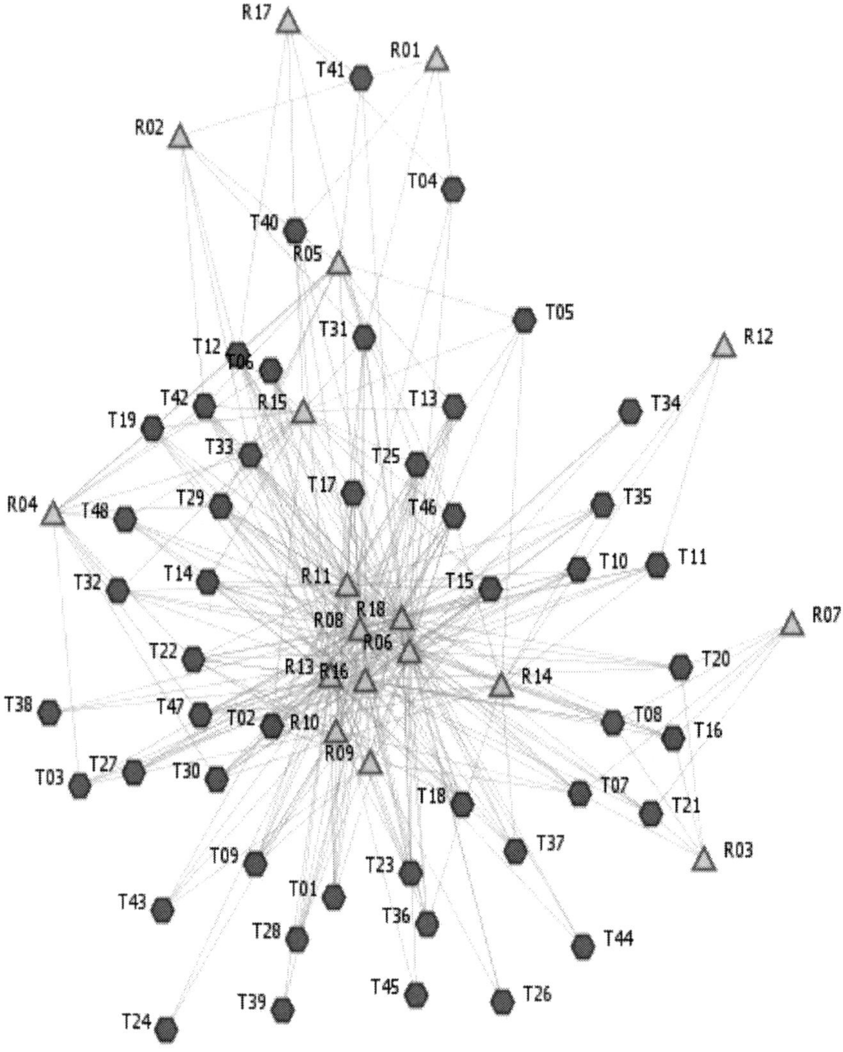

Figure 5.11 Resource–task network

and proposed value (elements of Connecto's business model) in the context of this study depend on intra-organizational relations and intangible resource management. Since the identified intangible resources are based on business processes, it would be useful to further examine in what way the knowledge, tasks, and resources are related to one another within a selected business process and which items have the largest impact on the fulfillment of business processes. As already stated on multiple occasions, an organization's performance and value creation depend on the

Table 5.2 Connecto strategic objectives, value proposition, and business processes

Strategic objectives	*Value proposition*	*Business processes*
• increase in subject matter knowledge (on IT and new technologies); • intra-organizational knowledge transfer; • further professionalization; • diversification of income; • generation of profit and company value.	• satisfying a wide range of customers' IT and IT-related needs; • long-lasting customer attachment through the professional character of services; • competing on quality, not price; • long-lasting cooperation with customers; • handling customers' issues that they need not be burdened with.	• commercial process, including advertising and telemarketing; • sales; • implementation process; • customer retention (service) process; • production process; • administrative process.

networks of relations identified in this study, their structure, and the positions of network nodes.

References

Adam, E. E., Hershauer, J. C., & Ruch, W. A. (1981). Developing quality productivity ratios for public sector personnel services. *Public Productivity Review*, *5*(1), 45–61. https://doi.org/10.2307/3380165

Anderson, J. V. (1987). Technology and mindset: A model for generating new product and service ideas. *National Productivity Review*, *6*(2), 111–124. https://doi.org/10.1002/npr.4040060203

Blackler, F., & Regan, S. (2009). Intentionality, agency, change: Practice theory and management. *Management Learning*, *40*(2), 161–176.

Boer, N.-I., Van Baalen, P. J., & Kumar, K. (2002). An activity theory approach for studying the situatedness of knowledge sharing. *Proceedings of the 35th Annual Hawaii International Conference on System Sciences* (pp. 1483–1492). IEEE. Retrieved from http://ieeexplore.ieee.org/xpls/abs_all.jsp?arnumber=994017

Borgatti, S. P. (2005). Centrality and network flow. *Social Networks*, *27*(1), 55–71. https://doi.org/10.1016/j.socnet.2004.11.008

Brooking, A. (1996). *Intellectual capital: Core asset for the third millennium* (1st ed.). London: International Thomas Business Press.

Buchanan, S., & Gibb, F. (1998). The information audit: An integrated strategic approach. *International Journal of Information Management*, *18*(1), 29–47. https://doi.org/10.1016/S0268-4012(97)00038-8

Burnett, S., Illingworth, L., & Webster, L. (2004). Knowledge auditing and mapping: A pragmatic approach. *Knowledge and Process Management*, *11*(1), 25–37. https://doi.org/10.1002/kpm.194

Burnett, S., Williams, D., & Grinnall, A. (2013). The strategic role of knowledge auditing and mapping: An organisational case study. *Knowledge and Process Management*, *20*(3), 161–176. https://doi.org/10.1002/kpm.1416

Burnett, S., Williams, D., & Illingworth, L. (2013). Reconsidering the knowledge audit process: Methodological revisions in practice. *Knowledge and Process Management*, *20*(3), 141–153.

Chan, P. C. W., & Lee, W. B. (2011). Knowledge audit with intellectual capital in the quality management process: An empirical study in an electronics company. *The Electronic Journal of Knowledge Management*, *9*(2), 98–116.

Cheung, C. F., Li, M. L., Shek, W. Y., Lee, W. B., & Tsang, T. S. (2007). A systematic approach for knowledge auditing: A case study in transportation sector. *Journal of Knowledge Management*, *11*(4), 140–158.

Cummings, J. N. (2004). Work groups, structural diversity, and knowledge sharing in a global organization. *Management Science*, *50*(3), 352–364.

Cummings, J. N., & Cross, R. (2003). Structural properties of work groups and their consequences for performance. *Social Networks*, *25*(3), 197–210.

Debenham, J., & Clark, J. (1994). The knowledge audit. *Robotics and Computer-Integrated Manufacturing*, *11*(3), 201–211.

Droege, S. B., & Hoobler, J. M. (2003). Employee turnover and tacit knowledge diffusion: A network perspective. *Journal of Managerial Issues*, 50–64.

Hansen, M. T. (1999). The search-transfer problem: The role of weak ties in sharing knowledge across organization subunits. *Administrative Science Quarterly*, *44*(1), 82–111.

Hemetsberger, A., & Reinhardt, C. (2009). Collective development in open-source communities: An activity theoretical perspective on successful online collaboration. *Organization Studies*, *30*(9), 987–1008.

Henczel, S. (2001). *The information audit: A practical guide*. Munich: K. G. Saur.

Hong, S., Van den Goor, G., & Brinkkemper, S. (1993). A formal approach to the comparison of object-oriented analysis and design methodologies. *Proceedings of the Twenty Sixth Annual Hawaii International Conference on Systems Sciences* (pp. 689–698). Los Alamitos, CA: IEEE Computer Society Press.

Kuutti, K. (1996). Activity theory as a potential framework for human-computer interaction research. In B. A. Nardi (Ed.), *Context and consciousness: Activity theory and human-computer interaction* (pp. 17–44). Cambridge, MA: MIT Press.

Law, J. (1992). Notes on the theory of the actor-network: Ordering, strategy, and heterogeneity. *Systems Practice*, *5*(4), 379–393. https://doi.org/10.1007/BF01059830

Levantakis, T., Helms, R., & Spruit, M. (2008). Developing a reference method for knowledge auditing. In T. Yamaguchi (Ed.), *Practical aspects of knowledge management* (Vol. 5345, pp. 147–159). Retrieved from http://link.springer.com/10.1007/978-3-540-89447-6_15

Liebowitz, J., Rubenstein-Montano, B., McCaw, D., Buchwalter, J., Browning, C., Newman, B., & Rebeck, K. (2000). The knowledge audit. *Knowledge and Process Management*, *7*(1), 3–10.

Maciel, C. O., & Chaves, C. E. L. (2017). Informational status in intra-organizational networks: The role of knowledge sharing and structural holes. *Revista de Administração*, *52*(2), 189–198.

Mertins, K., Wang, W. H., & Will, M. (2007). How to ensure the quality and reliability of intellectual capital statements? *Electronic Journal of Knowledge Management*, *5*(4), 437–447.

Orna, E., & Orna, E. (1990). *Practical information policies: How to manage information flow in organizations*. Aldershot, UK: Gower.

Osterwalder, A., & Pigneur, Y. (2010). *Business model generation: A handbook for visionaries, game changers, and challengers*. Hoboken, NJ: John Wiley & Sons.

Penrose, E. T. (1995). *The theory of the growth of the firm*. Oxford, UK: Oxford University Press.

Perez-Soltero, A., Barcelo-Valenzuela, M., Sanchez-Schmitz, G., Martin-Rubio, F., Palma-Mendez, J. T., Vanti, A. A., & others. (2007). A model and methodology to knowledge auditing considering core processes. *ICFAI Journal of Knowledge Management*, *5*(1), 7–23.

Phelps, C., Heidl, R., & Wadhwa, A. (2012). Knowledge, networks, and knowledge networks a review and research agenda. *Journal of Management*, *38*(4), 1115–1166.

Ragsdell, G., Probets, S., Ahmed, G., & Murray, I. (2014). Knowledge audit: Findings from the energy sector. *Knowledge and Process Management*, *21*(4), 270–279. https://doi.org/10.1002/kpm.1435

Susskind, A. M., Miller, V. D., & Johnson, J. D. (1998). Downsizing and structural holes their impact on layoff survivors' perceptions of organizational chaos and openness to change. *Communication Research*, *25*(1), 30–65.

Conclusion

Dynamically changing environments drive dynamic approaches to management, including intangible resource auditing. Traditional information, knowledge, and intellectual capital audit instruments have been rendered obsolete by the dynamic nature of organizational intangible resources and the associated risks, as these resources are becoming increasingly dynamic and tacit, based on experience and interpersonal relationships.

The subject of intangible resource audit has not been extensively discussed, either in Polish or in worldwide literature. The present study allowed for developing a *meta-model* of intangible resource audit, which enables a diagnosis of internal relations existing among such resources and their dynamics in the context of intangible resource management and effectiveness. This is by no means a simple issue, since intangible resources must be identified and relations between their components must be analyzed, as was the case in the discussed intangible resource audit methodology.

The integrated organizational intangible resource audit concept, termed the *meta-model*, was developed on the basis of a range of precepts from network theory, actor–network theory, activity theory, and resource-based approaches—selected to explain the interrelations among network nodes and their configurations (interactions). In no way does this imply that these are the only theories and views that could have been adopted. Most certainly, however, they form a foundation of a newly emerging *network-based view*, which requires comprehensive research to be considered a fully-fledged theory, as was the case for the popular resource-based view. Network theories were discussed in connection with resource-based views focusing on knowledge and intellectual capital, which provide natural context for intangible resources, well defined and empirically verified in literature.

Following a literature review, the integrated organizational intangible resource audit concept was developed, comprising five principal stages. Due to high complexity, the implementation stage has not yet been verified and therefore requires a separate publication. For the performance stage, a set of network metrics was specified, providing a basis for analyzing intangible resources and the effectiveness of their use. These metrics were selected in accordance with the nature of intangible resources, including information, knowledge, structural capital, and inherently associated tasks. Organizational and dynamic network analysis comprise a much broader range of instruments (Altman, Carley, & Reminga, 2018), though their selection and use in studies must be preceded with a thorough examination of theoretical precepts. Network metrics are useful tools for measuring network effectiveness, and their analysis provides managing staff with tools for organizational management in the areas of relationship dynamics, flows, and intangible resource use and sharing.

Organizational network analysis was used, incorporating elements of dynamic network analysis strictly related to organizational intangible resources (information and knowledge flows, structural capital associated with tasks), which enabled an analysis of the resource relation network and an assessment of the effectiveness of their use. The study was limited to information networks, knowledge networks, resource networks (based on structural capital), and task networks. The number of potential nodes and relations in an organizational network and thus the number of network combinations, is much larger, depending on the node categories used. Larger numbers of different nodes will entail a larger diversity of the organizational relation networks comprising the meta-network. Of course, many other areas may be subjected to organizational network analysis, including the identification of knowledge leaders, peripheral resources and their (tacit) potential and impact on the organization, cliques, clusters, or analysis of project teams from the perspective of intangible resource management and use.

One important objective of the present study was demonstrating the application of organizational network analysis techniques in intangible resource auditing in an organization. The study did not aim at analyzing business processes and value creation, even though such analysis is a key component of the audit performance stage, being both the result and the rationale of the audit. This methodology primarily focuses on knowledge and skills, including the ability to perform certain actions. In order to diagnose this knowledge, its use, and its associations with tasks, employees, and resources (structural capital), surveys and semi-structured interviews were used. Knowledge associated with tasks and business processes is potentially tacit (it is known to the employees, but not codified, formalized, or otherwise made explicit). The proposed intangible resource audit model, as opposed to traditional models involving the creation of a static knowledge inventory (typically in the form of a table), includes defining the network of associations between resources and creating an intangible resource map as an important step. In the study, business process is not structured, sequential, and linear, and is not shown as block diagrams. Core business processes were identified during interviews with managing directors, and the identified business processes provided context for knowledge, tasks, resources, and employees involved in each process, even if this involvement was due to performing a specific activity or having a specific item of knowledge. The analysis mainly focuses on network nodes and their interactions. Without a definition of core business processes in the organization, the identified knowledge, skills, resources, and tasks would become polarized, and there would be no indication as to how the knowledge, resources, and tasks are to be included in the analysis.

In a changing, turbulent environment, the range of business processes is bound to evolve, and the required knowledge, resources, and tasks are bound to change accordingly. The analysis of network node relation dynamics requires diagnosis at regular intervals, in a longitudinal study form (with an annual or shorter cycle, depending on the needs and employee fluctuation). Hence the inclusion of a re-auditing stage, in which the entire procedure is relaunched. Repeating the audit in a specified time frame (e.g., annually) is required in any control or advisory activity, as it enables the diagnosis of the extent, scope, and intensity of changes in the resources and their dynamics in the period of analysis.

The added value of the study consists in illustrating the analyses performed at three levels: entire network, dyads, and individual nodes, and exemplifying a network simulation based on immediate impact analysis (IIA) and node removal. Of course, many more scenarios of network changes may be proposed, as any of the nodes and relations listed can be modeled (by removal or addition), and changes in metrics following their removal or addition can be analyzed.

The study allows for evaluating the prominence (influence or importance) of specific human and nonhuman actors—but does it verify whether a resource (its properties) is as unique in other organizations? Findings from the selected case study (an IT company) cannot be discussed in the context of other organizations, as a single case study does not warrant such generalization. The weakness of one-mode information and knowledge networks is that they do not show what information and knowledge employees do exchange, but only what interactions they declare.

In this study, three techniques were presented: social network analysis, organizational network analysis, and dynamic network analysis. Though the cross-sectional study format was used, a longitudinal study would have provided a more comprehensive view of the dynamics of changes in network nodes and relationships, and their impact on value creation, by identifying those factors that affect these changes in the long term. This weakness of the cross-sectional approach is compensated for by simulation of changes using IIA. For researchers and practitioners interested in information exchange initiatives or encouraging knowledge exchange, resource sharing, or joint task performance within and outside of an organization, such a comprehensive approach to organizational intangible resources is appropriate and offers many potential benefits with regard to intangible resource management.

Unfortunately, the dysfunctions or risks associated with network organizations have not been broadly discussed. Researchers typically focus on prominent nodes rather than the peripheral ones and disregard network modeling for scenarios negative for the organization, dealing with high employee turnover and resource loss. The understanding of risks can provide a balanced view of the relationship network and its functioning in an intra- and inter-organizational setting. Network organizations are evolving, which makes risk analysis particularly difficult, as traditional social network analysis is static (Carley, 2003). Inclusion of risks associated with the loss of resources (e.g., information flows between actors, knowledge and skills, ICT infrastructure and specialized software, technology, or tasks) in the network simulation would allow for measuring the risks and the impact of such negative events on the shape of the network.

The observations made may assist managers in understanding factors critical to performance, such as information and knowledge flows between people, influencing the speed, quality, and accuracy of organizational decision-making. Information silos are usually associated with poor communication and recurring problems, which make organizations less efficient and flexible. Based on organizational network analysis and intangible resource audit results, managers may decide to establish interdisciplinary teams, encouraging teamwork through tasks that require distributed decision-making.

The examination of the relation network or the mutual interactions of network nodes involves a different perspective—a network perspective that allows for demonstrating the interrelations between network nodes in a way that is not possible in traditional statistical analysis, where observations are statistically independent, and producing insight that is not achievable by simply formulating data as matrices. The analysis would additionally benefit from the inclusion of a moderator variable (e.g., experience, education, location) in the investigation of network structure and its impact on actors' behaviors. Not all network node configurations that can be used for detailed analyses have been used here. Specific network structures were found to vary in density, depending on network size and type of relations (flows). It has been pointed out that the denser the network, the more relations can be identified. However, the optimum network density or distribution for an IT organization has not been established, as more extensive research is required for any conclusions in this aspect. This book presents metrics allowing for identifying prominent network nodes that may influence other nodes, based on the direct relations, incoming and outgoing, a node has. Such nodes may play various roles in the network, from activating information, knowledge, resource, and task flows to preventing them. Therefore, an in-depth analysis of specific nodes and their roles in each network is required.

Information and knowledge sharing occurs at all levels: interpersonal (micro), intra-organizational (meso), and inter-organizational (macro) (see Yang & Maxwell, 2011). So far, information and knowledge audits had mainly been performed in an organizational setting, without including external relations. Therefore, the inclusion of intellectual capital audit offers more possibilities for operationalization of the external dimension (customers, partners, stakeholders, etc.) and diagnosis of the flow and exchange of information, knowledge, resources, or even tasks between them. This is not an easy process, as organizations have their own operating procedures, control mechanisms, and workflows, which increase the difficulty involved in information and knowledge exchange. The intangible resource audit methodology may become a platform for a formalized process of information, knowledge, resource, and task exchange between organizations. In a typical audit, the customers play a passive role, as they are not involved in the study—processes critical to the fulfillment of an organization's objectives and customers' needs are analyzed, but without actual customer participation. Intangible resource audit should go beyond the internal state of the organization and include external relations and stakeholders. Organizational context analysis is not sufficient; it is only a starting point for the audit, providing understanding of the business objectives and their basis. This, however, requires the inclusion of stakeholders in the investigation (using questionnaires and interviews) and demonstration of inter-organizational resource flows and relations.

In the context of future research, relational capital (as a component of intellectual capital) and its association with the network-based view are particularly interesting. The present study was limited to intra-organizational relations, excluding the studied organization's external relations, which may thus become a potential area for a broader investigation including an analysis of the intangible resource network of an organization's stakeholders. One important aspect for further studies is an examination of the impact of intangible resources on enterprise value creation—which will be operationalized using organizational and dynamic network analysis in a separate publication by the author.

The present study is valuable both for management theorists and practitioners An attempt was made to fill in the identified gaps in resource theories. The results, including definitions of concepts related to intangible resources, audit, and auditing; and an understanding and interpretation of their relations, associations, complexity, and dynamics; contribute to the development of organization and management theory. Intra-organizational networks and their dynamics may be viewed as an intangible resource in themselves—one that is manageable and unique to a specific organization. A thorough review of available literature and theories in social and management studies was performed as a basis for developing an instrument suitable for use in any organization, regardless of industry or sector. Questions used in analysis and interviews apply to all organizations, which enables their operationalization in further, empirical studies.

The proposed intangible resource audit methodology is an attractive tool for decision-makers, as it allows for identifying isolated actors in the network who may absorb knowledge or control the incoming and outgoing flows of information and knowledge between groups and within the entire organization, as well as employees with the most social relationships with others. This knowledge empowers decision-makers to stimulate intangible resource sharing and effective use in the organization. Organizational processes can be modeled to minimize the risk of losing intangible resources by increasing connectivity among employees. The proposed methodology also enables managers to find out who knows whom. This basic knowledge may allow them to organize project teams and task groups and increase their innovation potential, suggest change leaders, respond and adapt to market changes, enhance collaboration and communication, and understand how the organization will change if it loses key intangible resources or resources directly related to them. The loss of resources (knowledge and skills) is directly associated with the loss of employees and of access to these resources by those who relied on these employees' support, which in turn may restrict the activity of the remaining staff.

As a consequence of intangible resource loss, a resource gap is formed that may or may not be promptly bridged, which affects the organization's efficiency. On the other hand, the introduction of new intangible resources (e.g., a new employee with new knowledge and skills) enables new reconfigurations in the relation network, potentially increasing resource accessibility for employees and enhancing task performance. The proposed methodology makes it possible to identify relation types that have an impact on the organization's performance and stability, as well as its flexibility in responding to the competitive environment.

This book presents a compilation of knowledge regarding information, knowledge, and intellectual capital audits, as well as a new *meta-model* for intangible resource audit. It has certain merits as well as limitations, which the author has attempted to address. The author believes that the integrated *meta-model* for organizational resource audit is a consistent and comprehensive instrument for auditing intangible resources and their relations and associations from the network perspective.

References

Altman, N., Carley, K. M., & Reminga, J. (2018). *ORA users guide 2018*. Pittsburgh: Carnegie Mellon University, School of Computer Science, Institute for Software Research.

Carley, K. M. (2003). Dynamic network analysis. In R. Breiger, K. Carley, & P. Pattison, (Eds.). *Dynamic social network modeling and analysis: Workshop summary and papers* (pp. 133–145). Washington, DC: National Academies Press.

Yang, T.-M., & Maxwell, T. A. (2011). Information-sharing in public organizations: A literature review of interpersonal, intra-organizational and inter-organizational success factors. *Government Information Quarterly*, *28*(2), 164–175.

Index